Multi-Objective Decision Making

The Institute of Mathematics and its Applications Conference Series

---

RECENT TITLES

Computational Methods and Problems in Aeronautical Fluid Dynamics, *edited by* B.L. Hewitt, C.R. Illingworth, R.C. Lock, K.W. Mangler, J.H. McDonnell, Catherine Richards and F. Walkden

Optimization in Action, *edited by* L.C.W. Dixon

The Mathematics of Finite Elements and Applications II, *edited by* J.R. Whiteman

The State of the Art in Numerical Analysis, *edited by* D.A.H. Jacobs

Fisheries Mathematics, *edited by* J.H. Steele

Numerical Software—Needs and Availability, *edited by* D.A.H. Jacobs

Recent Theoretical Developments in Control, *edited by* M.J. Gregson

The Mathematics of Hydrology and Water Resources, *edited by* E.H. Lloyd, T.O'Donnell and J.C. Wilkinson

Mathematical Aspects of Marine Traffic, *edited by* S.H. Hollingdale

Mathematical Modelling of Turbulent Diffusion in the Environment, *edited by* C.J. Harris

Mathematical Methods in Computer Graphics and Design, *edited by* K.W. Brodlie

Computational Techniques for Ordinary Differential Equations, *edited by* I. Gladwell and D.K. Sayers

Stochastic Programming, *edited by* M.A.H. Dempster

Analysis and Optimisation of Stochastic Systems, *edited by* O.L.R. Jacobs, M.H.A. Davis, M.A.H. Dempster, C.J. Harris and P.C. Parks

Numerical Methods in Applied Fluid Dynamics, *edited by* B.Hunt

Recent Developments in Markov Decision Processes, *edited by* R. Hartley, L.C. Thomas and D.J. White

Power from Sea Waves, *edited by* B. Count

Sparse Matrices and their Uses, *edited by* I.S. Duff

The Mathematical Theory of the Dynamics of Biological Populations II, *edited by* R.W. Hiorns and D. Cooke

Floods due to High Winds and Tides, *edited by* D.H. Peregrine

Third IMA Conference on Control Theory, *edited by* J.E. Marshall, W.D. Collins, C.J. Harris and D.H. Owens

Numerical Methods in Aeronautical Fluid Dynamics, *edited by* P.L. Roe

Numerical Methods for Fluid Dynamics, *edited by* K.W. Morton and M.J. Baines

Multi-Objective Decision Making, *edited by* S. French, R. Hartley, L.C. Thomas and D.J. White

Multi-Objective Decision Making

Based on the proceedings of a conference on Multi-Objective Decision Making organised jointly by The Institute of Mathematics and its Applications and The Department of Decision Theory, University of Manchester and held at the University of Manchester, 20-22 April, 1982.

Edited by

S. FRENCH R. HARTLEY
L. C. THOMAS D. J. WHITE
Department of Decision Theory
University of Manchester, Manchester, UK

1983

ACADEMIC PRESS
A Subsidiary of Harcourt Brace Jovanovich, Publishers
London New York
Paris San Diego San Francisco São Paulo
Sydney Tokyo Toronto

ACADEMIC PRESS INC. (LONDON) LTD.
24/28 Oval Road
London NW1

United States Edition published by
ACADEMIC PRESS INC.
111 Fifth Avenue
New York, New York 10003

British Library Cataloguing in Publication Data
Multi-Objective Decision Making.—(The Institute of Mathematics and its Applications conference series)
1. Decision making—Mathematical models—Congresses
I. French, S.
II. Series
658.4'033 HD30.23

ISBN 0-12-267080-9

Printed in Great Britain by
Whitstable Litho Ltd., Whitstable, Kent

CONTRIBUTORS

E.E. BISCHOFF: *Department of Management Science, University College Swansea, Singleton Park, Swansea SA2 8PP.*

Y. CRAMA: *Faculté de Droit, d'Economie et de Sciences Sociales, Université de Liége, Boulevard de Rectorat 7 - Bte 31, 4000 Liége, Belgium.*

R. DE NEUFVILLE: *Ecole Central des Arts et Manufactures, Grande voie des Vignes, 92290 Chatenay-Malabry, France.*

H.L. DHINGRA: *Dept. of Finance and Management Science, University of Saskatchewan, Saskatoon, Saskatchewan, Canada S7N OWO.*

S. FRENCH: *Department of Decision Theory, University of Manchester, Manchester M13 9PL.*

P. HARRISON: *Joint Consultancy on Patterns and Systems Limited, Bishops Stortford, Herts.*

R. HARTLEY: *Department of Decision Theory, University of Manchester, Manchester M13 9PL.*

A. JAEGER: *Ruhr University, D-4630 Bochum, West Germany.*

M. McCORD: *Massachusetts Institute of Technology, Cambridge, MA, USA.*

W. MICHALOWSKI: *Instytut Organizacji Zarzadzania i Doskonalenia Kadr, ul. Wawelska 56, 02-067 Warsaw, Poland.*

A. PIOTROWSKI: *Instytut Organizacji Zarzadzania i Doskonalenia Kadr, ul. Wawelska 56, 02-067 Warsaw, Poland.*

M.L.R. PRICE: *Operational Research Group, Wales Gas, Snelling House, Bute Terrace, Cardiff CF1 2UF.*

F.H. RUIZ-DIAZ: *Department of Decision Theory, University of Manchester, Manchester M13 9PL.*

B. RUSTEM: *Control Section, Department of Electrical Engineering, Imperial College of Science and Technology, London SW7.*

P. SERAFINI: *International Centre for Mechanical Sciences, 1-33100 Udine, Palazzo del Torso, Piazza Garibaldi 18, Italy.*

E. THANASSOULIS: *School of Industrial and Business Studies, University of Warwick, Coventry CV4 7AL.*

L.C. THOMAS: *Department of Decision Theory, University of Manchester, Manchester M13 9PL.*

M.K.-S. TSO: *Department of Mathematics, University of Manchester Institute of Science and Technology, P.O. Box 88, Manchester M60 1QD.*

M. VASSILOGLOU: *Department of Decision Theory, University of Manchester, Manchester M13 9PL.*

D.J. WHITE: *Department of Decision Theory, University of Manchester, Manchester M13 9PL.*

H.P. WYNN: *Department of Mathematics, Imperial College of Science and Technology, London SW7.*

PREFACE

In 1896 Pareto [1] began a study of efficient solution theory providing, perhaps, the earliest recognition of the difficulty of reducing decision problems to forms involving a single objective. Although there has been a continued interest in this area, primarily by economists, it was not until the mid 1960's that there was any serious study of multi-objective problems by management scientists and operational researchers. For some time prior to this, however, the difficulties encountered in the practice of these disciplines because of the multi-objective nature of problems had been well recognised. The growth of interest was given its initial momentum by the conference organised by Cochrane and Zeleny [2]. Since then there have been six conferences and multi-objective decision making has become one of the central themes of management science and operational research. The present conference is the first one to be held in the U.K. We hope that in its modest way it contributes usefully to a vast and growing literature.

About one half of the main papers given relate to a family of procedures, which are popularly known under the collective title: multi-objective interactive programming. These combine a process of learning about aspects of a decision maker's preference structure with a surrogate optimisation, or similar, procedure based on the information acquired. White gives an introduction to a selection of the better known procedures, illustrating their different assumptions and properties. Crama delivered a paper which examines some properties of the many STEM-like methods in terms of quasi balanced solutions. Bischoff studies the performance of several methods in terms of the quality of solutions obtained and the sensitivity to information provided.

In addition several speakers discussed special methods they had developed. Michalowski and Piotrowski provided a paper, presented by White, which was on a STEM-like procedure applied to a national problem of machinery manufacture. Thanassoulis presented and established convergence results for an interactive procedure, PASEB, which is based on concavity of the utility function and a polyhedral action space, and which is related to Geoffrion's well known procedure. Serafini presented a joint paper with Pascoletti, based on cone orders, which establishes convergence to efficient solutions along improving paths. Rustem described a method involving the adjustment of weighting factors using a quadratic performance index. White discusses a method in which the decision maker is assumed to behave as if he had a set of possible linear objective functions and was prepared to make preference statements between two alternatives only if one was at least as good or better than the other for all objective functions in the set. The set is unknown and the analytic properties of the method are examined.

No multi-objective interactive programming procedure, in the sense described in the second paragraph, exists which explicitly considers utility theory and coherence ideas in their use or development. This seems to be a considerable omission from this area. French raises this point explicitly in his survey. In addition he discusses his own philosophy concerning the role of utility and coherence in multi-objective problems, as well as providing information on discussions and other surveys in this area. De Neufville and McCord add to the existing disquiet concerning the validity of expected utility theory. Their experiments with various methods indicate, in particular, that in situations of certainty non-probabilistic-gamble methods produce results somewhat at variance with probabilistic-gamble methods. It remains to examine the significance of these results for multi-objective interactive programming methods. Vassiloglou and French look at the problem of examination marks in terms of a multi-criteria decision problem. Here the objectives are the marks in the different papers and the problem is to combine these different objectives to give an overall ranking or grade to the candidates. They look especially at the problem when not all the candidates take the same paper.

Central to all multi-objective methods, to some degree or other, is the set of efficient solutions. Hartley gives a survey of algorithms designed to obtain this set or a subset. Most of the methods fall roughly into two classes viz. those which attempt to reduce the problem to a parametric family of scalar valued problems, and those which attempt to generalise known scalar algorithms, such as dynamic programming, to vector algorithms.

The remaining papers of Thomas, Wynn and Ruiz-Diaz introduce novel ideas of a special kind related to multi-objective problems. Thomas shows how a Markov decision process, in which the same decisions must be taken for states within specified classes, may be looked at as a multi-objective problem, and examines this in the context of known and new multi-objective Markov decision process results. Wynn surveys and categorises several families of problems that occur in statistics and all of which involve the selection of some optimum (or efficient) subset.

Ruiz-Diaz and French give a survey of the recent but rapidly expanding area of multi-objective scheduling problems.

They describe the theoretical results obtained and comment on the work performed on these problems.

Finally a small number of short papers were presented. White discussed a multi-objective Boolean problem, and develops a branch and bound method which falls into Hartley's second category quite nicely. Harrison discusses his method for dealing with multi-objective problems in the furniture industry arising from the cutting stock problems in which waste, pattern complexity and number of different patterns constitute some objectives. Tso and Price discuss how a blending with uncertain parameters can be re-expressed as a problem in efficient set theory. Jaeger makes a plea for the use of graphical representations of multi-criterion problems as a way of describing the problem and possible solutions to non-specialists. Dhingra looks at the conflicting objectives that an agent, who acts on behalf of others (the principals) and the principals might have in the context of manager-share holder relationships. He points out both have multi-objective criteria to satisfy.

The Editors would like to thank the Institute of Mathematics and its Applications, especially Catherine Richards, Marian Smith and the other staff for their contributions to the financing, organising and running of the conference and also Kate Baker for the hard work done before, at, and after the conference on our behalf. We also thank the authors for their most welcome contributions.

January 1983

S. French
R. Hartley
L.C. Thomas
D.J. White

[1] V. Pareto, Cours d'Econome Politique, Rouge, Lausanne, 1896.

[2] J.L. Cochrane, M. Zeleny, Eds., Multiple Criteria Decision Making, University of South Carolina Press, 1973.

ACKNOWLEDGEMENTS

The Institute thanks the authors of the papers, the editors Dr. S. French (University of Manchester), Dr. R. Hartley (University of Manchester), Dr. L.C. Thomas (University of Manchester) and Professor D.J. White (University of Manchester) and also Mrs. S. Hockett and Mrs. J. Parsons for typing the manuscript.

CONTENTS

SURVEY OF ALGORITHMS FOR VECTOR OPTIMISATION PROBLEMS

Roger Hartley

(Department of Decision Theory, University of Manchester)

1. Introduction

In its most general form, the multiple objective programming problem can be written

$$\begin{aligned} \text{Vmax } & f_1(x) \\ & \vdots \\ & f_p(x) \\ \text{subject to } & g_1(x) \leqq b_1 \\ & \vdots \\ & g_m(x) \leqq b_m \\ & x \in X \end{aligned}$$

where X is some subset of R^n, the f_k's are objective functions and the g_i's are constraints. If no further information on the decision-maker's preferences is available, either initially or interactively, the furthest one can go in analysing the problem is to look for the set of efficient (non-dominated, admissible, Pareto optimal) solutions. A feasible $x \in X$ is *efficient* if and only if there is no feasible $y \in X$ satisfying

$$f(y) \geq f(x)$$

where f is the vector-valued function whose i'th component at x is $f_i(x)$ and $\geqq$, $>$ denote, respectively, weak and strict component-wise inequality whilst $\geq$ denotes "$\geqq$ but not $=$". Subscripts denote components of vectors.

Our intention here is to undertake a selective review of some algorithms available for determining either the whole set of efficient solutions, or some well-defined subset or, in one case, a close approximation to the efficient set.

Before looking at specific types of optimisation problem we shall indicate some broad categories into which algorithms may be classified. Such classification schemes have several uses including suggesting possible methods for solving new problems and new methods for old problems as well as offering some criteria for assessing the value of competing algorithms.

Firstly we can partition the class of algorithms as follows.

(I) A characterisation of efficiency is used to transform the multiple objective problem into a family of single objective problems specified in terms of a number (usually p-1), of parameters. Well-known single objective optimisation techniques coupled with parametric methods can then be used to find all solutions of this family.

(II) A standard single objective optimisation method is modified to cope with multiple objective problems. It is necessary, of course, to establish conditions for the validity of such extensions. To date the most favoured technique for this treatment is dynamic programming.

(III) The final class contains all methods which do not correspond to any standard single objective method. Clearly, any such method can be specialised to the single objective case and, therefore, the presumption would be that the specialisation is inferior, in this case, to standard methods. However if the reason for this is that computation time is not as heavily dependent on the number of objectives as in other methods, a compensating advantage may be that the approach becomes relatively more attractive for problems with a large number of objective functions.

It is perhaps worth remarking that, if a computer code is available for parametric programming, algorithms of class I can be particularly easy to implement.

Another way of classifying algorithms is by the manner in which they construct the efficient set.

(A) Each iteration generates a subset of the efficient set (or whatever set we are aiming to find). The union of the subsets is the efficient set.

(B) At each iteration there is a set containing the efficient set. The intersection of these sets is the efficient set.

(C) The penultimate stage of the algorithm is a set S of feasible solutions containing the efficient set, and the final step is to find the efficient subset of S which is obviously the efficient set.

(D) Other methods.

The importance of (A) is that premature termination of the calculations, due to the size of the problem or for any other reason, at least gives feasible solutions, known to be non-dominated and this may be of some use to the decision maker. Conversely, failure to complete an algorithm in class (B) leaves us not even knowing one efficient solution. However, if our objective in finding the efficient set is to discard dominated solutions on the grounds that they would not be optimal for any sensible utility function, then we could, instead, discard the complement of the set with which we terminate our algorithm. We will still not have thrown away any potential optima but we may have retained more solutions than necessary.

Class (C) possesses similar advantages and disadvantages as (B) but with the additional difficulty that the final step involves selecting the efficient subset of a finite set expressed as a list of members. If the efficient set has many elements this step could be extremely time-consuming and is rarely discussed explicitly by authors proposing algorithms in class (C).

Methods in section (D) display none of the advantages of either class (A) or class (B).

Class (I) algorithms seem naturally to fall also in class (A) and this is true for the selection considered here. Otherwise, there is no necessary relationship between the two classification schemes.

For future use we will include a couple of extra definitions here. Let us say that $x, y \in X$ are *equivalent* if

$$f(x) = f(y).$$

For any subset $S \subseteq X$ we shall call $T \subseteq S$ a *complete representative* of S if every $s \in S$ is equivalent to some $t \in T$. Both T and S generate the same set (efficient frontier) in the objective function space.

We shall also say that feasible $x \in X$ is *weakly efficient* if there is no feasible $y \in X$ satisfying

$$f(y) > f(x)$$

The set of all such solutions will be called the *weak efficient set*.

Many algorithms, particularly those in class (I), naturally produce a complete representative of the efficient set but are easily modified, if desired, at some computational cost, to generate the complete set. In some cases the weak efficient set is produced. This can be used to obtain the efficient set, but in many cases the weak efficient set itself may be adequate.

Linear programming is discussed in sections 2 and 3 with the former concentrating on finding efficient vertices. Sequential problems via dynamic programming are studied in section 4 and integer problems covered in section 5. Finally, in section 6, combinatorial structures, particularly routing and assignment problems are investigated. Non-linear problems, involving more sophisticated characterisation theorems and few algorithms are not discussed here.

2. Linear multi-objective problems - Finding efficient vertices

We can write the problem as

$$\text{LVMP:} \quad V \max \; Cx$$

$$\text{subject to} \quad Ax \leq b$$

$$x \geq 0$$

and in this section we will describe how to obtain all efficient basic feasible solutions. The approach we describe, though coinciding with none of the published methods is close to all of them and we will endeavour to point out where such methods differ from the description below. For comparison with subsequent sections we note that all the algorithms in this and the next section can be classified as IA according to the schemes described in the last section.

The methods can be seen to turn upon the following characterisation theorem. Proofs may be found in many places, e.g. [37].

Theorem 2.1

A feasible x in LVMP is efficient if and only if it is optimal in $LP(w)$ for some $w \in R^p$ with $w > 0$ where

$$LP(w): \quad \text{maximise} \quad w^T Cx$$
$$\text{subject to} \quad Ax \leqq b \quad (Ax+s=b, \quad s \geq 0)$$
$$x \geqq 0.$$

Suppose B is a basic matrix* i.e. it is a non singular $m \times m$ submatrix of (A,I) and that by permuting the coefficients of (x,s) we can write (A,I) as (B,N); (x,s) as (x_B, x_N) and C as (C_B, C_N). Then we will say B is *efficient* if and only if there is some $w>0$ such that

$$w^T(C_B B^{-1} N - C_N) \geqq 0 \qquad (2.1)$$

In order to handle strict inequalities like $w>0$ computationally it is only necessary to observe that since (2.1) is homogeneous, as will be all the sets of inequalities in which it occurs, we can write the inequality as $w \geqq e$ where e is a k-vector of 1's. Using theorem 2.1 and the fact (easily proved from the lexicographic simplex method) that (2.1) for some B is necessary and sufficient for $(x_B, x_N) = (B^{-1}b, 0)$ to be optimal in $LP(w)$ we get a valuable corollary.

Corollary 2.2

A feasible $\hat{x}$ in LVMP is an efficient basic feasible solution if and only if there is an efficient basis matrix B such that $\hat{x} = (\hat{x}_B, \hat{x}_N) = (B^{-1}b, 0)$.

A useful consequence of this result is that we can concentrate our search on finding efficient bases which will, in turn, yield efficient solutions. Such an approach, suggested by Evans and Steuer [18] avoids problems with degeneracy encountered by other authors. Using a theorem of the alternative it can be shown that (2.1) is equivalent to the inconsistency of the set of inequalities

$$(C_B B^{-1} N - C_N)u \leq 0; \qquad u \geqq 0$$

* We will assume, *for simplicity of presentation only*, that no two columns of (A,I) are identical. Thus B specifies and is specified by the index set of columns defining it.

and this can be tested by solving the subsidiary LP

$$\begin{aligned} \text{maximise} \quad & e^T v \\ \text{subject to} \quad & (C_B B^{-1} N - C_N)u + v = 0 \\ & u, v \geqq 0 \end{aligned}$$

which either has $(u,v) = (0,0)$ as its optimal solution or is unbounded. The former is a necessary and sufficient condition for the efficiency of B.

The basic idea of the algorithm is to first find an efficient basis, B, if one exists. Then one *processes* B by testing adjacent bases (i.e. those obtainable from B by a single pivot) for efficiency. Continuing in this way, we look for an unprocessed efficient basis B' and test any previously unencountered bases adjacent to B'. If all efficient bases so far discovered have been processed we stop and the following result ensures us that no efficient bases remain to be discovered.

Theorem 2.3

The graph $G_1 = (V, E_1)$ with vertex set V and edge set E_1 given by

$$V = \{B \mid B \text{ is an efficient basis}\}$$

$$E_1 = \{\{B_1, B_2\} \mid B_1 \text{ and } B_2 \text{ are adjacent}\}$$

is connected.

This is easily proved by parametric methods; a little care is necessary to cope with the fact that we are dealing with bases, not vertices (two adjacent degenerate bases may define the same vertex).

The algorithm can be improved by refining the adjacent basis test as follows. Suppose B is efficient, $\bar{B}$ is adjacent to B and a^j is the unique column of $\bar{B}$ not occurring in B. Let us say that $(B, \bar{B})$ is an *efficient pair* if and only if there is some $w > 0$ such that

$$w^T(C_B B^{-1} N - C_N) \geqq 0 \qquad (2.2a)$$

$$w^T(C_B B^{-1} a^j - c^j) = 0 \qquad (2.2b)$$

where c^j is the column of C corresponding to a^j. Note that (2.2a) guarantees the efficiency of B. By making x_j basic in the tableau corresponding to B for LP(w), where w is any solution of (2.2), it is easy, using the simplex method criterion for alternative optimal solutions, to see that the result is an optimal tableau corresponding to $\bar{B}$. This yields the next result.

Theorem 2.4

If $(B,\bar{B})$ is an efficient pair of bases then $\bar{B}$ is efficient and $(\bar{B},B)$ is an efficient pair. Further, if B is non-degenerate the edge specified by B and x_j is efficient if and only if $(B,\bar{B})$ is an efficient pair.

With this result in mind we can modify the algorithm by testing bases adjacent to B to see if they make an efficient pair with B. Corresponding to theorem 2.3 we have

Theorem 2.5

The graph $G_2 = (V,E_2)$ with V defined as in theorem 2.3 and

$$E_2 = \{\{B_1,B_2\} \mid (B_1,B_2) \text{ is an efficient pair}\}$$

is connected.

The proof of theorem 2.3 referred to above also establishes theorem 2.5 (which, of course, implies theorem 2.3).

Using a theorem of the alternative we can again express (2.2) as a dual LP problem

$$\begin{aligned} LP_j : \text{maximise } & e^T v \\ \text{subject to } & (C_B B^{-1} N - C_N)u - (C_B B^{-1} a^j - c^j)w + v = 0 \\ & u,w,v \geqq 0 \end{aligned}$$

and the maximal solution being bounded (equivalent to $(u,w,v) = (0,0,0)$ being optimal) is necessary and sufficient for $(B,\bar{B})$ being an efficient pair.

The method outlined is essentially "algorithm 2" of Evans and Steur [19]. Unfortunately, as pointed out by Ecker and Kouada [17], Evans and Steuer appear to base their method on the incorrect assertion that boundedness of LP_j is necessary and sufficient for efficiency of $\bar{B}$. The approach taken above shows that algorithm 2 is correct. This algorithm builds upon similar but slightly cruder versions due to Charnes and Cooper [10], Evans and Steuer [18], Yu and Zeleny [51] and Zeleny [52]. Ecker and Kouada [17] suggest a neat method for examining the feasibility of (2.2) for all j indexing non-basic variables, simultaneously, which can easily be incorporated in the algorithm. (Ecker and Kouada's overall approach requires a special treatment of degeneracy.)

It is worth noting that the basis exploration approach used here requires that we store, for each unprocessed efficient basis, the inverse basis matrix, assuming a revised simplex method is used. The storage requirements involved are potentially very large and Zeleny [52] suggests that we only store one basis and don't just explore adjacent bases. The computational implications of this method have not been evaluated but do not appear promising. One way of easing storage requirements is to associate with each efficient pair of bases $(B,\bar{B})$, where $\bar{B}$ has not been listed before, the η-vector [25] and an index which perform the pivot from B^{-1} to $\bar{B}^{-1}$. Whatever method is used to record inverse bases, if G_2 has a large diameter or, in almost all situations if Zeleny's suggestion is employed, a long sequence of pivots may have to be performed. This can lead to an accumulation of inaccuracies as observed by Evans and Steuer. This suggests that some consideration of errors and basis re-inversion should be made. No author so far appears to have pursued this point.

Many authors work directly with vertices rather than bases. The difficulty with this approach arises from the fact that (2.1) is not necessary, although it is sufficient, for $(x_B, x_N) = (B^{-1}b, 0)$ to be efficient. Furthermore, finding the edges emanating from a degenerate vertex is a non-trivial problem. This is considered in some detail by Evans and Steuer [19] in presenting their algorithm 1 and more cursorily by other authors but the approach appears to offer no obvious advantages except possibly for particular examples with a high degree of degeneracy.

Another approach, discussed by Yu and Zeleny [51] and Zeleny [52], is to decompose the w-parameter space into polyhedra associated with efficient vertices, or, in more generality, faces. The considerable computational cost of obtaining these regions would seem to rule out such methods in an algorithm to find efficient vertices but it may have more potential for finding the complete efficient set.

The final topic we shall discuss in this section is the first with which the algorithm itself must deal: finding an efficient basis or showing that none exists. If the feasible region is known to be bounded or can be made so by putting "realistic" upper bounds on the variables then we can simply solve LP(e). Otherwise using theorem 2.1 and the basic duality result that a feasible LP is bounded if and only if its dual problem is feasible we obtain the following result.

Theorem 2.6

Suppose LVMP is feasible and consider the inequalities

$$\begin{aligned} A^T y &\geqq C^T w \\ y &\geqq 0, \quad w > 0 \end{aligned} \qquad (2.3)$$

(i) If $(\hat{y},\hat{w})$ is feasible in (2.3) then $LP(\hat{w})$ has an optimal (efficient) solution.

(ii) If (2.3) is infeasible the efficient set is empty.

When solving LP(w) by the simplex method it is possible that some of the bases encountered may be efficient. One could test for this using (2.1), either every iteration, or only in occasional tableaux. Evans and Steuer's computational experiments [19] indicate that the former strategy is a poor one and, although the latter may be more successful, bearing in mind we are only considering the initialisation phase of a method in which, for most problems, the bulk of computation will be devoted to searching for further efficient bases, it is debatable whether it is worthwhile to introduce such refinements. Indeed, in view of these considerations the number of papers on this problem is rather surprising. Evans and Steuer [18] use a complicated sequential procedure. This avoids considering the inequalities (2.3) but only by searching for bounded objective functions and only then if such objectives exist. Ecker and Kauada [16] show that a single LP can be used to find an efficient feasible solution or show that there is none. However, this LP involved adding the constraints $Cx \geq Cx_0$ and there is no obvious reason why the single LP should necessarily be quicker to solve than the two-stage procedure described above. Furthermore, the LP will not in general yield an efficient vertex. Ecker and Hegner [14] show how an efficient basis (and its inverse) may be derived from the efficient point but again some additional computation is involved. Isermann [30] proposed a two-stage procedure similar to but more complicated than the above. However, Ecker and Hegner [14] show that his method could fail. Benson [3] gave conditions under which the Isermann procedure works as well as a two-stage procedure of his own, valid in all circumstances. It is still more complicated than the above.

3. Linear multiobjective problems - Further considerations

If the decision-maker has a non-linear utility function increasing in the objectives, his optimal decision will be efficient but may not be a vertex. For this reason we may be interested in finding the complete efficient set and not just the efficient vertices. From theorem 2.1 we have immediately the following property.

Theorem 3.1

The efficient set is a union of faces.

As an immediate corollary:

Corollary 3.2

A point in the relative interior of a face is efficient if and only if the whole face is efficient.

Faces can be defined in at least three ways. To explain these we need to define a $(m+n)$-vector $u = (x, b-Ax)$. Let X denote the feasible region

$$X = \{x \mid u \geqq 0\}.$$

Then, (i) if $J \subseteq \{1,2,\ldots,m+n\}$, any set of the form

$$F_J = \{x \mid u \geqq 0, \quad u_j = 0 \quad \text{for} \quad j \in J\}$$

which is non-empty, is a face and any face can be expressed (not necessarily uniquely) in this form, for some J. Alternatively

(ii) if $a \in R^n$ satisfies $a \neq 0$ and $a \in R$ then

$$\{x \in X \mid a^T x = \alpha\}$$

is a face if it is non-empty and $a^T x \leq \alpha$ for all $x \in X$. Furthermore, with any face can be associated (a, α) which define the face as above. Finally

(iii) any face can be defined by specifying its vertices, (which are also vertices of X).

We shall mainly use form (i) here but also indicate how the faces found can be expressed in the other forms outlined above. All three forms have been used in the literature

Suppose B is a basis and $J_B \subseteq \{1,2,\ldots,m+n\}$ indexes the *non-basic* variables. We will say that $J \subseteq J_B$ is *efficient* if there is some $w > 0$ such that

$$w^T(C_B B^{-1}N - C_N) \geqq 0 \quad (3.1a)$$

$$w^T(C_B B^{-1}a^j - c^j) = 0 \quad \text{for } j \in J_B \setminus J \quad (3.1b)$$

Theorem 2.1 and corollary 3.2 lead to the following result.

Theorem 3.3

A face F_J is efficient if and only if there is some efficient basis B and $J \subseteq J_B$, such that J is efficient. Furthermore F_J can be defined in form (ii) by taking $a = C^T w$ and $\alpha = w^T C_B B^{-1} b$ where w solves (3.1).

The most convenient representation of the complete efficient set is to specify the *maximal* efficient faces. To do this we must find minimal sets J satisfying (3.1). Both Isermann [30] with a test which is essentially the dual of (3.1) and Ecker, Hegner and Kouada 15 with (3.1) itself, describe methods for doing this. The approach of Ecker et al. is more explicit and takes account of information gained from other bases incident to some face. Both approaches essentially assume non-degeneracy and Ecker et al assume X is bounded.

Bitron and Magnanti [7] give an interesting characterisation of efficient faces incident to a given vertex by specifying hyperplanes as in form (ii). The parameters of these hyperplanes, which contain all maximal efficient sets incident to the vertex, are given by the extreme points of the optimal solution set of an auxiliary LP associated with the vertex.

Except in the trivial sense of avoiding duplication, no use is made of information from other vertices. The actual algorithm described by these authors does not make clear how all extreme points (which are also needed to find new efficient vertices) are to be generated and so direct comparison with the previous methods is not easy. A result along these lines, but not stated in this form by Bitran and Magnanti is the following.

Theorem 3.4

Suppose B is a basis and $\hat{w}$ is an extreme point of the set of inequalities

$$w^T(C_B B^{-1}N - C_N) \geqq 0$$

$$w \geqq e$$

then

$$\{x \in X \mid w^T Cx = w^T C_B B^{-1} b\}$$

is an efficient face. Furthermore all maximal efficient faces can be obtained in this way.

The efficient set algorithm then proceeds as in the algorithms of the preceding section, generating new maximal efficient faces (if there are any) whenever new efficient bases are discovered. If the Ecker et al./Isermann-type characterisation is used, efficient pairs of bases are automatically generated. With the Bitran-Magnanti approach one must pivot to an adjacent basis in one of the efficient faces found from the current basis. As outlined no difficulties over degeneracy or unboundedness occur. Careful recording of the efficient bases makes the listing of the vertices defining each efficient face straightforward. This is covered explicitly by Isermann [29].

Gal [21] has a somewhat underspecified approach which associates a set of vectors with each efficient vertex. By selecting a vector and the bases whose sets contain that vector the maximal efficient faces can be constructed. Yu and Zeleny [51] and Zeleny [52] propose testing sets of efficient vertices assuming these have already been determined, to see if their convex hull forms an efficient face. Such an approach does not appear computationally atractive.

We now turn to a special case of the LVMP. This is the vector transportation problem which can be written as

$$\begin{aligned}
\text{VTP:}\quad \text{V max}\quad & f(x) = -\sum_{i,j}^{m,n} c^{ij} x_{ij} \\
\text{subject to}\quad & \sum_{j=1}^{n} x_{ij} = a_i \qquad i = 1,\dots,m \\
& \sum_{i=1}^{m} x_{ij} = b_j \qquad j = 1,\dots,n \\
& x_{ij} \geqq 0
\end{aligned}$$

where c^{ij} is a k-vector, $a_i, b_i > 0$ and $\sum_i a_i = \sum_j b_j$. This can be solved by modifying the basic approach outlines in the last two sections to enable the theory underlying the transportation method to be used. Standard tricks, involving perturbations of the right hand sides, can be used to break degeneracy and therefore we shall assume no degeneracy.

However, problems with degeneracy can also be side-stepped by the techniques outlined above.

Let $\{\hat{x}_{ij}\}$ be a feasible solution of the constraints. Under our non-degeneracy assumption there are unique k-vectors u^i, v^j for $i = 1,\ldots,m;\ j = 1,\ldots,n$ satisfying $u^1 = 0$ and

$$u^i + v^j = c^{ij} \qquad \text{whenever } \hat{x}_{ij} > 0.$$

The LP duality theorem with theorems 2.1 and 2.2 establish the next result.

Theorem 3.5

(i) $\{\hat{x}_{ij}\}$ is efficient if and only if there is some $w > 0$ such that

$$w^T(c^{ij}-u^i-v^j) \geqq 0 \qquad \text{for all } i,j.$$

(ii) If $\hat{x}_{k\ell} = 0$ then the edge of the feasible region defined by making $x_{k\ell}$ basic is efficient if and only if there is some $w > 0$ such that

$$w^T(c^{ij}-u^i-v^j) \geqq 0 \qquad \text{for all } i,j$$

$$w^T(c^{k\ell}-u^k-v^\ell) = 0.$$

Using these results and, of course, the standard labelling methods [25] for finding adjacent solutions, the procedure of the previous section can be modified in an obvious way to generate all efficient basic feasible solutions. This, with some modifications of detail is essentially Phase II of the method proposed by Isermann [31]. Phase I is easy once it is noted that the feasible region is bounded since this means that we have only to solve the transportation problem with cost function

$$\sum_{i,j=1}^{m,n} e^T c^{ij} x_{ij}$$

and the same constraints as VTP. This is simpler than the lexicographic minimisation method which has been proposed.

We can also generalise (3.1) to the case of the transportation problem and use it to calculate maximal efficient faces. Isermann gives details.

The transportation problem with two objectives is studied by Aneja and Nair [1] who present an algorithm that involves solving at least one complete transportation problem for each vertex (often more) and therefore seems uncompetitive. These authors also consider the three objective problem in which the third objective function is of bottleneck (minimax) type. This is easily allowed for by right hand side parametrisation but we will omit the details.

In general, bicriterion problems (i.e. those with $p=2$) essentially involve only one parameter since the weighting vector $w = (w_1, w_2) > 0$ can be scaled so that $w_1 + w_2 = 1$ in which case w can be written as $w = (w_1, 1-w_1)$ for $0 < w_1 < 1$. Standard parametric programming [25] can be used to find the optimal solutions for all w_1 in the unit interval. A little care is needed if dual degeneracy occurs since all optimal solutions must be found for all dual degenerate tableau. However, if a complete representative of the efficient set is acceptable, such difficulties disappear. Choo [11] outlines a procedure for both bicriterion linear and transportation problems which, although not stated explicitly, adopts the parametric programming approach. Because of the relative ease with which bi-criterion problems can be solved it is suggested that all algorithms designed for the general problem should be tested on examples with at least three criteria.

Steuer [40], [41] considers the problem LP(w) in which each component of w is constrained to lie in an (open) interval which we write $w \in W$. He shows how this problem can be transformed into a LVMP with the same constraint set. Unfortunately the number of objective functions rises from p to 2^p and this could be computationally disadvantageous. However, if (2.1), (2.2) and (3.1) are modified so that we require $w \in W$ instead of $w > 0$, it is easy to adapt the algorithms described above, using bounded variable methods, to apply directly to this problem.

Bitran [6] considers the family of LVMP's in which $\ell_{ij} \leq c_{ij} \leq u_{ij}$, which we will write $C \in \Phi$. He solves the problem of evaluating $\bigcap_{C\in\Phi} \text{Eff } C$, where Eff C is the efficient set corresponding to C. However, the most natural set for the decision maker would appear to be $\bigcup_{C\in\Phi} \text{Eff } C$ and no results are offered for this problem. More general sensitivity analysis is discussed by Gal [23] who addresses the problem of the range of parameter variation, when either C or b is parametrised, which does not change the efficient set. Gal [22] and Gal and Leberling [24] also show how redundant objective functions (i.e. those whose removal does not change the efficient set) can be identified.

Schachtman [39] offers an algorithm to find the efficient set when the feasible set (which must be bounded) is specified as the convex hull of a given finite set of vectors. This is particularly pertinent to statistical descision theory. He also shows how a polytope with the same efficient set but more easily analysed may be constructed. This problem is also discussed by Zionts and Wallenius [53].

4. Sequential Problems

We now consider problems which have a natural sequential form or can be transformed to such a form. The type of sequential problem we shall be discussing in this section can be specified by

$$\text{Vmax} \quad f(x^1, x^2, \ldots, x^R) = \sum_{r=1}^{R} g^r(z^r, x^r)$$

where z^1 is given and

$$z^{r+1} = h^r(z^r, x^r) \qquad r = 1,2,\ldots,R-1$$

and $x^1, x^2, \ldots, x^R$ are to be chosen by the decision-maker subject to $x^r \in X_r$, for $r = 1,2,\ldots,R$, where x^r, z^r, g^r, h^r are vectors, appropriately dimensioned, for $r = 1,2,..,R$.

The natural tool to use in the analysis of such problems is the backward recursion procedure of dynamic programming. We shall firstly write down the natural generalisation of the recursive inductive equations to the vector case. These involve the sets $E_r(z^r)$ which we would hope to be the set of efficient values over the stages $r, r+1, \ldots, R$ when the process starts from state z^r. We shall see that this hope is only fulfilled under appropriate conditions although it is, of course, correct in the single objective case. We write "+" for the usual sum of sets and "Eff A" for the efficient set of A.

$$E_R(z^R) = \text{Eff} \bigcup_{x^R \in X_R} \{g^R(z^R, x^R)\}$$

$$E_r(z^r) = \text{Eff} \bigcup_{x^r \in X_r} \{\{g^r(z^r, x^r)\} + E_{r+1}(h^r(z^r, x^r))\}$$

for $r = 1,2,..,R-1$.

We would then hope that $E_1(z^1)$ would be the set of efficient f i.e. the efficient set in the objective function space which we shall write E. Furthermore, to identify the set of efficient solutions F, we might expect to calculate, firstly, the x^r's giving rise to members of $E_r(z^r)$. To be precise, this gives the sets

$$F_R(z^R) = \{x^R \in X_R | g^R(z^R, x^R) \in E_R(z^R)\}$$

$$F_r(z^r) = \{x^r \in X_r \mid \text{There is a } y \in E_{r+1}(h^r(z^r, x^r)) \text{ such that } (g^r(z^r, x^r) + y) \in E_r(z^r)\}$$

which arise naturally in the course of calculating the $E_r(z^r)$'s. We must then construct F*, where

$$F^* = \{(x^1, x^2, \ldots, x^R) | x^1 \in E_1(z^1),\ x^r \in F_r(h^{r-1}(z^{r-1}, x^{r-1})) \text{ for } r = 2, 3, \ldots, R\}$$

and hope that $F^* = F$.

Unfortunately, as indicated in the introduction and in contradiction of the single objective case, we cannot guarantee that $E_1(z^1) = E$ or $F^* = F$. The following pathological example illustrates this point.

Counter-example 4.1

Take $X_1 = \{\binom{-2}{2}, \binom{2}{-2}\}$

$$X_2 = \{x \in R^2 | |x_1| < 3, |x_2| < 3\} \cup \{\binom{-3}{3}\}$$

$$g^1(x) = g^2(x) = x$$

$$z^1 = 0$$

$$h^1(z^1, x^1) = 0 \quad \text{for all } z^1, x^1.$$

Then $E_2(z^2) = \{\binom{-3}{3}\}$ for all z^2

$$E_1(z^1) = E_1(0) = \{\binom{-5}{5}, \binom{-1}{1}\}$$

$$F_2(z^2) = \{\binom{-2}{2}, \binom{2}{-2}\} \quad \text{for all } z^2$$

$$F^* = \{(\binom{-2}{2}, \binom{-3}{3}), (\binom{2}{-2}, \binom{-3}{3})\}$$

However, it is not hard to see that

$$E = \{\binom{-5}{5}\}$$

$$F = \{(\binom{-2}{2}, \binom{-3}{3})\}$$

We see that backward induction fails here, although it can be shown that forward induction is successful. However, it is possible to construct examples for which neither method works.

In the example $E \subseteq E_1(z^1)$, $F \subseteq F^*$, which is true in general, but, in order to achieve equality, extra conditions are needed. Let A be the set of achievable objective function values given z^1:

$$A = \{ \sum_{r=1}^{R} g^t(z^r,x^r) \,|\, z^{r+1} = h^r(z^r,x^r) \quad \text{for } r = 1,2,..,R-1;$$
$$x^r \in X_r \quad \text{for } r = 1,2,...R\}.$$

Then $E = \text{eff } A$ and we will say that E is a *kernel* if and only if, for any $y \in A$ there is $y' \in E$ such that $y' \geqq y$.

Theorem 4.2

$E \subseteq E_1(z_1)$, $F \subseteq F^*$. If, in addition, E is a kernel then $E = E_1(z_1)$, $F = F^*$.

The proof is straightforward and the result was first stated in greater generality by Yu and Seiford [50]. They allowed much more general combination operations to get f from $g^1, g^2, ..., g^R$, the only requirements being monotonicity and decomposability for each component. They also consider a much more general domination structure in the objective function space. Moreover, they exhibit a counter-example showing that some extra condition is needed in theorem 4.2 but their example used a more complicated combination operator than simple addition and a more complicated combination structure than componentwise ordering. The counter-example given here contradicts the claims of Villareal and Karwen [44] who, in the context of an application to integer programming, claim that $E = E_1(z^1)$ without extra conditions. The example shows that even in applications to integer programming care is needed unless the feasible region is known to be bounded.

Conditions for E being a kernel (or in Yu and Seiford's terminology the problem being non-dominance bounded) are given by Hartley [27] under quite general order relations and for cone-generated orders. Results in [27] can be used to prove the following which can be used in conjunction with theorem 4.2.

Theorem 4.3

E is a kernel if any of the following holds

(i) X_r is finite for $r = 1,2,\ldots,R$.

(ii) X_r is a polyhedral set, g_r and h_r are linear for $r = 1,2,\ldots,R$.

(iii) X_r is a compact set, g_r and h_r are continuous for $r = 1,2,\ldots,R$.

(iv) X_r is a closed set, g_r is inf-compact and h_r is linear for $r = 1,2,\ldots,R$.

Of course, unless the sets $E_r(z^r)$ can be expressed in some convenient analytic way it may be impossible to perform the calculations for (iii) and (iv).

When this generalised dynamic programming procedure works, it is a class IID method.

A special case of the above scheme is to find the efficient set of a sum of sets and a DP-type procedure was given by Moskowitz [33] for the case of finite sets. This was generalised by White [47] to infinite sets. His condition for the procedure neither implies nor is implied by E being a kernel, but does use similar concepts. It seems rather difficult to apply when $R \geq 3$. The case of finite sets was also considered by Daellenbach and de Kluyuer [12].

Stochastic sequential problems have been discussed by several authors and we refer to the paper by Thomas, [43] in the present volume, which gives a brief survey of some of the results.

5. Integer multiple objective programming

The integer, linear, vector maximum problem can be written

$$\text{ILVMP}: \quad V \max \; Cx$$
$$\text{subject to} \quad Ax \leqq b$$
$$x \geqq c, \quad x \in X$$

where $X = Z^n$ and Z is the set of integers. The zero-one or binary problem, BLVMP, is specified in the same way except that $X = \{0,1\}^n$.

In some ways this is an attractive problem in that the efficient set is finite, at least if the feasible region is bounded, and can therefore be listed explicitly. However, this Janus-like advantage, can create difficulties. To see this, consider the problem

$$\begin{aligned} &V \max \quad Ix \\ &\text{subject to} \quad e^T x \leqq b \\ &\qquad\qquad\quad x \geqq 0, \quad x \in Z^n \end{aligned}$$

where I is a unit matrix, e is a vector of 1's and $b>0$ satisfies $b \in Z$. Then the cardinality of the efficient set is $\binom{b+n}{n-1}$, whereas, if $x \in Z^n$ is dropped we have n efficient vertices, and 1 efficient face. When $b=19$, $n=6$ these numbers become 42504, 6, 1, respectively. Thus a virtually trivial problem in the LP case can become unmanageable when the variables are integer-valued. Of course in some cases, particularly for binary problems, the opposite can happen and an efficient set that is highly complicated without the integer constraints can result in a relatively short list of efficient solutions.

The second problem is that the weighting factor characterisation of theorem 2.1 does not carry over to the integer case. We will give an example to show this in section 6.

Unless the utility function is known to be linear we must appeal to different characterisations and we shall describe some of these now. The proofs are straightforward and are omitted. The first theorem is a slight extension of work of Klein and Hannan [32].

We will first define some new notation. We shall write, for any integers α,β with $\beta \geqq \alpha$,

$$\bigvee_{i=\alpha}^{\beta} (c^{iT} x \leqq e_i)$$

for the conjunctive constraint which says that at least one of the following inequalities must hold

$$\begin{aligned} c^{\alpha T} x &\leqq e_\alpha \\ c^{(\alpha+1)T} &\leqq e_{\alpha+1} \\ &\vdots \end{aligned}$$

$$\vdots$$

$$c^{\beta T}x \leqq e_\beta,$$

where c^{iT} is the ith row of C (which we take to be $p \times n$).

Theorem 5.1

If $y^1, y^2, \ldots, y^r$ are efficient in ILVMP then any optimal solution of ILP_r:

$$\text{maximise } c^{1T}x$$

$$\text{subject to } Ax \leqq b$$

$$\bigvee_{i=2}^{p} (c^{iT}x \leqq c^{iT}y_j - 1) \quad \text{for } j=1,2,..r$$

$$x \geqq 0, \quad x \in Z^n$$

is also efficient. Furthermore, if the feasible region of ILVMP is bounded then, for any y^1, if y^{r+1} is an optimal solution of ILP_r, the sequence $\{y^1, y^2, \ldots\}$ is finite and a complete representative of the efficient set.

The algorithm which arises from this theorem is obvious. To choose y_1 we could solve ILP(e) if the feasible region is bounded. This seems a simpler procedure than that suggested by Klein and Hannan. The conjunctive constraints can be handled directly particularly in binary problems. Full details of an algorithm for the binary case based on the Balas additive algorithm for a single objective function can be found in [32]. It is a class IA method.

For the next result, due to the author, we need a further definition. If $d^1, d^2 \in Z^{p-1}$ we will say that d^2 is an *ancestor* of d^1 if $d^2 \geqq d^1$ and $e^T d^2 = e^T d^1 + 1$. This says that d^2 equals d^1 in all components except one and exceeds it by one in that component.

For any $d \in Z^{p-1}$ let us write

$$ILP^*(d): \quad \text{maximise } c^{1T}x$$

$$\text{subject to } Ax \leqq b$$

$$c^{iT}x \leqq d_i \quad \text{for } i=2,\ldots,p$$

$$x \geqq 0, \quad x \in Z^n$$

and $\chi(d)$ for its optimal value function. We adopt the convention that $\chi(d) = \infty$ if the problem is unbounded and $\chi(d) = -\infty$ if it is infeasible.

Theorem 5.2

If x is feasible in ILVMP it is efficient if and only if there is some $d \in Z^{p-1}$ such that

(i) x is optimal in $ILP^*(d)$

(ii) $\chi(d) \neq \chi(d')$ for all ancestors d' of d.

One way of turning this result into an algorithm, in the case when ILVMP has a bounded feasible region, is to find the maxima $m_2, m_3, \ldots, m_p$ of $c^{2T}x, c^{3T}x, \ldots, c^{pT}x$ over the feasible region. Then solve $ILP^*(d)$ for $(d^2, d^3, \ldots d^p) \leqq (m^2, m^3, \ldots, m^p)$ choosing a sequence which ensures all ancestors of d have been processed before $ILP^*(d)$ is solved. Note that if $d_i > m_i$ then $\chi(d) = -\infty$. To make the algorithm effective maximal use should be made of parametric procedures to solve $ILP^*(d)$ when $ILP^*(d')$ has already been solved and d' is an ancester of d.

This method, which is also class IA, may involve solving more problems than the previous procedure but avoids conjunctive constraints which could be awkward to handle, particularly for non-binary problems. It also orders the efficient set in a natural way.

As outlined, both methods give a representative set of the efficient set. If the complete efficient set is needed it will be necessary, whenever ILP_r of theorem 5.1 or $ILP^*(d)$ of theorem 5.2, has alternative optimal solutions, to determine the complete set of optimal solutions.

When $p=2$ and an appropriate starting value y' is chosen in the first algorithm, the two methods become the same. The conjunctive constraint in ILP_r reduces to a single standard constraint. The effect of both characterisations is that one has to solve a parametrised family of ILP's with a single right hand side parameter varying. This is a much easier problem than is the one when $p \geq 3$. As in LP, the bicriterion problem deserves to be considered as a special case. The binary case of this result was also discussed by Pasternak and Passy [36].

Our final two characterisation results arise from the work of Bowman [8]. For any $d \in R^p$ define

$$||d||_\infty = \max_{i=1,2,\ldots,p} |d_i|$$

$$\max\{d\} = \max_{i=1,2,\ldots,p} d_i$$

Note that $\max\{d\}$ is *not* a norm. Consider the sequence of ILP's in which we first maximise $c^{1T}x$ over the feasible set of ILVMP. Then we maximise $c^{2T}x$ over the optimal set and then sequentially maximise each of the objective functions over the residual optimal sets. Let f^* be the optimal objective function value at the end of this lexicographic procedure. Define $IP(d)$, for $d \in R^p$, to be the problem

$$IP(d) : \quad \text{minimise} \quad \max\{f^*+d-Cx\}$$
$$\text{subject to} \quad Ax \leqq b$$
$$x \geqq 0; \quad x \in X.$$

Theorem 5.3

x^* is weakly efficient if and only if it is optimal in $IP(d)$ for some $d \geqq 0$ with $d_1=0$.

Bowman used $||.||_\infty$ instead of $\max\{.\}$, but then the characterisation is necessary, but may not be sufficient. The effect of this is that extra solutions, which are not weakly efficient, may be generated and then have to be eliminated at the end.

Now let f^+ be any element in R^p such that $f^+ \geqq Cx$ for all feasible x in ILVMP. Define, for any $w>0$ the problem $IP^+(w)$ by

$$IP^+(w) : \quad \text{minimise} \quad ||W(f^+-Cx)||_\infty = \max\{W(f^+-Cx)\}$$
$$\text{subject to} \quad Ax \leqq b$$
$$x \geqq 0; \quad x \in Z^n$$

where

$$W = \begin{pmatrix} w_1 & & & 0 \\ & w_2 & & \\ & & \ddots & \\ 0 & & & w_p \end{pmatrix}$$

Theorem 5.4

x^* is weakly efficient if and only if it is optimal in $IP(w)$ for some $w>0$.

Note that we can normalise w so that $w_1=1$. This shows that $IP^+(w)$ involves $p-1$ parameters. Bowman's characterisation was for efficient points but he needed an extra condition to guarantee that the efficient and weakly efficient sets are the same, which we will not state here.

In order to solve $IP(d)$ it is useful to rewrite it, by a straightforward transformation, as

$$\begin{aligned} &\text{minimise} && \mu \\ &\text{subject to} && Cx + \mu e \geqq f^*+d \\ & && Ax \leqq b \\ & && x \geqq 0, \quad x \in Z^n \qquad (d_1 = 0) \end{aligned}$$

and $IP^+(w)$ as

$$\begin{aligned} &\text{minimise} && \mu \\ &\text{subject to} && c_i^T + w_i^{-1}\mu \geqq f_i^+ \qquad i = 1,2,..,p; \quad w_1=1 \\ & && Ax \leqq b \\ & && x \geqq 0, \quad x \in Z^n. \end{aligned}$$

Noting that theorems 5.3 and 5.4 characterise weakly efficient solutions, any algorithm based on these characterisations will, at best, generate the weak efficient set or a representative set of it. This means that they may be classed as IC methods for finding the efficient set.

Banker, Guignard and Gupta [2] follow a quite different strategy. They show that if s satisfies

$$Cs \leq 0, \qquad s \in Z^n \tag{5.1}$$

then the efficient set is a subset of

$$\begin{aligned} &Ax \leqq b \\ &\bigvee_{i=1}^{m} (a^{iT}x \geqq b_i + a^{iT}s+1) \end{aligned}$$

where a^i is the ith row of A.

The authors propose that an s satisfying (5.1) be chosen "as near as possible" to the origin in some sense presumably hoping that this will reduce the number of non-efficient solutions to the inequalities. They then essentially enumerate the integer solutions of the inequalities in a systematic but computationally expensive manner and eliminate dominated solutions. Part of the computational difficulty arises from the hard-to-handle conjunctive constraints. This use of their result rather throws away a major advantage of this approach, viz. that the efficient set is nearly expressed as a set of integer inequalities, partly obviating the difficulty of the large size of the efficient set for simple problems, as discussed earlier. Indeed, it can be shown that, for any C, there is a finite set S satisfying

$$S \subseteq \{s | Cs \leq 0, \quad s \in Z^n\}$$

and, for any A and b, the efficient set E, satisfies

$$E = \{x \in Z^n \mid Ax \leqq b, x \geqq 0, \bigvee_{i=1}^{m} (a^{iT}x \geqq b_i + a^{iT}s + 1) \; \forall \; s \in S\}$$

Unfortunately, to find S could be more computationally costly than solving the original problem, although if A and b vary and C is fixed the result might be useful. There is the potential here for the construction of an interesting class III B algorithm.

A special form of the integer problem arises when the problem of selecting the efficient vectors out of a list of vectors is considered. An algorithm, polynomial in the number of vectors and known to be best possible for two or three objective functions, is given by Kung, Luccio and Preparata [33]. This algorithm seems the natural one to use for class C methods and to combine with the approach of Banker et.al. When the initial set of vectors for this problem is known to be the weak efficient set, as is the case for Bowman's characterisations, for example, one might hope for a speedier method. However, other than in the trivial bicriterion case this problem does not appear to have been discussed.

Bitran [4] describes a class III algorithm, which he extends in [5], for binary multi-criteria problems. His method starts by looking at the set of binary vectors efficient when the constraints $Ax \leqq b$ are dropped. The change in this set when the constraints are restored is then calculated. The details are too complicated to describe here.

We will conclude by mentioning the papers of Villareal and Karwen [44,45,46] who adopt a dynamic programming approach In spite of the errors, discussed in the last section, in their underlying multi-objective dynamic programming theory, the problems they discuss are solvable by their procedures. They also show how some of the dimensionality problems arising in the dynamic programming technique can be partially mitigated as well as discussing ways of combining their technique with other approaches.

6. Multiple-objective combinatorial optimisation

Although a well-established area in the single objective case, combinatorial optimisation has not been very intensively investigated from the multiple objective standpoint. In this section I shall describe some general points which arise when this subject is pursued and also note some unsolved problems. Two specific areas, routing problems and assignment problems, which have been discussed by some authors, will be used to illustrate these points but details of algorithms will not be given. Multiple objective machine scheduling has also been studied and the results are surveyed by Ruiz-Diaz and French [38] in their paper in this volume.

The multiple objective routing problem is defined in terms of a network N, two distinct vertices s and t in N and the set $\mathcal{P}$ of paths from s to t in N. To any arc (i,j) of N we assign vector $c(i,j)$ and this allows us to define, for any $P \in \mathcal{P}$, a length

$$c(P) = \sum_{(i,j)\in P} c(i,j)$$

Our problem is then to determine the set of efficient paths, i.e. those $P \in \mathcal{P}$ for which there is no $Q \in \mathcal{P}$ such that

$$c(Q) \leq c(P).$$

The multiple objective assignment problem starts from the set Π_n of permutations on $\{1,2,...,n\}$. To each distinct pair $i,j \in n$ we assign a vector cost c^{ij} and this allows us to define, for any $\pi \in \Pi_n$

$$c(\pi) = \sum_{i=1}^{n} c^{i,\pi(i)}$$

Our problem is then to determine the set of efficient

permutations, i.e. those $\pi \in \Pi_n$ for which there is no $\pi' \in \Pi_n$ such that

$$c(\pi') \leq c(\pi)$$

Both problems in the single objective case have two features in common, and in common with a large class of other problems. Firstly, there exist algorithms for both problems which will find an optimal solution in polynomial time (i.e. with maximum computation time a polynomial in the number of bits required to specify the data). Secondly, if the problems are written as integer programming problems in a natural way, the set of optimal vertices of the linear programming relaxation (the problem in which the integer requirement on the variables is dropped) is equal to the set of optimal integer solutions. Indeed, it follows from the recently discovered polynomial algorithm for linear programming that the second property implies the first, although the linear programming algorithm is not necessarily a competitive procedure. The linear programming relaxation for routing problems is a little too complicated to describe here but full details can be found in [48]. For assignment problems, by putting $x_{ij} = 1$ if $j = \pi(i)$ and $x_{ij} = 0$ otherwise we can write the assignment problem as

$$V \max \quad \sum_{i,j=1}^{n} c^{ij} x_{ij}$$

$$\text{subject to} \quad \sum_{i=1}^{n} x_{ij} = 1$$

$$\sum_{j=1}^{n} x_{ij} = 1$$

$$x_{ij} \geqq 0, \quad \text{integer.}$$

The result just referred to says that in the single objective case, any optimal solution of this problem becomes an optimal vertex, if the variables are not restricted to being integers.

We would naturally hope that both these results would carry over in some way to the multiple objective case. Unfortunately these hopes are dashed. Let us start by considering the second property for the assignment problem. If it were true that the efficient set was a subset of the efficient set of the relaxed problem it would follow from the results of section 2 that any efficient permutation was optimal in the scalar problem obtained by using an appropriate set of positive scalar multipliers. However, consider the following problem in which n=3 and the objective vectors are two-dimensional. The c^{ij}'s are displayed in tabular form.

	1	2	3
1	$\binom{3}{0}$	$\binom{0}{3}$	$\binom{0}{0}$
2	$\binom{0}{3}$	$\binom{3}{0}$	$\binom{1}{2}$
3	$\binom{0}{0}$	$\binom{0}{2}$	$\binom{2}{2}$

Writing a permutation π as $(\pi(1),\pi(2),\pi(3))$ (N.B. *not* cycle notation), we have

$$c(1,2,3) = \binom{8}{2} \qquad c(2,1,3) = \binom{2}{8}$$

$$c(1,3,2) = \binom{4}{4} \qquad c(2,3,1) = \binom{1}{5}$$

$$c(3,1,2) = \binom{0}{5} \qquad c(3,2,1) = \binom{3}{0}$$

Hence (1,2,3), (2,1,3), (1,3,2) are efficient. However, if we put $x_{ij} = \frac{1}{2}$ for $i,j = 1,2,$; $x_{33} = 1$ and $x_{ij} = 0$ otherwise it is easy to check that

$$\sum_{i,j=1}^{n} c^{ij}x_{ij} = \binom{5}{5}$$

so that no set of weighting factors would make (1,3,2) optimal in the LP relaxation. Indeed, it is easy to check graphically that (1,2,3) and (2,1,3) are the only efficient vertices of the relaxed problem. This example also shows that the mutli-objective transportation method of section 3 cannot be applied to this problem. Once again, this is different from the single objective case.

Similar results can be deduced for the routing problem; we refer to [48] for details.

One way round these difficulties is to ignore the efficient solutions, such as (1,3,2) above, which are dominated in the relaxed problem. This approach is adopted by White for the routing problem in [48], where he gives an LP algorithm to determine the remaining efficient solutions. However, having adopted such an approach it may be preferable to use a parametric version of a special purpose algorithm. A suitable parametric procedure for routing problems, where only one parameter is involved, is described in [28] and can be extended to the multi-parametric case. Nevertheless there seems to be no particularly compelling reason for concentrating on this subset of the efficient set. We are therefore thrown back on right hand side parametrisation or class II methods. Assignment problems are discussed in [48]. For routing problems Hansen [25] gives a generalisation of Dijkstra's algorithm to the bicriterion case and Hartley [29] shows how dynamic programming can be used in the general multi-criterion case. These are both class IID algorithms. Unfortunately, although both polynomial algorithms in the single objective case, these methods become exponential in the multiple objective case. In the special case where all but one of the objective functions is a maximum, i.e. respectively for shortest path and assignment problems we have

$$[c(P)]_k = \max_{(i,j)\in P} [c(i,j)]_k$$

$$[c(\pi)]_k = \max_{i=1,..,n} [c^{i,\pi(i)}]_k$$

for $k = 2,...,p$. then the right-hand-side parametrised problem ILP*(d) of section 5 can be easily solved by standard methods. In the shortest path case we simply have to remove certain arcs and solve a single objective shortest path problem and, in the assignment case, by increasing certain $[c^{ij}]_1$'s to a large number we can reduce the problem to a standard assignment problem. Furthermore, the resulting method is pseudopolynomial, i.e. execution time is polynomial in n and $\max_{i,j,k} [c^{ij}]_k$.

None of these useful features carries over to the standard case and this reinforces a belief that a number of "easy" single objective problems turn "hard" in the multi-objective case. We would like to be able to capture these results more precisely by using the concept of NP-completeness, incidentally showing that there is no way in which the polynomial methods of the single objective case can be extended to "polynomial", in some suitably defined sense, methods for the multiple objective problem. Let us recall that, roughly speaking, a problem is NP-complete if it is as hard to solve as the travelling salesman's problem and a wide range of other difficult problems. For practical purposes it means that we would not spend time looking for a polynomial algorithm. Unfortunately there is some ambiguity as to the way in which the NP-completeness concept should be generalised. We will conclude by briefly examining some possible ways this could be achieved.

An immediate difficulty is that, as shown by Hansen [25] the number of efficient paths in the routing problem may be exponential in the data and a similar result can be shown for the assignment problem. Thus, any algorithm will be exponential but we wish to explore the fact that certain problems become even harder than this would imply. We might also note that a single efficient path or permutation can be found in polynomial time simply by taking any set of positive weighting factors and solving the consequential single objective problem. The difficulty arises because of our desire to find all efficient solutions.

If right-hand-side parametrisation is used on the bi-criterion routing problem the resulting problem is known to be NP-complete and I suspect, although I have been unable to find a reference that the same is true for assignment problems. These results can be reinterpreted as stating that the problem of testing whether a path is efficient or not is NP-complete. As a criticism of this criterion we might object that in the vector LP method, having found an efficient vertex we tested "adjacent" vertices for efficiency and thus, if we can find an adjacency concept with the right properties an adjacent solution efficiency test is the right procedure to look at. For right hand side parametrisation, an adjacent problem may be one involving only a unit change in one objective function or the smallest change required to alter the optimal solution. Nevertheless, all such approaches to extending NP-completeness make some implicit presupposition about the method to be used if our interest is in the complete efficient set, although they do throw light on the difficulties encountered in finding suitable algorithms.

Another possibility is to examine the time required per efficient point. Thus, if a problem has M efficient points and takes time T we might ask that T/M be a polynomial in the data. Indeed, White [49] discusses a special case of the multi-objective assignment problem, in which $p=n$ and

$$[c^{ij}]_k = 0 \quad \text{for} \quad j \neq k$$

and the author has found an algorithm for this case, in which T/M is polynomial in n. To date no result for the general problem, linking T/M with execution times for hard single objective problems have been obtained.

Finally, one way round some of these difficulties is to ask only for approximate solutions and [26] gives an algorithm for the bicriterion shortest path problem, allowing a specified error $\varepsilon>0$, which is polynomial in the data and $1/\varepsilon$. Since the scaling method used to derive this algorithm is quite widely applicable one might expect similar results to be obtainable for other multi-objective combinatorial problems.

References

[1] Aneja, Y.P. and Nair, K.P.K. Bicriteria Transportation Problem, *Man.Sci.*, 25, 73-78, (1979).

[2] Banker, R.L., Guignard, M. and Gupta, S.K. An Algorithm for Generating Efficient Solutions to the Multiple Objective Integer Programming Problem. Applied Research Centre, The Warton School U. of Pennsylvania (1978).

[3] Benson, H. Finding an Initial Efficient Extreme Point For a Linear Multiple Objective Program. *J.O.R.S.* 32, 495-498, (1981).

[4] Bitran, G.R. Linear Multiple Objective Programs with Zero-One Variables. *Math.Prog.* 13, 121-139,(1977).

[5] Bitran, G.R. Theory and Algorithms for Linear Multiple Objective Programs with Zero-One Variables. *Math.Prog.* 17, 362-390, (1979).

[6] Bitran, G. Linear Multiple Objective Problems with Internal Coefficients. *Man.Sci.* 26, 694-706, (1980)

[7] Bitran, G.R. and Magnanti, T.L. Duality based Characterizations of Efficient Facets. M.I.T. Preprint, O.R. 092-79 (1979)

[8] Boffey, T.B. (Ed.) Proceedings of CP77-Combinatorial Programme Conference. University of Liverpool

[9] Bowman, V.J. On the Relationship of the Tchebycheff Norm and the Efficient Frontier of Multiple Criteria Objectives. In Thiriesz & Zionts [42].

[10] Charnes, A. and Cooper, W.W. *Management Models and Industrial Applications of Linear Programming.* Wiley, N.Y. (1961).

[11] Choo, E.U., Linear Bicriteria Simplex Algorithm, Santa Clara University Preprint (1981).

[12] Cochrane, J. and Zeleny, M. (Eds), *Multiple Criteria Decision Making*, University of South Carolina Press, Columbia, S.C. (1973).

[13] Daellenbach, H.G. and De Kluyver, C.A. Note on Multiple Objective Dynamic Programming, *J.O.R.S.*, 31, 591-594, (1980).

[14] Ecker, J.G. and Hegner, Nancy S. On Computing an Initial Efficient Extreme Point. *J.O.R.S.*, 2, 1005-1008, (1978).

[15] Ecker, J.E., Hegner, N.S. and Kouada, I.A. Generating all Maximal Efficient Faces for Multiple Objective Linear Programs. *J.O.T.A.*, 30, 353-381, (1980).

[16] Ecker, J.G. and Kouada, I.A. Finding Efficient Points for Linear Multiple Objective Programs. *Math.Prog.* 8, 375-377 (1975).

[17] Ecker, J.G. and Kouada, I.A. Finding all Efficient Extreme Points for Multiple Objective Linear Programs. *Math.Prog.* 14, 249-261 (1978)

[18] Evans, J.P. and Steuer, R.E. A Revised Simplex Method for Linear Multiple Objective Programs. *Math. Prog.* 5, 54-72 (1973).

[19] Evans, J.P. and Steuer, R.E. Generating Efficient Extreme Points in Linear Multiple Objective Programming: Two Algorithms and Computational Experience. In Cochrane, J. and Zeleny, M. [12].

[20] Fandel, G. and Gal, T. (eds.) *Multiple Criteria Decision Making Theory and Application.* Proceedings, Hagen/ Konigswinter, W. Germany (1979). Springer-Verlag, Berlin (1980).

[21] Gal, T. A General Method for Determining the Set of all Efficient Solutions to a Linear Vectormaximum Problem. *E.J.O.R.* 1, 307-322 (1977).

[22] Gal, T. A Note on Size Reduction of the Objective Functions Matrix in Vector Maximum Problems. In Fandel and Gal [20].

[23] Gal, T. Postefficient Sensitivity Analysis in Linear Vector-Maximum Problems. In Nijkamp & Spronk [35].

[24] Gal, T. and Leberling, H. Redundant Objective Functions In Linear Vector Maximum Problems and their Determination. *E.J.O.R.* 1, 176-184, (1977).

[25] Hadley, G. *Linear Programming*. Addison-Wesley, New York, 1962.

[26] Hansen, P. Bicriterion Path Problems, In Fandel & Gal [20].

[27] Hartley, R. Aspects of Partial Decisionmaking - Kernels of Quasi Ordered Sets. *Econometrica* 44, 605-608 (1976).

[28] Hartley, R. Sensitivity Analysis in Shortest Path Problems, In Boffey (ed.) [8].

[29] Hartley, R. Dynamic Programming in Vector Networks, Decision Theory Note 86, University of Manchester (1979).

[30] Isermann, H. The Enumeration of the Set of all Efficient Solutions for a Linear Multiple Objective Program. *O.R.Q.* 28, 711-725 (1977).

[31] Isermann, H. The Enumeration of all Efficient Solutions for a Linear Multiple-Objective Transportation Problem. *N.R.L.Q.* 26, 123-139, (1979).

[32] Klein, D. and Hannan, E. A Branch and Bound Algorithm for the Multiple Objective Zero-One Linear Programming Problem. Florida International University (1979).

[33] Kung, H.T., Luccio, R. and Preparata, F.P. On Finding the Maxima of a Set of Vectors. *J.A.C.M.*, 22, 469-476, (1975).

[34] Moskowitz, H. A Recursion Algorithm for Finding Pure Admissible Decision Functions in Statistical Decisions, *Opns. Res.* 23, 1037-1042 (1975).

[35] Nijkamp, P. and Spronk, J. (Eds.) *Multiple Criteria Analysis*, Gower, Aldershot, Eng. (1981).

[36] Pasternak, H. and Passy, U. Bicriterion Mathematical Programs with Boolean Variables, In J. Cochrane & M. Zeleny [12].

[37] Philip, J. Algorithms for the Vector Maximum Problem, *Math.Prog.* 2, 207-229 (1979).

[38] Ruiz-Diaz, F. and French, S. A Survey of Multi-Criteria Problems in Combinatorial Scheduling Problems. In present volume.

[39] Schachtman, R. Generation of the Admissible Boundary of a Polytope. *Opns.Res.* 22, pp.151-159 (1974).

[40] Steuer, R.E. Multiple Objective Linear Programming with Internal Criterion Weights, *Mgmt.Sci.* 23, 305-316, (1976).

[41] Steuer, R.E. A Five Phase Procedure for Implementing a Vector-Maximum Algorithm for Multiple Objective Linear Programming Problems.

[42] Thiriesz, H. and Zionts, S. (Eds.) *Multiple Criteria Decision Making* (Jouy-en-Josas, France, 1975). Springer-Verlag, Berlin (1976).

[43] Thomas, L.C. Constrained Markov Decision Processes as Multi-objective Problems. In Present Volume.

[44] Villareal, B. and Karwan, M.H. Dynamic Programming Approaches for Multi-criterion Integer Programming, State U. of N.Y. at Buffalo, Buffalo, N.Y. (1978).

[45] Villareal, B. and Karwan, M.H. Mutli-criterion Integer Linear Programming: A Hybrid Dynamic Programming Recursive Approach. State U. of N.Y. at Buffalo, Amherst, N.Y. (1978).

[46] Villareal, B. and Karwan, M.H. Multi-criterion Integer Linear Programming: Some Extensions. State U. of N.Y., Buffalo, Amherst, N.Y. (1978).

[47] White, D.J. Generalised Efficient Solutions for Sums of Sets. *Opns.Res.* 28, 844-846, (1980).

[48] White, D.J. The Set of Efficient Solutions for Multiple Objective Shortest Path Problems. *Computers and O.R.*, 9, 101-107, (1982).

[49] White, D.J. A Special Multi-Objective Assignment Problem. Notes in Decision Theory No. 113 (1982).

[50] Yu, P.L. and Seiford, L. Multi-stage Decision Problems with Multiple Criteria. In Nijkamp and Spronk, M.C.A. (1981).

[51] Yu, P.L. and Zeleny, M. The Set of all Non-Dominated Solutions in Linear Cases and a Multi-Criteria Simplex Method. *J.Math.Anal.Appl.* 49, 430-468 (1975).

[52] Zeleny, M. *Linear Multi Objective Programming*. Lecture Notes in Econ. & Math. Systems No 95, Springer-Verlag, Berlin (1974).

[53] Ziontz, S. and Wallenius, J. Identifying Efficient Vectors: Some Theory and Computational Results. *Opns. Res.* 28, 785-793, (1980).

REACHABILITY OF VECTOR OPTIMA THROUGH DYNAMIC PROCESSES

P. Serafini

(Institute of Mathematics, Computer and System Science, University of Udine, Italy)

1. SUMMARY

This paper deals with the determination of vector optima through dynamic processes, both discrete and continuous. In particular the following problems are investigated: convergence of the defined processes toward vector optima, possibility of interaction between the optimizer and the procedure itself, choice of suitable policies in order to converge toward specified optima.

It is shown that convergence is assured under a rather large degree of interaction. Some ways of improving this interaction are also suggested by applying techniques of optimal control and mathematical programming.

2. INTRODUCTION

In this paper we are given:

(i) a twice continuously differentiable map $F: R^n \to R^m$;

(ii) a closed convex cone $\Lambda \subset R^m$, with non empty interior $\overset{0}{\Lambda}$.

The cone Λ defines a partial ordering in R^m. Accordingly we have the following definition:

Definition A point $x \in R^n$ is Λ optimal (or vector optimal or briefly optimal) if there exists a neighbourhood (nbhd) N of x so that:

$$F(x') - F(x) \notin \Lambda \setminus \{0\}$$

for any $x' \in N$.

Of course Λ optimality reduces to Pareto-optimality if

$\Lambda = R^m_+$. The components F_i of F can be thought of as scalar objectives which have to be simultaneously "optimized", and the cone Λ takes into account the degree of intercomparison allowed among the objectives.

In this paper we shall be interested in finding Λ optima through dynamic processes, both discrete and continuous. These processes look like the familiar steepest ascent processes for scalar optimisation. However, by the very nature of vector optimisation, these processes are governed by difference or differential inclusions rather than equations.

For us a discrete dynamic process is a sequence $\{x_k\} \subset R^n$, $k = 1, 2, \ldots$ and a continuous dynamic process is a piecewise differentiable function

$$x : [0,\infty) \to R^n.$$

Our aim is to find dynamic processes converging toward Λ optima, i.e., $x_k \to x$ or $x(t) \to x$, with x Λ optimal. Therefore it makes sense to require:

$$\begin{aligned} &F(x_{k+1}) - F(x_k) \in \Lambda \qquad \text{(discrete process)} \\ &DF(x(t))\,\dot{x}(t) \in \Lambda \qquad \text{(continuous process)} \end{aligned} \tag{1}$$

where DF(x) is the derivative of F evaluated at x and $\dot{x}(t)$ is the (right) derivative of x(t).

Processes satisfying (1) are called monotone. They have been investigated by several authors (see Smale(1973, 1976), Aubin-Cellina-Nobel (1977), Clarke-Aubin (1977), Cornet (1979) and Aubin (1979)).

Of course it is not strictly necessary to satisfy (1) for a generic process to converge toward optima. However, in order to obtain meaningful results, a condition like (1) is very desirable, since it mounts to "improving" F as the process goes on. There is also another justification for (1). Dynamic processes satisfying (1) often represent economic planning procedures aimed at driving the economy from an initial non-optimal state to an optimal one through a monotone path.

3. CONVERGENCE OF DISCRETE PROCESSES

It is important to remark that condition (1) alone is not enough to guarantee convergence toward Λ optima of discrete processes. Actually it has been proved in Pascoletti-Serafini

(1982) that if:

(a) $F(x_{k+1}) - F(x_k) \in \Lambda$

(b) $\{x_k\}$ is in a compact subset

(c) there exists a continuous function $\in(x)$ such that

(i) $\in(x)>0$ for $x\notin\Omega$, where Ω is any set containing the set of Λ optima,

(ii) $\|F(x_{k+1}) - F(x_k)\| \geqslant \in(x_k)$,

then any convergent subsequence of $\{x_k\}$ converges to some point in Ω.

A quite efficient way to generate sequences satisfying the above conditions is the following.

Let $\Lambda^* = \{\pi \in R^m: \Pi\lambda \geqslant 0 \ \forall\lambda\in\Lambda\}$ (elements of Λ^* are considered row vectors).

It is a known fact that at an optimal x there exists $\pi\in\Lambda^*$ such that $\pi DF(x) = 0$.

Hence if $x_{k+1} = x_k + \Delta x_k$, $\Delta x_k = \alpha_k h_k$ with steplength α_k and direction h_k, it makes sense to choose $h_k = DF^T(x_k)\pi_k^T$ (^{T} denotes transpose) for some $\pi_k\in\Lambda^*$, which amounts to weighting the objectives through π_k. Note also that, since range DF^T is orthogonal to ker DF, the direction h_k has no "irrelevant" component along ker $DF(x_k)$.

Now, taking into account (1), we have:

$$\begin{array}{l}\pi_k\in\Lambda^* \\ DF(x_k)\ DF^T(x_k)\ \pi_k^T\in\Lambda\end{array} \qquad (2)$$

The steplength α_k can be chosen according to:

$$\alpha_k = \inf_{\alpha} DF(x_k + \alpha h_k)\ h_k \notin \Lambda.$$

Condition (2) is not strong enough to guarantee existence of convergent processes.

Let $S(x) = \{\pi\in\mathring{\Lambda}^*: DF(x)\ DF^T(x)\pi^T\in\mathring{\Lambda},\ \|\pi\| = 1\}$ where $\mathring{\Lambda}$ and $\mathring{\Lambda}^*$ denote the cone interiors. The condition $\|\pi\|=1$ is simply a normalisation which is useful for technical purposes.

Let $\theta = \{x\in R^n: \exists\pi\in\Lambda^*,\ \|\pi\| = 1,\ \pi DF(x) = 0\}$ and

$$\mathring{\theta} = \{x\in R^n: \exists\pi\in\mathring{\Lambda}^*,\ \|\pi\| = 1,\ \pi DF(x) = 0\}.$$

Points of θ are usually referred to in the literature as critical points. As already noted Λ-optima lie in θ. It is easy to prove that $S(x)$ is empty if and only if x is in θ.

It has been proved in Pascoletti-Serafini (1982) that if $\sigma(x)$ is a point-to-set mapping which is uppersemicontinuous outside θ and $\phi \neq \sigma(x)\subset S(x)$, then the process governed by the difference inclusion

$$\begin{aligned} x_{k+1} &= x_k + \Delta x_k \\ \Delta x_k &= \alpha_k\ DF^T(x_k)\pi_k^T, \pi_k\in\sigma(x_k) \\ \alpha_k &= \inf_{\alpha}\ DF(x_k + \alpha DF^T(x_k)\pi_k^T)\notin\Lambda \end{aligned} \qquad (3)$$

is convergent toward some $\bar{x}$ in θ. Moreover if $\bar{x}\in\mathring{\theta}$ also $\pi_k\to\bar{\pi}$ where $\bar{\pi}DF(\bar{x}) = 0$. This last property is particularly important and will be exploited later. The uppersemicontinuous mapping $\sigma(x)$ can be constructed through linear programming. Of course the freedom of choice of π_k in $\sigma(x_k)$ can be exploited at each step, thus allowing some interaction between the optimiser and the process.

4. CONVERGENCE OF CONTINUOUS PROCESSES

So far as the continuous process is concerned we are led by the same line of thought to consider the following differential inclusion:

$$\begin{aligned} \dot{x} &= DF^T\ (x(t))\ \pi^T(t) \\ \pi(t) &\in \overline{S(x(t))}\ \text{(i.e. the closure of } S(x(t))) \end{aligned} \qquad (4)$$

We shall only limit to sketch the proof of the following theorem.

<u>Theorem</u>
There exists a differentiable $x :[0,\ a) \to R^n$ which is solution of (4) for an initial condition $x(0) = x_0$ and for some $a>0$.

If moreover $x(t)$ is contained in a compact subset then $a = \infty$ and $x(t)$ tends to some $\bar{x}$ in θ as t tends to infinity.

Proof

First define a function π: $R^n \setminus \theta \to R^m$ such that $\pi(x) \in S(x)$. Such a function clearly exists. We want to show that there exist continuous functions π. This can be done (as suggested by Smale (1976) for a related problem) by choosing for any x a suitable neighbourhood N_x such that a particular constant value π_x is in $S(x')$ for any x' in N_x. Since R^n is locally compact and satisfies the second axiom of countability, the family of N_x, which is an open covering of $R^n \setminus \theta$, has a locally finite refinement $\{V_i\}_{i \in I}$ with I some index set. Let $\gamma_i : R^n \setminus \theta \to R$ be any smooth function strictly positive on V_i and zero outside V_i.

Now the function

$$\pi(x) = \frac{\sum_{i \in I} \gamma_i(x) \pi_x}{\| \sum_{i \in I} \gamma_i(x) \pi_x \|}$$

is well defined and $\pi(x) \in S(x)$. (See Golubitski-Guillemin 1973, pp. 15-17 for the related mathematical topics.)

We are therefore left to consider the differential equation $\dot{x} = f(x)$ with $f(x) = DF^T(x)\, \pi^T(x)$ continuously differentiable and the first part of the theorem is proved.

Now the compactness assumption, the differentiability of $f(x)$ and the monotonicity of the solution imply the second part of the theorem.

Actually a little more could be proved with $\pi(x)$ simply a piecewise continuous function.

We note that only existence of solutions for analogous differential inclusions have been proved under stricter hypotheses in Clarke-Aubin (1977) and Cornet (1977) for instance.

The fact that in the dynamic processes described above convergence toward critical points rather than optima is achieved should not be surprising. This is due to the use of derivatives for the generation of the process. However this is not a serious limitation. In fact a critical non-optimal point is not stable, in the sense of Smale (1973), for the processes (3) and (4). Conversely an optimal $\bar{x}$ characterized by (a) rank $DF(\bar{x}) = m-1$; (b) $\bar{x} \in \overset{0}{\theta}$; (c) $\bar{\pi} D^2 F(\bar{x})$ negative definite on $\ker DF(\bar{x})$, is stable (see Smale (1973) or Marzollo-Pascoletti-Serafini (1979)). We recall that (c) is the second order sufficiency condition for Λ-optimality (Wan (1975)), Marzollo-Pascoletti-Serafini (1979)) and that Λ-optimality at $\bar{x}$ implies $\bar{\pi} D^2 F(\bar{x})$ negative semi-definite on ker $DF(\bar{x})$. For a discussion of the role played by the second order conditions see Marzollo-Pascoletti-Serafini (1978).

Therefore, taking into account stability, we may say that, apart from exceptional cases, (3) and (4) generate processes convergent toward stable optima.

5. CONTROL OF THE DYNAMIC PROCESS

It is natural to look at the process described by (3) and (4) as control problems, where the control variable is π and is constrained to belong to a set depending in turn on the achieved state.

If it is indifferent to the optimizer which Λ-optimum will be achieved by the process, then there are no further problems: it is enough to choose any control π satisfying (3) or (4).

However it may typically happen that some optima are "preferred" to others and therefore some suitable control of the process, i.e., a suitable interaction between the optimizer and the process itself is needed.

Now the following questions arise: (i) given an initial state x_o does there exist a process converging to these preferred optima?; (ii) if so, is there any feedback law $\pi(x)$ yielding this process?

So far as the first question is concerned this is a problem of controllability, known also as accessibility in economic contexts; the results in Cornet (1979) cannot however be applied here because (3) and (4) are monotone processes defined differently. In the continuous case note that:

$$\frac{d}{dt} F(x(t)) = DF(x(t))\, DF^T(x(t))\, \pi^T(x(t)).$$

Hence a necessary condition for a point x to be reachable from x_o is that

$$F(x) - F(x_o) \in \overset{0}{\Lambda}$$

(the same condition holds for the discrete process).

This condition is certainly not sufficient because of the additional requirement $\pi \in \Lambda^*$.

If $\bar{x} \in \overset{0}{\theta}$, it is not difficult to show that there exists a nbnh N of $\bar{x}$ such that $DF(x')DF^T(x')\pi^T \in \Lambda$ implies $\pi \in \Lambda^*$ for any x' in N. Now consider the set $W(x) = \{x' : x' = z(t)$ for some t and some z solution of $\dot{z} = - DF^T(z)\pi^T(z)$, $\pi \in \overline{S(z)}$ and initial condition $z(0) = x\}$. Let $V(\bar{x}) = \{x \in N_{\bar{x}} : F(\bar{x}) - F(x) \in \overset{0}{\Lambda}\}$. In view of the above remarks the results in Cornet (1979), $\bar{x}$ is reachable from any point in $V(\bar{x})$. Therefore the set of points for which $\bar{x}$ is reachable is simply $\bigcup_{x \in V(\bar{x})} W(x)$. An analogous result for the discrete case cannot be given because of the asymmetry in time of the discrete process.

So far the second question above, we note that if (3) and (4) are dynamic processes aimed at finding a particular vector optimum, then this optimum has to be characterized in some way with respect to other not preferred optima, even if it is necessarily unknown in advance. Perhaps the simplest characterization is to specify the value of the associated optimal dual π. If the dynamic process is thought of as a planning procedure, then it still makes sense, because of its economic interpretation to characterize an optimum, i.e. an economic equilibrium state, through the optimal dual π viz. through the marginal gains of the objective functions at the equilibrium.

These motivations lead us to consider the following problem.

Problem A

Given an initial state x_0 control the dynamic process (3) or (4) so as to go as close as possible to an (unknown) optimum whose associated optimal dual has some assigned value.

The naive approach to Problem A is to control the process by exploiting the information carried by the past state trajectory the fact that π is the dual variable and $DF\ DF^T\pi^T$ yields the direction of the image of the trajectory in R^m, can help in the choice of a suitable control. This approach however can be very unsatisfactory.

Let us give a brief account of the difficulties involved in Problem A. Let $\bar{x}$ be a stable optimum and x_0 a point sufficiently near $\bar{x}$ with $F(\bar{x}) - F(x_0) \in \overset{0}{\Lambda}$. Let $\bar{\pi}\ DF(\bar{x}) = 0$ $\bar{\pi} \in \overset{0}{\Lambda^*}$. We have already remarked that $DF(x_0)DF^T(x_0)\pi^T \in \Lambda$. We are , therefore, tempted to control the dynamic process with a constant control π, motivated by the fact that $\pi(t)\to\bar{\pi}$ for any dynamic process converging to $\bar{x}$. In other words we have to study stability of the differential equation

$$\dot{x} = DF^T(x)\,\bar{\pi}^T \tag{5}$$

in the proximity of the equilibrium $\bar{x}$. But $\bar{x}$ is locally stable for (5) if $\bar{\pi}D^2F(\bar{x})$ is negative definite on the whole space rather than on a sub-space as it is required for stability of (4).

As an illustrative example consider:

$\Lambda = R^2$

$F: R^2 \to R^2 \quad F_1 = \exp(-x_1^2 + x_2) \qquad F_2 = \exp(-x_1^2 - x_2)$

$\hat{F}: R^2 \to R^2 \quad \hat{F}_1 = -\exp(x_1^2 + x_2) \qquad \hat{F}_2 = -\exp(x_1^2 - x_2).$

The set of optima is both for F and for $\hat{F}$ the axis $x_1=0$, whose images are the positive branch of the hyperbola $F_1F_2 = 1$ and the negative branch of the hyperbola $\hat{F}_1\hat{F}_2 = 1$, respectively. At (0,0) the optimal dual is (1,1) in both cases. It is easy to see that near the origin $\dot{x}=DF_1+DF_2$ is unstable whilst $\dot{x}=D\hat{F}_1+D\hat{F}_2$ is stable. This difference is because the image of F is convex whilst the image of F is not.

This is indeed a general statement. Actually Problem A becomes often trivial in convex cases.

A possibility of handling Problem A in non-convex cases is offered by applying techniques of optimal control. The next development is concerned with the continuous case only since it is analytically more tractable. Therefore consider the following control problem:

$$\inf_{\pi\in\Pi(x_o)} \ \lim_{\tau\to\infty} \ \| DF^T(x(\tau))\,\bar{\pi}^T \|$$

$$\dot{x}(t) = DF^T(x(t))\,\pi^T(t) \tag{6}$$

$$x(0) = x_o$$

where $\pi(x_0)$ is the set of piecewise continuous function $\pi(t)$ which is feasible for (6), i.e., $\pi(t) \in \overline{S(x(t))}$.

This is a control problem of Mayer type. If $\bar{x}$ such that $\bar{\pi}\, DF(\bar{x}) = 0$, is reachable from x_0, then certainly the optimal control of (6) will drive the state to $\bar{x}$. We note that if we fix τ (instead of taking the limit to infinity), a solution of the above problem is assured to exist by a theorem in Cesari (1968), with a non-substantial modification of the definition of $S(x)$.

Let us venture for the moment in a heuristic discussion of the properties of optimal solutions of (6).

Let us define the function:

$$V(x) = \inf_{\pi \in \Pi(x)} \lim_{\tau \to \infty} \| DF^T(x(\tau))\, \bar{\pi}^T \| .$$

Note that V is independent of time because the control is over an infinite time horizon. By a simple application of the principle of optimality one get:

$$V(x) = \inf_{\pi \in \overline{S(x)}} V(x + DF^T(x)\, \pi^T\, dt).$$

If we suppose that V has Gateaux derivative, then we have:

$$\inf_{\pi \in \overline{S(x)}} DV(x, DF^T(x)\pi^T) = 0$$

which is the Hamilton-Jacobi-Bellman equation for the case in consideration. Hence if we may write

$$DV(x, h) = DV(x)\, h$$

we have the following characterization:

$$\begin{aligned} &DV(x)\, DF^T(x)\, \pi^T \geq 0 \quad \text{for any } \pi \in \overline{S(x)} \\ &DV(x)\, DF^T(x)\, \hat{\pi}^T = 0 \quad \text{for the optimal } \hat{\pi}. \end{aligned} \tag{7}$$

If we denote by $\Gamma^*(x)$ the cone generated by $\overline{S(x)}$, then (7) implies $DF\, DV^T \in \partial\Gamma$ ($\partial\Gamma$ is the boundary of Γ). It is not difficult to see that $\gamma \in \partial\Gamma$ implies either $\gamma \in \partial\Lambda$ or $\gamma = DF\, DF^T \mu^T$ with $\mu \in \partial\Lambda^*$ (or both). Hence
either $DF\, DV^T = DF\, DF^T\, \mu^T$ with $\mu \in \partial\Lambda^*$ and $DF\, DF^T \pi^T \in \partial\Lambda$

or DF $DV^T \in \partial\Lambda$ $\pi \in \partial\Lambda^*$.

These relationships, together with the boundary conditions, allow us in principle to solve the Hamilton-Jacobi-Bellman equation.

We are more interested however in the qualitative behaviour of optimal solutions as displayed by (7). Unless $\overline{DV(x)} = 0$, the optimal control $\pi(x)$ is a boundary point of $\overline{S(x)}$. If $DV(x) = 0$ any control in $\overline{S(x)}$ is optimal. Note that, for well behaved problems, $V(x) = 0$ is likely to define a region A in R^n, whilst $V(x) > 0$ a region B of equicost surfaces. We may then interpret the above result as: any control is optimal in A, but if the optimal trajectory will intersect $\partial A (= \partial B)$ then a boundary control is needed and the trajectory will always remain in ∂A.

The practical difficulties of finding an optimal policy make a search for a suboptimal policy convenient. First we make the following observation: if the optimal dual $\bar{\pi}$ is "inside" $\underline{S}(x)$ throughout the process, then $\pi(t)$ will eventually tend to $\bar{\pi}$. Hence if we are able to keep $\bar{\pi}$ as the most inside of $S(x)$ as possible during the process, we have found an optimal policy for Problem A.

In order to formalize these concepts let us consider the following function:

$$d(\bar{\pi}) = \begin{cases} \min\limits_{\pi \in \partial\Gamma^*} \|\bar{\pi} - \pi\| & \text{if } \bar{\pi} \in \Gamma^* \\ -\min\limits_{\pi \in \partial\Gamma^*} \|\bar{\pi} - \pi\| & \text{if } \bar{\pi} \notin \Gamma^* \end{cases}$$

Clearly $d(\bar{\pi})$ is a kind of measure of how much inside $\bar{\pi}$ is of Γ^*, and hence of $S(x)$. From the convexity of Γ^*, $d(\bar{\pi})$ can be expressed in a more convenient form as follows:

$$d(\bar{\pi}) = \min_{\substack{\gamma \in \Gamma \\ \|\gamma\| = 1}} \bar{\pi}\gamma$$

These observations will now be exploited for the discrete process (3).

If Δx_k is an increment at step k, admissible according to (3), an optimal policy is one which solves:

$$\max_{\Delta x_1} \max_{\Delta x_2} \cdots\cdots \min_{\substack{\gamma \in \Gamma(x+\Sigma \Delta x_k) \\ \|\gamma\| = 1}} \bar{\pi}\gamma$$

A suboptimal policy of order n can therefore be defined as the one which chooses at each iteration step k, the admissible Δx_k which solves the following mathematical programming problem:

$$\max_{\Delta x_k} \max_{\Delta x_{k+1}} \cdots\cdots \max_{\Delta x_{k+n-1}} \min_{\substack{\gamma \in \Gamma(x + \sum_{k}^{k+n-1} \Delta x_i) \\ \|\gamma\|=1}} \bar{\pi}\gamma \tag{8}$$

where of course Δx_k has to be admissible for the cone $\Gamma(x + \sum_{i}^{k-1} \Delta x_i)$. Policies of this type allow a great deal of interaction between the optimizer and the process itself. To illustrate this concept consider that a suboptimal policy of order n generates at each step also n-1 predictions of optimal increments at next iterations. According to the discrepancy between the predictions and the actual increments, the optimizer can decide to raise or to lower the order of the suboptimal policy. As already noted, a simple policy of order zero is sufficient for convex problems.

6. CONCLUSIONS

In this paper both discrete and continuous processes have been treated. Of course a practical procedure aimed at finding vector optima will be very likely based on a discrete process. Nevertheless, since continuous processes are easier to handle analytically and they can be viewed as the limit case of discrete ones, it is still convenient to investigate their properties in order to gain useful insight into the problem.

Also we have not taken into account possible constraints. Clearly constraints will be present in a real problem. However we have concentrated our attention only on the aspects inherent to the vector nature of the optimization problem. The (non-trivial) problems connected with the presence of constraints are the same as in the usual scalar optimization and therefore we have disregarded them (see also for the constrained case Pascoletti-Serafini (1982)). We note however that the theorem stated at the beginning of section 3 is rather general, allowing for any type of constraints and only requiring continuity of the objective function F.

One of the aims of this paper was to point out that in non-convex cases the interaction between the optimizer and the process cannot be based on the simple information from the current solution. Some sort of prediction on the future trajectory is needed. If this prediction is based only on local information then it certainly leads to a suboptimal policy only. If instead it is based on the global characteristics of the trajectory, as it can be done by applying techniques of optimal control, then an optimal policy will be achieved. It is worth noting however that, depending on the particular problem, this last approach can present considerable difficulties.

In case the problem exhibits some kind of convexity, the procedure suggested in Pascoletti-Serafini (1982) can work satisfactorily.

We also note that even if the cone Λ was assumed fixed from the beginning, it could be changed at any iteration step according to the new information available to the optimizer. Of course the procedure will converge to those Λ-optima where Λ is the last defined cone.

It can also be shown that the rate of convergence of the above processes is linear with ratio depending on the eigenvalues of the quadratic form $\pi D^2F(x)$ restricted to $\ker DF \times \ker DF$.

REFERENCES

AUBIN, J.P. 1979 Monotone evolution of resource allocation, *J. of Mathematical Economics,* **6**, pp. 43-62.

AUBIN, J.P., CELLINA, A. and NOHEL, J. 1977 Monotone trajectories of multivalued dynamical systems, *Annali di Matematica Pura ed Applicata,* **115**, pp. 99-117.

CESARI, L. 1968 Existence theorems for optimal controls of the Mayer type, *SIAM J. Control,* **6**, pp. 517-552.

CLARKE, F.H. and AUBIN, J.P. 1977 Monotone invariant solutions to differential inclusions, *J. London Math. Soc.,* **16**, pp. 357-366.

CORNET, B. 1979 Monotone planning procedures and accessibility of Pareto optimal, "New Trends in Dynamic System Theory and Economics" (Aoki, M. and Marzollo, A.,Eds) Academic Press, New York.

GOLUBITSKI, M. and GUILLEMIN, V. 1973 Stable Mappings and Their Singularities, Springer, New York.

MARZOLLO, A., PASCOLETTI, A. and SERAFINI, P. 1978 "Genericity and Singularities in Vector Optimization", Recent Developments in Variable Structure Systems, Economics Biology (Mohler, R.R. and Ruberti, A. Eds) Springer, Berlin.

MARZOLLO, A., PASCOLETTI, A. and SERAFINI, P. 1979 "Differential techniques for cone optimality and stability", New Trends in Dynamic System Theory and Economics (Aoki, M. and Marzollo, A. Eds) Academic Press, New York.

PASCOLETTI, A. and SERAFINI, P. 1982 An iterative procedure for vector optimization, *J. of Mathematical Analysis and Application.*

SMALE, S. 1973 "Global analysis and economics I: Pareto optimum and a generalization of Morse Theory", Dynamical Systems (Peixoto, M.M. Ed) Academic Press, New York.

SMALE, S. 1976 Exchange processes with price adjustment, *J. of Mathematical Economics*, **3**, pp. 211-226.

WAN, Y.H. 1975 On local Pareto optima, *J. of Mathematical Economics*, **2**, pp. 35-42.

OPTIMUM SUBSET PROBLEMS IN STATISTICS AND OPERATIONAL RESEARCH

H.P. Wynn

(Imperial College, London)

1. INTRODUCTION

The purpose of this paper is to give a brief taxonomy of an important group of problems which occur in certain branches of applied mathematics. A rough heading for these problems is "optimum subset problems". We shall place special emphasis on statistics and operational research. It is no accident that the principal source of such problems is multiple decision-making of some kind, or at least decision-making in which the action space is of a complex multidimensional nature. Here are some examples.

(1) Hypothesis testing or zero-one decision making. Here the optimum subset is called the critical region (or the acceptance region). The Neyman-Pearson lemma is perhaps the best known optimum subset result.

(2) Optimum design of experiments or optimum designs of sample surveys. An optimum selection of observation points (treatment combinations, sampling units) is required from a set of allowable observation points. (See Silvey, 1980).

(3) Cluster analysis. Clusters may be composed of points which are in some optimum sense close to each other.

(4) Optimum subset selection in regression. An optimum subset of the parameters is selected to give an optimum regression. (See Boyce, Farhi and Weischedel, 1974).

(5) Optimum subset selection of statistical populations according to the size of their mean. This often goes under the name of rank order selection. (See Gupta and Panchapakesan, 1979).

(6) The class of admissible decision rules in classical Wald decision theory is an optimum class of rules out of a class of

allowable decision rules. (See Berger, 1981, for a recent account).

(7) In mathematical programming many problems can be phrased as optimum subset problems, for example, a shortest path through a directed graph.

(8) Social choice theory, developed by Arrow, Sen and others, has a well developed theory of optimum subsets using choice functions to construct social orderings from individual orderings. (See Sen, 1970, Kelly, 1978).

In trying to present a classification of these problems we have been forced to divide the subject into discrete and continuous problems. One reason for this is historical, but the main reason is that the continuous problems sometimes allow the use of measure-theoretic results which are not available in discrete cases. This dichotomy goes over also to algorithmic considerations where conversely some discretisation may be necessary for programming the continuous problems. It is too easy to take the way out of saying that all optimum subset problemsare merely variational problems in disguise. However, we shall see in the Section 3 that certain continuous problems can certainly be set up as convex programming problems and lead to Kuhn-Tucker type solutions which are a direct generalisation of the Neyman-Pearson lemma. These solutions are the so-called "separation theorems". It is these which, as yet, have no discrete analogue. For discrete problems we shall attempt a rough classification using some of the notation from social choice theory.

2. DISCRETE PROBLEMS

Let X be a finite set and consider all possible subsets namely the power set 2^X. Typical members of 2^X are called U, V etc. Let every subset U have a unique subset C(U). We shall call this set the optimum subset of U. The set function C(.) is called the choice function. Sometimes C(U) is called the choice set. The uniqueness of C(U) is a convenience to allow more compact axiomatisation. It can be overcome in an obvious way by taking unions, but we omit this development.

The first axiom which is universal is that for all U in 2^X

$$C(U) \subset U.$$

We now list a number of other axioms which might be used in a discrete optimum subset theory. They are given labels so as to be recognisable to readers knowledgeable in social choice theory.

All the axioms listed below should be prefixed by "for all U, V in 2^X". A very desirable property is

$$C(U \cup V) = C(C(U) \cup C(V)) \qquad (PI)$$

This can be read as "the optimum subset of the union is the optimum subset of the union of optimum subsets". It is usually referred to as "path independence". A weaker version of this is weak path independence

$$C(U \cup V) \subset C(C(U) \cup C(V)) \qquad (WPI)$$

A host of other axioms are available. We merely list four more.

$$U \subset V \Rightarrow (U \cap C(V)) \subset C(U) \qquad (\alpha)$$

$$C(U \cup V) \subset C(U) \cup C(V) \qquad (\alpha)'$$

$$U \subseteq V \Rightarrow C(V) \text{ is not strictly contained in } C(U) \qquad (SS)$$

$$C(U) \cap C(V) \subset C(U \cup V) \qquad (\gamma)$$

The axiom (SS) is referred to as the "superset" property. It can be shown that (WPl), (α) and (α)$'$ are all equivalent. A key theorem is that (WPl) together with (SS) are equivalent to PI. This makes (SS) a second desirable property.

We now give some examples to give a feel for the axioms and theorems as they apply to wider settings than social choice theory.

Example 1. If the U and V are closed sets in a topological space then the boundary $\delta(.)$ satisfies (WPI) for it is elementary that

$$\delta(U \cup V) \subset \delta(U) \cup \delta(V)$$

Although most topological spaces studied are infinite this suggests that "boundary" is a useful conceptualisation of the optimum subset idea.

Example 2. Consider a linear statistical model with standard notation: $E(Y) = \theta_1 x_1 + \ldots + \theta_m x_m$. Let us index submodels by their parameter suffix set $U \subset \{1,\ldots,m\}$. For any submodel U let C(U) be the largest fully estimable submodel of U, that is, a submodel C(U) for which every parameter has a linear unbiased estimator. Then it is easy to verify that (WPI) holds but not necessarily (WP): i.e., the identifiable (estimable) parts of the union are contained in the union of the identifiable parts but may be a proper subset. (See Stewart and Wynn, 1981, for an axiomatic development of this problem).

Example 3. Convex hulls. Let $X=\{x_1,\ldots,x_N\}$ be a set of points in Euclidean space R^P. For any subset $U \subset X$ let C(U) be the subset of U which are extreme points of the convex hull of U. Then it can easily be shown that (PI) holds. This forms the basis for a number of algorithms for "peeling" in cluster analysis a technique which peels off successive convex hulls of a set of points to obtain a picture of the shape of the cluster. (Barnett, 1979, Eddy, 1977).

Example 4. Additive set functions. Let C(U) be the subset $U' \subset U$ which achieves the maximum of a set function $\Phi(U')$ subject to a size constraint $\#(U') = n < \#(U)$. If Φ is additive, that is

$$\Phi(U') = \Sigma_{x \varepsilon U'} \Phi(x),$$

then it is clear that (PI) holds. We merely put into U' the n points with the best Φ-values. We ignore the uniqueness problem which could be resolved by relaxing the size restriction. This points to (PI) being a weaker condition than additivity.

The approach in Example 4 of defining C(.) in terms of a set function defined on singletons $x \in X$ points to the following idea which is somewhat weaker. Thus suppose that we have a partial ordering on X: "$\geqslant$". Then this gives rise to a number of alternative definitions of C(.). For example

$$C(U) = \{x \;\varepsilon\; U \;/\; \nexists\; y \;\varepsilon\; U \text{ such that } y \geqslant x\} \tag{1}$$

$$C(U) = \{x \;\varepsilon\; U \;/\; x \geqslant y, \text{ for all } y \;\varepsilon\; X\} \tag{2}$$

Conversely given a choice function U we could define the ordering "$\geqslant$" in the following way using the two member set $\{x,y\}$.

$$x \geqslant y \text{ if and only if } x = C(\{x,y\}). \tag{3}$$

If such a definition leads to a proper partial ordering then C(.) is said to have a rationalisation (other definitions are possible). In social choice theory choice functions defined in this way were the first to be studied. The weaker axioms given above were a later development. Theorems are available (see Kelly, 1978) which tie up the two approaches. For example it can be shown that rationalisation is possible if and only if (PI) and (γ) hold. Thus, roughly, rationalisation lies between additivity and path independence.

Example 5. Let $X = \{x_1,\dots,x_n\} \in R^P$. Define C(U) as the positive (Pareto) boundary of U by defining $x \geqslant y$ as the usual component-wise ordering and taking definition (1) above. Then we certainly have a rationalisation of C(.). It is easy to verify that (PI) and (γ) hold. This example compared to example 4, where no rationalisation is possible, shows the strength of the extra condition (γ).

Example 6. Admissible decision rules. One decision rule d is said to be better than a decision rule d' in a class of decision rules D if (using standard notation) the risk functions of d and d' satisfy $R(\theta,d') \geqslant R(\theta,d)$ for all parameter values θ in the parameter space Θ with strict inequality at at least one value of θ. Although the class of decision rules is usually continuous we can define the class of admissible decision rules, D_O, exactly according to definition (1) above identifying U with D and C(U) with D_O. The elementary theorems on admissible decision rules given first by Abraham Wald are remarkably similar to the theorems on rationalisation in social choice theory (See Berger, 1981). Finally, in this section, we note that the stronger properties of (PI) and rationalisation allow the construction of much faster algorithms for finding optimum subsets. In particular any algorithm based on the rationalisation property will be close in spirit to the simple sort of algorithms which would be used if the ordering were strong (linear) or if additivity held. There is much work to be done on the NP-programmability of finite optimum subset algorithms in relationship to the various axioms listed above. Also, hidden in the existing literature on optimum subset algorithms is the use of these axioms often without any formal development of interrelations between them.

3. CONTINUOUS SUBSET THEORY

In a series of papers the author (Wynn, 1976, 1977, 1981) developed a theory of optimum subsets with special reference to problems in experimental design and sampling theory. This came out of the optimum theory of experimental designs developed by

Kiefer and Wolfowitz (1959, and later papers), (see Silvey, 1980). However we have been aware for some time that the theory had application outside that rather specialised one. An important contribution to the subject is that of Morris (1979a,b), although he does not mention the wide application of the theory to decision problems. The basic approach of all this work is to replace sets by measures. The main advantage of this idea, which has its roots in classical decision theory, is that additivity and convexity are more easily introduced. Additive set functions become integrals and convex combinations of measures are easier to define than convex combinations of sets. Thus we now take X to be probability space $(X,\mathcal{A},\xi_0)$. The concept of a subset is replaced by a measure ξ strictly dominated by the measure ξ_0 in the following sense. For any measurable set A in $\mathcal{A}$

$$0 \leqslant \xi(A) \leqslant \xi_0(A).$$

If this holds we write $0 \leqslant \xi \leqslant \xi_0$. This certainly implies that ξ is absolutely continuous with respect to ξ_0. Thus in terms of densities with respect to ξ_0 we can write equivalently

$$0 \leqslant f_\xi\,(x) \leqslant 1.$$

We could use the notation $\xi \leqslant \xi_0$. Thus intuitively ξ never exceeds ξ_0. A special case of ξ of ξ_A the measure for which for some measurable A the density satisfies (with probability one with respect to ξ_0)

$$f_{\xi_A}\,(x) = 1 \text{ for all } x \text{ in } A$$
$$= 0 \text{ otherwise;}$$

that is the indicator function of the set A. This is precisely the approach taken in hypothesis testing: f_ξ is then a decision rule which is only non-randomized if $f_\xi \in \{1,0\}$ with probability one.

The optimum subset problem can be reformulated as follows. Minimise $\Phi\,(\xi)$ subject to $0 \leqslant \xi \leqslant \xi_0$, where $\Phi(\cdot)$ is a function on ξ. The pure optimum subset problem is then the special case when $\xi = \xi_A$ as above. The important class of set functions we shall consider will be those which can be expressed as functions of a set of moments

$$m_i(\xi) = \int_X g_i d\xi = \int_X g_i f_\xi \, dx \qquad (i=1,\ldots,k)$$

where the g_i are k given integrable functions on X.

An immediate advantage of this special case is the use of the Liapounov theorem on the range of a vector measure (see, for example, Lindenstrauss, 1966). This enables us to prove the following theorem. We omit the proof. First, let $m(\xi) = (m_1(\xi),\ldots,m_k(\xi))$ be the vector of moments.

Theorem 1

Let ξ_0 be a non-atomic measure. Then given any $m(\xi)$ with $0 \leq \xi \leq \xi_0$ there exists a measurable set A such that $m(\xi) = m(\xi_A)$.

This firmly links the optimum measure problem with the optimum subset problem of which it is a special case. For if we find an optimum measure ξ^* whose density is not an indicator, then provided the non-atomicity condition holds there is a set A such that $m(\xi^*) = m(\xi_A)$: that is the optimum solutions expressed in terms of the m(.) vectors are the same.

The main advantage in dealing with measures is that the class of measures dominated by ξ_0 in the above sense is convex, that is closed under the operation of taking convex combinations $\xi = (1-\alpha)\xi_1 + \alpha\xi_2$ of two measures ξ_1 and ξ_2 $(0 \leq \alpha \leq 1)$. The convexity of measure space, and indeed the Liapounov theorem itself gives us that, under suitable conditions, the set of all moment vectors $m(\xi)$ is a closed convex set in R^P. Suppose then that this set is closed and convex and that Φ is a convex function on it. Then we can write down conditions for optimality expressed in terms of directional derivatives, as in the derivation of Kuhn-Tucker conditions.

Theorem 2. A necessary and sufficient condition for $\xi \leq \xi_0$ to minimise $\Phi(m(\xi))$ is that

$$\nabla\Phi(m,m') = \frac{\partial}{\partial\alpha}\Phi((1-\alpha)m + \alpha m')\Big|_{\alpha=0} \geq 0 \text{ for all } \xi \leq \xi_0$$

where $m = m(\xi)$ and $m' = m(\xi')$.

Writing $\nabla\Phi$ for the gradient vector of Φ the condition reduces to

$$\int_X d(\xi,x) f_\xi \, dx \geq \int_X d(\xi,x) f_{\xi'} \, dx \text{ for all } \xi' \leq \xi_0,$$

where

$$d(\xi,x) = - \nabla\Phi(m(\xi))^T g(x),$$

and $g = (g_1,\ldots,g_k)$.

This last condition can be converted to a "separation theorem" on the function $d(\xi,x)$. Recall that the Neyman-Pearson lemma characterises the acceptance region for a test of hypothesis as a region in which a certain function (the likelihood ratio) is larger than a constant. Thus the critical region separates the function into large and small values. More precisely we say that a function $h(x)$ separates disjoint measurable sets A and B if there is a constant c such that $h \geq c$ on A and $h \leq c$ on B (with probability one). Using this idea Theorem 2 can be adapted. Here supp(ξ) refers to the support of ξ. We now include a simple size constraint analogous to the one in Example 4. This says that the total amount of mass allowed to ξ is v where $0 < v < 1$ $(= \xi_0(X))$. We obtain (Wynn, 1982)

Theorem 3. A measure $\xi \leq \xi_0$ satisfying $\xi(X) = v$ $(0 < v < 1)$ minimizes $\Phi(m(\xi))$ if and only if $d(x,\xi)$ separates supp(ξ) and supp($\xi_0 - \xi$).

More general theorems are to be found in Morris (1979 a,b). The side constraint in Theorem 3 is generalised to more general moment constraints or even more generally convex constraints. The Neyman-Pearson lemma is a simple special case. The separation theorems, Theorem 3 or its generalisations, seem to be related to the rationalisation results referred to in the last section. The optimum subsets are given by the level sets of some function defined on X. However the key point about the general convex theory is that the function, $d(x,\xi)$ in Theorem 3, depends on the optimum subset itself. Despite this the shape of the function will give much information about the shape of the optimum subset. If for example the function is quadratic then the level sets and hence the optimum subsets are ellipsoids. We give a simple example of such a case.

Example 7. Let X be the unit square $[0,1]^2$. Let $x = (x_1, x_2)$. Consider the moments $m_{ij} = \int_X x_1^i x_2^j \, d\xi$. $(0 \leq i, 0 \leq j, i+j \leq 2)$. We shall assume also the constraint $m_{00} = v$. These moments together form a moment matrix $M = \{m_{ij}\}$. Maximising the determinant of M is equivalent to minimising $-\log \det M$. This is a problem that could arise in the optimal design of experiments. The function $d(x,\xi)$ is given by

$$d(x,\xi) = (1, x_1, x_2)^T M^{-1} (1, x_1, x_2).$$

This is clearly quadratic in (x_1, x_2). The level sets are ellipses. Suppose now that ξ_0 is uniform over X. Symmetry considerations tell us immediately that the optimum ξ, subject to $\xi \leq \xi_0$, (and hence the optimum subset) is obtained by removing from ξ_0 all the mass inside a circle centred at $(\frac{1}{2},\frac{1}{2})$.

REFERENCES

Barnett, V. 1976 "The ordering of multivariate data", *J. Roy. Statist. Soc.*, **139**, 318-354.

Berger, J.O. 1980 Statistical decision theory. Springer Verlag, Berlin.

Boyce, D.E., Farhi, A. and Weischedel, R. 1974 Optimal subset selection. Springer Verlag, Berlin.

Eddy, W.F. 1977 "A new convex hull algorithm for planar sets". *ACM Trans. Math. Software*, **3**, 398-403.

Gupta, S.S. and Panchapakesan, S. 1980 Multiple decision procedures. Wiley, New York.

Kelly, J.S. 1978 Arrow Impossibility Theorems. Academic Press, New York.

Kiefer, J. and Wolfowitz, J. 1959 "Optimum designs in regression problems" *Ann. Math. Statist.*, **30**, 271-294.

Lindenstrauss, J. 1966 "A short proof of Liapounoff's convexity theorem". *J. Math. and Mech.* **15**, 971-972.

Morris, R.J.T. 1979a "Optimisation with nonadditive set functions". 18th Conference on Decision and Control, **1**, 445-450.

Morris, R.J.T. 1979b "Optimal constrained selection of a measurable subset". *J. Math. Analysis and Appl.*, **70**, 546-562.

Sen, A.K. 1970 Collective choice and social welfare. Oliver and Boyd, London.

Silvey, S.D. 1980 Optimal design. Chapman and Hall, London.

Stewart, I. and Wynn, H.P. 1981 "The estimability structure of linear models and submodels". *J. Roy. Statist. Soc. B*, **43**, 197-207.

Wynn, H.P. 1976 "Minimax purpose survey sampling design". *J. Amer. Statist. Assoc.*, **72**, 655-657.

Wynn, H.P. 1977 Optimum designs for finite populations sampling. Statistical decision and related topics, II, Academic Press, New York.

Wynn, H.P. 1982 Optimum submeasures with application to finite population sampling. Statistical decision and related topics, III, Academic Press.

A SURVEY OF MULTI-OBJECTIVE COMBINATORIAL SCHEDULING

Fernando Ruiz-Diaz and Simon French

(Department of Decision Theory, University of Manchester)

ABSTRACT

Combinatorial scheduling problems with a single objective are notoriously difficult; in fact, the majority are NP-hard. So it is not surprising to find that until recently there was little research into multi-objective scheduling problems. In this paper we give a state-of-the-art survey, concentrating mainly on single machine problems. We suggest a number of avenues for future research.

1. INTRODUCTION

Combinatorial scheduling concerns itself with the optimal sequencing of a fixed set of jobs through limited processing resources. In common with other areas of combinatorial optimisation, it is assumed that the data is known and deterministic; there is no uncertainty involved. And also in common with other areas of combinatorial optimisation, the problems are typically very, very difficult. In fact, the majority are NP-hard; i.e. it is conjectured that they can never be solved in a computationally efficient manner and that the time required by solution algorithms will always grow exponentially with the problem size. Given that these extreme computational demands can occur with even the simplest of objective functions, it is not surprising to find that there have been few attempts to find schedules either that are efficient (Pareto optimal, admissible, V-optimal) with respect to multiple conflicting objectives or that optimise a multi-attribute value function, which explicitly allows for trade-off between objectives.

In this paper we survey the state-of-the-art in multi-objective scheduling, concentrating first on the problem of finding efficient schedules and then on that of optimising multi-attribute value functions. At the end of the paper we make some general remarks about the computational requirements of the algorithms and also point to promising areas for future research.

At the outset we would remark on an unfortunate, but quite unavoidable confusion of terms. Efficient will have two distinct meanings throughout this paper: one derived from the theory of multi-objective optimisation, the other from the theory of computation. A schedule is efficient if it is undominated within a partial order defined over the multiple objectives. An algorithm is efficient if the time required to solve a particular instance of a problem grows polynomially with the size of the instance. In an attempt to avoid the confusion we will use the term computationally efficient for the latter case.

We begin with a brief statement of a general combinatorial scheduling problem.

2. COMBINATORIAL SCHEDULING

Suppose that n jobs $\{J_1, J_2, \ldots, J_n\}$ require processing on a single machine. We shall assume that the processing of J_i requires t_i time-units and that once begun it must not be interrupted before completion. We use C_i to denote the time that J_i completes under a particular processing sequence. Our task is to find a processing sequence which minimises some measure of performance. For regular measures of performance, which are defined to be those that are non-decreasing in the processing times, it may be shown that there is no advantage in considering inserted idle time, i.e. having the machine idle when there are still jobs to be processed. In consequence, the schedule is completely defined by the permutation of $\{J_1, J_2, \ldots, J_n\}$ which gives their processing order. Throughout this paper we shall confine our attention to such regular measures of performance. The only significant restriction which this entails is that we are prohibited from considering the inventory costs of completed jobs.

Figure 2.1 illustrates a schedule for a single machine problem and introduces the main quantities of interest, which are defined briefly below.

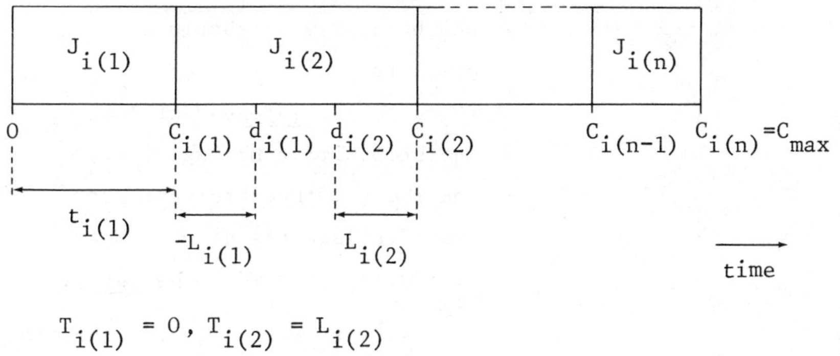

Figure 2.1 A diagram of a typical schedule for a single machine problem.

Glossary of Notation and Terms

$\{J_1, J_2, \ldots, J_n\}$ - the set of jobs to be processed.

$(J_{i(1)}, J_{i(2)}, \ldots, J_{i(n)})$ - a particular processing sequence, i.e. a permutation of $\{J_1, J_2, \ldots, J_n\}$.

t_i - the processing time of J_i.

C_i - the completion time of J_i.

C_{max} - $\max_{i=1}^{n} \{C_1, C_2, \ldots, C_n\}$, the completion time of the last job in the processing sequence and hence of all the processing. C_{max} is known as the make-span of a schedule. Generally the subscript "max" will denote the maximum of a set of subscripted quantities.

$\bar{C}$ - $(1/n) \sum_{i=1}^{n} C_i$, the mean completion time. Generally an overbar will denote the mean of a set of subscripted quantities.

d_i - the due date of J_i, is the time by which ideally J_i should be completed.

L_i - $(C_i - d_i)$, the lateness of J_i. L_i may be positive or negative.

T_i - $\max\{0, L_i\}$, the tardiness, or positive lateness of J_i. When $T_i > 0$, J_i is said to be tardy.

r_i - the ready time of J_i, i.e. the time at which J_i is ready for processing; no processing of J_i may occur before r_i. Unless stated otherwise, we shall assume that $r_i = 0 \ \forall i$.

F_i - $(C_i - r_i)$, the flow time of J_i. When $r_i = 0$, $F_i = C_i$ and the terms flow-time and completion time are used interchangeably.

Typical of the objective functions that we shall be seeking to minimise are: T_{max}, $\bar{C}$, $\bar{F}$, $\bar{T}$, $\sum \alpha_i C_i$, $\sum \alpha_i F_i$, $\sum \alpha_i T_i$, where in the last three cases the α_i are weights.

In the above we have assumed that there is only one machine on which the jobs may be processed. We have done so because most of the work in multi-objective scheduling have made the same assumption. However, this assumption is neither necessary nor usual within the general field of scheduling. Various classes of problem with several machines have been studied: job shop problems in which each job must be processed on a number of machines and, moreover, it must pass from one machine to another in an order particular to the job; flow shop problems in which each job must be processed on the first machine, then the second, then the third,....; and parallel processor problems in which each job requires to be processed on just one machine and any of the machines have the capability of processing it. We shall not need to describe such problems in greater detail here, but those interested may find a comprehensive survey in French (1982).

3. THE APPROACH TO VAN WASSENHOVE AND GELDERS

The first paper to explicitly introduce the concept of efficiency into the context of scheduling was that of Van Wassenhove and Gelders (1980). They considered a single machine problem with two objectives: the vector minimisation of mean flow time and maximum tardiness.

$$\underset{\pi \in \Pi}{\text{V-min}} \ (T_{max}, \bar{F}) \tag{3.1}$$

Here and throughout Π is the set of permutation schedules.

Their algorithm is based on some earlier work of Smith (1956), which solved the problem of minimising $\bar{F}$ subject to the constraint that $T_{max} = 0$ assuming that this constraint on T_{max} can be achieved. Heck and Roberts (1972) extended the approach to the minimisation of $\bar{F}$ subject to $T_{max} \le \Delta$ for some $\Delta \ge 0$. (Thus we may note for interest the introduction of goal programming ideas into scheduling.) Apparently unaware of Heck and Roberts' earlier work, Gelders and Van Wassenhove modified Smiths' algorithm similarly but in such a way as to ensure that it produced an efficient schedule. We shall not explicitly describe their algorithm for minimising $\bar{F}$ subject to $T_{max} \le \Delta$ here; see Van Wassenhove and Gelders (1980), and French (1982) for details. However, we shall describe the procedure whereby they repeatedly use their algorithm to generate the efficient frontier in $(T_{max}, \bar{F})$ space. Note that their procedure assumes that all data are integers.

<u>Step 0</u>. Set $\Delta = \sum_{i=1}^{n} t_i$. (N.b. T_{max} can never exceed the total processing time, assuming $d_i \ge 0 \quad \forall i$.)

<u>Step 1</u>. Find a schedule π^* to minimise $\bar{F}$ subject to $T_{max} \le \Delta$. If no schedule with $T_{max} \le \Delta$ exists, <u>stop</u>. (N.b. their method ensures π^* is efficient.)

<u>Step 2</u>. Compute T_{max} for π^* and reset $\Delta = T_{max}(\pi^*) - 1$. (N.b. it is here that the demand for the data to be integers is essential.)

<u>Step 3</u>. If $\Delta \ge 0$ go to <u>Step 1</u>; otherwise <u>stop</u>.

We can make a number of immediate comments. Firstly, the need for the data to be integers can be removed by resetting

Δ to $T_{max}(\pi^*) - \delta$ in Step 2, where δ is the g.c.d. of all the data. Secondly, although all the efficient frontier in (T_{max}, $\bar{F}$) space is found, only a representative set of efficient schedules is found, i.e. only one of possibly many efficient schedules is found at each efficient (T_{max}, $\bar{F}$) point. Moreover the algorithm can be modified to find all efficient schedules if desired (Van Wassenhove and Gelders, 1980). Thirdly, the procedure constructs the efficient frontier in a straightforward pass, working from lower right to upper left in the (T_{max}, $\bar{F}$) plane. Finally, we defer a full discussion of the computational demands of the algorithm to a later section, but note here that the number of cycles is at most $(1 + \sum_{i=1}^{n} t_i)$ and that the reduction of Δ to $T_{max}(\pi^*) - 1$ in Step 2 means that this is usually a very poor upper bound.

Smith (1956) suggested that his algorithm could be extended to minimise $\sum \alpha_i F_i$ subject to $T_{max} \leq 0$; unfortunately his suggestion was ill-founded. Burns (1976) presented a counter example and was unable to produce an alternative algorithm to solve the problem optimally, although he did develop a heuristic method. Miyazaki (1981) has produced a better heuristic method, but it seems that the problem can only be solved optimally by recourse to implicit enumeration. Bansal (1980) has published a branch and bound method. It seems impractical, therefore, to generalise Gelders and Van Wassenhove's method to find schedules that are efficient with respect to (T_{max}, $\sum \alpha_i F_i$). Firstly, the method is likely to be computationally inefficient since implicit enumeration seems necessary at Step 1. Secondly, simply minimising $\sum \alpha_i F_i$ subject to $T_{max} \leq \Delta$ does not necessarily find an efficient point in the (T_{max}, $\sum \alpha_i F_i$) plane, and it is not clear how to modify Bansals' branch and bound algorithm so that it would. Thus Gelders and Van Wassenhove's procedure might find some inefficient points as well as all the efficient points in the (T_{max}, $\sum \alpha_i F_i$) plane. These extra inefficient points may, of course, be discarded without a substantial increase in computation, but in that they are found in the first place the method's computational efficiency is further questioned.

Emmons (1975) has considered the problem of minimising $\bar{F}$ subject to $g_{max} \leq g^*$, where $g_i(C_i)$ is some non-decreasing cost function based on the completion times, $g_{max} = \max_{i=1}^{n} g_i(C_i)$, and $g^* = \min_{\pi\in\Pi} g_{max}(\pi)$. In fact, Emmons' approach will actually minimise $\bar{F}$ subject to $g_{max} \leq \Delta$ for any $\Delta \geq g^*$. So providing that the g_i are all integer-valued, the method of Van Wassenhove and Gelders will generalise immediately to find the efficient frontier in the $(g_{max}, \bar{F})$ plane.

Nunnikhoven and Emmons (1977) have considered the problem of minimising the number of parallel machines required to process n jobs such that $T_{max} \leq \Delta$ for some Δ. Their problem is NP-hard, and so their solution is necessarily enumerative. We mention their paper here because combined with the approach of Gelders and Van Wassenhove it may be developed to find the efficient frontier in (m, T_{max}) space, where m is the number of the machines, although it should be noted that the method may find some inefficient points as well and these would need to be checked for and discarded.

3. EFFICIENT SCHEDULES WITH CONTROLLABLE PROCESSING TIMES

We have assumed until now that the processing times of the jobs are fixed as part of the data, but in practice it is usually possible to expedite processing of a job within certain limits and at a cost. To typify this we shall consider situations in which the processing times must lie in the interval

$$a_i \leq t_i \leq b_i \quad , \qquad i = 1,2,\ldots,n,$$

but within the range any t_i may be selected at a cost $c_i(b_i-t_i)$. We let $\sum = \sum_{i=1}^{n} c_i(b_i-t_i)$ be the total cost of processing, and note that when $t_i < b_i$ J_i is said to have been crashed by (b_i-t_i). Van Wassenhove and Baker (1980) have developed two greedy algorithms to solve two bicriterion problems when $\sum$ is one of the criteria.

Consider first their method to construct the efficient frontier

$$\text{V-}\min_{\pi\in\Pi} \quad (T_{max}, \textstyle\sum)$$

for a single machine problem. Their method is very intuitive. It assumes the jobs are sequenced in order of non-decreasing due-date.

<u>Step 0</u>. First set $t_i = b_i \;\; \forall_i$ and identify J_k such that $k = \min \{i | T_i = T_{max}\}$. If $T_k = 0$, <u>stop</u>.

<u>Step 1</u>. For J_j such that $j \leq k$, $t_j > a_j$, and $c_j = \min\{c_i | i \leq k, t_i > a_i\}$. If no such job exists, <u>stop</u>.

<u>Step 2</u>. Crash J_j until one of the following happens:

a) $t_j = a_j$: return to <u>Step 1</u>.

b) $T_k = T_r$, where $r = \min \{i | T_i = \max_{\ell<j}\{T_\ell\}\}$: reset $k = r$ and return to <u>Step 1</u>.

c) $T_k = 0$: <u>stop</u>.

Van Wassenhove and Baker prove that the algorithm traces out the efficient frontier in $(T_{max}, \sum)$ space. Their proof is indirect, via an equivalent linear programming formulation. A direct proof is possible; but is long and involved.

The second greedy algorithm finds the efficient frontier in the more general problem:

$$\text{V-min} \quad (g_{max}, \textstyle\sum),$$

where $\sum = \sum_{i=1}^{n} c_i(b_i - t_i)$ as before, $g_{max} = \max_{i=1}^{n} \{g_i(C_i)\}$, and $g_i(C_i)$ is a non-decreasing cost function for J_i. Their algorithm is only applicable when the $g_i(.)$ are such that the jobs can be indexed so that

$$g_1(t) \geq g_2(t) \geq \ldots \geq g_n(t) \quad \text{for all } t \geq 0.$$

Moreover, they require that the jobs are so indexed.

Their method is based upon a two-pass algorithm which minimises $\sum$ subject to $g_{max} \leq G$. In the first pass the algorithm calculates for each job J_i the amount of crashing D_i that must have occurred by its completion C_i so that $g_i(C_i) \leq G$.

The second pass meets these crashing requirements D_i by means of straightforward greed; it works through the D_i in sequence, achieving them by the simple expedient of crashing the cheapest jobs no later in the sequence than J_i.

When the $g_i(.)$ are general non-decreasing functions, the efficient frontier in $(g_{max}, \sum)$ space may have curved segments. Thus the algorithm cannot find all the frontier in finite time. In such cases Van Wassenhove and Baker suggest applying the algorithm for $G = G_{min}, G_{min}+\gamma, G_{min}+2\gamma, \ldots, G_{max}$, where γ is some suitably small increment and G_{min} and G_{max} are the extremes of g_{max} found when respectively all $t_i = a_i$ and all $t_i = b_i$. When the $g_i(.)$ are piecewise linear, the efficient frontier is also piecewise linear and it is possible to use their method to just find the efficient vertices, and hence, by implication, all the efficient frontier. In this piecewise linear case the time required to find the efficient frontier is $O(n^3)$ for an n job problem. However, this statement masks a difficulty.

The method requires that the jobs are sequenced such that $g_1(t) \geq g_2(t) \geq \ldots \geq g_n(t)$ for all t. How may this be achieved? Van Wassenhove and Baker suggest applying Lawlers' algorithm (Lawler, 1973; French, 1982) with all the $t_i = b_i$, but this will only be satisfactory if all the inequalities between the $g_i(.)$ are <u>strict for all t</u>. If ever there were equality, Lawlers' algorithm would allow an arbitary choice where, in fact, there were none. No computationally efficient algorithm may be designed to order the jobs in order of non-increasing $g_i(.)$ <u>unless</u> some analytical properties of the $g_i(.)$ are known. Now once the $g_i(.)$ are restricted to known analytical forms, it may well be possible to improve upon the computational efficiency of this general purpose greedy algorithm. For instance, when $g_i(C_i) = \max\{C_i-d_i, 0\} = T_i$ the problem V-min $(g_{max}, \sum)$ reduces to the earlier V-min $(T_{max}, \sum)$ problem. The earlier greedy algorithm specifically designed for that problem requires $O(n^2)$ time for an n job problem, not the $O(n^3)$ time required by this more general algorithm. In other words, this algorithm may be rendered computationally inefficient through the $g_i(.)$ not having sufficient structure and in cases where they do it may be an inefficient algorithm by comparison with ones designed for the particular forms of the $g_i(\cdot)$

5. INTEGER PROGRAMMING FORMULATIONS

The constraints, the structure, and many of the objectives in combinatorial scheduling, and here we do not limit ourselves to single machine problems or zero ready times, can be formulated as a multi-objective mixed integer linear programme. Huckert et al. (1980) have suggested using an integer programming formulation due to Manne (1960), but clearly they could have used any other equivalent formulation and several others do exist (French, 1982; Rinnooy Kan, 1976). To solve the multi-objective mixed integer programme Huckert et al. propose using an interactive approach, thus allowing the decision-maker to explore a restricted region of the efficient surface that is of particular interest to him without the necessity of computing the whole efficient set. In their work they have selected the interactive approach known as the step method (STEM) (Benayaum et al., 1971). However, again this is, in a sense, an arbitrary choice and other methods could be used.

The advantage of integer programming formulations is that they enable one to translate problems in multi-objective scheduling, an area into which there has been little research, into multi-objective integer programmes, into which there has been some research. It apparently obviates the need to develop new methods. However, there is a problem. There are no computationally efficient algorithms for multi-objective integer programmes. Huckert et al. admit that their formulation of a 20 job, 10 machine problem has 1900 binary variables, 201 continuous variables and 4000 constraints, and, therefore, is too large to solve with present-day computers. The computational intractability of integer programming formulations of multi-objective scheduling problems should not be surprising; such formulations have already proved a very poor approach for solving single objective problems (French, 1982).

6. MULTI-ATTRIBUTE VALUE FUNCTION APPROACHES

We turn now from the problem of finding efficient schedules with respect to a number of criteria to that of finding an optimal schedule with respect to a multi-attribute value function, which explicitly weights and allows for trade-off between conflicting objectives.

Vickson (1980) has investigated a single machine problem, in which the processing times are controllable. His objective function is a weighted sum of processing costs and weighted mean flow time:

$$TC = w_1 \sum_{i=1}^{n} c_i (b_i - t_i) + w_2 \sum_{i=1}^{n} \alpha_i F_i .$$

For conceptual clarity we have included w_1 and w_2 in this expression, but obviously we may take $w_1 = w_2 = 1$ w.l.o.g. Moreover, let us write $s_i = b_i - t_i$ so that the objective function becomes:

$$TC = \sum_{i=1}^{n} (c_i s_i + \alpha_i F_i)$$

Although he was unable to prove that this problem is NP-hard, Vickson was unable to discover a polynomial time algorithm for its solution. He did, however, develop a branch and bound technique and some heuristic approaches with outstanding performances. Without delving too deeply into the theory of these solutions, let us note that they derive their performance entirely from the simple structure of the objective function TC.

Consider any sequence of jobs $(J_{i(1)}, J_{i(2)}, \ldots, J_{i(n)})$ and remember that

$$F_{i(k)} = \sum_{j=1}^{k} t_{i(j)} = \sum_{j=1}^{k} (b_{i(j)} - s_{i(j)}).$$

Thus

$$TC = \sum_{i=1}^{n} (c_i s_i + \alpha_i F_i)$$

$$= \sum_{k=1}^{n} (c_{i(k)} s_{i(k)} + \alpha_{i(k)} F_{i(k)})$$

$$= \sum_{k=1}^{n} \sum_{j=k}^{n} \alpha_{i(j)} b_{i(k)} + \sum_{k=1}^{n} (c_{i(k)} - \sum_{j=k}^{n} \alpha_{i(j)}) s_{i(k)} .$$

Hence, for a given sequence, TC is minimised by choosing

$$s_{i(k)} = \begin{cases} 0 & \text{if } c_{i(k)} > \sum_{j=k}^{n} \alpha_{i(j)}, \\ (b_{i(k)} - a_{i(k)}) & \text{if } c_{i(k)} \leq \sum_{j=k}^{n} \alpha_{i(j)}. \end{cases}$$

So in an optimal sequence each job will be either fully crashed or completely uncrashed. It is this fact together with further conditions that may be deduced from this form of the objective function that enable Vickson to solve the problem. Without wishing to detract from Vickson's achievement, we note that his objective function, although a weighted sum of two criteria, simplifies to a weighted average of the $s_{i(k)}$, albeit only when the sequence is known. In a sense, therefore, he is not faced by all the complications and difficulties that we may expect as typical within multi-objective scheduling.

Gelders and his co-workers have developed algorithms for a variety of problems in which the sum of weighted flow-times and weighted tardinesses, viz $\sum_{i=1}^{n} (\alpha_i F_i + s_i T_i)$, is to be minimised (Gelders and Kleindorfer, 1974, 1975; and Sambandan, 1978; and Van Wassenhove and Gelders, 1978). Moreover, in the single machine case they also allow for a possibility of using overtime to expedite the processing. In this sense, the processing times are controllable. Both branch and bound and heuristic methods are developed for the problems. However, the algorithms are specifically designed to optimise this particular objective function with its linear weighting of flow times and tardiness; lower bounds, elimination schemes, etc. rely on this linear structure. What can be done to optimise a general non-linear multi-attribute value function?

Kao (1980) considers a n-job, single machine problem in which the objective is to maximise an additive value function:

$$u(x_1, x_2, \ldots, x_m) = \sum_{m=1}^{M} u_m(x_m).$$

Here the $x_1, x_2, \ldots, x_m$ are M measures of performance, e.g. T_{max}, $\bar{F}$, etc., and the $u_m(.)$ are monotonic decreasing single attribute value functions. In fact, Kao's methods extend to a non-additive value function, providing that it is decreasing in all its arguments. His approach is that of branch and bound.

Let $D_k^i = (i(n-k+1),....,i(n-1), i(n))$ be the ith node at the kth level in the elimination tree. D_k^i specifies the <u>last</u> k jobs in the processing sequence. At D_k^i the lower bounds are calculated as follows. For each $m, 1 \le m \le M$, x_m is minimised among the processing sequences which have the specified ordering of the last k jobs. For this minimising sequence $u(x_1,x_2,....,x_m)$ is calculated; call its value $u_k^i(m)$. The lower bound at D_k^i is taken as $\alpha_k^i = \max_{m=1}^{M} \{u_k^i(m)\}$. As well as lower bounds at each node, a global lower bound at each level is also calculated:

$$LB_k = \max \{LB_{k-1}, \max \{\alpha_k^i\}\}.$$

Finally an upper bound is calculated at each node by $UB_k^i = \sum_{m=1}^{M} u_m(\hat{x}_m)$, where $\hat{x}_m$ is the minimum value of x_m obtained at D_k^i when x_m is minimised independently of the other performance measures. Clearly if $UB_k^i < LB_{k-1}$ there is no point in searching below node D_k^i and it is therefore fathomed. Kao also indicates how to develop elimination criteria for comparing and eliminating unfathomed nodes at the same level which represent final subsequences of the same k jobs. These elimination criteria, in fact, correspond to the recursions that would be used in a dynamic programming approach to the problem. In this sense he is combining a branch and bound search of the elimination tree with dynamic programming.

Kao's computational results are promising, but a number of points should be noted. Firstly, at each node M single objective problems have to be solved. Each of these may be a time consuming operation; for instance, one must use implicit enumeration to minimise mean tardiness on a single machine. Secondly, the major problem with dynamic programming is that it requires much core store to maintain tables of intermediate calculations. Kao's use of dynamic-programming-like elimination criteria will make similar storage demands, yet without them his computational results indicate poor time performance. Nonetheless, Kao is to be congratulated for taking the first step in tackling a very general multi-attribute scheduling problem.

7. DISCUSSION

The literature on single-objective scheduling is vast, while that on multi-objective scheduling is minute in comparison. Undoubtedly, the major reason for this discrepancy is that the extreme difficulty of single-objective problems discourages one from tackling still more difficult multi-objective problems. However, we do not believe that this is the only reason. We feel that part of the explanation is that there is no general approach to multi-objective combinatorial scheduling, and indeed to the whole field of multi-objective combinatorial optimisation. Admittedly, there have been many papers on multi-objective integer programming; a number have been mentioned at this conference. But these papers implicitly assume that the number of variables and constraints are within reasonable limits - a fair assumption if the underlying practical problem has a natural expression as an integer programme. Unfortunately, when other combinatorial problems are reformulated as integer programmes they typically require many variables and constraints, and the existing literature does not help us solve them. With this in mind let us look back at the work surveyed above.

The methods described in sections 3 and 4 have much in common. Firstly, they all deal with bicriteria problems. In two dimensions the efficient frontier is a line, and it is both possible and natural to explore it by starting at one end and working through to the other. All the methods referred to do precisely this, and we may note in passing that they do so by what are essentially greedy algorithms. It is not at all clear how such ideas can be generalised to three or more dimensions because there is no natural ordering of efficient vertices in an efficient surface. Doubtless, other bicriteria problems will be solved by developments of these methods (the principles underlying Hartley, 1979, may also be relevant), but they do not seem to embody a general approach to the finding of efficient schedules in n-dimension ($n \geq 3$). We have already suggested that there are considerable problems with the approach of Huckert et al. (1980).

Within the field of single objective combinatorial optimisation the theory of computational complexity and NP-completeness has been remarkably successful at delineating classes of problems of comparable difficulty, and to a certain extent suggesting algorithmic approaches to their solution (Rinnooy Kan, 1976). There does not seem to be a useful, parallel theory in the field of efficient solutions. For a single objective problem a good algorithm is one whose computational requirements increase polynomially with the instance size. What is a good algorithm for finding efficient solutions? Since the number of efficient solutions usually increases exponentially with the instance size when binary encoding is used, should we say that a good efficient solution algorithm has pseudo-polynomial computational requirements? The algorithms of section 3 and 4 all have pseudo-polynomial behaviour. But such a definition may be too naive. Perhaps we should distinguish between the time an algorithm takes to find its first efficient solution and the time it takes to move to subsequent ones.

Turning now to the problem of optimising a multi-attribute value function, we should admit that there is little distinction here between this and the more usual single-objective scheduling problems; there is only one function to optimise. Nonetheless, there is some distinction. The underlying theme of multi-attribute value theory is that of functional forms and it seems to us that there is further work to be done following on that of Kao to develop general combinatorial algorithms for optimising the most common additive and multiplicative forms.

8. REFERENCES

1. Bansal, S.P. "Single machine scheduling to minimise weighted sum of completion timed with secondary criteria - a Brand and Bound approach", *Eur. J. Opl. Res.*, 5, 177-181, (1980).

2. Benayoun, R., de Montgelfier, J., Tergny, J., and Laritchev, O., "Linear Programming with Multiple Objective Functions: Step Method (STEM)", *Mathematical Programming 1*, 366-375, (1971).

3. Burns, R.N., "Scheduling to minimise the weighted sum of completion timed with secondary criteria", *Nav. Res. Log. Quart.*, 23, 125-129, (1976).

4. Emmons, H., "A note on a scheduling problem with dual criteria", *Nav. Res. Log. Quart.*, Vol. 22, No. 3, 615-616, (1975).

5. French, S., *Sequencing and Scheduling*, Ellis Harwood Ltd., Chichester (1982).

6. Gelders, L.F. and Kleindorfer, P.R., "Coordinating aggregate and detailed scheduling in a one machine job shop Part I", *Theory Ops. Res. 22*, 46-60 (1974).

7. Gelders, L.F. and Kleindorfer, P.R., "Coordinating aggregate and detailed scheduling in a one machine job shop, Part II, computation and structure", *Theory Ops. Res. 23*, 312-324 (1975).

8. Gelders, L.F. and Sambandam, N., "Four single heuristics for scheduling a flow shop", *Int. J. Prod. Res., 16*, 221-231 (1978).

9. Hartley, R., "An Algorithm for Bicriterion Integer Programming", *Notes in Decision Theory*, Note number 64, Department of Decision Theory, University of Manchester, (1979).

10. Heck, H. and Roberts, S., "A note on the extension of a result on scheduling with secondary criteria", *Nav. Res. Log. Quart., 19*, 403-405 (1972).

11. Huckert, K., R. Rhode, O. Roglin and Weber, R., "On the interactive solution of a multicriteria scheduling problem", 2, *Z.Ops.Res., 24*, 47-60 (1980).

12. Kao, E.P.C., "A multiple decision theoretic approach to one machine scheduling problem", *Comput. and Ops. Res., 7*, 251-259 (1980).

13. Lawler, E.L., "Optimal sequencing of a single machine subject to precedence constraints", *Mgmt. Sci., 19*, 544-546 (1973).

14. Manne, A.S., "On the job-shop scheduling problem", *Ops. Res., 8*, 219-223 (1960).

15. Miyazaki, S., "One machine scheduling problem with dual criteria", *J. of Ops. Res. Society of Japan, 24*, 37-50 (1981).

16. Nunnikhoven, T.S. and Emmons, H., "Scheduling on parallel machines to minimise two criteria related to job tardiness", *A.I.I.E. Trans., 9*, 288-296 (1977).

17. Rinnooy Kan, A.H.G., *Machine Scheduling Problems*, Martinus Nijhoff, The Hague (1976).

18. Smith, W.E. "Various optimisers for single stage production", *Nav. Res. Logist. Quart., 3*, 59-66 (1956).

19. Van Wassenhove, L.C. and Gelders, L.F., "Four solution techniques for a general one-machine scheduling problem", *Eur. J. Opl. Res.*, *2*, 281-290 (1978).

20. Van Wassenhove, L.C. and Gelders, L.F., "Solving a Bi-criterion scheduling problem", *Eur. J. Opl. Res.*, *4*, 42-48 (1980).

21. Van Wassenhove, L.N. and Baker K.R., "A Bicriterion approach to time/cost trade-offs in sequencing". Paper presented at the 4th European Congress on Operational Research, Cambridge, England, July 22-25, 1980. Submitted to *Eur. J. Opl. Res.*

22. Vickson, R.G. "Choosing the job sequence and processing times to minimise total processing plus flow cost on a single machine", *Ops. Res.*, *28*, 1155-1167 (1980).

CONSTRAINED MARKOV DECISION PROCESSES AS MULTI-OBJECTIVE PROBLEMS

L.C. Thomas

(Department of Decision Theory, University of Manchester)

1. INTRODUCTION

Consider a Markov decision process with state space $S \times M$ where S and M are finite sets. In normal Markov decision processes, the system can choose an action k from a set of possible actions, $K_{(s,m)}$. If action k is chosen, there is an immediate reward $r^k(s,m)$ and with probability $p^k_{(s,m),(s',m')}$ the system moves to state (s',m'). The aim is to choose a strategy π that maximises the reward under some criterion. A strategy π specifies for all stages n and all possible histories h_n the probability $\pi_n(k|h_n)$ of choosing action k. The history h_n equals the sequence of states and actions in the past together with the present state.

$$h_n = ((s_1,m_1), k_1,(s_2,m_2), k_2,\ldots, k_{n-1},(s_n,m_n)) \quad (1.1)$$

where (s_i,m_i) is the state of the system at the ith stage and k_i is the action chosen at this stage. C is the class of all such strategies.

In the case of constrained Markov decision processes, the action set in state (s,m) is K_s - that is depends only on the s component of the state. Moreover, we are only allowed to consider strategies where the choice of action depends only on the S-component of the history. Thus we would only allow policies π where

$$\begin{aligned}\pi_n(k|(s_1,m_1),k_1,(s_2,m_2),k_2,\ldots,k_{n-1},(s_n,m_n))\\ = \pi_n(k|(s_1,\tilde{m}_1),k_1,(s_2,\tilde{m}_2),k_2\ldots,k_{n-1},(s_n,\tilde{m}_n))\end{aligned} \quad (1.2)$$

no matter what the $\tilde{m}_i$ are. We denote the set of such strategies by C^s. So for the strategies in C^s, if we choose action k in state (s,m) at some stage, we are constrained to choose the same action in state $(s,\tilde{m})$ at that stage.

Constrained Markov decision processes have not received much attention apart from a paper by Hastings and Sadjadi [6] who suggest how using the bounds from ordinary value iteration might shorten the enumerative procedure of calculating the average reward under each stationary policy in order to find the optimal one. However there are several different types of problems which are constrained M.D.P.'s. In section two we give three such examples.

The object of this paper is to show how these constrained Markov Decision Processes are equivalent to multi-objective Markov Decision Processes on a state space S, where the rewards are given in the vector space M. The trick we use is in some sense the reverse of what White and Kim [14] did in transferring multi-objective M.D.P.'s into partially observable ones. However as the objectives in the problem we end up with intertwine whereas White and Kim started with ordinary multi-objective M.D.P.'s the results are very different. In section three we describe this equivalence between constrained M.D.P.'s and multi-intertwining objective Markov decision processes (M.I.O.M.D.P.) and show that a strategy is optimal for constrained M.D.P.'s if and only if it gives the only efficient value for the corresponding M.I.O.M.D.P. We concentrate throughout the paper on the average reward case, because this is the more appropriate criterion for many of the examples, but analogous results hold in the discounted case.

In section four we look at the relationships, or rather the lack of them, that exist between the special types of strategies such as the deterministic, the stationary and the Markov strategies, in M.I.O.M.D.P. These have implications for which type of strategy can be optimal in the corresponding constrained problem.

Three general methods have been used to solve ordinary multi-objective Markov decision processes over an infinite horizon. The first [5,13] is to use the weighting factor approach to translate them to scalar M.D.P.'s that can then be solved by linear programming etc. The second is to use the multi-objective version of value iteration [8,15] and the third is to apply the multi-objective version of policy iteration [4]. In section five we generalise policy iteration again to find all the efficient points of a M.I.O.M.D.P., and also use it to check if a particular strategy is the unique efficient strategy. We end by applying this algorithm to a library problem example.

2. EXAMPLES OF CONSTRAINED MARKOV DECISION PROBLEMS

(A) The Library Problem.

Consider n books $B_1, B_2, \ldots, B_n$, placed in a line along a bookshelf. When a book is requested it is removed from the shelf, but replaced before the next request is dealt with. If the book was the ith one from the front then it is replaced in position $\tau(i)$ - irrespective of which book it was - and the books between i and $\tau(i)$ move up or down a place depending if $i < \tau(i)$ or $i > \tau(i)$. The problem is to find which replacement scheme τ minimises the average position of the book chosen, when p_i, the probability that book B_i is chosen next is not known for any i. Hendricks [7] introduced this problem, and Phelps and Thomas [11] showed for a special class of probabilities that the transposition replacement scheme - $\tau(1) = 1$, $\tau(i) = i-1$, $i \geq 2$ - was optimal. The conjectures are (1) that for all probability distributions and all starting positions of the books, transportation is optimal for all forward moving replacement schemes - $\tau(1) = 1$, $\tau(i) < i$ - and (2) that if we take all possible starting positions of the books as equally likely then the transposition scheme is optimal over all schemes. For details see the survey article of Nelson [10].

In this case the state space is the position of the books and the position of the book chosen. Thus it is of the form $S \times M$ where $M = \{B_{\sigma(1)}, B_{\sigma(2)} \cdots B_{\sigma(n)} \mid \text{for all permutations } \sigma\}$ and $S = \{i \mid 1 \leq i \leq n\}$. The action space K in each state is the position the book can be replaced so $K = \{j \mid 1 \leq j \leq n\}$ and the immediate cost $r^k(i,\sigma)$ is i and

$$p^k_{(i,\sigma),(j,\sigma')} = p_{\sigma'(j)} \quad \text{if} \begin{cases} \sigma'(j)=\sigma(j) & \text{for } j<\min(i,k) \text{ and } j>\max(i,k). \\ \sigma'(k)=\sigma(i) & \\ \text{and } \begin{array}{l} \text{if } i\leq k \quad \sigma'(j)=\sigma(j+1) \quad i\leq j\leq k-1 \\ \text{if } i\geq k \quad \sigma'(j)=\alpha(j-1) \quad k+1\leq j\leq i \end{array} \end{cases} \tag{2.1}$$

$$p^k_{(i,\sigma),(j,\sigma')} = 0 \qquad \text{for any other } \sigma'.$$

Obviously the replacement schemes are C^S type policies, and we can ask which among this class of policies is optimal.

(B) Design Problems.

This problem looks at systems, like queues, which can be described in terms of a Markov chain. The problem is to choose *a priori* the values of the parameters that can be varied so that it maximises the average expected reward per period. One is designing the system to produce the maximum reward. Thus in a queueing problem one may be able *a priori* to determine the service rate or the number of servers to operate. Evans [3] described a gradient search algorithm to solve such a specific queue design problem. If M is the state space of the chain and K the set of possible values of the variable parameters of the problem, we can define this as a constrained Markov decision process. Let $S = \{s_o\}$ - just one point - and $r^k(s_o,m)$ is $r^k(m)$ the reward when the system is in state m with parameters set at k. Similarly $p^k_{(s_o,m),(s_o,m')} = p^k_{mm'}$ - the probability of transition from m to m' of the original chain when the parameter values are k. Policies in C^s are then simply those that are fixed *a priori*.

(C) Partially Observable Problems.

Partially observable M.D.P.'s are generalisations of ordinary M.D.P.'s where there is uncertainty about the state of the Markov process, but one is allowed to acquire information about the state. Monahan [9] in his survey gives many examples of such processes. Consider a slightly different problem where the state space of the system is given by $S \times M$. We can observe accurately the S-component of the space, but have no idea, of the M-component, nor are we allowed to make inferences about it. This might arise in a replacement problem where S are the observable components and M the unobservable ones, and we require 'easy-to-operate' strategies, which depend only on the known observations. These are nothing but the constrained policies C^s.

3. MULTIPLE-INTERTWINING OBJECTIVE MARKOV DECISION PROCESSES.

Consider the constrained Markov decision process described in section one which has a finite state space $S \times M$, finite action spaces K_s which depends only on the S-component of the state space, and strategies restricted to the class C^s of non-anticipative strategies constrained to satisfy (1.2). For each such strategy π, we define the average reward starting in state (s,m) by,

$$g^{\pi}(s,m) = \liminf_{n \to \infty} n^{-1} \, \mathrm{Exp}^{\pi}\{ \sum_{k=1}^{n} r^{A_k}(X_k) \,|\, X_1 = (s,m)\} \quad (3.1)$$

where X_k and A_k are the random variables describing the state and action chosen at the kth stage using policy π. This is equivalent to defining

$$g^{\pi}(s,m) = \liminf_{n \to \infty} n^{-1} \, \mathrm{Exp}^{\pi}\{v_{n,1}^{\pi(h_1)}(s,m)\} \quad (3.2)$$

where $v_{n,k}^{\pi(h_k)}(X_k)$ is the total further reward obtainable when at stage k of a problem, where one is using policy π over a total of n stages (thus $n-k+1$ to go), and the history up to stage k is h_k and the state at stage k is X_k. Thus

$$v_{n,k}^{\pi(h_k)}(X_k) = r^{\pi(h_k)}(X_k) + \sum_{X_{k+1}} p_{X_k,X_{k+1}}^{\pi(h_k)} \, v_{n,k+1}^{\pi(h_k,\pi(h_k),X_{k+1})}(X_{k+1}) \quad 1 \leq k \leq n-1 \quad (3.3)$$

$$v_{n,n}^{\pi(h_n)}(X_n) = r^{\pi(h_n)}(X_n).$$

We say that π^* is optimal in class $C_{\cdot}^S$, where $C_{\cdot}^S$ is some subset of C^S if

$$g^{\pi^*}(s,m) = \sup_{\pi \in C_{\cdot}^S} g^{\pi}(s,m) \qquad \text{for all } (s,m) \in S \otimes M. \quad (3.4)$$

We write C_M^S for the set of Markov strategies in C^S, i.e. those where the choice of action depends only on the present S-component of the state space and the number of stages that have elapsed. C_S^S is the set of stationary policies which are the strategies in C_M^S where the choice of action is independent of the stage and C_D^S is the set of deterministic policies. For any stationary strategy π, let $P_*^{\pi}(.,.)$ be the stationary distribution of the corresponding chain, then

$$g^{\pi}(s,m) = \sum_{(s',m') \in S \times M} P_*^{\pi}((s,m),(s',m')).r^{\pi(s')}(s',m') \quad (3.5)$$

where $P_*^{\pi}((s,m),(s',m'))$ is the long run probability of being in state (s',m') given the chain started in (s,m). Brown [1] showed that these definitions of gain in (3.2), (3.1) and (3.5) coincide for stationary policies, and there is always an optimal policy that is stationary.

We now present a multi-objective Markov decision process which gives the same rewards as the above problem. Its state space is S and for each state s in S, the action space is the K_s described above. If action k is chosen in state s, the immediate reward R is a $|M|$-dimensional vector with coordinates given by

$$R^k(s)_m = r^k(s,m) \tag{3.6}$$

and the probability that the system moves to state s' is given by the $|M| \times |M|$ matrix with elements

$$P^k(s,s')_{mm'} = P^k_{(s,m),(s',m')}. \tag{3.7}$$

This definition implies that the transition probability of going from s to s' can be different for different components of the objective function. Moreover the value of a component at one stage is the immediate reward in that component added to the weighted sum of the values of other components at the next stage. Since the components of the objective function at each stage depend on future values of each other, we call these processes multi-intertwining objective Markov Decision Processes (M.I.O.M. D.P.). Let C, (C_M, C_S, C_D) be the set of non-anticipative (Markov, stationary, deterministic) policies for such processes. For any policy π in C we can define the average reward stating in state s by mimicking (3.2), (3.3). Thus

$$\underline{G}^\pi(s) = \liminf_{n \to \infty} n^{-1} \operatorname{Exp}\{ \underline{V}_{n,1}^{(h_1)}(s) \} \tag{3.8}$$

where

$$\underline{V}_{n,k}^{\pi(h_k)}(X_k) = \underline{R}^{\pi(h_k)}(X_k) + \sum_{s:X_{k+1}=s} P^{\pi(h_k)}(X_k, X_{k+1}) * V_{n,k+1}^{\pi(h_k,\pi(h_k),X_{k+1})}(X_{k+1}) \tag{3.9}$$

$$\underline{V}_{n,n}^{\pi(h_n)}(X_n) = \underline{R}^{\pi(h_n)}(X_n) \tag{3.10}$$

and

$$\left(\sum_{s'} P(s,s')*V(s')\right)_m = \sum_{s'} \sum_{m'} P(s,s')_{mm'} V(s')_{m'} \tag{3.11}$$

For $\pi \in C_S$ let $\underline{P}^\pi_*(s,s')$ be the stationary distribution of the corresponding chain, then the average reward starting in state s is

$$\underline{G}^\pi(s) = \sum_{s' \in S} \underline{P}^\pi_*(s,s') * \underline{R}^\pi(s') \tag{3.12}$$

We define the partial orders $\succ$, $\succcurlyeq$ on $R^{|M|}$ by $\underline{x} \succcurlyeq \underline{y}$ if $x_i \geq y_i$ $\forall$ $i = 1,\ldots,|M|$, and $\underline{x} \succ \underline{y}$ if $\underline{x} \succcurlyeq \underline{y}$ and $\underline{x} \neq \underline{y}$. A policy $\pi \in C$ is efficient for state s in C if there is no $\underline{\pi}' \in C$ satisfying

$$\underline{G}^{\pi'}(s) \succ \underline{G}^{\pi}(s) \qquad (3.13)$$

The set of efficient policies is denoted $E(C.(s))$. The relationships between the two models can be made plain in the following lemma.

Lemma 3.1

If $(S \otimes M,\ r^k(.).p^k_{(.),(.)},\ C^S)$ is a constrained Markov decision process and $(S,\underline{R}(.),P(\ ),C)$ the corresponding M.I.O.M.D.P. then

(a) every strategy $\pi \in C^S$ corresponds to a strategy π in C and vice versa,

(b) $g^{\pi}(s,m) = (G^{\pi}(s))_m$.

(c) $C^S_M = C_M$, $C^S_S = C_S$, $C^S_D = C_D$.

(d) π is optimal in $C^S(C^S_M, C^S_S, C^S_D)$ if and only if the corresponding strategy in C is the unique efficient policy in $C(C_M, C_S, C_D)$ for all states s.

Proof

The proof of all four parts follows trivially from the definitions once one identifies π in C^S with the strategy in C, which at the nth stage with history $(s_1,k_1,s_2,k_2\ s_n)$ chooses action k with probability $\pi_n(k|(s_1,m_1),k_1,\ldots(s_n,m_n))$ for any $m_1,m_2,\ldots m_n$. The condition of equation (1.2) ensures this is well defined.

Thus the problem of looking for optimal strategies in the constrained problem can be translated into looking for uniquely efficient ones in the M.I.O.M.D.P.

4. PROPERTIES OF M.I.O.M.D.P.

We are interested in the relationship between the four sets

$$Y(s)[Y_M(s),Y_S(s),Y_D(s)] = \{G^{\pi}(s) \mid \pi \in C[C_M,C_S,C_D]\} \quad (4.1)$$

Derman and Strauch [2] showed that in the ordinary M.D.P. case, which is a special case of M.I.O.M.D.P. $Y(s) = Y_M(s)$ and if all the policies give rise to ergodic chains $N\,Y_D(s) = Y_S(s) = Y_D(s)$ where N denotes the convex hull of the set. Hartley [5] shows that a similar result holds for discounted M.O.M.D.P.'s, and we can prove the same result in the average cost M.O.M.D.P. case (A.M.O.M.D.P. is a M.I.O.M.D.P. where $P^k(s,s')_{mm'} = p^k_{ss'}\delta_{mm'}$, $\forall\, k,s,s',m,m'$).

<u>Theorem 4.1</u>

If every strategy in a M.P.M.D.P. forms an ergodic chain (so all states are in the same persistent class), then

$$Y_D(s) = Y_S(s) = Y_M(s) = Y(s) = \underset{s}{\cup} Y(s). \quad (4.2)$$

<u>Proof</u>

Every stationary policy π has a stationary distribution $P^{\pi}_*(s)$ which is the long run probability of being in state s and $\underline{G} = \sum_{s\in S} P^{\pi}_*(s)\underline{R}^{\pi}(s)$. First we show $Y_S(s)$ is convex. Suppose σ and ρ are stationary policies and choose λ, $0 < \lambda < 1$. We must find a stationary policy τ so that

$$\underline{G}^{\tau} = \lambda\underline{G}^{\sigma} + (1-\lambda)G^{\sigma} = \lambda \sum_{s\in S} P^{\sigma}_*(s)\underline{R}^{\sigma}(s) + (1-\lambda)\sum_{s\in S} P^{\rho}_*(s)\underline{R}^{\rho}(s) \quad (4.3)$$

Let τ be the policy that in state s chooses σ with probability $k_s^{-1}\lambda_s P^{\sigma}_*(s)$ and ρ with probability $k_s^{-1}(1-\lambda)P^{\rho}_*(s)$ where $k_s = P^{\sigma}_*(s) + (1-\lambda)P^{\rho}_*(s)$. Then

$$k_s P^{\tau}(s,s') = \lambda P_*(s)P^{\sigma}(s,s') + (1-\lambda)P^{\rho}_*(s)P^{\rho}(s,s') \quad (4.4)$$

So

$$\sum_s k_s P^{\tau}(s,s') = \lambda P^{\sigma}_*(s') + (1-\lambda)P^{\rho}_*(s') = k_{s'} \quad (4.5)$$

Then $P^{\tau}_*(s) = k_s$ so

$$\underline{G}^{\tau} = \sum_s P^{\tau}_*(s)\left(k_s^{-1}\lambda P^{\sigma}_*(s)\underline{R}^{\sigma}(s) + k_s^{-1}(1-\lambda)P^{\rho}_*(s)\underline{R}^{\rho}(s)\right)$$

$$= \lambda \sum_s P_*^{\sigma}(s)\underline{R}^{\sigma}(s) + (1-\lambda) \sum_s P_*^{\rho}(s)\underline{R}^{\rho}(s)$$

$$= \lambda\underline{G}^{\sigma} + (1-\lambda)\underline{G}^{\rho} \tag{4.6}$$

Thus $\mathcal{N} Y_D(s) \subseteq \mathcal{N} Y_S(s) = Y(s)$. If we can show $Y(s) \subseteq \mathcal{N} Y_D(s)$, the result holds. Suppose there is a $\underline{G}^{\pi}(s) \in Y(s)$ which is not in $\mathcal{N} Y_D(s)$. Then by the separating hyperplane theorem there is a $\underline{w}$, so

$$\underline{w}.\underline{G}^{\pi}(s) > \underline{w}.\underline{G}^{\delta}(s)$$

for all deterministic policies δ. But $\underline{w}.\underline{G}(s)$ is the average cost for an ordinary M.D.P. and if all the policies are ergodic, Ross [12] shows that there must be an optimal policy that is deterministic. Hence the contradiction.

This result is useful because if we find the efficient set in C_S we have also found the efficient set in C. However for M.I.O.M.D.P. the result does not hold, even if we require the equivalent of ergodicity on the enlarged space $S \times M$.

A M.I.O.M.D.P. is state ergodic if all the policies in C_S partition $S \times M$ into the same classes P_k of persistent aperiodic states and these are all of the form $P_k = \{S \times M_k\}$.

This incorporates both the ergodic M.O.M.D.P. described above and the completely irreducible M.I.O.M.D.P. when there is only one class, $S \times M$. In the rest of the paper we will assume the M.I.O.M.D.P are state ergodic and so the average cost is independent of the starting state. We give examples to show none of the equalities in 4.2 holds for these processes.

Example 1

$Y_D \neq Y_S$, $Y_D \neq Y_M$, $Y_D \neq Y$.

Let $|S| = 1$, $|M| = 2$, $C_D = \{1,2\}$ where

$$P_{11}^1 = \begin{pmatrix} \frac{1}{2} & \frac{1}{2} \\ \frac{1}{2} & \frac{1}{2} \end{pmatrix} \qquad R_1^1 = \begin{pmatrix} 0 \\ 2 \end{pmatrix} \qquad P_{11}^2 = \begin{pmatrix} \frac{1}{3} & \frac{2}{3} \\ \frac{1}{3} & \frac{2}{3} \end{pmatrix}$$

$$R_1^2 = \begin{pmatrix} 2 \\ 0 \end{pmatrix}.$$

For any $\tau \in C_S$ where one chooses 1 with prob τ, 2 with prob $(1-\tau)$ we have

$$P_{11}^{\tau} = \begin{pmatrix} \frac{1}{3}+\frac{1}{6}\tau & \frac{2}{3}-\frac{1}{6}\tau \\ \frac{1}{3}+\frac{1}{6}\tau & \frac{2}{3}-\frac{1}{6}\tau \end{pmatrix} ; \quad R_1 = \begin{pmatrix} 2-2\tau \\ 2\tau \end{pmatrix}$$

$$P_{\tau}^{*}(1,1) = \frac{1}{6}\begin{pmatrix} 2+\tau, & 4-\tau \\ 2+\tau, & 4-\tau \end{pmatrix}, \quad \underline{G}^{\tau} = \frac{4+6\tau-4\tau^2}{6}\begin{pmatrix}1\\1\end{pmatrix}$$

As $\underline{G}^1 = \begin{pmatrix}1\\1\end{pmatrix}$, $\underline{G}^2 = \frac{2}{3}\begin{pmatrix}1\\1\end{pmatrix}$, $Y_D = \{ x\begin{pmatrix}1\\1\end{pmatrix} / 2/3 \leq x \leq 1\}$, but $\underline{G}^{3/4} = 25/24\begin{pmatrix}1\\1\end{pmatrix} \notin N.Y_D$ and yet this policy is in C_S, C_M and C.

Example 2 $\quad Y_s \neq Y_M$, $\quad Y_s \neq Y$

$$|S| = 1, \quad |M| = 2, \quad C_D = \{1,2\} \text{ where}$$

$$P_{11}^{1} = \begin{pmatrix} \frac{1}{8} & \frac{7}{8} \\ \frac{1}{8} & \frac{7}{8} \end{pmatrix} \quad R_1^1 = \begin{pmatrix}0\\0\end{pmatrix} ; \quad P_{11}^{2} = \begin{pmatrix} \frac{7}{8} & \frac{1}{8} \\ \frac{7}{8} & \frac{1}{8} \end{pmatrix} \quad R_1^2 = \begin{pmatrix}-6\\1\end{pmatrix}$$

So for mixed τ

$$P_{11}^{\tau} = \begin{pmatrix} \frac{7}{8}-\frac{6}{8}\tau, & \frac{1}{8}+\frac{6}{8}\tau \\ \frac{7}{8}-\frac{6}{8}\tau, & \frac{1}{8}+\frac{6}{8}\tau \end{pmatrix} \qquad R_1 = (1-\tau)\begin{pmatrix}-6\\1\end{pmatrix}$$

$$\underline{G}^{\tau} = \frac{-42\tau^2+83\tau-41}{8}\begin{pmatrix}1\\1\end{pmatrix}$$

As τ varies $0 \leq \tau \leq 1$, we get $Y_S = \{x\begin{pmatrix}1\\1\end{pmatrix}; \ \frac{-41}{8} \leq x \leq \frac{1}{164}\}$ whereas the policy 1,2,1,2,1,2 gives rewards $\begin{pmatrix}0\\0\end{pmatrix}$, $\begin{pmatrix}\frac{1}{8}\\ \frac{1}{8}\end{pmatrix}$, $\begin{pmatrix}0\\0\end{pmatrix}$, $\begin{pmatrix}\frac{1}{8}\\ \frac{1}{8}\end{pmatrix}$,... so has $G = \frac{1}{16}\begin{pmatrix}1\\1\end{pmatrix}$.

Example 3.

$Y_M \neq Y$.

$|S| = 3, \quad |M| = 2, \quad |K_1| = 2, \quad |K_2| = |K_3| = 1.$

$$P^i_{12} = \begin{pmatrix} \frac{1}{4} & \frac{1}{4} \\ \frac{1}{4} & \frac{1}{4} \end{pmatrix}, \quad P^i_{13} = \begin{pmatrix} \frac{1}{4} & \frac{1}{4} \\ \frac{1}{4} & \frac{1}{4} \end{pmatrix} \quad i = 1,2,. \quad R^1_1 = \begin{pmatrix} 12 \\ 0 \end{pmatrix}, \quad R^2_1 = \begin{pmatrix} 0 \\ 12 \end{pmatrix}$$

$$P^1_{22} = \begin{pmatrix} \frac{1}{4} & \frac{1}{4} \\ \frac{1}{4} & \frac{1}{4} \end{pmatrix}, \quad P^1_{21} = \begin{pmatrix} \frac{1}{2} & 0 \\ \frac{1}{2} & 0 \end{pmatrix} \quad R^1_2 = \begin{pmatrix} 0 \\ 0 \end{pmatrix}$$

$$P^1_{33} = \begin{pmatrix} \frac{1}{4} & \frac{1}{4} \\ \frac{1}{4} & \frac{1}{4} \end{pmatrix}, \quad P^1_{31} = \begin{pmatrix} 0 & \frac{1}{2} \\ 0 & \frac{1}{2} \end{pmatrix} \quad R^1_3 = \begin{pmatrix} 0 \\ 0 \end{pmatrix}.$$

The movement of the system through the states space S is independent of the policy chosen, and the only rewards occur when the system reaches state 1. The expected number of stages until return to 1 is 3. The policy which in state 1, says choose action 1 if previous state was 2 and action 2 if previous state was 2, guarantees a reward of 12 to both components each time the state enters one. Thus average reward for this non-Markov policy is $G = 4\begin{pmatrix} 1 \\ 1 \end{pmatrix}$. Since at each stage, the chance the process arrives at state 1 from state 2 is the same as it arriving at state 1 from state 2, any Markov policy gives an expected reward of $6\begin{pmatrix} 1 \\ 1 \end{pmatrix}$ when the system arrives at state 1. Hence expected average reward for any Markov policy is $2\begin{pmatrix} 1 \\ 1 \end{pmatrix}$.

These counter examples have two obvious implications. Firstly in constrained M.D.P.'s the optimal policy need not be Markov or stationary let alone deterministic. In the design of queueing or inventory problems we often optimise over the deterministic policies, but there is no reason to suppose a random policy or even a non-stationary one might not be better. Secondly the result in ordinary M.O.M.D.P.'s that the efficient set of stationary policies is efficient for all policies is false. Looking at the class of all non-anticipative policies to find efficiency is very difficult, so we will concentrate on C_D - the deterministic policies - and find an algorithm for finding efficient set among deterministic policies. We will then modify this to test if a policy is the unique efficient deterministic policy and so optimal amongst deterministic policies in the constrained problem.

5. POLICY ITERATION ALGORITHM

Let $E(Y_D)$ be the efficient set of Y_D. We modify Furukawa's [4] policy iteration algorithm to find this set, again recalling that all our policies are state ergodic. Any policy $f \in C_D$ is determined by its choice of action $f(s)$ in state s. For such a policy we can define its gain $\underline{G}^f$ and bias $\underline{V}^f(s)$ by solving

$$\underline{G}^f + \underline{V}^{f(s)} = \underline{R}^{f(s)}(s) + \sum_{s' \in S} P^{f(s)}(s,f')*\underline{V}^f(s') \tag{5.1}$$

with $(V^f(s^*))_{m^*} = 0$ for some fixed $s^* \in S$ and a fixed m^* in each M_k of the partition of $S \otimes M$ into persistent classes. We can check this gives correct gain by multiplying all terms in (5.1) by $P_*^f(s)$ to get $\underline{G}^f = \sum_s P_*^f(s)*\underline{R}^{f(s)}(s)$. Define

$$\underline{\gamma}_f^g(s) = \underline{R}^{g(s)}(s) + \sum_{s' \in S} P^{g(s)}(s,s')*\underline{V}^f(s') \tag{5.2}$$

then we get the following lemma.

Lemma 5.1

Let $\gamma_f^g(.) > \gamma_f^f(.)$ if for all s, m $\gamma_f^g(s)_m \geq \gamma_f^f(s)_m$ with at least one inequality strict then

(i) If $\gamma_f^g(.) > \gamma_f^f(.)$ then $\underline{G}^g \succ \underline{G}^f$

(ii) If $\gamma_f^g(s) = \gamma_f^f(s)$ for all s, $\underline{G}^g = \underline{G}^f$

(iii) If $\gamma_f^g(.) < \gamma_f^f(.)$ then $\underline{G}^g \prec \underline{G}^f$.

Proof

$$\gamma_f^g(s) - \gamma_f^f(s) = R^{g(s)}(s) + \sum_{s'} P^{g(s)}(s,s')*V^f(s') - \underline{G}^f - \underline{V}^f(s) \tag{5.3}$$

Multiplying 5.3 by $P_*^g(s)$ and summing over all s gives

$$\sum_s P_*^g(s)*(\gamma_f^g(s) - \gamma_f^f(s)) = \underline{G}^g - \underline{G}^f \tag{5.4}$$

and since $P_*^g(s)_{mm'} \geq 0$ for all m,m', with strict inequality for each m (for at least one m') from state ergodicity, the result holds.

This is the basis for the following algorithm, where E_k is a set of policies whose values are possible efficient after stage k and F_k the set of non-efficient policies.

Algorithm.

1. Set $E_o = F_o = \{\phi\}$. Choose any policy $f_1 \in C_D$.

2. For policy f_n calculate

$$\underline{G}^{f_n} + \underline{V}^{f_n}(s) = \underline{R}^{f_n(s)}(s) + \sum_{s' \in S} P^{f_n(s)}(s,s') * \underline{V}^{f_n}(s') \tag{5.5}$$

for all states s.

3. Calculate $\underline{\gamma}_f^k(s)$ for all s, and $k \in K_s$. Define

$$F_{f_n} = \{g \mid \gamma_{f_n}^{g(s)}(s) \prec \gamma_{f_n}^{f_n(s)} \forall s\} \tag{5.6}$$

$$E_{f_n} = \{g \mid \gamma_{f_n}^{g(s)}(s) \succcurlyeq \gamma_{f_n}^{f_n(s)} \forall s \text{ with } \gamma_{f_n}^{g(s)} \succ \gamma_{f_n}^{f_n(s)} \text{ for at least one } s\}. \tag{5.7}$$

4. If $E_{f_n} \neq \{\phi\}$, let $F_n = F_{n-1} \cup F_{f_n}$, $E_n = E_{n-1} \cap F_{f_n}^c$ and choose $f_{n+1} \in E_{f_n}$. Return to Step 2.

If $E_{f_n} = \{\phi\}$ let $F_n = F_{n-1} \cup (F_{f_n} - \{f_n\})$, $E_n = (E_{n-1} \cap F_{f_n}^c) \cup \{f_n\}$. Choose $f_{n+1} \in (F_n \cup E_n)^c$ [Furakawi [4] suggests choosing $f_{n+1}(s)$ so that $\gamma_{f_n}^{f_{n+1}(s)} \not\prec \gamma_{f_n}^{f_n(s)}$ if possible, but this is not necessary, and there is as yet no computational experience to show it is quicker, than an arbitrary choice]. Return to Step 2.

5. When $F_n \cup E_n = C_D$, notice that for all policies $f \in E_n$ we have calculated $\underline{G}^f$ at some point. Let $E = \mathcal{E}\{\underline{G}^f \mid f \in E_n\}$ where $\mathcal{E}\{X\} = \{\underline{x} \in X \mid \nexists, y \in X, \underline{y} \succ \underline{x}\}$, then these are the efficient average reward vectors.

Theorem 5.2

$$E = \mathcal{E}\{\underline{G}^f \mid \underline{f} \in C_D\}.$$

Proof

From Lemma 5.1, for every $\underline{g} \in F_n$ there is an $f \in C_D$ with $\underline{G}^g \prec \underline{G}^f$. Thus

$$E\{\underline{G}^f \mid f \in C_D\} = E\{\underline{G}^f \mid f \in F_n \cup E_n\} = E\{\underline{G}^f | f \in E_n\} = E \tag{5.8}$$

We are interested when there is a unique average value.

Corollary 5.3

If for some f_n $F_{f_n} = C_D$ then $\underline{G}^{f_n}$ is the unique efficient value.

Proof

This follows trivially from Lemma 5.1.

This is a sufficient condition not a necessary one, and usually the result is not so clear cut. Suppose we want to check whether the average reward corresponding to a given policy f is the unique efficient reward, we can modify the above algorithm as follows.

Algorithm 2

1. Calculate $\underline{G}^f$, $\underline{V}^f(s)$ for all s as in (5.1).

2. Calculate $\gamma_f^k(s)$ for all s and all $k \in K_s$. Find E_f, F_f.

3(a). If $E_f \neq \{\phi\}$ then $\underline{G}^f$ is not efficient let alone uniquely efficient.

3(b). If $F_f = C_D$ then $\underline{G}^f$ is the unique efficient average reward.

3(c). If $E_f = \{\phi\}$ $F_f \neq C_D$, for each $g \in C_D \cap F_f^c$; let

$$d_g^1 = \sum_{s'} P^g(s,s') * (\gamma_f^{f(s)}(s') - \gamma_f^{g(s)}(s')), \tag{5.9}$$

$$d_g^{n+1}(s) = \sum_{s'} P^g(s,s') * d_g^n(s') \tag{5.10}$$

Repeat until either (a) $\underline{d}_g^{n+1}(s) \succcurlyeq \underline{0}$ $\forall s$, or

(b) $(d_g^{n+1}(s))_m \leq 0$ for $\forall$ $(s,m) \in P_k$, one of the persistent classes in the partition of $S \times M$.

If (a) occurs $\underline{G}^f \succcurlyeq \underline{G}^g$ and we repeat with another g from C_D F_f^c and continue until we have tested all $g \in C_D \cap F_f^c$. If (a) occurs in every case, $\underline{G}^f$ is the unique efficient value.

If (b) ever occurs, $\underline{G}^f \not\succcurlyeq \underline{G}^g$ and so $\underline{G}^f$ is not the unique efficient average reward value.

6. EXAMPLE

Consider the library problem described in section two and suppose there are three books with $p_1 = .5$, $p_2 = .4$, $p_3 = .1$. So $S = \{1,2,3\}$ $M = \{\pi(1),\pi(2),\pi(3) \mid \pi \text{ any permutation}\}$. We will show that the policy T where $T(1) = 1$, $T(2) = 1$, $T(3) = 2$ is optimal amongst all forward moving policies, using the second algorithm described above. There is only one other, namely τ where $\tau(i) = 1$, and both these have $S \times M$ as the only ergodic class. Solving (5.1) for T we get $\underline{G}^T = 1.7313\,\underline{e}$ where $e^T = (1,1,1,1,1,1)$ and $v(1)_{123} = 0$, $\overline{v}(1)_{132} = 0.\overline{7}69$, $v(1)_{213} = 0.136$, $v(1)_{231} = 1.129$, $v(1)_{312} = 2.156$, $v(1)_{321} = 2.409$. Note that $v(2)_{a_1a_2a_3} = 1 + v(1)_{a_2a_1a_3}$ and $v(3)_{a_1a_2a_3} = 2 + v(1)_{a_1a_3a_2}$. Then taking components in the order 123, 132, 213, 231, 312, 321, we get

$$\gamma_T^1(1) = \begin{pmatrix} 1.731 \\ 2.500 \\ 1.867 \\ 2.860 \\ 3.887 \\ 4.140 \end{pmatrix} \qquad \gamma_T^2(1) = \begin{pmatrix} 1.867 \\ 3.887 \\ 1.731 \\ 4.140 \\ 2.500 \\ 2.860 \end{pmatrix} \qquad \gamma_T^3(1) = \begin{pmatrix} 2.860 \\ 4.140 \\ 2.500 \\ 3.887 \\ 1.731 \\ 1.867 \end{pmatrix}$$

$$\gamma_T^1(2) = \begin{pmatrix} 2.867 \\ 4.887 \\ 2.731 \\ 5.140 \\ 3.500 \\ 3.860 \end{pmatrix} \quad \gamma_T^2(2) = \begin{pmatrix} 2.731 \\ 3.500 \\ 2.867 \\ 3.860 \\ 4.887 \\ 5.140 \end{pmatrix} \quad \gamma_T^3(2) = \begin{pmatrix} 3.500 \\ 2.731 \\ 3.860 \\ 2.867 \\ 5.140 \\ 4.887 \end{pmatrix}$$

$$\gamma_T^1(3) = \begin{pmatrix} 5.887 \\ 3.867 \\ 6.140 \\ 3.731 \\ 4.860 \\ 4.500 \end{pmatrix} \quad \gamma_T^2(3) = \begin{pmatrix} 4.500 \\ 3.731 \\ 4.860 \\ 3.867 \\ 6.140 \\ 5.887 \end{pmatrix} \quad \gamma_T^3(3) = \begin{pmatrix} 3.731 \\ 4.500 \\ 3.867 \\ 4.860 \\ 5.887 \\ 6.140 \end{pmatrix}$$

Thus $E_T = \{\phi\}$, $F_T = \{T\}$. So for τ we must test using the method of 3(c).

The symmetry of the matrices $P^\tau(1,s')$, $P^\tau(2,s')$, $P^\tau(2,s')$ means that $d_\tau^n(1)$, $d_\tau^n(2)$, $d_\tau^n(3)$ are permutations of one another, so we only give $d_\tau^n(1)$.

$$d_\tau^2(1) = \begin{pmatrix} 0.0678 \\ 0.0272 \\ 0.0512 \\ -0.0272 \\ -0.0784 \\ -0.0678 \end{pmatrix} \quad d_\tau^3(1) = \begin{pmatrix} 0.0465 \\ 0.0262 \\ 0.0476 \\ 0.0162 \\ -0.0512 \\ -0.0041 \end{pmatrix} \quad d_\tau^4(1) = \begin{pmatrix} 0.0418 \\ 0.0316 \\ 0.0419 \\ 0.0293 \\ 0.0191 \\ 0.0192 \end{pmatrix}$$

Thus $\underline{G}^\tau > G^T$ and so T is the optimal forward mixing policy. It is easy to check that T is better than any other policy which has only one ergodic class $S\otimes M$. If τ_{abc} is the policy where $\tau(1) = a$, $\tau(2) = b$, $\tau(3) = c$, these policies are τ_{111}, τ_{112}, τ_{131}, τ_{211}, τ_{212}, τ_{222}, τ_{231}, τ_{232}, τ_{311}, τ_{312}, τ_{313}, τ_{322}, τ_{322}, τ_{331}, τ_{332} and τ_{333}.

REFERENCES

[1] BROWN, B.: On the iterative method of dynamic programming on a finite state space, discrete time Markov process; Ann. Math.Stat. 36, 1279-1285, (1965).

[2] DERMAN, C., STRAUCH, R.: A note on memoryless rules for controlling sequential control processes; Ann. Math. Stat. 37, 276-278 (1966).

[3] EVANS, R.V.: Markov chain design problems; Op.Res. 29, 959-970, (1981).

[4] FURUKAWA, N: Vector valued Markovian decision processes within countable state space; Recent Developments in Markov Decision Process, pp.205-223, ed. by Hartley, Thomas, White, Academic Press, New York (1980).

[5] HARTLEY, R.: Finite, Discounted, Vector Markov Decision Processes. Notes in Decision Theory, No. 85, University of Manchester, (1979).

[6] HASTINGS, N.A.J., SADJADI, D.: Markov programming with policy constraints; E.J.O.R. 3, 253-255, (1979).

[7] HENDRICKS, W.J.; The stationary distribution of an interesting Markov chain; J.Appl. Prob. 9, 231-233 (1972).

[8] HENIG, M.I.: Dynamic Programming with returns in partially ordered sets, Faculty of Commerce and Business Administration, University of British Columbia, Vancouver (1980).

[9] MONAHAN, G.E.: A survey of partially observable Markov decision processes: theory, models and algorithms. College of Industrial Management, Georgia Institue of Technology, Atlanta (1981).

[10] NELSON, P.R.: The transposition replacement policy with partial memory, Department of Statistics, Ohio State University (1981).

[11] PHELPS, R.I., THOMAS, L.C.: On optimal performance in self-organising paging algorithms. J.Inf.and Opt. Sci. 1, 80-93, (1980).

[12] ROSS, A.M. Applied Probability Models with Optimisation Applications, Holden Day, San Francisco (1970).

[13] VISWANATHAN, B., AGGARWAL, V.V., NAIR, K.P.K.: Multiple Criteria Markov Decision Processes, pp 263-272 in Multiple Criteria Decision Making ed. by Storr and Zeleny, North-Holland, Amsterdam (1977).

[14] WHITE, C.C., III, KWANG, W.K.: Solution procedures for vector criterion Markov decision processes: Large Scale Systems 1, 129-140 (1980).

[15] WHITE, D.J.: Multi-objective, infinite horizon, discounted Markov decision processes. To appear in J.M.A.A.

A BRANCH AND BOUND METHOD FOR MULTI-OBJECTIVE BOOLEAN PROBLEMS

D.J. White

(Department of Decision Theory, University of Manchester)

The following brief discussion is based upon the fuller version of White [1].

The Problem

$Z = \{0, 1\}^n$

$X = \{x \in Z: g(x) = 0\}$

$g: \mathbb{R}^n \to \mathbb{R}^1$ is non-negative and integer valued on Z

$\{f^i(x)\}$, $i=1,2,\ldots m$, $x \in Z$, are the objective functions

For $Y \subseteq Z$, $h: \mathbb{R}^n \to \mathbb{R}^m$,

$E(Y,h) = \{x \in Y: h(y) \geqq h(x) \to h(y) = h(x)\}$.

To find

$$E(X,f)$$

Notes

1. Any equality $h(x) = 0$ may be written as $g(x) = 0$, g non-negative on Z, with $g = h^2$.

2. Any set of equalities $\{g_i(x) = 0, i=1,2,\ldots p\}$ may be reduced to a single one $g(x) = 0$, g non-negative on Z, e.g. $g = \sum_{i=1}^{p} g_i^2$, or, if $\{g_i\}$ are integer valued and non-negative, $g = \sum_{i=1}^{p} \mu_i g_i$ for some $\mu \in \mathbb{R}^p$, $\mu \geqq 0$ will do.

3. Although this paper assumes that g is integer valued, it is easy to modify the method when this is not the case. The crucial property is the finiteness of Z.

THE LAGRANGIAN

Let ℓ, $u \in R^1$ be such that

$$\ell \leqq f^i(z) \leqq u, \quad \forall i, \forall z \in Z$$

and $$\lambda \in \mathbb{R}^1, \quad \lambda \geqq u - \ell + 1.$$

Define $$f_\lambda : Z \to \mathbb{R}^1 \text{ by}$$

$$f_\lambda(z) = f(z) - \lambda\, g(z) e$$

$$e^T = (1,1,1, \ldots 1) \in \mathbb{R}^m$$

Theorem

$$E(X, f) = E(Z, f_\lambda).$$

This is an extension of the corresponding scalar result of Hammer and Rudeanu [2].

The method assumes $\{f^i\}$, g are all polynomial on Z, and hence linear in z_k, $\forall k$. λ is to be found a priori by finding appropriate ℓ and u.

The Method

It finds $E(Z, f_\lambda)$ via three operations applied iteratively. It uses the following alternative representations

$$f_\lambda(z) = z_k \beta_k(z) + \gamma_k(z), \quad k=1,2,\ldots m.$$

$\{\beta_k\}$, $\{\gamma_k\}$ are polynomial in $\{Z_j\}$, $j \neq k$ i.e. $\{\beta_k\}$, $\{\gamma_k\}$ are independent of z_k.

Assume that at some stage we have three subsets, viz.

S : a subset of z;

F : a subset of $\{k\}$ for which the corresponding $\{z_k\}$ have been fixed at 0 or 1;

Z_F : the subset of Z determined by F.

S, F, Z_F will be dependent on the sequence of calculations prior to this stage. F will be a set of variable indices {k} together with the specification that for each such k, $z_k = 0$ or $z_k = 1$. F may be looked upon as $F = (F_1, F_0)$, where F_1 is the set of k for which $z_k = 1$ and F_0 is the set of k for which $z_k = 0$. Then

$$Z_F = \{z \in Z : z_k = 1, \forall k \in F_1, z_k = 0, \forall k \in F_0\}$$

We use the single symbol F throughout.

The following steps I, II, III are carried out at each stage of the algorithm. Initially $F = \emptyset$, $Z_F = Z$, $S = \{z^1\}$, z^1 arbitrary in Z.

I EXTENDING F via S

For $k \notin F$ let:

$\overline{\alpha_{k1}}$ be an upper bound for f_λ on Z for $z_k = 1$;

$\overline{\alpha_{k0}}$ be an upper bound for f_λ on Z for $z_k = 0$.

If $\exists\ z \in E(S, f_\lambda)$ with $f_\lambda(z) \geq \overline{\alpha_{k1}}$, fix $z_k = 0$.

If $\exists\ z \in E(S, f_\lambda)$ with $f_\lambda(z) \geq \overline{\alpha_{k0}}$, fix $z_k = 1$.

Add k to F, i.e. add k to F_1 or to F_0 depending on the above.

II EXTENDING F VIA Z

For $k \notin F$ let:

$\overline{\beta_k}$ be an upper bound for β_k on Z;

$\underline{\beta_k}$ be a lower bound for β_k on Z;

If $\overline{\beta_k} \leq 0$, fix $z_k = 0$

If $\underline{\beta_k} \geq 0$, fix $z_k = 1$.

i.e. if $\beta_k \leq 0$, $\forall z \in Z$ set $z_k = 0$, and if $\beta_k \geq 0$ $\forall z \in Z$ set $z_k = 1$.

Add k to F i.e. add k to F_1 or to F_0 depending on the above.

III EXTENDING S

Consider each $z \in S$ and each $k \in \{1,2,\ldots m\}$.

If $z_k = 0$ and $\beta_k(z) \geq 0$, set $z'_j = z_j$, $\forall j \neq k$, $z'_k = 1$ and add z' to S. We have $f_\lambda(z') \geq f_\lambda(z)$.

If $z_k = 1$, and $\beta_k(z) \leq 0$, set $z'_j = z_j$, $\forall j \neq k$, $z'_k = 0$, and add z' to S. We have $f_\lambda(z') \geq f_\lambda(z)$.

These operations are repeated iteratively until no more extensions may be obtained using them. If we reach such a position, with some S, F, Z_F, and $Z_F \subseteq S$, we simply find $E(S, f_\lambda)$ which is calculated at any stage in any case, and this gives $E(X, f)$. Otherwise select $z \in Z_F \setminus S$, replace S by $S \cup \{z\}$ and iterate. Since Z is finite the process ends in a finite number of moves.

In White [1] the method is used for 0 - 1 portfolio analysis problems.

REFERENCES

1. White, D.J. "A Branch and Bound Method for Multi-Objective Boolean Problems", to be published in *E.J.O.R.*

2. Hammer, P.L. and Rudeanu, S. 1968 Boolean Methods in Operations Research, Springer.

A SELECTION OF MULTI-OBJECTIVE INTERACTIVE PROGRAMMING METHODS

D.J. White

(Department of Decision Theory, University of Manchester)

1. INTRODUCTION

Since the pioneering work of Dyer, Geoffrion and Feinberg [18] a considerable number of approaches to the multi-objective interactive problem have been developed. Some of these have highly common features. Others have quite distinct frameworks underlying the methods. The purpose of this paper is merely to look at a selection of these approaches to give the reader some idea of the nature of methods developed. No critique is given. Indeed it is the belief of the author that all methods known to him have deficiencies in some form or other and that a proper approach to the critique issue must involve a more comprehensive coverage of existing methods. Nor is it intended to give a survey of existing methods. A list of papers known to the author is appended to offset this deficiency and the reader can follow these up.

A multi-objective problem is defined by:

(i) a feasible action space X with generic element x;

(ii) a set of m objective functions $\{f^i\}$ mapping X into the real line $\mathbb{R}^1$;

(iii) the requirement to find a best, or acceptable, $x \in X$.

In all the methods the decision maker is assumed to be able to express preferences or indifferences between some members of X. We will use the following notation, viz. for $x, y \in X$

$x\ Ry \rightleftarrows$ x is at least as good as y

$x\ Py \rightleftarrows$ x is preferred to y

$x\ Iy \rightleftarrows$ x is indifferent to y

With the exception of the method of Stewart [63] these are quite consistent with the methods. Stewart distinguishes between the physical act of choosing between x and y and the notion of true preference which might not be reflected by individual choices. The remainder of this introductory section excludes Stewart's framework.

For most of the methods preferences are assumed to be monotone non-decreasing in the objectives $\{f^i\}$. Indeed the use of the word "objective" implies such a monotonicity property. Those methods using efficient solution ideas require much monotonicity.

When studying multi-objective problems in general there are, broadly speaking, three forms of analysis which may be carried out. These are as follows.

(1) <u>Closed Form of Analysis</u>

This applies when it is possible to combine the m objectives into a single objective function $u(f) = u(f^1, f^2, \ldots f^m)$. This is referred to as a "value function"; and is such that

$$x\ Ry \rightleftarrows u(f(x)) \geqq u(f(y)).$$

For such problems the problem reduces to a standard optimisation problem, viz

$$\max_{x \in X} [u(f(x))].$$

The existence of such a u is not strictly necessary, and if R is a total order (complete and transitive) all we require is to find

$$x \in X \text{ such that } x\ Ry, \quad \forall\ y \in X.$$

The two concepts are equivalent in most realistic situations.

The use of the term "closed" reflects the putting together of the "objective system", as described by f, and the "subject system", as described by u.

This is the ideal situation. However there can be practical problems in achieving this level of completion, indeed, it may not be strictly necessary to do so in order to meet requirement (iii) of our problem.

(2) Open Form of Analysis

This arises when all that is done is to present to the decisionmaker the set f(X) where

$$f(X) = \{t \in \mathbb{R}^n : t = f(x) \text{ for some } x \in X\}$$

This corresponds to a study of the object system largely, although the subject system is involved to the extent that the $\{f^i\}$ have to be identified.

This is the easiest, and most common, approach and does not involve the difficult issues in identifying preference structures. In effect, however, it does restrict any sensible X to having a small number of members and it is wasteful of information which will exist, in some cases, on preferences, which can be used to search larger X sets.

(3) Partially Open/Closed Form of Analysis

This form of analysis is intermediate between the extreme forms given previously. It forms the basis for multi-objective interactive programming methods, the subject of this paper. The simplest case is the efficient solution analysis in which the problem is reduced to finding

$$E(X,f) = \{x \in X : \not\exists\, y \in X, yPx\}$$

where yPx is by definition, yRx, $x \not R y$.

For the usual vector order $\geqq$ over $\mathbb{R}^m$ this is equivalent to finding

$$E(X,f) = \{x \in X : \not\exists\, y \in X,\ f(y) \geq f(x)\}$$

where $f(y) \geq f(x)$ is, by definition $f(y) \geqq f(x)$, $f(y) \neq f(x)$

Multiple-objective interactive programming methods use a combined optimisation/decisionmaker interactive questioning process which, in general, only searches a subset of X, and only to the extent that part (iii) of the multi-objective problem specification is achieved. It uses what information it can glean from preferences as they evolve to direct the search. The search involves the use of a surrogate optimisation process, for other options to be considered, and then additional preference information on these is used to refine the surrogate procedure.

The term "optimisation" is to be interpreted in a broad sense so as to include, for example, the determination of the efficient set of a subset of options.

The schematic in Fig. 1 depicts the general framework underlying multi-objective methods. In this framework the following constructs are used.

(a) S^r is the set of options at iteration r of the method which are used to establish preference information.

It is usually, but not always, a subset of X (e.g. see Morris and Oren [4]). Sometimes it is a singleton (e.g. see Marcotte and Soland [39]). Sometimes it is a subset of $E(X,f)$ (e.g. see Wallenius and Zionts [68]). Indeed, given monotonicity this need only be so for many problems (e.g. compact action spaces, and continuity conditions).

(b) $v^r = u^r(f)$ is a surrogate value function obtained on the basis of preference information from S^r, and is used to modify S^r to produce S^{r+1} for the next iteration.

R^r is a surrogate order relation obtained, as an alternative to u^r, on the basis of preference information from S^r, and is likewise used to produce S^{r+1} for the next iteration (e.g. see Yu [76]).

Given these points, the schematic is self explanatory (see Fig. 1).

Let us now look at the selected methods which form the substance of the paper. The format for each will be

(1) Assumptions

(2) Method

(3) Results

(4) Notes.

2. THE SELECTED METHODS

I The method of Dyer, Geoffrion and Feinberg [*18*]

(1) <u>Assumptions</u>

(i) $X \in \mathbb{R}^n$ is compact and convex;

(ii) $v = u(f)$ is concave and continuously differentiable on X;

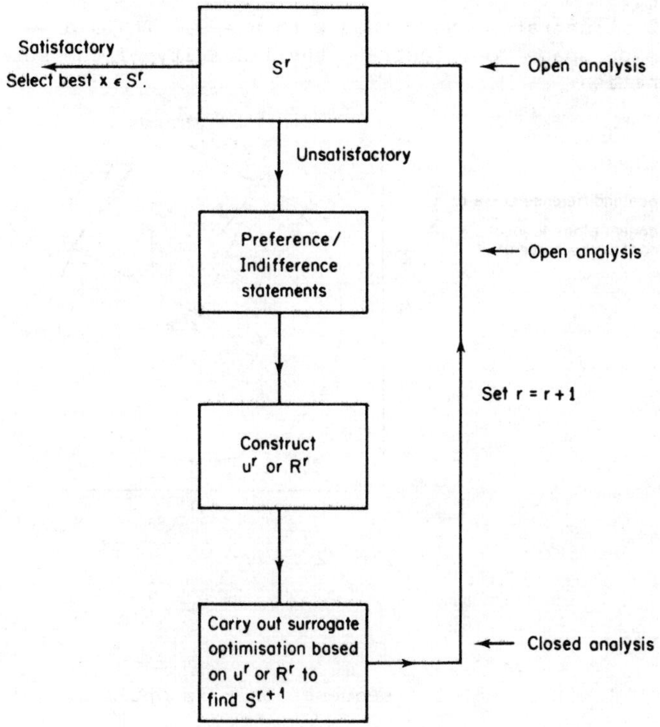

Fig. 1

(iii) v is unknown explicitly.

(2) <u>Method</u>

(i) Set $r = 1$. Select $x^1 \in X$. Go to (ii).

(ii) If x^r is acceptable to the decisionmaker, stop. Otherwise go to (iii).

(iii) Assume we have arrived at x^r. Find $\nabla v(x^r)$ by finding $\nabla u(f)$ at $f(x^r)$ by interaction with the decisionmaker. Go to (iv).

(iv) Find y^r to maximise $\nabla v(x^r)x$ on X. Go to (v).

(v) Find a best point x^{r+1} on the line segment $\overline{x^r y^r}$ by interaction with the decisionmaker. Set $r = r + 1$. If $x^{r+1} = x^r$ stop. x^r is optimal. Otherwise go to (ii).

Fig. 2 illustrates the method with n = 2. It is drawn in the decision space to illustrate the linearity of the surrogate value function.

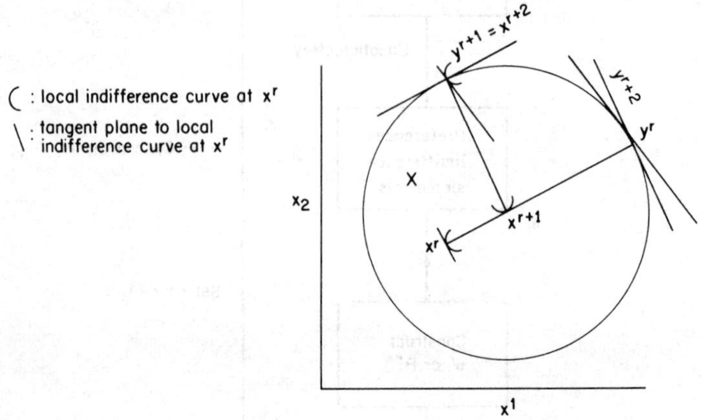

Fig. 2

(3) Results

(i) Any limit point of a sequence $\{x^r\}$ is optimal.

(ii) Such a limit point will exist.

(iii) x^{r+1} is at least as good as x^r.

(iv) If $x^{r+1} = x^r$, x^r is optimal.

(4) Notes

(i) Compactness is used only to ensure the existence of optimisers and for (ii) above.

(ii) S^r is a suitable neighbourhood of x^r, large enough to estimate $\nabla u(f)$.

(iii) In practice step (iv) must be replaced by

"find some better point x^{r+1} than x^r on $\overline{x^r y^r}$"

but this need not give convergence to an optimum without control of step sizes.

(iv) The reading list contains papers which extend the method and look at the line search problem in step (v).

II The Method of White [73]

(1) Assumptions

(i) $X \subseteq \mathbb{R}^n$ is compact.

(ii) $\{f^i\}$ are continuous on X.

(iii) $u(f) = \lambda^* f$ for some $\lambda^* \in \Lambda = \{\lambda \in \mathbb{R}^m : \lambda \geqq 0, \sum_{i=1}^{m} \lambda_i = 1\}$.

(iv) λ^* is unknown explicitly.

(2) Method

(i) Set r = 1. Select $x^1 \in X$. Go to (ii).

(ii) Assume that we have arrived at the rth iteration with a set $S^r = \{x^r, x^{r-1}, \ldots x^1\}$, with z^r a best point in S^r with $\Lambda^r = \{\lambda \in \Lambda$, determined by inequalities or equalities in λ derived from the knowledge of all preferences and indifferences over S^r expressed in "at least as good as" form$\}$ and its vertices $\{\lambda^{rk}\}$, $1 \leqq k \leqq K_r$. If z^r is acceptable to the decisionmaker, stop. Otherwise go to (iii).

(iii) Find

$$\sigma_r = \max_{x \in X} \max_{1 \leqq k \leqq K_r} [\lambda^{rk}(f(x) - f(z^r))]$$

If $\sigma_r = 0$, stop. z^r is optimal. Otherwise go to (iv).

(iv) Let x^{r+1} realise σ_r. Set $r = r + 1$, $S^{r+1} = S^r \cup \{x^{r+1}\}$, and go to (ii).

Fig. 3 illustrates the method with m=2. In this case it is drawn in the objective function space f(X) to emphasise the linearity of u(f). The points x^{r1}, x^{r2} are, respectively the points which maximise $\lambda^{r1} f(x)$ and $\lambda^{r2} f(x)$ over X. In this case $\sigma_r > 0$ and we set $x^{r+1} = x^{r2}$. The hypothetical optimum is at x^*, and $z^{r+1} = x^{r+1}$.

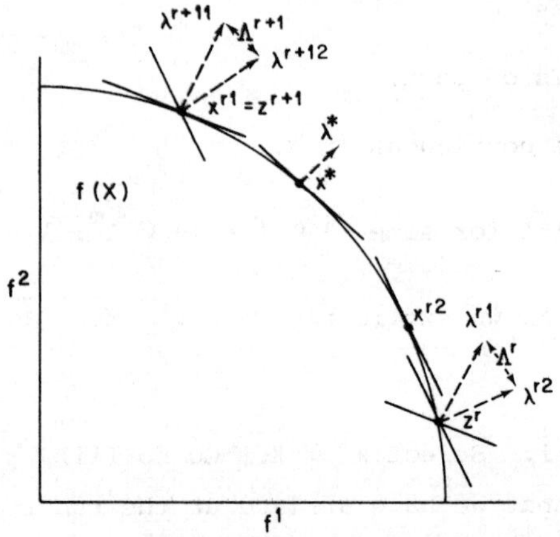

Fig. 3

(3) Results

(i) For any subsequence $\{x^{r_t}\} \subseteq \{x^r\}$ which converges, the corresponding subsequence $\{z^{r_t}\} \subseteq \{z^r\}$ converges to an optimal solution.

(ii) Such a convergent subsequence will exist.

(iii) If the procedure terminates at step (ii), and z^r uniquely maximises $\lambda^{rk}(f(x) - f(z^r))$ for $k = k_q$, $q = 1,2,\ldots \ell$, then:

either $\lambda^* = \sum_{k \neq k_q} \mu_k \lambda^{rk}$ for some μ with $\mu \geqq 0$, $\sum_{k \neq k_q} \mu_k = 1$

or z^r is a unique optimal solution.

If $\{k_q\} = \{1,2,\ldots K_r\}$, then z^r is a unique optimal solution

(iv) z^{r+1} is at least as good as z^r.

(4) Notes

(i) Compactness is only used to ensure the existence of optimisers and for (ii) above.

(ii) For linear f, polyhedral X or finite problems, the process is finite.

(iii) The method can reach an optimal solution without recognising this, and can continue indefinitely.

III The Method of Wallenius and Zionts [68]

(1) <u>Assumptions</u> (see Notes)

(i) $X \subseteq \mathbb{R}^n$ is a polytope.

(ii) f is linear an X.

(iii) $u(f) = \lambda^* f$ for some $\lambda^* \in \Lambda = \{\lambda \in \mathbb{R}^n : \lambda \geqq 0, \sum_{i=1}^{m} \lambda_i = 1\}$.

(iv) λ^* is unknown explicitly.

(2) <u>Method</u>

(i) Set r = 1. Select $x^1 \in E(X,f)$. Go to (ii).

(ii) Assume that we have arrived at the rth iteration with a point $x^r \in E(X,f)$, a set S^r of previous points considered, and a set $\Lambda^r = \{\lambda \in \Lambda$, determined by the preferences and indifferences already established over $S^r\}$. If the best point in S^r is acceptable stop. Otherwise go to (iii).

(iii) Determine all the adjacent vertices, A^r, to x^r in X which are in $E(X,f)$. If none of these is preferred to x^r, stop. x^r is optimal. Otherwise go to (iv).

(iv) For all such vertices compare them with x^r.

If $x \in A^r$ and $x \, P \, x^r$ set $\lambda f(x) \geqq \lambda f(x^r) + \varepsilon$.

If $x \in A^r$ and $x^r \, P \, x$ set $\lambda f(x) \leqq \lambda f(x^r) - \varepsilon$.

If $x \in A^r$ and $x^r \, I \, x$ set $\lambda f(x) = \lambda f(x^r)$.

ε is a small positive number.

Form Λ^{r+1} by adding these constraints to Λ^r. Go to (v).

(v) Choose $\lambda \in \Lambda^{r+1}$, adding small quantities to ensure that $\lambda > 0$. Find x^{r+1} to maximise λf over X. Set $S^{r+1} = S^r \cup A^r \cup \{x^{r+1}\}$ and go to (ii).

Fig. 4 illustrates the method. It assumes $f(x) = x, \forall x \in X$. x^* is the hypothetical optimum. For this illustration $x^{rl} P x^r$, where x^{rl} is the only adjacent vertex to x^r which is efficient.

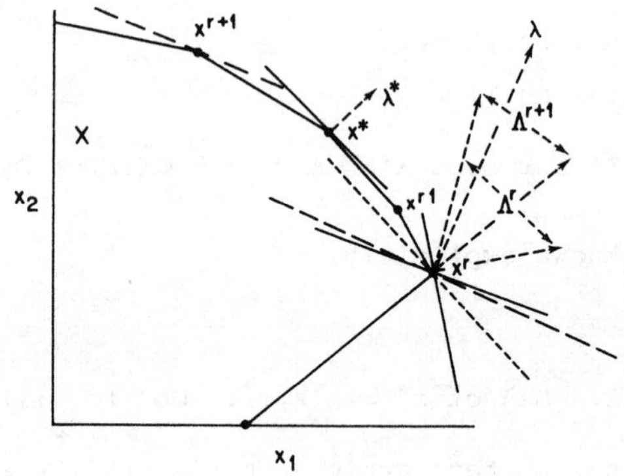

Fig. 4

(3) Results

Providing ε is small enough an optimal solution will be achieved in a finite number of moves.

(4) Notes

(i) As indicated by the authors, only efficient edges at x^r need be considered, and X need only be polyhedral. Their actual method uses this.

(ii) The method has been extended to cater for pseudo concave f (see [70]).

(iii) x^{r+1} need not be at least as good as x^r.

(iv) Paired comparisons do not make use of the whole of S^r as defined in this paper.

(v) There might be a problem of choosing ε. If ε is too large it can exclude λ^*, and x^* might not be reached.

IV The Method of Steuer [59]

(1) Assumptions

(i) $X \subseteq \mathbb{R}^n$ is polyhedral.

(ii) f is linear on X.

(iii) $u(f) = \lambda^* f$ for some $\lambda^* \in \Lambda = \{\lambda \in \mathbb{R}^m \; \sum_{i=1}^{m} \lambda_i = 1,$

$\ell_i < \lambda_i < \mu_i, \; \forall_i\}$.

(iv) Λ is known, λ^* is unknown explicitly.

(2) Method

(i) Set $r = 1$ and $f^1 = f$. Go to (ii).

(ii) Assume we have arrived at the rth iteration with f^r. Go to (iii).

(iii) By interaction with the decisionmaker find if he wishes to determine $E_v(X, f^r)$ i.e. the efficient part of X with respect to f^r which are vertices in X. If so, do this and stop. Otherwise go to (iv).

(iv) Determine a trial subset of $E_v(X, f^r)$ (see the paper for details of this step). Go to (v).

(v) By interaction with the decisionmaker find if he is satisfied with a best member of this subset. If so, stop. Otherwise go to (vi).

(vi) Determine a new f^{r+1}, related to f^r, in a specified manner (see papers for details). Set $r = r + 1$, replace f^r by f^{r+1} and go to (ii).

(3) Results

(i) The work is experimental and contains no theoretical results.

(ii) The objective is to find an approximater to a vertex optimiser of $\lambda^* f$. This is done by looking at all vertex optimisers of λf, $\lambda \in \Lambda$, in principle. To do this a previous result of Steuer [60] is used i.e. the initial problem can be converted to an equivalent one of finding $E_v(X, f^0)$, where $f^0 : \mathbb{R}^n \to \mathbb{R}^q$, $q = 2^m$. The method attempts to approximate f^0 by the sequence $\{f^r\}$, where f^r has far less components than f^0

(iii) $E_v(X, f^{r+1}) \subseteq \varepsilon_v(X, f^r)$

(iv) $\nexists\, E_v(X,f^r) \geqq \varepsilon_v(X,f^0)$

(4) Notes

Although it is clear that $E_v(X,f^0) \subseteq \varepsilon_v(X,f^1)$ it is not clear that $E_v(X,f^0) \subseteq E_v(X,f^r)$, $r > 1$.

V The Method of Gabbani and Magazine [22]

(1) Assumptions

(i) $X \subseteq \mathbb{R}^n$ is the integer subset of a polytope.

(ii) f is linear on the polytope.

(iii) $u(f) = \lambda^* f$ for some $\lambda^* \in \Lambda = \{\lambda \in \mathbb{R}^m : \lambda \geqq 0, \sum_{i=1}^{m} \lambda_i = 1\}$.

(iv) λ^* is unknown explicitly.

(2) Method

(i) Set r = 1. Choose $\{\lambda^{1k}\} \subseteq \mathbb{R}^m$, k=1,2,... 2m+1, in a specified manner (see Fig. 5 for an illustration for the case m = 3). Find $\{x^{1k}\}$, k=1,2... 2m+1 so that x^{1k} maximises $\lambda^{1k}f$ on X. By interaction with the decisionmaker find the most preferred $z^1 \in \{x^{1k}\}$. Go to (ii).

(ii) Assume we have reached iteration r with a point z^r and with λ^r equal to the λ^{rk} which gave rise to z^r at the previous iteration. Generate a new set $\{\lambda^{r+1k}\}$ k=1,2,... 2m+1 with λ^r as the reference point in a specified manner (see Fig. 5 for an illustration for the case m = 3). Go to (iii).

(iii) Find $\{x^{r+1k}\}$, k=1,2... 2m+1, so that x^{r+1k} maximises $\lambda^{r+1k}f$ on X. Small positive quantities are added to components of $\{\lambda^{r+1k}\}$ to ensure $\{x^{r+1k}\} \subseteq E(X,f)$. Go to (iv).

(iv) By interaction with the decisionmaker find the most preferred $z^{r+1} \in \{x^{r+1k}\}$, and the λ^{r+1} corresponding to the λ^{r+1k} which gives z^{r+1}. Set r=r+1. Go to (ii).

Fig. 5 illustrates how λ^r is used to generate $\{\lambda^{r+1k}\}$ in the case m = 3. Triangular coordinates are used. The figure shows, for each of the 7 points which might be λ^r, the next simplex which will be chosen to generate $\{\lambda^{r+1k}\}$, each of the latter being chosen in the simplex in the same relative manner as for the previous simplex.

The new simplices S_1, S_4, S_7 are indicated. Simplices are similar within the groups {1, 2, 3}, {4, 5, 6}, {7}.

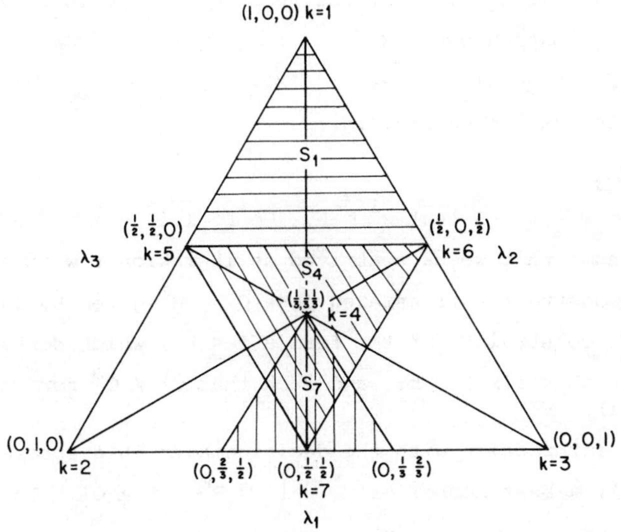

Fig. 5

(3) Results

Providing the maximiser of $\lambda^{r+1k}f$ corresponding to λ^r is kept at z^r, z^{r+1} is at least as good as z^r.

(4) Notes

(i) No specification of stopping rules is given.

(ii) No analysis of the behaviour of the method is given.

(iii) No significant information on preferences gleaned in the analysis is used to guide future searches.

(iv) $S^r = \{x^{rk}\}$, k=1,2,.. 2m+1.

IV The Method of Morris and Oren [41]

(1) <u>Assumptions</u>

(i) $X = \{x \in \mathbb{R}^n : Af(x) \leqq b, f(x) \geqq 0\}$, $A \in \mathbb{R}^{p \times m}$, $p > m$, and a^i is the ith row of A.

Implicitly it is also assumed that $C^r \cap \{f \in \mathbb{R}^m : f \geqq 0\}$, as defined in the method, is compact, $\forall r$. The form of $\bar{\bar{X}}$ chosen ensures that the feasible objective function set is polyhedral.

(ii) f is continuous on X.

(iii) u(f) is quasi concave on f(X).

(iv) u is unknown explicitly.

(2) <u>Method</u>

(i) Set r = 1. Select $x^1 \in X$. Go to (ii).

(ii) Assume that we have arrived at iteration r with some $x^r \in X$. Construct a translated cone $C^r \subseteq \mathbb{R}^m$ given by identifying a set of m constraints of the form $a^i f \leqq b_i$, which contain all {i} for which $a^i f(x^r) = b_i$, and such that $C^r \neq C^s$ for any $s < r$. Go to (iii).

(iii) By interaction with the decisionmaker in a special way find $f(y^r)$, a best member of $C^r \cap \{f \in \mathbb{R}^m : f \geqq 0\}$. Go to (iv).

(iv) If $y^r \in X$, stop. y^r is optimal. Otherwise go to (v).

(v) Set

$$f(x^{r+1}) = \alpha_r f(y^r) + (1 - \alpha_r) f(x^r)$$

where

$$\alpha_r = \min_{i \in J_{r+1}} [a^i(f(x^r) - f(y^r))/(a^i f(x^r) - b_i)]$$

$$J_r = \{i : i \notin I_r, a^i(f(y^r) - f(x^r)) > 0\}$$

$$I_r = \{i \text{ which define } C^r\}$$

Set r = r + 1, replace x^r by x^{r+1} and go to (ii).

Fig. 6 illustrates the method for $m = 2$, $p = 4$. x^* is the hypothetical optimum. $\{\pi^i\}$ denote the hyperplanes $a^i f(x) = b_i$, $i=1,2,3,4$. v^r denotes the vertex of C^r. At x^* we have drawn the local $u(f)$ curve touching π^3.

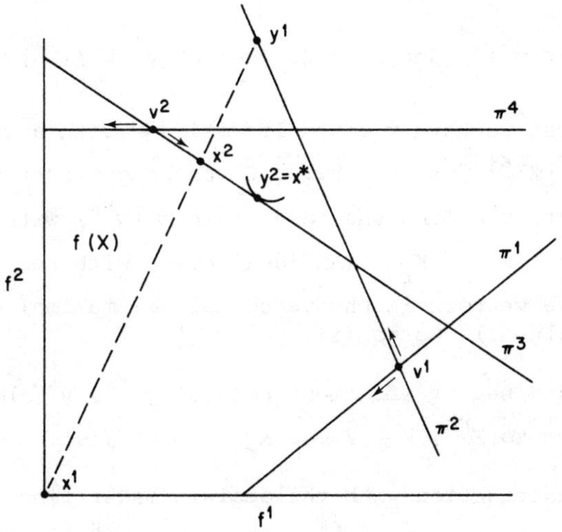

Fig. 6

(3) Results

(i) The method converges to an optimal solution in a finite number of iterations.

(ii) x^{r+1} is at least as good as x^r.

(4) Notes

(i) $f(S^r) = C^r \cap \{f \in \mathbb{R}^m : f \geqq 0\}$

(ii) $f(X) \subseteq f(S^r)$. This constitutes a significant difference with all the other methods. The authors introduce their own special interactive method for S^r using a "bucket and chip" method of allocation of resources. The usefulness of the method must depend on how much easier it is to handle S^r than it is to handle X.

(iii) The authors say that the restriction $p > m$ may be removed.

VII The Method of Marcotte and Soland [38]

(1) Assumptions

(i) X finite.

(ii) preferences are monotone non-decreasing in f.

(2) Method

(i) Set r = 1. Set $X^1 = X$. Select $y^1 \in E(X^1)$. Set $z^1 = y^1$. Go to (ii).

(ii) Suppose we have reached iteration r with a set of non-empty sets $\{X^{rk}\} \subseteq X$, $k=1,2,\ldots K_r$ to be considered and a best point to date z^r. Find the ideal points $\{w^{rk}\}$ with respect to $\{f(X^{rk})\}$, $k=1,2,\ldots K_r$. (An ideal point with respect to a set of objective vectors is the vector of all maximal objective function values.) Go to (iii).

(iii) Find a set of efficient points $\{y^{rk}\}$, y^{rk} being efficient with respect to X^{rk}, $k=1,2,\ldots K_r$. Go to (iv).

(iv) By interaction with the decisionmaker find a best point $\tilde{z}^{r+1}$ of the points $\{z^r, \{y^{rk}\}, \{\text{feasible } w^{rk}\}\}$. Go to (v).

(v) If by interaction with the decisionmaker $\tilde{z}^{r+1}$ is at least as good as w^{rk} for any k, delete X^{rk} from further consideration. If all $\{X^{rk}\}$ are deleted, stop. $\tilde{z}^{r+1}$ is optimal. Otherwise go to (vi) with $\tilde{K}_r$ as the non-deleted set of k values.

(vi) Set $\tilde{\tilde{K}}_r$ to be the set of $k \in \tilde{K}_r$ for which w^{rk} is not feasible. Go to (vii).

(vii) For each $k \in \tilde{\tilde{K}}_r$ and each i, set

$$X_i^{rk} = \{x \in X^{rk} : f^i(x) > f^i(y^{rk})\}$$

By renumbering all these sets construct a set of sets $\{X^{r+1k}\}$, $k=1,2,\ldots K_{r+1}$. Set r = r + 1, replace z^r by z^{r+1} where z^{r+1} is a best point in the set $\{\tilde{z}^{r+1}\} \cup \underset{k\in\tilde{K}_r/\tilde{\tilde{K}}_r}{\{\text{ideal } x \text{ in } X^{rk}\}}$, $\{X^{rk}\}$ by $\{X^{r+1k}\}$ and go to (ii).

Note that if $X_i^{rk} = \emptyset, \forall_i$, then y^{rk} gives a feasible ideal point and $k \notin \tilde{\tilde{K}}_r$.

(3) Results

(i) The process terminates when z^r is at least as good as all the ideal points $\{w^{rk}\}$.

(ii) Termination takes place in a finite number of iterations at an optimal solution.

(4) Notes

(i) The method merely uses the fact that optimal solutions may be found in the efficient set.

(ii) It makes little use of preference information other than to eliminate subsets from further consideration.

(iii) $S^r = \{z^r, \{y^{rk}\}, \{\text{feasible } w^{rk}\}\}$.

(iv) The actual paper assumes compactness and continuity conditions and extends the work to convex sets, although there are some technical issues about this.

VIII The Method of Stewart [63]

(1) Assumptions

(i) X finite.

(ii) $\exists\, u(f, \Pi)$ (called a "utility function") on $f(X) \times \Pi$, where Π is a set of possible parameters $\{\pi\}$.

(iii) $\exists$ prior distribution F over Π,

(iv) $\exists$ true parameters $\pi \in \Pi$, $c \in \mathbb{R}^1$, $c > 0$ and when the decisionmaker is presented with the choice between $x, y \in X$ he will choose x with probability

$$(1 + \exp(-c(u(f(x), \pi) - u(f(y), \pi))))^{-1}$$

(v) The form of $u(f,\pi)$ is known, but π is unknown explicitly.

(2) The Method

(i) Set $r = 1$. Choose $x^1 \in X$. Set $S^1 = \{x^1\}$, $F^1 = F$. Go to (ii).

(ii) Assume we have reached iteration r with a set $S^r = \{x^r, x^{r-1}, \ldots, x^1\} \subseteq X$ and a posterior distribution F^r. Go to (iii).

(iii) If $r = m$ go to (vii). Otherwise go to (iv).

(iv) Find $x^{r+1} \in X$ to maximise

$$\Sigma_{k=1}^{r} \| f(x^k) - f(x) \|^2$$

where $\| \; \|$ is the Euclidean norm. Go to (v).

(v) Set $S^{r+1} = S^r \cup \{x^{r+1}\}$. Go to (vi).

(vi) By interaction with the decisionmaker compare x^{r+1} with $\{x^k\}$, pairwise, and update F^r until all such comparisons have been completed, to produce a new posterior distribution, F^{r+1}. Set $r = r + 1$, replace S^r, F^r by S^{r+1}, F^{r+1} respectively and go to (ii).

(vii) Order X according to

$$E_\pi(u(f(x), \pi))$$

using the posterior distribution F^r. Go to (viii).

(viii) Select a $\delta \in R^1$, $\delta > 0$, and find, using F^m,

$$u_r = \max_{x \in X} [E_\pi(u(f(x), \pi))]$$

$$X^r = \{x \in X : E_\pi(u(f(x), \pi)) \geqq u_r - \delta\}.$$

Go to (ix).

(ix) By interaction with the decisionmaker compare any pairs $\{x,y\} \subseteq X^r$ which have not been yet compared and update F^r until all such comparisons have been made, to produce a new posterior distribution, F^{r+1}. Set $r = r + 1$, replace F^r by F^{r+1} and go to (vii).

(3) <u>Results</u>

There are no theoretical results. Experiments with a specific $u(f, \pi^O)$ tend to produce a result in line with an ordering based on $u(f, \pi^O)$.

(4) Notes

(i) The parameter c is recognised as being a crucial one in the method. If c is small, there are many iterations, and, if c is large, the process terminates early.

(ii) There is a question of interpretation of the model. The "utility function" $u(f,\pi)$ is not a utility function in the usual sense of the word since it relates to "probabilistic choice". The question of what is meant by "x being better than y" is interpreted implicitly as "$u(f(x), \pi) > u(f(y), \pi)$" (assuming that the posterior distribution converges to a lump distribution at the true π), and this is equivalent to "the probability that x is chosen rather than y is greater than ½".

IX The Method of Yu [76]

(1) Assumptions (Constant Cone Case)

(i) $f(x) = x, \forall x \in X \subseteq \mathbb{R}^n$.

(ii) $\exists$ dominance cone $\Lambda \subseteq \mathbb{R}^n$, with vertex 0, such that $\lambda \in \mathbb{R}^1, \lambda > 0, d \in \Lambda/\{0\}, x = y + \lambda d \rightarrow y \text{ P} x$.

(iii) Λ is unknown explicitly.

(iv) $E(X, \Lambda) = \{x \in X : \nexists\, y \in X, d \in \Lambda/\{0\} \text{ with } x = y + d\}$

(2) Method

(i) Set $r = 1$, $S^1 = X$. Go to (ii).

(ii) Assume we have arrived at iteration r with a set $S^r \subseteq X$. Go to (iii).

(iii) By interaction with the decisionmaker find an estimate $\tilde{\Lambda}^r$ of $\Lambda^r = \{d \in \mathbb{R}^n : \text{whenever } x,y \in S^r, x - y = \lambda d, \text{ for some } \lambda > 0, \text{ then } y \text{ P} x\}$. Go to (iv).

(iv) Set $S^{r+1} = E(S^r, \tilde{\Lambda}^r)$. If $S^{r+1} = S^r$ stop. Accept S^r as an estimate of $E(X, \Lambda)$. Otherwise set $r = r + 1$, replace S^r by S^{r+1} and go to (ii).

(3) Results

(i) $S^{r+1} \subseteq S^r$

(ii) It is possible to ensure that $\tilde{\Lambda}^r \subseteq \tilde{\Lambda}^{r+1}$.

(4) Notes

(i) Some guidance is given for the estimation step (ii).

(ii) If $E(X, P)$ is the efficient set with respect to the underlying preference structure P then

$$E(X, P) \subseteq E(X, \Lambda).$$

(iii) Yu allows for $y, x \in X$, $y\,Px$ but $x \neq y + \lambda d$ for any $\lambda \in \mathbb{R}^1$, $\lambda > 0$, $d \in \Lambda/\{0\}$, whereas White [74] requires that the P structure be exactly equivalent to a Λ cone structure. Fig. 7 illustrates this in the case m = 2. The shaded region depicts a range of objective functions $\{\lambda f\}$, $\lambda \in \mathbb{R}^2$, $\lambda \geq 0$, whose coefficient vectors are given by $\Lambda/\{0\}$. For Yu it is only required that, for x, y as shown, y Px i.e. if y is at least as good as x for all the objective functions and better for at least one, then y Px. For White this is an "if and only if" requirement.

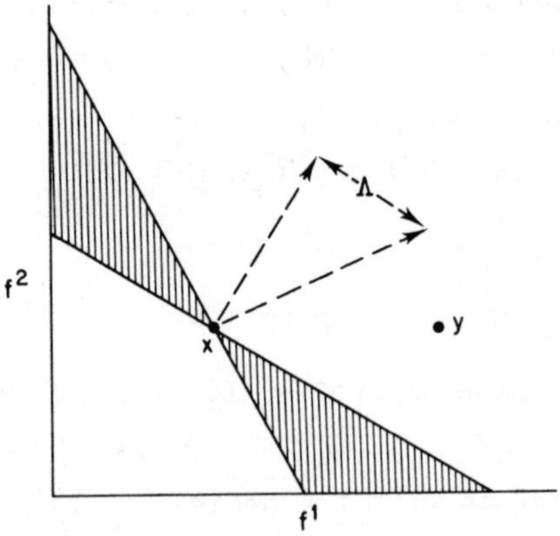

Fig. 7

3. SUMMARY

The paper has briefly discussed a selection of nine multi-objective interactive methods which appear in the literature. Although a few notes have been added, the paper is not intended to provide a critique. Indeed all methods are subject to critique from some points of view.

The introductory section provides a framework within which the general motives of multi-objective interactive methods may be viewed. Each of the methods, via the assumptions made, requires prior information of different kinds; and the power of the method depends on the strength of these assumptions.

Methods II-V for example, require value functions which are linear in the objectives. The assumptions are very strong, but the results are also very strong as well. Within this class of methods, the individual methods try to use specific features of the problem class to get solutions. Method II uses, in effect, ideal solution ideas (at stage r, a new set of objective functions $\{g^{rk}\} = \{\lambda^{rk} f\}$ is used, and the method treats these from the ideal solution point of view), and the convergence of the $\{\sigma_r\}$ sequence may be used to study suboptimality. Method III uses efficient solution theory for linear problems to maximal effect. Method IV uses an equivalence result for efficient solutions in an approximating manner, which tries to get a representative set of transformed objective functions from among the larger set. Method V tries to direct the decisionmaker towards a decreasing feasible region for the weighting factors using a pivoting method oriented around the previous best solution and the weighting factors which gave this. It is a simplicial method.

Method I weakens the requirement of a linear value function to that of concavity and uses the concavity property to progressively cut down the region of search.

The unusual feature of method VI is that it moves outside the feasible space X for the decisionmaker interactive phase, the authors feeling that this makes the interactive phase easier to handle (see the paper for fuller details). It assumes quasi concavity of the value function.

The only other method assuming that a value function exists is method VII. This makes almost the weakest assumptions in that it only requires that preferences are monotone in f. Correspondingly it is the most demanding to operate in terms of the amount of effort on behalf of the decisionmaker and in terms of computations. Its learning capacity is minimal of all the methods discussed in this paper; but it is least likely to operate on the basis of false premises.

The remaining two methods do not work on the basis of a value function as defined in this paper since they involve a measure of unsureness on the part of the decisionmaker when making his choice.

Method VIII introduces the ideas of probabilistic choice, and allows the possibility of intransitivities of choice arising in a systematic way, whereas other methods (e.g. method III) use ad hoc ways of resolving such inconsistencies. It introduces the learning effect in a Bayesian manner, and the assumptions are very strong.

Method IX allows for unsureness on the part of the decision-maker by allowing him only to make preference judgements when he is absolutely sure, and hence some attempts to compare options give no information. Again the assumptions are strong, but by no means as strong as the linearity assumptions of methods II-V, which are special cases.

As will be obvious the methods throw up some very leading questions, e.g. how are we to know that the prior assumptions hold? Questions such as these will be examined by the author in a subsequent paper.

4. REFERENCES

1. Agarwal, S.K. 1973 Optimising Techniques for the Interactive Design of Transportation Networks under Multiple Objectives, Ph.D., North Western University, Evanston.

2. Atkins, D.R. and Chou, E.U. 1977 "An Interactive Algorithm for 'Multi-Criteria' Programming", *Comp. and O.R.*, **1**, 81-87.

3. Baum, S., Carlson, R.C. and Shukla, P.R. 1979 Interactive Solution of Discrete Multi-criterion Problems: An Algorithm for Computational Results for the Binary Variable Case, Technical Report 79-82, Department of Industrial Engineering and Engineering Management, Stanford University.

4. Belenson, S. and Kapur, K. 1973 "An Algorithm for Solving Multi-criterion Linear Programming Problems with Examples", *O.R.Q.*, **24**, 65-77.

5. Benayoun, R., Larichnev, O., de Montgolfier, J. and Tergny, J. 1971 "Linear Programming with Multiple Objective Functions: Stem Method", *Mathematical Programming*, **1**, 366-375.

6. Benayoun, R. and Tergny, J. 1970 "Mathematical Programming with Multiple Objective Functions: A Solution by P.O.P.", *Revue Metra*, **9**, 279-299.

7. Benito, F. 1980 Optimising Markov Decision Processes and Linear Aggregation: A Dialogue Algorithm, European Operational Research Conference.

8. Bischoff, E. 1982 Comparing Approaches for Multi-Criterion Optimisation, Conference on Multi-Objective Decision Making, Manchester, April.

9. Bowman, J. 1976 On the Relationship of the Tchebychef Norm and the Efficient Frontier in Multiple-Criteria Objectives. In: "Multiple Criteria Decision Making", (H. Thiriez and S. Zionts, Eds.), Springer.

10. Boyd, W. 1973 Interactive Preference Assessment for Decisions with Multiple Attribute Outcomes, 4th Research Conference on Subjective Probability Utility and Decision-making, Rome.

11. Bragard, L. 1982 A Critical Analysis of STEM like Solutions to Multi-Objective Programming Problems, Conference on Multi-Objective Decision Making, Manchester, April.

12. Buyanov, B.B., Ozernoy, V.M. 1974 "A Decision Method Using Vector Criterion", *Eng. Cyb.*, **12**, 49-54.

13. Carlson, R.C. and Shukla, P.R. 1979 Analysis and Solution of Discrete Multi-criterion Problems with Ranged Trade-offs, Technical Report 79-84, Department of Industrial Engineering and Engineering Management, Stanford University.

14. Dendrou, B.A., Dendrou, S and Houstis, E. 1980 "Multi Objective Decision Analysis for Engineering Systems", *Comp. and O.R.*, **7**, 301-312.

15. Depraetere, P., Muller, H. and de Sambonckx, S. 1981 Critical Considerations Concerning the Multi-criteria Analysis by the Method of Zionts and Wallenius, CORS-ORSA-TIMS Conference, Toronto, (Rijksuniversiteit, Gent).

16. Duckstein, L., Monarchi, D. and Weber, J. 1976 An Interactive Multiple Objective Decision-Making Aid Using Non-linear Goal Programming. In: "Multiple-criteria Decision Making", (M. Zeleny, Ed.), Springer.

17. Dyer, J.S. 1972 "Interactive Goal Programming", *Man. Sc.*, **19**, 62-70.

18. Dyer, J.S., Feinberg, A. and Geoffrion, A.M. 1972 "An Interactive Approach for Multi-Criterion Optimization, with an Application to the Operation of an Academic Department", *Man. Sc.*, **19**, 357-368.

19. Dyer, J.S. 1974 "The Effects of Errors in the Estimations of the Gradient on the Frank-Wolfe Algorithm with Implications for Interactive Programming", *Operations Research,* **22**, 160-174.

20. Dyer, J.S. 1973 An Empirical Investigation of a Man Machine Interactive Approach to the Solution of the Multiple Criterion Problem. In: "Multi-Criteria Decision Making", (M. Zeleny and J.L. Cochrane, Eds.), University of South Carolina Press.

21. Dyer, J.S. 1973 "A Time Sharing Computer Program for the Solution of the Multiple Criteria Problem", *Man. Sc.,* **19**, 1379-1383.

22. Gabbani, D. and Magazine, M.J. 1981 An Interactive Heuristic Approach for Multi-Objective Integer Programming Problems, Working Paper 148, Department of Management Sciences, University of Waterloo, Ontario.

23. Gaft, M.G. and Ozernoi, V.M. 1977 Multi-criterion Decision Problems. In: "Conflicting Objectives in Decisions", (D.E. Bell, R.L. Keeney and H. Raiffa, Eds.), Wiley.

24. Geoffrion, A.M. 1971 Vector Maximal Decomposition Programming, Working Paper No. 164, Western Management Science Institute, University of California, Los Angeles, June.

25. Haimes, Y.Y. and Hall, W.A. 1976 The Surrogate Worth Trade-Off Method with Multiple Decision-makers. In: "Multiple Criteria Decision Making", (M. Zeleny, Ed.), Springer.

26. Harris, F. and Steuer, R. 1980 "Intra-Set Point Generation and Filtering in Decision and Criteria Space", *Comp. and O.R.,* **7**, 41-53.

27. Hemming, T. 1976 A New Method for Interactive Multi-Objective Optimisation: A Boundary Point Ranking Method. In: "Multiple Criteria Decision Making", (H. Thiriez and S. Zionts, Eds.), Springer.

28. Hopkins, D.S.P., Massey, M.W.F. and Wehrung, D. 1978 "Interactive Preference Optimisation for University Administrators", *Man. Sc.,* **24**, 599-611.

29. Huckert, K., Rhode, R., Roglin, O. and Weber, R. 1980 "On the Interactive Solution to a Multi-criteria Scheduling Problem", *Zeitschrift für Operations Research,* **24**, No. 1, 47-60.

30. Hwang, C.L. and Masud, A.S. 1981 "Interactive Sequential Goal Programming", *J.O.R.S.,* **32**, 391-400.

31. Hwang, C.L., Masud, A.S., Paidy, S.R. and Yoon, K. 1979 Multiple Objective Decision Making, Methods and Applications, Springer.

32. Inagaki, T., Inone, K. and Akashi, H. 1978 "Interactive Optimisation of Systems Reliability Under Multiple Objectives", *IEEE Trans. Reliability,* R-**27**, No. 4,

33. Karwan, M.H., Villarreal, B. and Zionts, S. 1980 An Interactive Branch and Bound Procedure for Multi-criterion Integer Linear Programming, Joint National Meeting of TIMS/ORS, Washington.

34. Korhonen, P., Wallenius, J. and Zionts, S. 1981 Some Theory and a Method for Solving the Discrete Multiple Criteria Problem, Working Paper No. 498, Helsinki School of Economics.

35. Lin, J.G. 1976 "Multiple Objective Problems: Pareto Optimal Solutions by Method of Proper Inequality Constraints", *IEEE Trans.*, A.C., **21**, 641-650.

36. Lin, J.G. 1977 "Proper Inequality Constraints and Maximisation of Index Vectors", *JOTA*, **21**, 505-522.

37. Lukka, M. 1979 "An Algorithm for Solving a Multiple Criteria Optimal Problem", *JOTA*, **28**, 435-438.

38. Marcotte, O. and Soland, R.M. 1980 Branch and Bound Algorithm for Multiple-Criteria Optimisation, Universities of Cornell and George Washington.

39. Marcotte, O. and Soland, R.M. 1981 An Interactive Branch and Bound Algorithm for Multiple Criteria Optimisation, Report T-442, School of Engineering and Applied Science, George Washington University.

40. Michalowski, W. and Piotrowski, A. 1982 Solving Multi-objective Production Planning Problem by an Interactive Procedure, Conference on Multi-Objective Decision-making, Manchester, April.

41. Morris, P. and Oren, S. 1980 "Multi Attribute Decision Making by Sequential Resource Allocation", *Operations Research*, **28**, 233-252.

42. Morse, J.N. 1980 "Reducing the Size of the Non-Dominated Set: Pruning by Clustering", *Comp. and O.R.*, **7**, 55-66.

43. Musselman, K. and Talavage, J. 1980 "A Trade-Off Cut Approach to Multiple Objective Optimisation", *Operations Research*, **28**, 1424-1435.

44. Nakayama, H., Tonino, T. and Sawaragi, Y. 1980 "An Interactive Optimisation Method in Multi Criteria Decisionmaking", *IEEE Trans.*, S.M.C., **10**, 163-169.

45. Oppenheimer, K.R. 1978 "A Proxy Approach to Multi-Attribute Decision Making", *Man. Sc.*, **24**, 675-689.

46. Oppenheimer, K.R. 1977 A Proxy Approach to Multi-Attribute Decision Making, Ph.D. Dissertation, Department of Engineering - Economic Systems, Stanford University.

47. Pascoletti, A. and Serafini, P. 1982 Reachability of Vector Optima through an Iterative Procedure, Conference on Multi-Objective Decision Making, Manchester, April.

48. Pearmann, A. 1977 "A Weighted Maximin and Maximax Approach to Multiple Criteria Decision Making", *Operational Research Quarterly*, **28**, 584-587.

49. Pollatscheck, M.A. 1976 "Personnel Assignment by Multi-objective Programming", *Zeitschrift für Operations Research*, **20**, 161-170.

50. Price, W.L. 1976 An Interactive Objective Function Generator for Goal Programming. In: "Multiple Criteria Decision Making", (H. Thiriez and S. Zionts, Eds.), Springer-Verlag.

51. Ravindran, A. and Sadagopan, S. 1980 Multi-criteria Mathematical Programming - A Unified Interactive Approach, Research Memorandum No. 80-3, School of Industrial Engineering, West La fayette.

52. Rivett, P. 1977 "Policy Selection by Structural Mapping", *Proceedings of the Royal Society, A.* **354**, 407-423.

53. Rosinger, E.E. 1980 Interactive Algorithm for Multi-Objective Optimisation. In: "Multiple Criteria Decision Making", (C. Fandel and T. Gal, Eds.), Springer.

54. Ross, G.T. and Soland, R.M. 1980 "A Multi-criteria Approach to the Location of Public Facilities", *E.J.O.R.*, **4**, 307-321.

55. Rustem, B. 1982 Multiple Objective Optimisation with Convex Constraints, Conference on Multi-Objective Decision Theory, Manchester, April.

56. Sakawa, M. and Seo, F. 1979 "A Methodology for Environmental Systems Management: Dynamic Application of the nested Lagrange Multiplier Method", *IEEE Trans.*, S.M.C., **9**, 794-805.

57. Sarin, R.K. 1977 Interactive Evaluation and Bound Procedures for Feliciting Multi-Attributed Alternatives. In: "Multiple Criteria Decision-Making", (M.K. Starr and M. Zeleny, Eds.), North-Holland.

58. Sawarka, M. 1982 "Interactive Multi-Objective Decision Making by the Sequential Proxy Optimization Technique: SPOT", *E.J.O.R.*, **9**, 386-396.

59. Steuer, R.E. 1977 "An Interactive Multiple Objective Linear Programming Procedure", T.I.M.S., *Studies in the Management Sciences*, **6**, (M.K. Starr and M. Zeleny, Eds.), North-Holland.

60. Steuer, R.E. 1976 "Linear Multiple Objective Programming with Interval Criterion Weights", *Man. Sc.*, **23**, 305-316.

61. Steuer, R.E. 1976 A Five Phase Procedure for Implementing a Vector-Maximum Algorithm for Multiple Objective Linear Programming Problems in Multiple Criteria Decision Making, (H. Thiriez and S. Zionts, Eds.), Springer-Verlag.

62. Steuer, R.E. and Schuler, A.T. 1978 "An Interactive Multiple-Objective Linear Programming Approach to a Problem in Forest Management", *Operations Research*, **26**, 254-269.

63. Stewart, T.J. 1981 An Interactive Approach to Multiple Criteria Decision Making Based on Statistical Inference, Tech. Rep. TWISK204, National Research Institute for Mathematical Sciences, Pretoria, South Africa.

64. Thanassoulis, E. 1982 "Paseb" A Solution Procedure for Multi-Objective Linear Programming Problems, Conference on Multi-Objective Decision Making, Manchester, April.

65. Törn, A.A. 1980 "A Sample-Search-Clustering Approach for Exploring the Feasible/Efficient Solutions of M.C. D.M. Problems", *Comp. and O.R.*, **7**, 67-79.

66. Walker, J. 1978 "An Interactive Method as an Aid in Solving Bicriterion Mathematical Programming Problems",*O.R.Q.*, **29**, 915-922.

67. Wallenius, J. and Zionts, S. 1977 A Research Project on Multi-criterion Decision Making. In: "Conflicting Objectives in Decisions", (D. Bell, R. Keeney and H. Raiffa, Eds.), Wiley.

68. Wallenius, J. and Zionts, S. 1976 "An Interactive Programming Method for Solving the Multiple Criteria Problem", *Man. Sc.*, **22**, 652-663.

69. Wallenius, J. 1975 "Comparative Evaluation of Some Interactive Approaches to Multi-criterion Optimisation", *Man. Sc.*, **21**, 1387-1396.

70. Wallenius, J. and Zionts, S. 1981 An Interactive Multiple Objective Linear Programming Method for a Class of Underlying Non-linear Utility Functions, Working Paper No. 451, School of Management, University of Buffalo.

71. Wehrung, D.A. 1979 "Multidimensional Line Search Using a Binary Preference Relation", *Operations Research*, **27**, 356-363.

72. Wehrung, D.A. 1978 "Interactive Identification and Optimisation Using a Binary Preference Relation", *Operations Research*, **26**, 322-332.

73. White, D.J. 1980 "Multi-Objective Interactive Programming", *J.O.R.S.*, 517-523.

74. White, D.J. 1982 Multi-Objective Interactive Programming for Efficient Sets, Conference on Multi-Objective Decision Making, Manchester, April.

75. White D.J. 1982 A Multi-Objective Interactive Programming Method for Finite Sets. Notes in Decision Theory, No. 132, University of Manchester.

76. Yu, P.L. 1973 Introduction to Domination Structures in Multi-criteria Decision Problems. In: "Multiple-criteria Decision Making", (J.L. Cochrane and M. Zeleny, Eds.), University of South Carolina Press.

77. Zionts, S. 1977 Multiple Criteria Decision Making for Discrete Alternatives with Ordinal Criteria, Working Paper No. 299, State University of New York at Buffalo, School of Management.

78. Zionts, S. 1979 "A Survey of Multiple Criteria Integer Programming Methods", *Ann. Disc. Math.*, **5**, 389-398.

79. Zionts, S. 1981 "A Multiple Criteria Method for Choosing Among Discrete Alternatives", *E.J.O.R.*, **7**, 143-147.

MULTIPLE OBJECTIVES WITH CONVEX CONSTRAINTS

B. Rustem

(Department of Electrical Engineering, Imperial College, London)

1. INTRODUCTION

Iterative approaches involving interactions with decision makers have often been advocated in multiple criterion optimization (see White, 1982) as well as in the specification of politicians' preferences in macro-economic decisions involving multiple objectives (see e.g. Frisch, 1981; Kornai, 1975, p. 420). This paper describes a method which uses such interactions to define a locally valid weighting matrix for a Euclidean norm. This norm measures the distance from a point at which the decision maker's objective levels are simultaneously and completely satisfied. Such points are known as "bliss" points, or desired values, and represent the desired but not necessarily feasible objectives of decision makers. The method is a generalisation of an approach for linear equality constraints, discussed in Rustem, Velupillai, Westcott (1978) to convex constraints. The present paper also discusses the effect of the method on the shadow prices. This allows the decision maker to moderate his requirements while interacting with the method if he does not find the corresponding shadow prices acceptable. Furthermore, with the exception of Theorem 2, the theoretical results in Section 4 are new.

Let $\underline{x} \in E^n$ be the vector of decision variables in the n-dimensional Euclidean space. Let the desired value, or bliss point, which the decision maker would ideally like to achieve be denoted by $\underline{x}^d$ and let $\underline{x}^d$ be bounded. Let R be the feasible set of $\underline{x}$. We assume that $x^d \notin R$. Hence, it is not feasible. Clearly, when $\underline{x}^d \in R$ the decision making problem with multiple objectives would have the obvious solution $\underline{x} = \underline{x}^d$. When $\underline{x}^d \notin R$, the relative importance of each element of $\underline{x}$ attaining its desired value has to be specified. This information can then be used to compute <u>the best feasible alternative</u> to $\underline{x}^d$ on R.

In mathematical terms this problem can be summarised as

$$\min \{q_c(\underline{x}) \mid \underline{x} \in R\} \tag{1}$$

where

$$q_c(\underline{x}) \triangleq \tfrac{1}{2}\langle \underline{x} - \underline{x}^d, Q_c(\underline{x} - \underline{x}^d)\rangle \tag{2}$$

$$= \tfrac{1}{2}\| \underline{x} - \underline{x}^d \|^2_{Q_c} \tag{3}$$

and Q_c is a symmetric positive definite weighting matrix which specifies the relative importance of each element of $\underline{x}$ attaining its desired value. The diagonal elements of Q_c penalise the departure of a variable from its desired value. The off-diagonal elements measure the importance attached to the deviation in one variable versus the deviation in another. Hence, these elements express nonlinear (quadratic) trade-offs between variables. Clearly, by specifying a positive definite Q_c, a measure of distance from $\underline{x}$ to $\underline{x}^d$ is defined (see (3)). The iterative method of this paper is aimed at tailoring Q_c to meet the requirements of the decision maker.

When R is convex, the solution of (1) has a simple geometric interpretation. As (1) minimizes the norm (3), the solution is the projection of $\underline{x}^d$ onto R, with respect to this norm (see Luenberger, 1969; Rustem, 1981). Let R denote a set of linear equality constraints,

$$R = \{\underline{x} \in E^n \mid N^T\underline{x} = \underline{b}\} \tag{4}$$

where $\underline{b}$ is an (m x 1) constant vector and N is an (n x m) matrix whose columns are assumed (for simplicity) to be linearly independent. This projection, and hence the solution of (1), is stated in the following lemma.

<u>Lemma 1</u>

When R is given by (4), the solution of (1) is given by

$$\underline{x}_c = \underline{x}^d - H_c N(N^T H_c N)^{-1}(N^T\underline{x}^d - \underline{b}) \tag{5}$$

where

$$H_c = Q_c^{-1}$$

and the Lagrange multipliers (or shadowprices) associated with (1) are given by

$$\underline{\lambda}_c = -(N^T H_c N)^{-1}(N^T \underline{x}^d - \underline{b}). \tag{6}$$

Proof

Writing the Langrangian associated with (1)

$$L_c(\underline{x}, \underline{\lambda}) = q_c(\underline{x}) - \langle N^T \underline{x} - \underline{b}, \underline{\lambda} \rangle$$

both (5) and (6) can be derived straightforwardly from the following first order conditions

$$Q_c(\underline{x}_c - \underline{x}^d) - N\underline{\lambda}_c = \underline{0} \tag{7}$$

$$N^T \underline{x}_c - \underline{b} = \underline{0} \tag{8}$$

□

The restrictive structure of (4) is relaxed in subsequent sections. However, expressions (5) - (8) are still used to illustrate various projection properties of the method.

Before discussing the iterative method for determining Q_c, it would be appropriate to introduce the underlying motivation which stems from concepts in numerical optimization. Suppose the decision maker has a globally valid true weighting matrix Q_t which is not known. The problem of determining Q_t can be resolved by generating a finite sequence of matrices that converge to Q_t. The following algorithm generates such a sequence:

Step 0: Given an initial positive definite matrix Q_0 and an initial value $\underline{x}_0 \in E^n$, set $k = 0$.

Step 1: Ask the decision maker to specify two vectors $\underline{\delta}, \underline{\gamma} \in E^n$ such that $\underline{x}_{k+1} = \underline{x}_k + \underline{\delta}$ (the significance of $\underline{\delta}$ will be discussed in Section 2) and $\underline{\gamma} = \nabla q_t(\underline{x}_{k+1}) - \nabla q_t(\underline{x}_k)$

where $q_t(\underline{x}) \triangleq \frac{1}{2}\langle \underline{x} - \underline{x}^d, Q_t(\underline{x} - \underline{x}^d)\rangle$ and hence

$\nabla q_t(\underline{x}) \triangleq Q_t(\underline{x} - \underline{x}^d)$.

Step 2: Update Q_k using the rank-one formula

$$Q_{k+1} = Q_k + \frac{(\underline{\gamma} - Q_k\underline{\delta})(\underline{\gamma} - Q_k\underline{\delta})^T}{\langle \underline{\gamma} - Q_k\underline{\delta}, \underline{\delta}\rangle}\text{; set } k = k + 1\text{, go to}$$

Step 1.

The rank-one formula in Step 2 is a member of the variable metric family widely used for computing approximations to second derivative matrices in function optimization (see Broyden, 1967; Davidon, 1968). The vector $\underline{\gamma}$ represents the change in the gradient vector of q_t evaluated at $\underline{x}_{k+1}$ and $\underline{x}_k$, respectively. In an unconstrained optimization framework the aim is to solve the problem $\min \{ q_t(\underline{x}) \mid \underline{x} \in E^n \}$. When Q_t is not known, increasingly accurate approximations to it is provided by the sequence $\{Q_k\}$ generated by the above rank-one formula. In this case, ∇q_t is known, the vector $\underline{\delta}$ is a descent direction at $\underline{x}_k$, implying that q_t is reduced along $\underline{\delta}$, and is usually given by $\underline{\delta} = -Q_k^{-1} \nabla q_t(\underline{x}_k)$. When $\underline{x}$ is further constrained by a feasible set the form of $\underline{\delta}$ clearly becomes more complicated. On the other hand, in a multiple objective decision making enviroment ∇q_t is generally not known and, as discussed in the above algorithm, $\underline{\delta}$ is specified by the decision maker. In this case, assigning values to $\underline{\gamma}$ is not a trivial problem and is discussed in Bray (1972, 1975). In Section 2, the approximation $\underline{\gamma} \simeq \phi\, Q_c\underline{\delta}$ is considered for some scalar $\phi \geq 1$.

The above algorithm is not dependent on the feasible region R since Q_t is assumed to be globally valid. It can, however, be made to be dependent on R by requiring $\underline{x}_k \in R$. The correction computed using the above updating formula has the property that it does not restrict the choice of the direction or magnitude of $\underline{\delta}$ in any way. The denominator needs to be safeguarded from becoming zero. This can be accomplished with small changes to $\underline{\delta}$ and/or $\underline{\gamma}$ within limits acceptable to the policy maker. Provided this is done, it can be shown that Q_{k+1} remains positive definite if Q_k is positive definite. Another interesting aspect of the algorithm is that after a finite number of steps the sequence of matrices $\{Q_k\}$ converge to the required true weighting matrix of the decision maker. This is stated in the following theorem:

Theorem (Fiacco and McCormick, 1968)

Assume $q_t(\underline{x})$ to be a positive definite quadratic form. Assume also that n linearly independent $\underline{\delta}$ vectors and corresponding values for $\underline{\gamma}$ may be specified by the decision maker. If no zero denominators occur in the updating formula then, starting with any positive definite weighting matrix, Q_0, the sequence of matrices generated by the algorithm converge (element-wise) to Q_t after at most n iterations. □

This result requires the specified $\underline{\delta}$ and $\underline{\gamma}$ vectors to be consistent with the true weighting matrix and hence with $q_t(\underline{x})$. In addition, there is no indication that there exists in reality a Q_t valid globally or just throughout R for the decision maker. Thus, Q_c in (2) can at best be seen as a local approximation to the weighting matrix of the decision maker. Furthermore, with $\underline{\gamma}$ approximated by $\underline{\gamma} \simeq \phi Q_c \underline{\delta}$, the above theorem can no longer be invoked. In subsequent sections the use of this approximation is explored for linearly constrained or in general convex R. The justification for this approximation is discussed in Section 3 where the properties of the resulting updating formula are analysed.

2. THE ITERATIVE METHOD FOR DETERMINING Q_c

Let $\Omega \in E^n$ denote the set of admissible, i.e. satisfactory or acceptable, values of $\underline{x}$ from the point of view of the decision maker. Given the desired value $\underline{x}^d$ and the region R, the "nearness" of the solution of (1) to $\underline{x}^d$ is only affected by the weighting matrix Q_c. Different values of this matrix define different points on R as the nearest point to $\underline{x}^d$. Thus, given $\underline{x}^d$, the only way of producing a solution of (1) that also satisfies Ω is to respecify Q_c.

It should be noted that, in contrast to the algebraic equalities and inequalities describing R, the set Ω is assumed to exist only in the mind of the rational decision maker. Rationality in the context of the method of this section is discussed in Section 3. In order to ensure the existence of a solution, $\underline{x}$, which simultaneously satisfies R and the decision maker, it is also necessary to assume that the "effective" feasible region, $\Omega \cap R$, is nonempty, i.e.,

$$\Omega \cap R \neq \phi \tag{9}$$

and that this intersection is convex. Clearly, this assumption is satisfied for convex R and Ω. Henceforth the subscripts k and t of Section 1 will not be used. Q_c can be taken as a local approximation to a Q_t which is locally valid in $\Omega \cap R$. Thus, problem (1) has to be solved a number of times, by respecifying Q_c, until a solution is found such that $\underline{x}_c \in \Omega \cap R$.

Let Q_c denote the current weighting matrix of (2). The solution of (1) using this matrix will be called the "current" optimal solution $\underline{x}_c$. This solution is presented to the decision maker who may decide that $\underline{x}_c \notin \Omega$ since some of the elements of $\underline{x}_c$ are not quite what he wants them to be. Consequently, an alternative solution of (1) has to be obtained by altering Q_c. In order to do this the decision maker is required to specify an $\underline{x}$ value which he would prefer instead of $\underline{x}_c$. This "preferred" value is denoted by $\underline{x}_p$ and obviously satisfies

$$\underline{x}_p \in \Omega \tag{10}$$

but <u>not necessarily</u>

$$\underline{x}_p \in R. \tag{11}$$

Thus, $\underline{x}_p$ incorporates all the alterations to $\underline{x}_c$ such that $\underline{x}_p$ is preferred, by the decision maker, to $\underline{x}_c$. Given $\underline{x}_c$ and $\underline{x}_p$ the displacement, or correction vector is defined as

$$\underline{\delta} \triangleq \underline{x}_p - \underline{x}_c. \tag{12}$$

Given $\underline{\delta}$, Q_c is altered to obtain the new weighting matrix Q_n using the rank-one correction

$$Q_n = Q_c + \mu \frac{Q_c \underline{\delta}\underline{\delta}^T Q_c}{\langle \underline{\delta}, Q_c \underline{\delta} \rangle} \tag{13}$$

where $\mu \geq 0$ is a scalar chosen to reflect the emphasis to be given to the update. It should be noted that (13) is obtained from the rank-one update in the previous section by using the approximation $\underline{\gamma} \approx \phi Q_c \underline{\delta}$. Hence $\mu = (\phi - 1)$ with $\phi \geq 1$. The new matrix Q_n is used in (1) to compute a "new" optimal solution $\underline{x}_n$. The rôle of μ in determining $\underline{x}_n$ and the desirable characteristics of $\underline{x}_n$, including the fact that it is an improvement on $\underline{x}_c$, are discussed in Sections 3 and 4. A single update of the form (13) does not necessarily yield a new optimal solution such that $\underline{x}_n \in \Omega$. Thus, (13) has to be utilized iteratively until $\underline{x}_n \in \Omega$. Such an iterative procedure, analogous to the algorithm discussed in Section 1, is summarized below.

Step 0: Given the desired value $\underline{x}^d$ and the feasible region R, assume some initial symmetric, positive definite weighting matrix Q_c.

Step 1: Using Q_c, solve (1) to obtain $\underline{x}_c$.

Step 2: [This step describes the interaction between the decision maker and the method.] If, according to the decision maker, $\underline{x}_c \in \Omega$ stop. Otherwise ask the decision maker to specify the changes, $\underline{\delta}$, required in the current optimal solution $\underline{x}_c$ to make it acceptable. The preferred value $\underline{x}_p$ is thus specified as

$$\underline{x}_p = \underline{x}_c + \underline{\delta}.$$

Alternatively, the decision maker might choose to specify $\underline{x}_p$ directly.

Step 3: Given Q_c and $\underline{\delta}$, choose a $\mu \geq 0$ and compute Q_n using (13). Set $Q_c = Q_n$ and go to Step 1.

The choice of μ is bounded from above and this bound is discussed in Section 3. It is also shown in Section 3 that Q_n remains symmetric positive definite if Q_c is symmetric positive definite.

An obvious choice for $\underline{x}_p$ is $\underline{x}_p = \underline{x}^d$. However, this choice does not add any further information about the decision maker's local preferences. It is already known from the outset that the decision maker prefers $\underline{x}^d$ to any $\underline{x} \in R$. Hence $\underline{x}^d$ is preferred to $\underline{x}_c$ ($\in R$). The fact that $\underline{x}_p$, $\underline{x}_p \neq \underline{x}^d$, is preferred to $\underline{x}_c$ constitutes additional information about the local preferences of the decision maker. The uselessness of setting $\underline{x}_p = \underline{x}^d$ is supported by the method and it is shown at the end of Section 3 that this choice does not alter the current solution, $\underline{x}_c$, in any way.

3. PROPERTIES OF THE METHOD: LINEAR EQUALITY CONSTRAINTS

The properties of the iterative procedure of the previous section can best be analysed by inspecting the effect of updating Q_c on the optimal solution. In this section the specific case arising when R is given by (4) is discussed. General convex constraints are considered in Section 4. However, it should be noted that the basic results for linear equality constraints considered in this section are also essential for the discussion in Section 4. The next theorem characterizes the effect of (13) as a corresponding update on the current optimal solution $\underline{x}_c$ and its corresponding multiplier $\underline{\lambda}_c$.

<u>Theorem 1</u>

Let Q_c be positive definite and R given by (4). Then, for any $\underline{\delta} \neq 0$ and $\mu \geq 0$, Q_n given by (13) is positive definite and the new optimal solution obtained using Q_n instead of Q_c is given by

$$\underline{x}_n = \underline{x}_c + \alpha P \underline{\delta} \tag{14}$$

where

$$P = I - H_c N(N^T H_c N)^{-1} N^T \tag{15}$$

$$H_c = Q_c^{-1}$$

$$\alpha = -\frac{\mu \langle \underline{\delta}, Q_c(\underline{x}_c - \underline{x}^d)\rangle}{\langle \underline{\delta}, Q_c \underline{\delta}\rangle + \mu \langle Q_c \underline{\delta}, PH_c(Q_c \underline{\delta})\rangle} \tag{16}$$

The corresponding Lagrange multiplier at $\underline{x}_n$ is given by

$$\underline{\lambda}_n = \underline{\lambda}_c - \alpha (N^T H_c N)^{-1} N^T \underline{\delta}. \tag{17}$$

Furthermore, $\alpha \geq 0$ for

$$<\underline{\delta}, Q_c(\underline{x}_c - \underline{x}^d)> \leq 0. \tag{18}$$

Proof

When Q_c is positive definite, the positive definiteness of Q_n follows trivially from (13). To derive (16) - (17), we apply (13) and the Sherman-Morrison formula (Householder, 1964) to

$$\lambda_n = -(N^T H_n N)^{-1}(N^T \underline{x}^d - \underline{b}) \tag{19}$$

$$= -(N^T(Q_c + \mu \frac{Q_c \underline{\delta}\underline{\delta}^T Q_c}{<\underline{\delta}, Q_c\underline{\delta}>})^{-1}N)^{-1}(N^T\underline{x}^d - \underline{b})$$

$$= \underline{\lambda}_c - \frac{\mu <\underline{\delta}, N(N^T H_c N)^{-1}(N^T \underline{x}^d - \underline{b})>(N^T H_c N)^{-1} N^T \underline{\delta}}{\mu <Q_c\underline{\delta}, PH_c(Q_c\underline{\delta})> + <\underline{\delta}, Q_c\underline{\delta}>} \tag{20}$$

Expressions (6) and (7) may be used to simplify (20) since

$$- <\underline{\delta}, N(N^T H_c N)^{-1}(N^T\underline{x}^d - \underline{b})> = <\underline{\delta}, N\underline{\lambda}_c>$$

$$= <\underline{\delta}, Q_c(\underline{x}_c - \underline{x}^d)> \tag{21}$$

and (20) with (21) yields the required result (17) with α given by (16).

To derive (14), we note from (5) and (6) that

$$\underline{x}_n = \underline{x}^d + H_n N \underline{\lambda}_n . \tag{22}$$

Applying (13), (17) and the Sherman-Morrison formula to (22) yields

$$\underline{x}_n = x^d + (H_c - \frac{u}{(\mu+1)} \frac{\underline{\delta}\underline{\delta}^T}{\langle\underline{\delta}, Q_c\underline{\delta}\rangle}) N(\underline{\lambda}_c - \alpha(N^T H_c N)^{-1} N^T \underline{\delta})$$

$$= x^d + H_c N\lambda \underline{c} - \alpha H_c N(N^T H_c N)^{-1} N^T \underline{\delta}$$

$$- \frac{\mu\ \underline{\delta}\underline{\delta}^T N\underline{\lambda}_c}{(\mu+1)\langle\underline{\delta}, Q_c\underline{\delta}\rangle} + \frac{\mu\alpha\ \underline{\delta}\underline{\delta}^T N(N^T H_c N)^{-1} N^T \underline{\delta}}{(\mu+1)\langle\underline{\delta}, Q_c\underline{\delta}\rangle}$$

$$+ \underline{x}^d + H_c N\underline{\lambda}_c + \alpha(I - H_c N(N^T H_c N)^{-1} N^T)\underline{\delta}$$

which, using (7) and (15), reduces to the required result (14).

Finally, it can be seen from (16) that if (18) is satisfied then $\alpha \geq 0$ since PH_c is symmetric positive semi-definite.

□

The matrix (15) is a well known projection operator which projects vectors in E^n onto the subspace

$$R_0 \triangleq \{\underline{x} \in E^n | N^T\underline{x} = \underline{0}\} \qquad (23)$$

(see, Goldfarb, 1969; Rustem, 1981). Thus, the correction term $\alpha P\underline{\delta}$ in (14) is along the projection of $\alpha\underline{\delta}$ onto R_0. Following the discussion in Section 1, this implies that $\underline{x}_n$ is as "near" to the preferred solution as allowed by the feasible region R. The magnitude of the stepsize α can be controlled using μ.

The inequality (18) may be interpreted as a "rationality condition" on the choice of $\underline{\delta}$. The reason for this lies in the form of (14). When (18) holds, then $\alpha \geq 0$ and thus the modification $\alpha P\underline{\delta}$ to the current optimal solution in (14) lies in the same direction as $\underline{\delta}$. This is the "best" alternative to $\underline{\delta}$, in the sense of the norm (3), allowed by the feasible region when $\underline{x}_c + \underline{\delta}$ is infeasible and lies outside R. Also, since $\underline{\delta}$ is given by (12), it should be a descent direction for $q_n(\underline{x})$ at $\underline{x}_c$ where

$$q_n(\underline{x}) \triangleq \tfrac{1}{2} \langle\underline{x} - \underline{x}^d, Q_n(\underline{x} - \underline{x}^d)\rangle.$$

Thus, the information that $\underline{x}_p$ is actually preferred to $\underline{x}_c$ is incorporated in $q_n(\underline{x})$. Using (13) with (18) establishes this result

$$\langle \underline{\delta}, \nabla q_n(\underline{x}_c)\rangle = \langle \underline{\delta}, Q_n(\underline{x}_c - \underline{x}^d)\rangle$$

$$= \langle \underline{\delta}, (Q_c + \mu \frac{Q_c \underline{\delta}\underline{\delta}^T Q_c}{\langle \underline{\delta}, Q_c \underline{\delta}\rangle})(\underline{x}_c - \underline{x}^d)\rangle$$

$$= (1 + \mu) \langle \underline{\delta}, Q_c(\underline{x}_c - \underline{x}^d)\rangle$$

$$= (1 + \mu) \langle \underline{\delta}, \nabla q_c(\underline{x}_c)\rangle.$$

Thus, $\underline{\delta}$ is a descent direction for $q_n(\underline{x}_c)$ if it is a descent direction for $q_c(\underline{x}_c)$ and condition (18) ensures the latter.

The convergence properties of the method, discussed in the next section, are dependent on the form of (14) which is used to show that for α bounded, using μ to control its size, the distance between $\underline{x}_n$ and $\underline{x}_p$ is less than the distance between $\underline{x}_c$ and $\underline{x}_p$.

As a note of warning it must be stressed that the method of Section 2 cannot be used to reveal the weighting matrix of (1) after the decision has been taken. The idea of "uncovering the objective function" once the decision has been made by others is an old and illusive one. It has arisen independently in control theory and in economics. The interest from the latter area is due to the desire to reveal the past preferences of decision makers. The iterative method of Section 2 may in this case be formulated, in the framework of Section 1, so that the desired value is set according to the desirable historical conditions, the feasible region R is set to be the model of the economy and the preferred value is set to be the actual historical value. The preferred value is fixed at the historical value throughout the procedure and is not changed as would normally be done in Step 2 of the procedure in Section 2.

In this setting the historical and, in this case, also the preferred value has to be a feasible point since, by definition, the model of the economy must explain the historical event.

Thus, for a linear model such as (4), the preferred value and all current optimal solutions are feasible and hence the $\underline{\delta}$ vector satisfies

$$N^T \underline{\delta} = \underline{0}.$$

Using this and (7), we can express the stepsize α in (14) as

$$\alpha = \frac{\mu \langle \underline{\delta}, Q_c(\underline{x}_c - \underline{x}^d) \rangle}{\langle \underline{\delta}, Q_c \underline{\delta} \rangle + \mu \langle Q_c \underline{\delta}, PH_c(Q_c \underline{\delta}_c) \rangle}$$

$$= \frac{\mu \langle \underline{\delta}, N\underline{\lambda}_c \rangle}{\langle \underline{\delta}, Q_c \underline{\delta} \rangle + \mu \langle Q_c \underline{\delta}, PH_c(Q_c \underline{\delta}_c) \rangle}$$

$$= 0.$$

Hence, if $\underline{\delta} \in R_0$ then the stepsize $\alpha = 0$. This is not a serious limitation of the method in general since if $\underline{x}_p$ is feasible ($\underline{x}_p \in R$), the decision maker can have exactly what he wants (i.e. since $\underline{x}_p \in \Omega \cap R$, setting $\underline{x}_n = \underline{x}_p$ the method stops). However, if the problem is to reveal the weighting matrix of a past decision, $\alpha = 0$ shows that the method is not suitable for this purpose.

Finally, consider the choice $\underline{x}_p = \underline{x}^d$ discussed in Section 2. From (14) and (17) we have

$$\underline{x}_n - \underline{x}_c = -\alpha(I - H_c N(N^T H_c N)^{-1} N^T)(\underline{x}_c - \underline{x}^d)$$

$$= -\alpha(I - H_c N(N^T H_c N)^{-1} N^T) H_c Q_c (\underline{x}_c - \underline{x}^d)$$

$$= -\alpha(I - H_c N(N^T H_c N)^{-1} N^T) H_c N \underline{\lambda}_c$$

$$= 0$$

which shows that this choice does not add any new information about the decision maker's preferences.

4. PROPERTIES OF THE METHOD: GENERAL CONVEX CONSTRAINTS

A desirable but local property of the method is that every time Q_c is updated and a new optimal solution is computed, the decision maker is more satisfied with the new optimal solution, $\underline{x}_n$, than he was with the current optimal solution $\underline{x}_c$. The following two theorems establish such results for the linear equality constrained case. These will then be extended to general convex constraints.

Theorem 2

For $0 \le \alpha \le 2$ in (14) the inequality

$$\| \underline{x}_n - \underline{x}_p \|_{Q_c} < \| \underline{x}_c - \underline{x}_p \|_{Q_c} \tag{24}$$

holds. Furthermore, for $0 < \alpha < 2$, (24) is a strict inequality.

Proof

The proofs of this and subsequent theorems and lemmas are omitted. They are available from the author. □

Theorem 3

For $0 \le \alpha \le 2$ in (14) the inequality

$$\| \underline{x}_n - \underline{x}_p \|_{Q_n} \le \| \underline{x}_c - \underline{x}_p \|_{Q_n} \tag{25}$$

holds. Furthermore, for $0 < \alpha < 2$, (25) is a strict inequality. □

The difficulty in establishing similar results in the case of general convex constraints arises from the fact that there may not be a point between $\underline{x}_c$ and $\underline{x}_n$, along $\underline{x}_n - \underline{x}_c$, which can be expressed as the projection of x^d onto R, with respect to the weighting Q_n, and hence solves the problem

$$\min \{ \tfrac{1}{2} \langle \underline{x} - \underline{x}^d, Q_n (\underline{x} - \underline{x}^d) \rangle \mid \underline{x} \in R \} \tag{26}$$

with some $\mu \ge 0$ defining Q_n via (13) and with convex R. The importance of this becomes clear when the above linear equality constrained case is considered. If for a given μ, $\underline{x}_n$ is such that $\alpha > 2$ in (14), in the linear equality case, reducing μ clearly reduces α given by (16) and for every value of μ, $\underline{x}_n$ can be expressed in terms of (13). Hence, if $\alpha > 2$, μ can be reduced to define an $\underline{x}_n$ for which the bound $0 \leq \alpha \leq 2$ is satisfied.

The main concept necessary for extending the results of Theorems 2 and 3 to general convex R is the line passing through $\underline{x}_n$ and $\underline{x}_c$. By considering the projection of $\underline{x}_p$ on this line, it is shown in Theorem 4 below that (24) and (25) hold for $\underline{x}_n$ close enough to $\underline{x}_c$. It is also shown that if this is not the case, reducing μ brings $\underline{x}_n$ close to $\underline{x}_c$ so that for small enough μ (24) and (25) hold.

The following two lemmas establish the basic results used in Theorem 4.

Lemma 2

For $\mu \geq 0$ in (13) and for $\underline{x}_c$ and $\underline{x}_n$ given by the solutions of (1) and (26), respectively, with convex R, the inequality

$$<\underline{x}_p - \underline{x}_c, Q_c(\underline{x}_n - \underline{x}_c)> \geq 0 \tag{27}$$

holds if $<\underline{\delta}, Q_c(\underline{x}_c - \underline{x}^d)> \leq 0$. □

Lemma 3

If the conditions of Lemma 2 hold then $\mu \rightarrow 0$ implies that $\|\underline{x}_c - \underline{x}_n\| \rightarrow 0$. □

Lemma 3 implies that the scalar μ can be used by the decision maker to control the size of the norm $\|\underline{x}_c - \underline{x}_n\|$. This result is utilized in the next Theorem.

Theorem 4

Let the conditions of Lemma 2 be satisfied and consider the line passing through $\underline{x}_c$ and $\underline{x}_n$. Let $\underline{x}_1$ be the projection of $\underline{x}_p$ onto this line. Thus

$$\underline{x}_1 = \underline{x}_c + P\underline{\delta}$$

where P is the operator projecting, under the norm $\|\cdot\|_{Q_c}$, vectors in E^n onto this line. Then for $\underline{x}(\alpha)$ given by

$$\underline{x}(\alpha) \triangleq \underline{x}_c + \alpha(\underline{x}_1 - \underline{x}_c)$$

and $0 \leq \alpha \leq 2$

$$\|\underline{x}(\alpha) - \underline{x}_p\|_{Q_c} \leq \|\underline{x}_c - \underline{x}_p\|_{Q_c} \tag{28}$$

$$\|\underline{x}(\alpha) - \underline{x}_p\|_{Q_n} \leq \|\underline{x}_c - \underline{x}_p\|_{Q_n}. \tag{29}$$

Also

$$\underline{x}_n - \underline{x}_c = \tau(\underline{x}_1 - \underline{x}_c) \tag{30}$$

with $\tau \geq 0$ which implies that both $\underline{x}_1 - \underline{x}_c$ and $\underline{x}_n - \underline{x}_c$ lie in the same direction. Furthermore, if

$$\underline{x}_n \notin X \triangleq \{\underline{x} | \underline{x} = \underline{x}_c + \alpha(\underline{x}_1 - \underline{x}_c), \ \alpha \in [0, 2]\}$$

then there exists a $\mu \geq 0$, small enough, so that the resulting solution of (26) satisfies X and thereby (28) and (29) with $\underline{x}_n = \underline{x}(\alpha)$. □

5. CONCLUDING REMARKS

The method discussed in this paper provides an interactive approach in which the decision maker can search for an acceptable solution of the multiple objective optimization problem.

The quadratic function used by the method allows the decision maker to express his trade offs in achieving each objective versus the others. Using a rank-one modification, the weighting matrix is tailored to meet the decision maker's requirements.

The effect of changing the weights are expressed in terms of optimal solution updates and in terms of updates to the shadow prices. If the decision maker is not prepared to accept the changes in the shadow prices corresponding to the new optimal solution, formulae (17), (16) and (14) provide the guidelines as to how he should moderate his requirements.

ACKNOWLEDGEMENT

This research was financed by a Science and Engineering Research Council Advanced Fellowship.

REFERENCES

Bray, J. 1972 "Some Considerations in the Practice of Economic Management", PREM Discussion Paper, No. 2.

Bray, J. 1975 "Optimal Control of a Noisy Economy with the UK as an Example", *J.R. Statistical Soc.*, Series A, Vol. **138**, Part 3.

Broyden, C. 1967 "Quasi-Newton Methods and their Application to Function Minimization", *Math. Comp.*, Vol. **21**, pp. 368-381.

Davidon, W.C. 1968 "Variance Algorithm for Minimization", *Comp. J.*, Vol. **10**, pp. 406-410.

Fiacco, A.V. and McCormick, G.P. 1968 "Nonlinear Programming: Sequential Unconstrained Minimization Techniques, J. Wiley, New York.

Frisch, R. 1981 "From Utopian Theory to Practical Applications", *American Economic Review,* Vol. **71**, N. 6, pp. 1-16.

Goldfarb, D. 1969 "Extensions of Davidon's Variable Metric Method to Maximize Under Linear Inequality and Equality Constraints", *SIAM J. Appl. Math.*, Vol. **17**, 739-764.

Householder, A.S. 1964 The Theory of Matrices in Numerical Analysis, Blaisdell, New York.

Kornai, J. 1975 Mathematical Planning of Structural Decisions, North Holland, Amsterdam.

Luenberger, D. 1969 Optimization by Vector Space Methods, John Wiley, New York.

Rustem, B., Velupillai, K. and Westcott, J.H. 1978 "Respecifying the Weighting Matrix of a Quadratic Objective Function", *Automatica,* Vol. **14**, pp. 567-582.

Rustem, B. 1981 Projection Methods in Constrained Optimization and Applications to Optimal Policy Decisions, Springer-Verlag, Berlin.

White, D.J. 1982 "A Selection of Multi-Objective Interactive Programming Methods", in this volume.

THE SOLUTION PROCEDURE "PASEB" FOR MULTI-OBJECTIVE LINEAR PROGRAMMING PROBLEMS

E. Thanassoulis

(School of Industrial and Business Studies, University of Warwick)

1. INTRODUCTION

In this paper, PASEB, a new method for the solution of multi-objective linear programming (MOLP) problems is presented.

In the last decade or so numerous methods have been proposed for the solution of MOLP problems. Some examples are Belenson and Kapur [1], Geoffrion et al. [2], Benayoun et al. [3], Zionts and Wallenius [4], Steuer [5] and White [6]. No method, however, has yet seen widespread application in practice and a practicable solution method for MOLP problems has yet to be found.

PASEB is an iterative and interactive solution procedure developed with special attention to its practicability. The basis of the method is the pattern search procedure proposed by Hooke and Jeeves [7] for unconstrained optimisation. The Hooke and Jeeves procedure will be referred to simply as the "Pattern Search" method.

In PASEB, to begin with, local search is carried out to determine a pattern of improving solutions. Then the decision maker's (DM's) preferred solution in the direction of the pattern becomes the current solution (a pattern move is made) and the foregoing procedure is repeated at the new solution, and so on, until at some current solution local search reveals no pattern of improving solutions. At such a solution, a preferred solution dominating the current, if it exists, is determined and local searches and pattern moves from the new solution are begun as before. If no feasible solution dominates the current, an attempt is made to determine a new solution preferred to the current one, by attempting to move on the efficient boundary (Benayoun et al. [8], p. 282) of the feasible region. If the attempt succeeds, local search and pattern moves as before are undertaken at the new solution. Otherwise a few suitably selected feasible directions ([9], p. 340) at the current solution are tested in an attempt to determine a solution preferred to the current one. If the attempt succeeds, local search and pattern moves are undertaken as before from the new solution. Otherwise, if the current solution is satisfactory, termination takes place, and if it is not, all feasible directions at the current solution are considered so that either a solution preferred to the current one is determined or the current solution is proved to be one of DM's most preferred solutions in the problem. Such a solution is referred to as a best compromise solution (BCS) to the problem.

While, in principle, PASEB can be used to determine a BCS to a MOLP problem, provided certain conditions referred to later are satisfied, this is time-consuming in practice and the method is intended primarily as a practicable procedure for obtaining quickly a "good" solution to a MOLP problem.

2. PRELIMINARY CONSIDERATIONS IN THE DEVELOPMENT OF PASEB

The MOLP Problem

Without loss of generality the MOLP problem can be written as follows:

$$\begin{aligned} &\text{Max } c_i \cdot x && i = 1 \ldots N \\ &\text{s.t. } a_i \cdot x \leq b_i && i \in I_1 \\ &\phantom{\text{s.t. }} a_i \cdot x = b_i && i \in I_2 \\ &\phantom{\text{s.t. }} x \geq 0 \end{aligned} \qquad \text{(P1)}$$

c_i is the (1 x n) constant gradient vector of the ith objective function, x is the (n x 1) decision vector, a_i is the (1 x n) constant gradient vector of the ith constraint and b_i is a scalar. We shall denote by X the set of feasible solutions to P1.

With respect to P1 the following are defined.

1. The ith individually optimal solution. This is an efficient (Gal [10]) solution at which the ith objective takes its optimal value over X. The ith individually optimal solution will be denoted by $\tilde{x}^i$.

2. The objective space of P1. Let $c(x) = \{c_i \cdot x,\ i = 1 \ldots N,\ x \in X\}$. The space in which $c(x)$ maps X is the objective space of P1.

It is assumed that the DM's preferences over solutions to P1 satisfy the necessary and sufficient conditions (Fishburn [11], ch. 3) so that in the objective space to P1 at least one function $U(c(x))$ exists having the following properties:

1. $U(c(x^1)) > U(c(x^2)) \rightleftarrows c(x^1)$ is preferred to $c(x^2)$;

2. $U(c(x^1)) = U(c(x^2)) \rightleftarrows c(x^1)$ and $c(x^2)$ are equally desired;

where $x^i \in X$, $i = 1, 2$. $U(c(x))$ is referred to as the DM's value function.

In view of this, a BCS to P1 is an optimal solution to the following probem:

$$\begin{aligned} &\text{Max } U(c(x)) \\ &\text{s.t. } x \in X \end{aligned} \tag{P2}$$

where x and X are as those defined in P1.

The distinguishing feature of P2 is that $U(c(x))$ is not known explicitly at the outset. However the DM can give certain information about solutions to P2 on the basis of his implicit feeling for his preferences over the objectives in P1. Thus, it can be said that $U(c(x))$ is implicitly known to the DM.

Practicability Requirements for MOLP Solution Methods

In view of the foregoing, in the MOLP situation depicted by P1, in principle a solution is desired to the single objective mathematical programming model P2 whose objective function is only implicitly known to a DM.

In general it is difficult to obtain an explicit statement, or even an approximation to $U(c(x))$, and then solve P2. (See Starr and Zeleny [12]). Instead, interactive iterative procedures are thought more practicable for solving P2 requiring the DM to give at preset points only limited, and local, information to some solution(s) about his value function.

PASEB has been developed to solve in principle P2 by an interactive iterative procedure. On the basis of the performance of some typical similar existing procedures (Geoffrion et al. [2],

Benayoun et al. [3], Zionts and Wallenius [4]) during some experiments with them using real decision makers (Wallenius [13], Zionts and Wallenius [14], Dyer [15]) it was thought that, for PASEB to prove practicable, it must incorporate the following features.

1. It must have practicable interaction and computational phases. A practicable interaction phase is one in which the DM is requested to give only such information as he can give with ease and confidence. Both phases for practicability must be of acceptably short duration.

2. It must have a high initial rate of convergence. A high initial rate of convergence provides the facility to determine a good solution to the problem fast. This is desirable because normally a good solution to the problem is sufficient as it is too time-consuming, and at any rate too difficult, to determine a BCS to the problem, given the uncertainty about the DM's structure of preferences in the problem.

3. It must not exclude solutions from further consideration during the solution process on the basis of information given by the DM. This is necessary to avoid the oversight of potentially good solutions due to the DM possibly occasionally giving information inconsistent with his structure of preferences.

4. It must converge to a BCS to the problem in principle.

Bearing in mind the foregoing practicability requirements for PASEB, Pattern Search was selected as a basis for PASEB's development. The suitability of Pattern Search for adaptation to form part of a MOLP solution process stems from two facts.

1. To optimise a function Pattern Search only requires pairwise comparison of solutions on the basis of the function being optimised. In the context of a MOLP solution method, this means that, at interaction phases, the DM need only use pairwise comparison of solutions. This, experiments (Dyer [15], Wallenius [13]) have shown, decision makers are able to do with ease and confidence.

2. The nature of Pattern Search is such that if it establishes a good approximation to the direction of improvement of the function being optimised, it can converge fast towards the best point in that direction. In the context of a MOLP solution method this could be exploited to provide the desired high initial rate of convergence for the method.

3. THE PASEB METHOD

Assumptions

All notation in this section is as defined in P1 and P2 unless otherwise stated. We assume in P1 and P2 the following to be true.

1. $U(c(x))$ is concave, differentiable with continuous first partial derivatives in X.

2. X is bounded and closed.

3. A dominating solution is always preferred to the solutions it dominates.

4. The objective function gradients c_i, $i = 1 \ldots N$ are linearly independent.

The implications of the above assumptions as well as the consequences of their relaxation are discussed later.

The PASEB Algorithm

1. Determine $\tilde{x}^i$, $i = 1 \ldots N$, and a starting feasible solution, to be the first current solution.

2. If the current solution is the sth consecutive "similar" solution go to 8. Otherwise carry out local search. If a pattern of improving solutions is established go to 7.

3. If the current solution is efficient go to 4. Else determine an efficient solution dominating the current solution and go to 2. (This step involves the solution of a modified P1 model to test for efficiency the current solution.)

4. Let x^k be the optimal solution to the step 3 efficiency testing model. If x^k is a basic solution to P1 go to 5, otherwise determine the DM's preferred solution in the direction of trade-offs between the objectives offered by some non-basic variable at x^k if they are attractive and go to 2. Otherwise repeat the foregoing for some other non-basic variable at x^k and so on. If no non-basic variable at x^k offers desirable trade-offs between the objectives go to 6.

5. If some non-basic variable at x^k does not generate feasible non-basic solutions to P1 when altered marginally, discard it. Otherwise determine the DM's preferred solution in the

direction of the trade-offs between the objectives offered by that variable, if they are desirable, and go to step 2. If the trade-offs in hand are undesirable repeat the foregoing process for some other non-basic variable at x^k and so on. If no non-basic variable at x^k offers desirable trade-offs between the objectives go to 6.

6. Ask the DM to specify one or more pairs of sets of objectives I_p and I_q he would wish to see improved and worsened, respectively, at the current solution. Determine a feasible direction at the current solution likely to offer objective value changes compatible with those expressed in some pair I_p, I_q. If the feasible direction determined offers desirable trade-offs between the objectives determine the DM's preferred solution along them and go to 2. Otherwise repeat the foregoing for some other pair I_p, I_q, if any, and so on. If no pair I_p, I_q leads to a solution preferred to the current, terminate at the current solution if it is thought satisfactory. Otherwise perform an "optimality check" at it. (The optimality check either leads to step 2 through some solution preferred to the current encountered, or proves the current solution to be a BCS.)

7. Determine the DM's preferred solution in the direction of the pattern of improving solutions established and go to 2.

8. Determine, if it exists, an efficient solution dominating the current. If the solution determined is the same or "similar" to the current, go to 6. Otherwise go to 2.

Detailed Description of PASEB Steps

Step 1

The ith individually optimal solution to P1, denoted $\tilde{x}^i$, is obtained as the optimal solution to the following problem:

$$\text{Max} \quad \lambda_i \frac{c_i \cdot x}{M_i} + \sum_{\substack{j=1 \\ j \neq i}}^{j=N} \lambda_j \frac{c_j \cdot x}{M_j} \tag{P3}$$

$$\text{s.t.} \quad x \in X$$

where λ_i, λ_j are scalars such that $\lambda_i >> \lambda_j$ and $\lambda_j > 0 \; \forall j$.* M_i is the maximal absolute value $c_i \cdot x$, $i = 1 \ldots N$, takes in X. $\tilde{x}^i$ is efficient (Gal [10]). In the event of alternative optimal solutions to P3 the most preferred basic one for the DM can be selected.

The first current solution in principle can be any feasible solution to the problem. However, it is advantageous if it is chosen as close to a BCS as can be, given any information the DM can supply about his over-all preferences over the objectives. If the DM cannot supply any such information, one of the individually optimal solutions to the problem can be used as the first current solution.

Step 2

In this step entry to step 8 takes place if it is felt that successive current solutions have been only marginally improving and it is desired to break the sequence of such solutions. "Similarity" of solutions and s in the context of the step are defined subjectively**. Their definition must strike a balance between too frequent interruptions of local search and pattern moves on the one hand and too many iterations of marginally improving solutions on the other. It is noted that local search and pattern moves in PASEB are expected to be the primary means of progress to improved solutions to the problem.

Local search in this step has the aim of determining a pattern of improving solutions and it is carried out over objective space directions.

With respect to P1, let $x^1, x^2 \in X$. The objective space direction defined by $c(x^1)$ and $c(x^2)$ is denoted $(c(x^1), c(x^2))$ and solutions lying on it are given by the following expression:

$$c(x) = c(x^1) + \lambda(c(x^2) - c(x^1)), \; \lambda \text{ scalar.} \qquad (1)$$

Local search is carried out as follows.

---

* λ_j can be set arbitrarily at 1 or a multiple thereof $\forall j$. While λ_i can be set at, say, 1000 λ_j.

** For convergence s must be finite and similarity must always be declared within some threshold (see Appendix).

If $c(x^k)$ is the current solution, the DM is asked to point out his preferred feasible solution $c(x^{kl})$ in the direction $(c(x^k), c(\tilde{x}^1))$. Then he is asked to point out in turn $c(x^{kr})$ in the directions $(c(x^{kr-1}), c(\tilde{x}^r))$, $r = 2 \ldots N$. If $c(x^k) \neq c(x^{kN})$ the pattern of improving solutions established is $(c(x^k), c(x^{kN}))$. If $c(x^k) = c(x^{kN})$ no pattern of improving solutions has been determined. (It is noted that at local search no movement from $c(x^k)$ is made unless a strictly preferred solution to it is encountered.)

To determine the DM's preferred solution in some objective space direction, say $(c(x^k), c(\tilde{x}^1))$ it is first necessary to determine all feasible solutions lying in that direction.

The feasible solutions in the direction $(c(x^k), c(\tilde{x}^1))$ are as follows:

$$c(x) = c(x^k) + \lambda(c(\tilde{x}^1) - c(x^k)), \quad \lambda^* \leqslant \lambda \leqslant 1, \qquad (2)$$

where λ^* is the minimum value of the scalar λ in the problem.

$$\begin{aligned} &\text{Min} \quad \lambda \\ &\text{s.t.} \quad c(x) = c(x^k) + \lambda(c(\tilde{x}^1) - c(x^k)) \\ &\qquad\; x \in X \\ &\qquad\; \lambda \text{ free.} \end{aligned} \qquad (P4)$$

Knowing λ^*, the DM can be shown $c(x)$ in expression (2) at small intervals of λ covering the range $[\lambda^*, 1]$. (x^{kl}) would then be the DM's preferred solution out of those shown to him. Alternatively, (see Geoffrion et al. [2], Figure 2) the DM can be shown on the same graph how each objective varies in value with λ, for $\lambda^* \leqslant \lambda \leqslant 1$, and he can then select his desired combination $c(x^{kl})$ of objectives values from the graph.

It is important to note certain aspects of the PASEB local search directions which led to their choice as local search directions.

Local search directions, as indeed all the PASEB directions of search, are in objective space. As in any real MOLP model variables exceed the objectives in number, by far, Objective space directions result in substantial interactive and computational savings when used instead of decision space directions. Decision space directions are immaterial in themselves to the DM whose preferences relate only to objective values at solutions to the problem.

It is noted that in PASEB, unlike in Pattern Search, local search directions have not been sought to be, each one in turn, parallel to one of the coordinate axes in the space the search takes place. This is because such local search directions would have implied looking for solutions preferred to the current one, keeping all but one of the objective values constant. In such a case, however, at no efficient current solution could local search reveal a pattern of improving solutions.

The chief advantage of the selected directions of local search is that they are likely to be well-diversified.

Each PASEB local search direction, in as much as it always allows an increase up to its maximal feasible value for the objective whose individually optimal solution, is used for defining that direction, and in any case it always allows a change to that objective's value. It is a direction which has a non-null projection in the direction of the coordinate axis of that objective, in objective space. In as much as PASEB local search directions do not ignore any objective space coordinate axis but are directions that attempt to approximate the objective space coordinate axes subject to allowing trade-offs between objectives, they can be said to be well-diversified.

A further reason why PASEB local search directions are likely to be well-diversified is because the individually optimal solutions used for defining the directions are "extreme" solutions to the problem because they are each obtained when one objective is given supreme importance over the remaining objectives. This means the individually optimal solutions are likely to be well-dispersed about the efficient boundary of the feasible region in the sense that such solutions would give approximate upper and lower bounds to the values each objective takes on the efficient boundary of the feasible region. The dispersed nature of the individually optimal solutions for a two-dimensional two objectives case, is illustrated in Fig. 1. There, the two individually optimal solutions of the problem bound precisely the range of values either objective takes over the efficient boundary of the feasible region. This, of course, is not generalisable, but is indicative of the nature of dispersion of individually optimal solutions that may be expected.

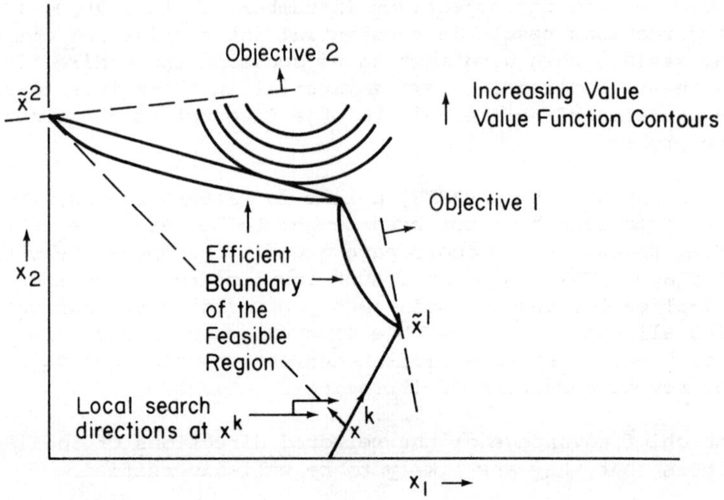

Fig. 1 $\tilde{x}^1$ and $\tilde{x}^2$ bound the values either objective takes in the efficient boundary of the feasible region

The diversified nature of the PASEB local search directions makes it likely that local search would normally reveal a pattern of improving solutions when the current solution is not close to a BCS. To see this it is noted that as any BCS to a MOLP problem lies in the efficient boundary of the feasible region, the isopreference contours of the DM's value function will be of higher and higher value as some part of that region is approached. The local search directions scanning towards well-dispersed points of that region are likely to meet contours of higher value than at the current solution, when the contour value at that solution is low. This can easily be illustrated at x^k in Fig. 1.

Step 3

In this step the fact is exploited that if the current solution is not efficient a dominating solution preferred to it exists and can be easily determined.

Let $c(x^k)$ be the current solution. Solve the following problem.

$$\text{Max} \quad Z = \sum_{i=1}^{i=N} e_i$$

$$\begin{aligned} \text{s.t.} \quad & c_i \cdot x - e_i = c_i \cdot x^k && i = 1 \dots N \\ & x \in X && \text{(P5)} \\ & e_i \geq 0 && i = 1 \dots N. \end{aligned}$$

Let x^{k+1} be an optimal solution to P5 and Z* the value of Z at x^{k+1}.

If $Z^* = 0$, $c(x^{k+1}) = c(x^k)$. The current solution is efficient and entry to step 4 takes place.

If $Z^* > 0$, $c(x^{k+1})$ dominates $c(x^k)$ and is preferred therefore to it. $c(x^{k+1})$ is the new current solution and entry to step 2 takes place. (It can easily be proved that $c(x^{k+1})$ is an efficient solution to P1.)

Step 4

In steps 4 and 5, a solution preferred to the current one is sought by attempting to move on the efficient boundary* of the feasible region, in the vicinity of the current efficient solution.

Let x^k be the optimal solution to P5, at which entry to step 4 takes place. When x^k is not a basic solution to P1, the DM's preferred solution in the direction of some desirable trade-offs between objectives offered by some non-basic variable at x^k is determined as follows. (A set of trade-offs between the objectives is desirable if for a marginal feasible move along them a solution preferred to the current is obtained).

Let a_{ij} be the coefficient of the jth non-basic variable in the row where e_i is basic for P5 at x^k. ($e_i = 0 \forall i$ at x^k.) Further, let $a_{ij} = 0$ if e_i is non-basic and $a_{ii} = -1$. Now it

* The possibility of the entire feasible region being efficient is ignored here. See however section 5.

can easily be seen that the vector of trade-offs between the objectives offered by the jth non-basic variable at x^k in P5 is:

$$c(a^j) = \{-a_{ij},\ i = 1 \dots N\}. \tag{3}$$

The set of feasible solutions lying in the objective space direction $c(a^j)$ at $c(x^k)$ are as follows.

$$c(x) = c(x^k) + \lambda c(a^j),\ \lambda_1 \leqslant \lambda \leqslant \lambda_2. \tag{4}$$

λ_1 and λ_2 are the minimal and maximal values of the scalar λ, respectively, in the following problem.

$$\begin{aligned} &\left.\begin{matrix}\text{Max}\\ \text{Min}\end{matrix}\right\}\ \lambda \\ &\text{s.t.}\quad c(x) = c(x^k) + \lambda c(a^j) \\ &\qquad\quad x \in X \\ &\qquad\quad \lambda \text{ free.} \end{aligned} \tag{P6}$$

If the jth non-basic variable under consideration at x^k is not an e_i variable, λ_1 in (4) is zero and P6 need only be solved to determine λ_2.

Knowing the range of feasibility of λ, the DM can be asked to point his preferred feasible solution in (4) in the same manner as at any local search direction in step 2.

It is recommended that, in step 4, non-basic e_i at x^k in P5 be the first to be checked for desirable trade-offs between the objectives. Such variables are, on the basis of the information generated in step 3, more likely than other non-basic variables at x^k to offer desirable trade-offs between the objectives.

This is for two reasons:

1. Solutions offered by non-basic e_i at x^k in P5 are likely to be efficient. As a non-basic e_i at x^k changes marginally in value, solutions generated will lie on the same face of

P1 (see Yu and Zeleny [16] expression (50) for the definition of a face of a MOLP model) as x^k, if no variable of P1, basic at zero level at x^k, changes value. Such solutions will be efficient because x^k is efficient and lies in the relative interior (for a definition of a relative interior point to a set, see Stoer and Witzgall [17], p. 88) of a face of P1, making that entire face efficient. (Yu and Zeleny [16], theorem 2.2). As there are no other a priori indications of what faces of P1 other than that of x^k are efficient, when attempting to move on the boundary of the feasible region it is clearly preferable to attempt to move over its face we know to be efficient rather than over other faces that may be inefficient*.

2. Under certain conditions, establishing whether the trade-offs between the objectives offered by the non-basic e_i at x^k in P5 are attractive is tantamount to establishing whether $c(x^k)$ is the DM's most desired solution on the face of P1 x^k lies. Clearly in such a case, the non-basic e_i at x^k provide an effective means to explore for further desirable solutions an efficient face of the feasible region.

The conditions referred to above are that all the non-basic e_i at x^k yield feasible solutions on the face of P1 on which x^k lies for a marginal both positive and negative value, and that the rank of the matrix of the gradients of the constraints defining the face in question is n - k*. (n is the dimension of x and k* is the number of non-basic e_i at x^k.) (For a formal proof, see Thanassoulis [18], Appendix 1.)

It is noted that it is not recommended that at x^k a check be carried out to establish whether the above conditions hold. This is too time-consuming simply to establish whether x^k is the DM's preferred solution on the face it lies. No conclusions can be drawn about global optimality of x^k, from a single face.

* It is not implied here that movement on the efficient boundary is always preferred to movement over inefficient interior solutions. Rather, if movement on the boundary is to be attempted, in the absence of further information about the DM's preferences, movement over the efficient boundary is preferred to movement over the inefficient boundary.

Step 5

The aim in this step is as in step 4. However, its implementation is slightly altered due to the following observation.

When x^k is a basic solution to P1, the P1 face on which it lies is a point. Thus, a non-basic variable at x^k in P5 will generate solutions different from x^k only if when it takes a marginal value a solution on a P1 face other than that of x^k is obtained. Such a solution will be a non-basic one to P1. A non-basic e_i variable at x^k in P5 now can only generate non-basic feasible solutions to P1 if, when it takes a marginal value, at least one of the P1 variables basic at zero at x^k in P5 takes a positive value. This implies such an e_i may take a marginal positive or negative value but never both.

On the basis of the foregoing observation, in step 5, for each non-basic variable at x^k in P5 the Simplex tableau is inspected to determine whether at a marginal value the variable generates non-basic feasible solutions to P1, and if the non-basic variable under consideration is an e_i variable, to determinein addition the sign of its marginal value for non-basic feasible solutions to P1. If, after this inspection, the non-basic variable is not discarded, the DM's preferred solution in the direction of the trade-offs between the objectives it offers is determined if the trade-offs are desirable. This is done in the same manner as for any non-basic variable at x^k in P5, in step 4. The only difference is that as now an e_i non-basic variable at x^k in P5 can only take a positive or negative value, but not both, P6 accordingly need only be maximised or minimised, respectively. Zero will form the lower or upper bound on λ in (4) accordingly. The e_i non-basic variables at x^k in P5 no longer have the same significance they had in step 4.

As x^k is now a basic solution to P1, in general, though not always, non-basic variables at x^k in P5 will lead to adjacent basic solutions to P1. Since x^k is an efficient basic solution to P1 at least one of its adjacent basic solutions is efficient (Yu and Zeleny [16], Theorem 3.7). If none of the directions at x^k leading to efficient adjacent basic solutions in P1 offers desirable trade-offs between the objectives, x^k is a BCS (Zionts and Wallenius [4], p. 657). Unfortunately not necessarily all such directions are generated by non-basic variables at x^k in P5.

Step 6

The theoretical basis of this step lies in Zoutendijk's [9] method of feasible directions for constrained optimisation.

The aim in step 6 is either to determine a solution preferred to the current and return to step 2, or failing that, to terminate at a satisfactory solution or a solution proved to be a BCS.

The execution of this step can be subdivided into two phases to be executed in the order outlined below.

Both of the phases use the linear model P7 below, which is described first.

Let x^k be the current solution and I_p and I_q index sets of objectives the DM wishes to see improve and worsen in value, respectively.

Consider the following models at x^k.

$$\text{Max } z_1 = \sum_{i \in I_p} c_i \cdot y - \sum_{i \in I_q} c_i \cdot y + \varepsilon \sum_{i \notin I_p \cup I_q} c_i \cdot y$$

or

$$\text{Max } z_2 = \nabla U(c(x^k)) . y$$

$$\begin{array}{lll}
\text{s.t.} & a_i \cdot y \leqslant 0 & i \in I_1 \text{ (b) } \cup AZ(t) \\
& a_i \cdot y = 0 & i \in I_2 \\
& 0 \leqslant y_j \leqslant 1 & j \in J \text{ (b) } \cup AZ(t) \qquad \text{(P7)} \\
& -1 \leqslant y_j \leqslant 1 & j \notin J \text{ (b) } \cup AZ(t) \\
& \Delta z_i - c_i \cdot y = 0 & i = 1 \ldots N \\
& \Delta z_i \text{ free.} & i = 1 \ldots N
\end{array}$$

y is a $(n \times 1)$ vector. $I_1(b)$, $J(b)$ are binding less than or equal constraints and non-negativity restrictions of P1 at x^k, respectively. I_2 is the set of equality constraints in P1. AZ(t) is the current set of anti-zigzagging restrictions defined below. ε is defined so that $0 < \varepsilon << 1$. Δz_i, $i = 1 \ldots N$ are the trade-offs between the objectives offered by y.

It can easily be seen that when AZ(t) = $\emptyset$, the feasible solutions to P7 are the feasible directions to P1 at x^k. (Hadley [19], p. 313, (9 - 19)). If AZ(t) $\neq \emptyset$, a subset of the feasible directions at x^k is defined by the constraints of P7. (Non-binding P1 constraints and non-negativity restrictions at x^k are ignored in P7 because they do not affect the set of feasible directions at x^k as they cannot be violated in the neighbourhood of x^k (Hadley [19], p. 360).)

The anti-zigzagging restrictions AZ(t) are progressively built as follows. Upon first entry to step 6, AZ(t) is set empty. At subsequent entries to step 6, the indices of those P1 constraints and non-negativity restrictions are retained in AZ(t), which upon entry to step 6 have been binding, non-binding and binding again, in that order, since the last time AZ(t) was set empty. AZ(t) is set empty, and P7 solved afresh if at some entry to step 6 it is found that P7, inclusive of AZ(t) $\neq \emptyset$, does not have a feasible solution offering desirable trade-offs between the objectives. Also, AZ(t) is set empty if P7, inclusive of AZ(t) $\neq \emptyset$, yields a solution offering desirable trade-offs between the objectives, but the DM's preferred solution is not at the maximum feasible step length from $c(x^k)$ along these trade-offs.

The purpose of the anti-zigzagging restrictions is to ensure convergence under certain assumptions, as will be seen later, as well as to speed up convergence. They speed up convergence because they ensure that constraints and non-negativity restrictions that appear repeatedly to limit movement in desired directions will not do so for the feasible direction to be determined next, as P1 restrictions treated as binding in P7 cannot limit movement in a feasible direction determined in P7.

With regard to the objectives of P7, only one is used at a time and they have the following meaning.

z_1 favours those feasible directions at x^k that improve and worsen, respectively, objectives in I_p and I_q. The third summation term in z_1 favours directions that can improve other objectives apart from those in I_p and I_q as well, but without prejudice to the desired changes for objectives in I_p and I_q. Clearly, if the DM could be expected to give relative weights to the desired changes for individual objectives in I_p and I_q, z_1 could be formulated accordingly to improve the likelihood of determining a good feasible direction at x^k. However, it is assumed that it is difficult for the DM to give such relative weighting.

z_2 cannot be explicitly formulated, but if it could, it is known (e.g. see Hadley [19], p. 302) that if P7 is solved to maximize z_2 when $AZ(t) = \emptyset$, if the optimal solution is y^* such that $z_2(y^*) \leqslant 0$, x^k would be a "constrained stationary point" to P2. Given $U(c(x))$ concave such a point would be the optimal solution to P2, (Hadley [19], p. 305), and therefore a BCS to P1. The optimality check, as will be seen shortly, is essentially based on this observation.

In both phases of this step it is necessary to determine the DM's preferred solution along the trade-offs between the objectives offered by some feasible solution y^* to P7. This is done as follows.

Let Δz_i^* be the values for Δz_i, $i = 1 \ldots N$ at y^*. The feasible solutions in the directions of the trade-offs between the objectives offered by y^* at $c(x^k)$ are as follows.

$$c_i \cdot x = c_i \cdot x^k + \lambda \Delta z_i^*, \; i = 1 \ldots N, \; 0 \leqslant \lambda \leqslant \lambda^*, \qquad (5)$$

where λ^* is the maximal value of λ in the following problem.

$$\begin{aligned} &\text{Max} \quad \lambda \\ &\text{s.t.} \quad c_i \cdot x - \lambda \Delta z_i^* = c_i \cdot x^k \qquad i = 1 \ldots N \\ &\qquad\quad x \in X \qquad\qquad\qquad\qquad\qquad\qquad \text{(P8)} \\ &\qquad\quad \lambda \leqslant 0. \end{aligned}$$

The DM's preferred solution from (5) is determined in the same manner as at any local search direction from (2).

The two phases of step 6 now are executed as follows.

During phase 1 P7 is solved with z_1 as the objective and the optimal solution is tested for desirable trade-offs between the objectives. If the test is successful the DM points out his preferred feasible solution along the trade-offs and entry to step 2 takes place. Otherwise the DM is asked to re-specify, if he so wishes, the sets I_p and I_q and the foregoing is repeated using z_1 accordingly modified for I_p and I_q. When the DM no longer wishes, to re-specify the sets I_p and I_q, if the current solution is satisfactory, termination occurs. Otherwise the optimality check (phase 2) begins.

It was observed earlier that the current solution x^k would be a BCS if it is the case that when $AZ(t) = \emptyset$*, the maximal value of z_2 in P7 is not positive. Since P7 is a bounded linear programming model, at least one of its basic solutions gives z_2 its maximal value in P7. z_2 will be positive at a basic solution to P7 if that solution offers desirable trade-offs between the objectives.

The optimality check is now performed as follows.

With respect to one of the basic solutions to P7, inclusive of its current set of AZ(t) restrictions, if any, the DM is asked to point out his preferred solution along the corresponding trade-offs between the objectives if they are desirable, and entry to step 2 occurs. If the trade-offs in question are not desirable the foregoing is repeated for the next basic solution to P7 and so on. If and when all basic solutions to P7 have been exhausted, if $A_z(t) = \emptyset$, termination occurs, the current solution having been shown to be a BCS. If $AZ(t) \neq \emptyset$, AZ(t) is set empty and step 6 is repeated from phase 1. (The DM this time need not specify the pairs of objectives I_p and I_q at the current solution as they are already available.)

It is interesting to note that if the DM is assumed capable of giving his marginal rates of substitution between the objectives at x^k, an approximation to $\nabla U(c(x^k))$ can be obtained in

---

* AZ(t) is of course not arbitrarily set empty, but only in accordance with the rules for building AZ(t) stated earlier.

the manner outlined by Geoffrion [2]et al. (p. 359) and z_2 in P7 can be formulated explicitly. Then in the context of the optimality check z_2 can be optimised directly in P7 to determine if some feasible solution to P7 offers desirable trade-offs between the objectives. However, it is assumed the DM would find it hard to give his marginal rates of substitution between the objectives and that is why instead the optimality check as outlined relies on the equivalent, more lengthy, but easier for the DM, task of checking a finite number of trade-offs between the objectives for desirability.

Step 7

Let $(c(x^k), c(x^{kN}))$ be the current pattern of improving solutions. The feasible solutions along $(c(x^k), c(x^{kN}))$ are as follows.

$$c(x) = c(x^k) + \lambda(c(x^{kN}) - c(x^k)), \ \lambda_1 \leqslant \lambda \leqslant \lambda_2, \qquad (6)$$

where λ_1 and λ_2 are, respectively, the minimal and maximal values of the scalar λ in the following problem.

$$\left.\begin{matrix}\text{Max}\\ \text{Min}\end{matrix}\right\} \lambda$$

$$\text{s.t.} \quad c(x) = c(x^k) + \lambda(c(x^{kN}) - c(x^k)) \qquad (P9)$$

$$x \in X$$

$$\lambda \quad \text{free}.$$

The DM is asked to select his preferred solution $c(x^{k+1})$ for $0 \leqslant \lambda \leqslant \lambda_2$ from (6) in the same manner as from (2) in any local search direction. Entry to step 2 takes places then with $c(x^{k+1})$ as the current solution.

The DM's preferred solution in (6) cannot be for $\lambda < 0$, because $c(x^{kN})$ is preferred to $c(x^k)$ and $U(c(x))$ is concave in X which is convex. (For proof, see Thanassoulis [18], Appendix 2). By the same token, if for some $0 < \lambda < 1$ in (6), a solution preferred to $c(x^{kN})$ exists, there cannot be some other solution in (6) for $\lambda > 1$ preferred to $c(x^{kN})$. However, to forestall the possibility of two interactions with the DM to determine his preferred solution in the direction of the pattern, it is suggested that P9 be solved first to determine λ_2.

Clearly, to economise on computing time, if the DM is amenable, he can first be asked to determine from (6), for $0 \leq \lambda \leq 1$, his preferred solution, and only if that is $c(x^{kN})$ itself need P9 be solved for λ_2, and if $\lambda_2 > 1$ a further interaction needs to take place to determine the DM's preferred solution in the direction of the pattern.

Step 8

The aim in this step is to break the sequence of similar current solutions at hand. This is attempted first by solving P5 at $c(x^k)$ to determine, if it exists, an efficient solution to P1 dominating $c(x^k)$. If the resulting solution is the same as $c(x^k)$ or similar to it, the sequence of similar current solutions has not been broken, and entry to step 6 takes place. Otherwise the sequence of similar current solutions has been broken and entry to step 2 takes place.

4. CONVERGENCE OF PASEB

PASEB can be shown to converge to a BCS under certain assumptions.

With reference to P2, let

$$U^k, \; k = 1 \; ... \tag{7}$$

be the value function values at consecutive PASEB current solutions. By the very nature of PASEB it is the case that

$$U^k > U^{k-1}, \; k = 2 \; ... \; . \tag{8}$$

In view of the continuity of the value function in P2, and the boundedness of X, (8) ensures that if the sequence (7) is finite, convergence to a BCS occurs.

If the sequence U^k is infinite, since X is bounded, in view of (8) U^k will have a finite limit, U*.

It can be shown in this case that U* is the maximal value of U(c(x)) in X under assumptions 1 and 2, stated in section 3, providing the sequence of decision space solutions corresponding to PASEB current solutions have a unique accumulation point. The sequence in question has at least one accumulation point but if more than one accumulation point exists convergence to a BCS cannot be proved. (See the Appendix.)

5. IMPLICATIONS OF RELAXING PASEB ASSUMPTIONS

Of the four assumptions about P1 and P2 made in section 3, the first two are sufficient to ensure that PASEB converges to a BCS to P2, under the proviso stated in the preceding section.

Assumption 3 implies that any BCS to a MOLP problem is an efficient one. This assumption is likely to hold for most real MOLP problems as an improved value for at least one objective at no deterioration to any other objective value should normally be desirable. If the assumption does not hold PASEB still progresses to improved solutions as before, but computational requirements could increase. This is because if assumption 3 does not hold steps 3 and 8 may occasionally yield a solution dominating the current, but not preferred to it. Such solutions should be rejected. Instead a solution in decision space terms should be determined corresponding to the current solution by solving P5 minimising Z, and entry from step 3 to step 4 or from step 8 to step 6 should take place. It must be noted that in such a case in step 4 non-basic e_i at an optimal solution to P5 may not offer efficient solutions as the current solution lies on an inefficient face. This, however, now is not too important as efficient solutions no longer have a special significance.

Assumption 4 is likely to hold for most MOLP problems (see Steuer [20], and Benayoun [8], p. 282). If it holds, the efficient solutions to the problem are on the boundary of the feasible region (Benayoun et al. [8]). If it does not hold, the entire feasible region of the problem may be efficient.* (Yu and Zeleny [16] - Remark 4.3).

If assumption 4 does not hold for a MOLP problem, PASEB still progresses to improved solutions as before. The only difference is that steps 3 and 8 cannot now yield dominating solutions and

---

* Such will be the case if and only if there exist scalars $\lambda_i > 0, i = 1 \ldots N$, such that $\sum_{i=1}^{i=N} \lambda_i c_i = 0$.

so preferred to the current one, if all feasible solutions are efficient. In such a case steps 3 and 8 are simply employed to yield a decision space solution corresponding to the current one before entry to the subsequent step takes place.

6. A NUMERICAL EXAMPLE

Consider the following MOLP model, solved also by Zionts and Wallenius [4] and White [6].

$$\begin{aligned}
\text{Max}\quad & c_1 \cdot x = 3x_1 + x_2 + 2x_3 + x_4 \\
\text{Max}\quad & c_2 \cdot x = x_1 - x_2 + 2x_3 + 4x_4 \\
\text{Max}\quad & c_3 \cdot x = -x_1 + 5x_2 + x_3 + 2x_4 \\
\text{s.t.}\quad & 2x_1 + x_2 + 4x_3 + 3x_4 \leqslant 60 \\
& 3x_1 + 4x_2 + x_3 + 2x_4 \leqslant 60 \\
& x_1, x_2, x_3, x_4 \geqslant 0 .
\end{aligned} \qquad \text{(P10)}$$

For convenience, the set of feasible solutions to P10 is denoted X.

It is assumed the DM's value function for P10 is as follows.

$$U(c(x)) = 0.58c_1 \cdot x + 0.21c_2 \cdot x + 0.21c_3 \cdot x. \qquad (9)$$

On the basis of the DM's value function, the BCS to P10 is

$$x^* = (12, 0, 0, 12) \qquad (10)$$

and

$$c(x^*) = (c_1 \cdot x^*, c_2 \cdot x^*, c_3 \cdot x^*) = (48, 60, 12). \qquad (11)$$

Using the DM's value function to answer interaction questions posed, PASEB progresses towards the BCS of P10 as follows.

Iteration 1

Step 1

Setting $\lambda_j = 0.001, \forall j$ and $\lambda_i = 1$ in P3, the following individually optimal solutions for the problem are obtained.

$$c(\tilde{x}^1) = (66, 30, -12) \tag{12}$$

$$c(\tilde{x}^2) = (20, 80, 40) \tag{13}$$

$$c(\tilde{x}^3) = (15, -15, 75). \tag{14}$$

Maximising $Z = c_1 . x + c_2 . x + c_3 . x$ on X yields the following first current solution:

$$c(x^1) = (24, 66, 66). \tag{15}$$

Step 2

The first local search direction is $(c(x^1), c(\tilde{x}^1))$.

In view of the linearity of $U(c(x))$ and the fact that $c(\tilde{x}^1)$ is preferred to $c(x^1)$, the DM's preferred feasible solution $c(x^{11})$ in the direction $(c(x^1), c(\tilde{x}^1))$ is

$$c(x^{11}) = c(\tilde{x}^1) = (66, 30, -12). \tag{16}$$

Similarly it is found that in the second local search direction $(c(x^{11}), c(\tilde{x}^2))$ the DM's preferred solution is

$$c(x^{12}) = c(x^{11}) = (66, 30, -12) \tag{17}$$

and in the final local search direction $(c(x^{12}), c(\tilde{x}^3))$ the DM's preferred solution is

$$c(x^{13}) = c(x^{12}) = (66, 30, -12). \tag{18}$$

Since $c(x^{13}) \neq c(x^1)$ entry to step 7 takes place.

Step 7

The pattern of improving solutions established is $(c(x^1), c(x^{13}))$ and the DM's preferred solution in the direction of the pattern is:

$$c(x^2) = c(x^{13}) = (66,\ 30,\ -12). \tag{19}$$

Iteration 2

Step 2

Since $c(x^2) = c(\tilde{x}^1)$ the first local search direction is trivial. Thus,

$$c(x^{21}) = c(x^2) = (66,\ 30,\ -12). \tag{20}$$

Since $c(x^{21}) = c(x^{11})$ the second and third local search directions of this step coincide with the second and third local search directions of step 2 in iteration 1, respectively. Clearly therefore we will have in the third and last local search direction of this step

$$c(x^{23}) = c(x^{13}) = (66,\ 30,\ -12). \tag{21}$$

Since $c(x^{23}) = c(x^2)$ no pattern of improving solutions has been established and step 3 is entered.

Step 3

P5 is now solved at $c(x^2)$, giving the following model.

$$\begin{aligned} \text{Max}\quad & Z = e_1 + e_2 + e_3 \\ \text{s.t.}\quad & c_1 \cdot x - e_1 = 66 \\ & c_2 \cdot x - e_2 = 30 \\ & c_3 \cdot x - e_3 = -12 \\ & x \in X \\ & e_i \geqslant 0 \qquad\qquad i = 1 \ldots 3. \end{aligned} \tag{P(11)}$$

At the optimal solution x^2 to P11 Z = O . x^2 is an efficient basic solution to P10. Entry to step 5 (via step 4) takes place.

Step 5

At x^2 in P11, e_1 is non-basic while e_2, e_3 and x_4 are basic at zero level.

If e_1 is made marginally negative, x_4 takes a positive value meaning for $e_1 < 0$ non-basic feasible solutions to P10 are generated. The trade-offs between the objectives offered by e_1 are desirable and they are as follows.

$$c(a^1) = (-1, 1.666, 1.333). \quad (22)$$

The feasible solutions along $c(a^1)$ at $c(x^2)$ are as follows:

$$c(x) = (66, 30, -12) + \lambda(-1, 1.666, 1.333) \quad 0 \leq \lambda \leq \lambda^*, \quad (23)$$

where λ^* is the maximal value of λ in the following model.

$$\begin{aligned} &\text{Max } \lambda \\ &\text{s.t. } c_1 \cdot x + \lambda = 66 \\ &\qquad c_2 \cdot x - 1.666\lambda = 30 \\ &\qquad c_3 \cdot x - 1.333\lambda = -12 \qquad \text{P(12)} \\ &\qquad x \in X \\ &\qquad \lambda \geq 0. \end{aligned}$$

P12 yields max $\lambda = \lambda^* = 18$. The DM's preferred solution from (23) is as follows.

$$c(x^3) = (48, 60, 12). \quad (24)$$

Iteration 3

We know that $c(x^3) = (48, 60, 12)$ is in fact the BCS to the problem. However, in the context of PASEB $c(x^3)$ has not yet been shown to be a BCS and termination does not take place until step 6 of this iteration is entered.

7. CONCLUSIONS

PASEB viewed in total may appear somewhat involved, particularly where the optimality check in step 6 is concerned. In practice, optimality as such hardly ever need be proved and the optimality check, if entered, would be merely to test for improving solutions some further feasible directions than hitherto tested at the current solution. Effectively shorn of its optimality check, PASEB is a relatively simple procedure for obtaining a "good" solution to a MOLP problem.

Viewed with respect to the practicability requirements laid down for it in section 2, PASEB can be expected to satisfy them by and large.

Interation phases in PASEB almost exclusively require the DM to make pairwise comparison of solutions only. This is an easy task as was argued in section 2. In step 6, the specification of the sets I_p and I_q, the only PASEB interaction not to rely on pairwise comparison of solutions, is similar but easier to the STEM interactive requirements where the DM must in addition state levels to which objectives must be relaxed. Wallenius [13] reports that in the STEM method decision makers had "some" difficulty stating levels to which objectives must be relaxed. In PASEB this difficulty is removed and the specification of the sets I_p and I_q should not prove too hard for the DM.

PASEB can be expected to exhibit a high initial rate of convergence. This is because using its optimal step length pattern moves the method climbs fast for the value function isopreference contours so long as it establishes patterns of improving solutions. The local search directions in the method were chosen, it was argued in section 3, to be well diversified so that they are likely to reveal a pattern of improving solutions when one exists. Therefore, PASEB can be expected to exhibit a fast initial rate of convergence.

Establishing constantly patterns of improving solutions is not only likely to lead to a high speed of convergence, but it will also mean low computational requirements. This is because in this case PASEB iterations would only consist of steps 2 and 7 (local search and pattern moves). Computational requirements in these two steps relate to determining the set of feasible solutions in various objective space directions. In this context, in step 7 if desired to reduce computational requirements only occasionally need P9 be solved to determine λ_2 as explained in section 3. In step 2 computational requirements can be reduced substantially as follows.

As an approximation, in (2), λ^* can be assumed always zero, eliminating computations in step 2. Alternatively, only if in (2) the solution for $\lambda = 0$ is preferred to all solutions for $\lambda \in [0,1]$ need λ^* be determined. (Otherwise it follows from Thanassoulis [18], Appendix 2 that the DM's preferred solution (2) cannot be for $\lambda < 0$.)

When local searches fail to reveal patterns of improving solutions PASEB iterations will involve steps 3, 4 or 5 and eventually 6. Each one of these steps naturally increases computational requirements. Thus, while under "normal" local search - pattern move progress computational requirements in PASEB should not prove severe, they can increase as that pattern of progress begins repeatedly to break down.

PASEB does not exclude solutions from further consideration during the solution process and so it can cope with an inconsistent DM.

Finally, under the qualifying assumptions discussed in section 4, PASEB can be shown to converge in principle to a BCS to the problem being solved.

Apart from the foregoing an important feature of PASEB is that using modern mathematical programming packages and a suite of small purpose-written computer codes, the method can be computerised effectively to eliminate the manual formulation of models in the context of PASEB steps. Solving a MOLP model by PASEB in that case reduces to running in the correct order a suite of computer programs with occasional intervention by the DM. (The author has one suite of such programs which are, however, problem specific.)

APPENDIX

CONVERGENCE OF AN INFINITE SEQUENCE OF PASEB CURRENT SOLUTIONS

With respect to P2 let the sequence U^k be as defined in (7), and let it be infinite with a limit U^*, as explained in section 4.

Let $\varepsilon > 0$ be such that if $c(x^k)$ and $c(x^{k+1})$ are two PASEB current solutions such that

$$U(c(x^{k+1})) - U(c(x^k)) \leqslant \varepsilon \qquad (A1.1)$$

the DM would treat $c(x^k)$ and $c(x^{k+1})$ as similar. ε is not explicitly stated by the DM nor need it be constant during the solution process. It is assumed however that there exists some very small $\varepsilon^0 > 0$ such that for $\varepsilon \leqslant \varepsilon^0$ the DM consistently treats $c(x^{k+1})$ and $c(x^k)$ as similar. Now in an infinite sequence U^k with U^* as a limit, clearly there will exist some k^0 such that

$$U(c(x^{k+1})) - U(c(x^k)) \leqslant \varepsilon^0 \quad \forall\, k \geqslant k^0. \qquad (A1.2)$$

In view of (A1.2) all current solutions after k^0 are similar. Given s finite in step 2, after k^0, the cycle of PASEB steps entered in each iteration will be 2 8 6 2 ... without local search taking place in step 2. The resulting solutions would be as follows then for the k^0th iteration on.

$$c(x^k_{b8}) \rightarrow c(x^k_{f8}) = c(x^k_{b6}) \rightarrow c(x^k_{f6}) = c(x^{k+1}_{b8}) \;\ldots \qquad (A1.3)$$

$c(x^k_{b8})$, $c(x^k_{f8})$ are the solutions at the beginning and finish of step 8, respectively. $c(x^k_{b6})$, $c(x^k_{f6})$ are the solutions at the beginning and finish of step 6, respectively.

Let an infinite sequence of solutions in (A1.3) associated with step 6, be as follows in decision space terms:

$$x^k_{b6},\; x^k_{f6},\; x^{k+1}_{b6},\; x^{k+1}_{f6} \;\ldots \qquad k = k^0 + 1,\; k^0 + 2 \;.. \qquad (A1.4)$$

In (A1.4) we may sometimes have $c(x^k_{f6}) = c(x^{k+1}_{b6})$ but we will always have $c(x^k_{f6})$ preferred to $c(x^k_{b6})$. Construct from (A1.4) an infinite sequence of solutions, omitting $c(x^{k+1}_{b_6})$ whenever it is not preferred to $c(x^k_{f_6})$

$$x^k, \ k = 1 \ldots . \tag{A1.5}$$

In view of the compactness of X the sequence (A1.5) has at least one accumulation point (Martos [21], p. 28, theorem 18). If the sequence (A1.5) has a unique accumulation point that point is shown below to be a constrained stationary point to P2. Such a point can then be shown to be a BCS to P2 due to the concavity of U(c(x)) and the convexity of X. (For proof see Hadley [19], p. 305).

Let x^* be a unique accumulation point to the sequence in (A1.5). Then $U^* = U(c(x^*))$. Moreover, x^* will be the limit to which the sequence (A1.5) converges. x^* can be shown to be a constrained stationary point to P2 by contradiction.

Let x^* not be a constrained stationary point to P2. At x^* there exists some small $\varepsilon > 0$ such that the following are true.

a) No constraint or non-negativity restriction not binding at x^* is binding at x, where $x \in \varepsilon(x^*) \cap X$. $\varepsilon(x^*)$ is the ε neighbourhood of x^*. However, some constraint or non-negativity restrictions binding at x^* may not be binding at some $x \in \varepsilon(x^*) \cap X$..

b) By the continuity of the gradient of U(c(x)) in X, and the fact that x^* is not a constrained stationary point, if r is a feasible direction at some $x \in \varepsilon(x^*) \cap X$ such that

$$\nabla U(c(x)) . \ r > 0 \tag{A1.6}$$

then, r satisfies (A1.6) at all $x \in \varepsilon(x^*) \cap X$. (See Zoutendijk [9], p. 343). $\nabla U(c(x))$ is the gradient of U(c(x)). A feasible direction r at some $x \in X$ satisfying (A1.6) is referred to at a usable direction.

In PASEB, each $c(x^{k+1})$ in (A1.5) which is an end of step 6 solution is determined as follows:

$$c(x^{k+1}) = c(x^k) + \lambda_k \ c(y^k), \tag{A1.7}$$

where $\lambda_k = \min(\lambda'_k, \lambda''_k)$. λ'_k is the maximal feasible and λ''_k the maximal desirable step length in the direction of the trade-offs between the objectives $c(y^k)$ at the current solution $c(x^k)$. y^k is a usable direction at x^k. Clearly in view of (A1.6) above, it is the case that for all solutions in (A1.5) within $\varepsilon(x^*)\cap X$ determined by (A1.7), $\lambda_k = \lambda_k'$.

If now the sequence (A1.5) is infinite and converges to x^*, there exists some k_1 such that x^k in (A1.5) is within $\varepsilon(x^*)\cap X, \forall\, k \geq k_1$.

Consider the following infinite sequence now derived from (A1.5).

$$x^k \quad k = k_1 + 1,\ k_1 + 2 \ldots \tag{A1.8}$$

where k_1 is as defined above.

Model P7 is set up at least at every other solution in (A1.8), with its anti-zigzagging restrictions if any. It can easily be seen that only constraints treated as non-binding in the context of P7 can restrict movement in any usable direction determined by that model. Hence, in view of a) above, only constraints binding at x^* but not yet treated as binding in the context of P7 may limit movement in usable directions determined by P7 at solutions from (A1.8). Thus, the anti-zigzagging restrictions can only increase in number progressively at solutions from (A1.8) P7 is set up, as some constraints binding at x^* are met each for the second time and retained as binding from then on. So long as step 6 yields solutions preferred to the current, the anti-zigzagging restrictions cannot be dropped because in (A1.7), $\lambda_k = \lambda_k'$. However, the constraints binding at x^* are finite in number and so after a finite number of solutions from (A1.8) at which P7 is set up, with its anti-zigzagging restrictions, it will be such that it contains all constraints binding at x^*. At that point the anti-zigzagging restrictions must be dropped as P7 cannot yield a usable direction. If it does, the next solution, since $\lambda_k = \lambda_k'$ in (A1.7), must be determined where that direction hits at least one constraint. That constraint, however, cannot be one binding at x^* and so the next solution in view of a) above cannot be in $\varepsilon(x^*)\cap X$.

After dropping its anti-zigzagging restrictions as above, model P7 will continue now to be set up at solutions from (A1.8) and its anti-zigzagging restrictions will increase as constraints binding at x^* are each met for the second time and retained.

The anti-zigzagging restrictions cannot now be dropped because always $\lambda_k = \lambda'_k$ in (Al.7) and in view of (Al.6) desirable and feasible directions exist at all solutions from (Al.8) P7 is set up. But the constraints binding at x* are finite in number and so after a finite number of iterations, P7 will comprise all constraints binding at x* and them alone. In view of (Al.6) P7 must yield a usable direction, but the new solution determined along it, in view of $\lambda_k = \lambda'_k$ in (Al.7) must be where the direction hits a constraint. Such a constraint cannot be binding at x* and the solution thus determined cannot be in $\varepsilon(x^*) \cap X$.

In view of the foregoing, if x* is not a constrained stationary point, there cannot be an infinite number of PASEB current solutions in its ε-neighbourhood, contrary to assumption.

If the sequence (Al.5) has more than one accumulation point each such point must give U(c(x)) the limit value U* of the sequence (7). However, U* cannot be now proved to be the maximal value of U(c(x)) in X.

REFERENCES

1. Belenson, S.M. and Kapur, K.C. 1973 "An Algorithm for solving multi-criterion linear programming problems with examples", *Op. Res. Q.*, **24**, 65-77.

2. Geoffrion, A.M., Dyer, J.S. and Feinberg, A. 1972 "An Interactive approach for multi-criterion optimisation, with an application to the operation of an academic department", *Mgt. Sci.*, **19**, 357-368.

3. Benayoun, R., de Montgolfier, J., Tergny, J. and Larichev, O.I. 1971 "Linear Programming with multiple objective functions: step method (STEM)", *Math. Prog.*, **1**, 366-375.

4. Zionts, S. and Wallenius, J. 1976 "An interactive programming method for solving the multiple criteria problem", *Mgt. Sci.*, **22**, 652-663.

5. Steuer, R.E. 1977 An interactive multiple objective linear programming procedure. In "Multiple Criteria Decision Making", (M.K. Starr and M. Zeleny, Eds.), TIMS Studies in the Management Sciences, North Holland, Amsterdam.

6. White, D.J. 1980 "Multi-objective interactive programming", *JORS*, **31**, 512-523.

7. Hooke, R. and Jeeves, J.A. 1965 "Direct Search solution of numerical and statistical problems", *J. Ass. Comput. Mach,* **8**, 212-229.

8. Benayoun, R. and Tergny, J. 1970 "Mathematical programming with multi-objective functions: A solution by P O P progressive orientation procedure", *Metra,* **9**, 279-299.

9. Zontendijk, G. 1959 "Maximising a function in a convex region", *J. Roy. Stat. B.,* **21**, 338-355.

10 Gal, T. 1977 "A general method for determining the set of all efficient solutions to a linear vector-maximum problem", *EJOR,* **1**, 307-322.

11. Fishburn, P.C. 1979 Utility Theory for Decision Making, R.E. Krieger Publishing Co.

12. Starr, M.K. and Zeleny, M. 1977 MCDM-State and future of the art. In "Multiple Criteria Decision Making", (M.K. Starr and M. Zeleny, Eds.), TIMS, North Holland, Amsterdam.

13. Wallenius, J. 1975 "Comparative evaluation of some interactive approaches to multicriterion optimisation", *Mgt. Sci.,* **21**, 1387-1396.

14. Zionts, S. and Wallenius, J. 1976 Some tests of an interactive programming method for multicriterion optimisation and an attempt at implementation. In "Multiple Criteria Decision Making", (S. Zionts and H. Thiriez, Eds.), pp. 319-331, Springer, Verlag, Berlin.

15. Dyer, J.S. 1973 An empirical investigation of a man-machine interactive approach to the solution of the Multiple Criteria Problem. In "Multiple Criteria Decision Making", (J.L. Cochrane and M. Zeleny, Eds.), pp. 202-216, University of South Carolina Press, Columbia.

16. Yu, P.L. and Zeleny, M. 1975 "The set of all non-dominated solutions in the linear case and a multi-criteria simplex method", *J. Math. Anal. Appl.,* **49**, 430-468.

17. Stoer, J. and Witzgall, C. 1970 Convexity and Optimisation in Finite Dimensions, I. Springer, Verlag, Berlin.

18. Thanassoulis, E. 1982 "PASEB: A Solution Procedure for Multi-Objective Linear Programming Problems," Warwick Papers in Industry, Business and Administration, Paper No. 1, CRIBA, University of Warwick.

19. Hadley, G. 1964 Non linear and dynamic programming, Addison-Wesley.

20. Steuer, R.E. 1976 "Multiple objective linear programming with interval criterion weights", *Mgt. Sci.*, **23**, 305-316.

21. Martos, B. 1975 Non linear Programming Theory and Methods, North Holland Publishing Company, Amsterdam.

MULTI-OBJECTIVE INTERACTIVE PROGRAMMING FOR EFFICIENT SETS

D.J. White

(Department of Decision Theory, University of Manchester)

1. Introduction

In White [2] the following problem is discussed. A decision maker has a compact action space $X \neq \phi$, and m continuous real valued objective functions $\{f^i\}$, $i=1,2,\ldots m$ defined on X. He also has a value function $\lambda^* f$ on X, with λ^* unknown, *a priori*, to the decision analyst. The decision maker cannot specify λ^* explicitly, but when presented with two actions $x,y \in X$, he will rank them implicitly, in terms of $\lambda^* f$. The following procedure is given for finding an optimal, or near optimal, $x \in X$, without necessarily finding λ^*.

(i) Choose $x \in X$. Set $S^1 = \{x^1\}$, z^1 to be the best point in S^1 $(= \{x^1\}$ in this case), $\Lambda^1 = \{\lambda \in R^m : \lambda \geqq 0, \sum_{i=1}^{m} \lambda_i = 1\}$, and let $\{\lambda^{1k}\}$ be the vertices of Λ^1, $k \in K^1$.

(ii) Let us assume that, at some stage, r, we have a feasible set $S^r = \{x^r, x^{r-1}, \ldots x^1\} \subseteq X$, with z^r a most preferred member of S^r, and a set $\Lambda^r = \{\lambda \in R^m : \lambda \geqq 0, \sum_{i=1}^{m} \lambda_i = 1$, and determined by preferences over S^r in 'at least as good as' form$\}$, with vertices $\{\lambda^{rk}\}$, $k \in K^r$. Then find $\sigma_r = \max_{x \in X} \max_{k \in K^r} [\lambda^{rk} f(x) - \lambda^{rk} f(z^r)]$. If $\sigma_r = 0$, stop. z^r is optimal in X. Otherwise if $\sigma_r > 0$, and x^{r+1} gives such a maximum, set $S^{r+1} = S^r \cup \{x^{r+1}\}$.

(iii) Find a best $z^{r+1} \in S^{r+1}$.

(iv) Set $\Lambda^{r+1} = \{\lambda \in \Lambda^r$: determined by any new preference knowledge on S^{r+1} obtained by bringing in $x^{r+1}\}$, and determine the generators $\{\lambda^{r+1k}\}$ of Λ^{r+1}. Return to step (ii).

The procedure may be interrupted to terminate at any acceptable solution.

It is shown in White [3] that, if the procedure terminates at some finite stage, then z^r is optimal for $\lambda^* f$. When termination is not finite, it is shown that if x^o is a limit point of the sequence $\{x^r\}$, then any subsequence $\{z^{r_t}\}$, corresponding to a convergent subsequent of $\{x^r\}$ with limit x^o, will converge to a point z^o, which is optimal for $\lambda^* f$.

In the present paper, we will relax the assumption concerning the existence of a value function, $\lambda^* f$, and replace the preference structure by something close to that studied in White [4] and related to that of Yu [5].

We will assume that the decision maker's implicit, unknown, preference structure, is determined by a set $\{\lambda\} = \Lambda \subseteq R^m$, $\lambda \geqq 0$, $\sum_{i=1}^{m} \lambda_i = 1$, $\forall \lambda \in \Lambda$, where Λ is a polytope, or the interior of a polytope, with vertex set $\{\lambda^k\}$, $k \in K$. The condition $\sum_{i=1}^{m} \lambda_i = 1$ is not necessary, but is a convenient normalising procedure. If R denotes 'at least as good as', when the decision maker is presented with two alternative actions $x, y \in X$, it is assumed that his response will be

$$xRy \rightleftarrows f(x) \geqq \lambda f(x), \quad \forall \lambda \in \Lambda. \qquad (1)$$

If P is strict preference, we will assume that P is identical with P_1 or P_2 where

$$xP_1y \rightleftarrows xRy, \quad y \not R x \qquad (2)$$

and

$$xP_2y \rightleftarrows \lambda f(y) > f(y), \quad \forall \lambda \in \Lambda. \qquad (3)$$

When $\Lambda = \{\lambda \in R^m : \lambda \geqq 0, \sum_{i=1}^{m} \lambda_i = 1\}$, definition (2) gives the usual efficient set, E_1 and definition (3) the 'weak efficient' set, E_2 (see Di Guglielmo [7]).

We are interested in finding the efficient set E, of X, with respect to P, i.e. Eff(X) where, for any subset $Y \subseteq X$,

$$\text{Eff}(Y) = E = \{x \in Y : \nexists\, y \in Y \text{ with } yPx\}. \quad (4)$$

In physical terms, for P_1, the decision maker, when given the choice between x and y, will only say 'x is at least as good as y', if it is at least as good as y for all possible objective functions $\{\lambda f\}$, $\lambda \in \Lambda$, and say 'x is preferred to y' if it is at least as good as y and preferred to y for some objective function. If one of the objective functions, $\{\lambda f\}$, subsequently turns out to be the right one, he loses nothing by keeping to E. A similar interpretation exists for P_2.

This framework has some similarities to that of Yu. Let

$$P = \{d \in R^m : d = f(y)-f(x), \text{ some } x,y \in X\}. \quad (5)$$

Then

$$xRy \rightleftarrows \lambda d \leqq 0, \quad \forall \lambda \in \Lambda. \quad (6)$$

If we assume Λ is a cone (by dropping the condition $\sum_{i=1}^{m} \lambda_i = 1$), with vertex 0, then Λ is the polar cone of P (see Rockafellar [6]). Hence we have

$$xRy \rightleftarrows f(y)-f(x) \in P. \quad (7)$$

In Yu, it is required that, for given cone, D,

$$f(y)-f(x) \in D / \{0\} \rightarrow xPy \quad (8)$$

This is similar to our definition of P_1, and Λ is the polar cone of D. It only operates in one direction however, and is a weaker requirement than that in this paper which is of an 'iff' form.

It is of interest to note that another difference lies in step (iii) of the main algorithm described in the next section, where E^{r+1} is replaced by the efficient set of S^{r+1} with respect to the approximating P^r at this stage. We will deal with the analogy of Yu's method in Section 5.

One can look at the set E in a slightly different way. Let $g^k = \lambda^k f$, $k \in K$. Then

$$E_1 = \{x \in X : \nexists\, y \in X, \lambda f(y) \geqq \lambda f(x), \ \forall \lambda \in \Lambda,$$
$$\lambda f(y) > \lambda f(x), \text{ some } \lambda \in \Lambda\}$$

$$= \{x \in X : \nexists\, y \in X, \quad g(y) \geq g(x)\} \tag{9}$$

$$= P_1 \tag{10}$$

where P_1 is the usual efficient set of $g(X)$ with respect to the usual vector order, $\geqq$, on R^q, if $\# K=q$, but where we do not know g in advance. Finding E_1 via our method would find P_1, but might not find g.

In what follows, for any subset $Y \subseteq X$, we define

$$I(Y) = \{x \in X : xIy, \text{ some } y \in Y\} \tag{11}$$

where

$$x,y \in X, \quad xIy \rightleftarrows xRy, yRx. \tag{12}$$

If we use E_2 for our efficiency, this would be equivalent to finding the weak efficient set P_2 (DiGuglielmo [7]) providing Λ is a polytope and not the interior of a polytope. We have

$$E_2 = P_2. \tag{13}$$

There is yet another interpretation we can place on E when X is convex and f is concave in its components.

If X is polyhedral and f linear in its components, then it is well known that if $V_1 = \{v=\mu g \in R^q, \mu>0, \sum_{k=1}^{q} \mu_k = 1\}$, and if M_1 is the set of all $x \in X$ which maximise v over X for some $v \in V_1$, then the efficient set of X with respect to g and the order $\geqq$ over R^q is identical with M_1. We thus obtain

$$M_1 = E_1. \tag{14}$$

Now

$$v = \mu g = \sum_{k=1}^{q} \mu_k g^k$$

$$= \gamma f \tag{15}$$

where

$$\gamma = \sum_{k=1}^{q} \mu_k \lambda^k \in R^m \tag{16}$$

$$\gamma_i = \sum_{k=1}^{q} \mu_k \lambda_i^k \geqq 0, \qquad i = 1,2,\ldots m \tag{17}$$

$$\sum_{i=1}^{m} \gamma_i = 1. \tag{18}$$

Thus if our initial problem is to find M_1, where $V_1 = \{v=\gamma f,$ for some $\gamma \in \Gamma\}$ and Γ is given by all solutions to (16), (17), (18) for some set $\{\lambda^k\}$ specified earlier on, taken over all μ specified above, then finding E_1 will be equivalent to finding M_1. In this case Γ is the interior of a polytope.

If we wish to use E_2, with X convex, and f concave in its components, we replace V_1 by a set $V_2 = \{v=\mu g \in R^q, \mu \geqq 0, \sum_{k=1}^{q} \mu_k = 1\}$. If M_2 is defined similarly to M_1, but relative to V_2 then the weak efficient set of X with respect to g and the order $>$ over R^q is identical to M_2. We then obtain

$$M_2 = E_2. \tag{19}$$

The analysis now follows in a similar manner to that of (15)-(18), except that '$\mu>0$' is replaced by '$\mu \geqq 0$', and Γ is a polytope.

Thus, although our original problem is to find E, or a suitable approximation to this, given the appropriate conditions, we equivalently find one or more of P_1, P_2, M_1, M_2.

Finally, if we know that P_2 prevails, it might be better to use strict inequalities for the set Λ^r at each stage, particularly if F^o, defined later, is desired. However we will, for the purposes of this paper, confine ourselves to the weaker inequalities.

2. The Procedure

The procedure is a modification of that given in the introductory section, *viz.*

(i) Choose $x^1 \in X$. Set $S^1 = \{x^1\}$, E^1 to be the efficient set of S^1 (= $\{x^1\}$ in this case), $\Lambda^1 = \{\lambda \in R^m : \lambda \geqq 0, \sum_{i=1}^{m} \lambda_i = 1\}$

and $\{\lambda^{1k}\}$ to be the vertices of Λ^1, $k \in K^1$.

(ii) Let us assume that at some stage, r, we have a feasible set $S^r = \{x^r, x^{r-1}, \ldots x^1\} \subseteq X$, with E^r as the efficient set of S^r, and a set $\Lambda^r = \{\lambda \in R^m : \lambda \geqq 0, \sum_{i=1}^{m} \lambda_i = 1$, and determined by known preferences over S^r in 'at least as good as' form$\}$, with vertices $\{\lambda^{rk}\}$, $k \in K^r$. Then find

$$\sigma_r = \max_{x \in X} \min_{z \in E^r} \max_{k \in K^r} [\lambda^{rk} f(x) - \lambda^{rk} f(z)]. \tag{20}$$

If $\sigma_r = 0$, stop. $I(E^r) = E$. Otherwise, if $\sigma_r > 0$, and x^{r+1} gives such a maximum, set $S^{r+1} = S^r \cup \{x^{r+1}\}$.

(iii) Find $E^{r+1} = \mathrm{Eff}\,(S^{r+1})$.

(iv) Set $\Lambda^{r+1} = \{\lambda \in \Lambda^r$: determined by any new preference knowledge on S^{r+1} obtained by bringing in $x^{r+1}\}$ and determine the vertices $\{\lambda^{r+1k}\}$ of Λ^{r+1}. Return to step (ii).

In determining Λ^{r+1} we only use the weak form given by R in (1), even though some preferences are elicited in strict P form.

3. Theory

Before dealing with the main results it is to be noted that E will be a kernel of X with respect to P under either definition of $P = P_1$ or P_2. A kernel is an efficient set which also has the property that $x \in X/E \rightarrow \exists\, y \in E$ with yPx. The fact that E_1 is a kernel comes from White [1], Theorem 6. The fact that E_2 is also a kernel may similarly be established, with a slight variation of the argument. Both proofs make use of Zorn's lemma. We henceforth assume E is a kernel.

We begin first of all with a lemma relating Λ, Λ^r and Λ^{r+1}. This in itself is useful if Λ is the prime aim, but as we shall see, in general $\Lambda \neq \Lambda^0 = \bigcap_{r=1}^{\infty} \Lambda^r$.

Lemma 1

$$\Lambda \subseteq \Lambda^{r+1} \subseteq \Lambda^r, \quad \forall\, r \geqq 1. \tag{21}$$

Proof

The right hand side inclusion is a consequence of the definition of Λ^{r+1}.

Now let $\Lambda(x,y) = \{\lambda \in R^m : \lambda \gtrsim 0, \sum_{i=1}^{m} \lambda_i = 1, \lambda f(x) \geq \lambda f(y)\}$, x, $y \in X$. If $x,y \in X$ and xRy we have $\Lambda \subseteq \Lambda(x,y)$. It is clear that $\Lambda^{r+1} = \bigcap_{x,y \in S^{r+1} : xRy} \Lambda(x,y)$. Hence $\Lambda \subseteq \Lambda^{r+1}$. Δ

Let us now look at a key feature of the algorithm which asserts that as long as there is a member of E which has not been included in E^r, either itself or some indifferent element, the process cannot terminate. For finite problems this is very useful. For infinite problems it is important but not quite so conclusive.

Since X is compact, and f is continuous, in its components, we may define, as in (20),

$$\sigma_r = \max_{x \in X} \min_{z \in E^r} \max_{k \in K^r} [\lambda^{rk} f(x) - \lambda^{rk} f(z)]$$

$$= \min_{z \in E^r} \max_{k \in K^r} [\lambda^{rk} f(x^{r+1}) - \lambda^{rk} f(z)]. \qquad (22)$$

We then have the following, which is the basis of step (ii) of the algorithm (see (ii) for definition of I).

Theorem 1

$$E \neq I(E^r) \rightarrow \sigma_r > 0. \qquad (23)$$

Equivalently

$$\sigma_r = 0 \rightarrow E = I(E^r). \qquad (24)$$

Proof

$E \not\subset I(E^r)$, since otherwise, since E is a kernel, we could reduce E^r.

Let $x \in E/I(E^r)$. Then

$$z \in E^r \rightarrow \exists\ \lambda \in \Lambda,\ \lambda f(x) > \lambda f(z)$$

$$\rightarrow \text{ (from lemma 1) } \exists\ \lambda \in \Lambda^r,\ \ \lambda f(x) > \lambda f(z)$$

$$\rightarrow\ \ \exists\ k \in K^r,\ \lambda^{rk} f(x) > \lambda^{rk} f(z). \tag{25}$$

From (25) we see that

$$\min_{z \in E^r}\ \max_{k \in K^r}\ [\lambda^{rk} f(x) - \lambda^{rk} f(z)] > 0. \tag{26}$$

Hence $\sigma_r > 0$ as required. Δ

Corollary 1

$$E \neq I(E^r) \rightarrow \sigma_r > 0 \rightarrow x^{r+1} \notin S^r. \tag{27}$$

Proof

Clearly $x^{r+1} \notin E^r$. If $x^{r+1} \in S^r/E^r$, then, since $\# S^r < \infty$, E^r is the kernel of S^r (see White [1], Theorem 3), and $\exists\ y \in E^r$ with yPx^{r+1}, and this implies that $\sigma_r \leqq 0$ contrary to hypothesis. Note that yPx^{r+1}, y, $x^{r+1} \in S^r \rightarrow \lambda f(y) \geqq \lambda f(x^{r+1})$, $\forall\ \lambda \in \Lambda^r \rightarrow \lambda^{rk} f(y) \geqq \lambda^{rk} f(x^{r+1})$, $\forall\ k \in K^r \rightarrow \sigma_r \leqq 0$.

It is possible to have $x^{r+1} \in I(S^r)/S^r$. Thus let: $X = \{x \in R^2 : x_1 + x_2 \leqq 1,\ x \geqq 0\}$, $f(x) = x$, $\forall\ x \in X$; $\Lambda = \{\lambda^*\}$, $\lambda^* = (\tfrac{1}{2}, \tfrac{1}{2})$; $x_1 = (1,0)$. Then $x^2 = (0,1)$ and $S^1 = \{x^1\}$, $x^2 \notin S^1$, but $x^2 I x^1$.

For many cases, $\sigma_r \neq 0$ for any finite r. When $\# X < \infty$, where $\# X$ is the number of elements in X, the procedure will terminate in a finite number of steps, as the following theorem gives.

Theorem 2

$\# X < \infty \rightarrow \exists\ r \geqq 1$ such that

$$\text{(i)}\ \ \sigma_r = 0 \tag{28}$$

$$\text{(ii)}\ \ E = I(E^r) \tag{29}$$

$$\text{(iii)}\ \ \Lambda^{r+1} = \Lambda^r. \tag{30}$$

Proof

Since $S^r \subseteq S^{r+1} \subseteq X$, $\forall\ r \geqq 1$, we must have $S^r = S^{r+1}$

for some $r \geq 1$. Hence $\Lambda^r = \Lambda^{r+1}$. Also, from Corollary 1, $\sigma_r = 0$, and then, from Theorem 1, $E = I(E^r)$. Δ

It is worth noting that, in general

(i) $\bigcap_{r=1}^{\infty} \Lambda^r \neq \Lambda$

(ii) $\sigma_r > 0 \nrightarrow E \neq I(E^r)$.

In order to illustrate this, let us consider the case when $K = \{1\}$ i.e. Λ consists of a single member λ^*, the case studied in White [2]. Let:

$$X = \{x \in R^2 : x_1+2x_2 \leqq 2,\ \ x_1 \geqq 0\},\quad f(x) = x,\ \forall\ x \in X,$$

$\Lambda = \{\lambda^*\} = \{(\frac{1}{2},\frac{1}{2})\}$, $P = P_1 = P_2$. Then $E = \{(2,0)\}$. Let us suppose that we begin with $\{x^1\} = (2,0)$, $S^1 = \{x^1\}$, $E^1 = \{x^1\}$. Then we generate the following sequence of results where $x^2 = (0,1)$.

$$S^1 = \{x^1\},\quad I(E^1) = \{x^1\} = E,\quad \Lambda^1 = \{\lambda \geqq 0,\ \lambda_1+\lambda_2=1\},$$

$$\lambda^{11} = (1,0),\quad \lambda^{12} = (0,1),$$

$$\sigma_1 > 0,\quad S^2 = \{x^2,x^1\},\quad E^2 = I(E^2) = \{x^1\} = E,$$

$$\Lambda^2 = \{\lambda \geqq 0:\ \lambda_1+\lambda_2 = 1,\ \ 2\lambda_1 \geqq \lambda_2\},$$

$$\lambda^{21} = (1,0),\quad \lambda^{22} = (\tfrac{1}{3},\tfrac{2}{3}),$$

$\sigma_2 = 0$. Process terminates.

Thus we obtain

(i) $\bigcap_{r=1}^{\infty} \Lambda^r = \Lambda^1 \cap \Lambda^2 = \Lambda^2 \neq \{\lambda^*\} = \Lambda$ (31)

(ii) $\sigma_1 > 0$, but $E = I(E^1)$. (32)

Theorem 2 gives us everything we might wish for in the case $\# X < \infty$. For $\# X = \infty$, the results are not so strong. A key set is E^o defined by

$$E^o = \bigcup_{r=1}^{\infty} E^r. \tag{33}$$

For any set $Y \subseteq X$ we define

$$\text{Eff}(Y) = \{x \in Y : \nexists\, y \in Y,\ yPx\} \tag{34}$$

where P may be equal to P_1 or P_2.

A set of central interest is $I(\text{Eff}(E^o))$. However even this is not strong enough in some ways. Thus it is possible to have some x in E but not in $I(\text{Eff}(E^o))$ or, indeed in $I(E^o)$. Thus let $X = \{x \in R^2 : x_1+x_2 \leqq 1,\ x_1 \geqq 0,\ x_2 \geqq 0\}$, $f(x)=(x_1,x_2)$ $\forall\, x \in X$, $\Lambda = \{\lambda \in R^2 : \lambda \geqq 0,\ \lambda_1+\lambda_2 = 1\}$, $\lambda^1 = (1,0)$, $\lambda^2 = (0,1)$, $P = P_1$ or P_2. Then it is easily seen that, with $x^1 = (1,0)$,

$$I(\text{Eff}(E^o)) = \text{Eff}(E^o) = E^o = \{(0,1)\} \cup \{(1,0)\} \cup \bigcup_{\substack{n \geqq 1 \\ 1 \leqq r \leqq 2^n - 1}} \{(r2^{-n}, 1-r2^{-n})\}, \tag{35}$$

and that

$$E = \{x \in X : x_1+x_2 = 1\}. \tag{36}$$

For the case $\# X < \infty$, we do get, from Theorem 2, the strongest result as follows.

<u>Theorem 3</u>

$$\# X < \infty \rightarrow E = I(\text{Eff}(E^o)) \tag{37}$$

<u>Proof</u>

For the r specified in Theorem 2, it is clear that $E^r = \text{Eff}(E^o)$, and the result follows from Theorem 2 again. Δ

For the case when $\# X = \infty$, it is natural to consider the closure $\bar{E}^o$ of E^o, and our subsequent analyses will be based on this. Even for this case it is to be noted that we can have an x which is a limit point of E^o but not in E.

Thus the last example, with X extended to include $\{x \in R^2 : x_2 = 0,\ 1 < x_1 \leqq 2\}$, and restricted to $P = P_1$ gives

$$E^o = \{(0,1)\} \cup \bigcup_{\substack{n \geqq 1 \\ 1 \leqq r \leqq 2^n - 1}} \{(r2^{-n}, 1-r2^{-n})\} \cup \{(2,0)\} \tag{38}$$

$$E = \{x \in X : x_1+x_2 = 1, \quad x_1 \neq 1\} \cup \{(2,0)\}. \quad (39)$$

Then the point $x = (1,0)$ is a limit point of E^o but not in E.

Let us now study the case when $\# X$ may be infinite. A crucial aspect is the behaviour of $\{\sigma_r\}$ given in (20).

<u>Lemma 2</u>

$\{\sigma_r\}$ is monotonic decreasing to 0 as r tends to ∞.

<u>Proof</u>

$$\sigma_r = \max_{x \in X} \min_{z \in E^r} \max_{k \in K^r} [\lambda^{rk} f(x) - \lambda^{rk} f(z)]$$

$$= \max_{x \in X} \min[\min_{z \in E^{r+1} \cap E^r} \max_{k \in K^r} [\lambda^{rk} f(x) - \lambda^{rk} f(z)],$$

$$\min_{z \in E^r / E^{r+1}} \max_{k \in K^r} [\lambda^{rk} f(x) - \lambda^{rk} f(z)]], \quad (40)$$

$$\sigma_{r+1} = \max_{x \in X} \min_{z \in E^{r+1}} \max_{k \in K^{r+1}} [\lambda^{r+1k} f(x) - \lambda^{r+1k} f(z)]$$

$$= \max_{x \in X} \min[\min_{z \in E^{r+1} \cap E^r} \max_{k \in K^{r+1}} [\lambda^{r+1k} f(x) - \lambda^{r+1k} f(z)],$$

$$\min_{z \in E^{r+1} / E^r} \max_{k \in K^{r+1}} [\lambda^{r+1k} f(x) - \lambda^{r+1k} f(z)]. \quad (41)$$

Now for any non-negative vector valued functions with $g(x,z) \in R^m$, we have, since $\Lambda^{r+1} \subseteq \Lambda^r$,

$$\lambda^{r+1k} g(x,z) = \sum_{k' \in K^r} \mu_{k'} \lambda^{rk'} \quad (42)$$

for some $\{\mu_{k'}\}$ such that $\sum_{k'} \mu_{k'} = 1$, and $\mu_{k'} \geqq 0$, $\forall\, k' \in K^r$.

Hence

$$\max_{k \in K^{r+1}} [\lambda^{r+1k} g(x,z)] \leqq \max_{k \in K^r} [\lambda^{rk} g(x,z)] \quad (43)$$

Since we can clearly ignore negative contributions to (40) and (41), for each $x \in X$, we see that the left hand side terms in (40) and (41), restricted to $E^{r+1} \cap E^r$, are at least as low in (41) as in (40).

Let us now consider the right hand side of (40) restricted to E^r/E^{r+1} and the right hand side of (41) restricted to E^{r+1}/E^r. Now if $E^{r+1}/E^r = \{x^{r+1}\}$, and if $z \in E^r/E^{r+1}$, then $x^{r+1}Pz$, and hence Λ^{r+1} is chosen so that $\lambda^{r+1k}f(x^{r+1}) \geqq \lambda^{r+1k}f(z)$, $\forall\, k \in K^{r+1}$. Then, using (43) again, we see that, for non-negative contributions,

$$\max_{k\in K^r} [\lambda^{rk}f(x) - \lambda^{rk}f(z)]$$

$$\geqq \max_{k\in K^{r+1}} [\lambda^{r+1k}f(x) - \lambda^{r+1k}f(z)]$$

$$\geqq \max_{k\in K^{r+1}} [\lambda^{r+1k}f(x) - \lambda^{r+1k}f(x^{r+1})]. \quad (44)$$

The only other possibility is $E^{r+1}/E^r = \phi$. In this case $E^{r+1} = E^r$, and the requisite result clearly holds.

We have thus established that $\sigma_r \geqq \sigma_{r+1}$ i.e. $\{\sigma_r\}$ is monotonic decreasing. Let us now prove that the limit is 0.

Since X is compact, we may choose a subsequence $\{r_t\}$ such that $\{x^{r_t+1}\}$ converges to a point $x^o \in X$. We have

$$0 \leqq \sigma_{r_{t+1}} = \min_{z\in E^{r_{t+1}}} \max_{k\in K^{r_{t+1}}} [\lambda^{r_{t+1}k} f(x^{r_{t+1}+1}) - \lambda^{r_{t+1}k} f(z)]. \quad (45)$$

Given $\varepsilon > 0$, we can find a t_o, such that

$$|x^{r_{t+1}+1} - x^{r_t+1}| \leqq \varepsilon \quad \text{for } t \geqq t_o. \quad (46)$$

If $x^{r_t+1} \in E^{r_{t+1}}$, from (45), (46), we have

$$0 \leqq \sigma_{r_{t+1}} \leqq \max_{k\in K^{r_{t+1}}} [\,|\lambda^{r_{t+1}k} f(x^{r_{t+1}+1}) - \lambda^{r_{t+1}k} f(x^{r_t+1})|\,]$$

$$\leqq \sigma(\varepsilon) \quad (47)$$

where $\sigma(\varepsilon)$ tends to 0 as ε tends to 0, from the continuity of the components f^i of f, $i = 1,2,..m$, and where $\sigma(\varepsilon)$ may depend on x^o.

If $x^{r_{t+1}} \notin E^{r_{t+1}}$, then $\exists\ z \in E^{r_{t+1}}$ with $zPx^{r_{t+1}}$. Then by definition of $\Lambda^{r_{t+1}}$ we have

$$\lambda^{r_{t+1}k} f(z) \geqq \lambda^{r_{t+1}k} f(x^{r_t+1}), \quad \forall\ k \in K^{r_{t+1}}. \tag{48}$$

In this case we still obtain (47).

Since we may make ε, and hence $\sigma(\varepsilon)$, as small as we wish, we obtain the desired result. Δ

We are now in a position to prove our main theorem which says that, in some limiting sense, the algorithm gives exactly E.

<u>Theorem 4</u>

$$E = I(\mathrm{Eff}(\bar{E}^{o})). \tag{49}$$

<u>Proof</u>

Let $x \in E$. Then

$$\begin{aligned}\sigma_r &\geqq \min_{z\in E^r} \max_{k\in K^r} [\lambda^{rk} f(x) - \lambda^{rk} f(z)] \\ &\geqq \min_{z\in E^r} \max_{k\in K} [\lambda^{k} f(x) - \lambda^{k} f(z)] \geqq 0, \quad \forall r.\end{aligned} \tag{50}$$

Then

$$\begin{aligned}0 &\leqq \inf_{z\in E^o} \max_{k\in K} [\lambda^{k} f(x) - \lambda^{k} f(z)] \\ &= \inf_r \min_{z\in E^r} \max_{k\in K} [\lambda^{k} f(x) - \lambda^{k} f(z)] \\ &\leqq \inf_r [\sigma_r] = 0.\end{aligned} \tag{51}$$

Since f is continuous in its components f^i, $i = 1,2,\ldots m$, and $\bar{E}^o$ is compact we see that $\exists\ z \in \bar{E}^o$ such that

$$\max_{k\in K} [\lambda^{k} f(x) - \lambda^{k} f(z)] = 0 \tag{52}$$

From (52) we have

$$\lambda^k f(x) \leqq \lambda^k f(z), \quad \forall\, k \in K \tag{53}$$

and hence

$$\lambda f(x) \leqq \lambda f(z), \quad \forall\, \lambda \in \Lambda. \tag{54}$$

Since $x \in E$, we must have

$$\lambda f(x) = \lambda f(z), \quad \forall\, \lambda \in \Lambda \tag{55}$$

and hence

$$xIz \in E\,. \tag{56}$$

This establishes that

$$E \subseteq I(\mathrm{Eff}(\overline{E}^{o})) \subseteq X. \tag{57}$$

Since E is a kernel of X with respect to R, we see from Thoerem 11 of White [1] that

$$= \mathrm{Eff}(I(\mathrm{Eff}(\overline{E}^{o}))) = I(\mathrm{Eff}(\overline{E}^{o})). \tag{58}$$

Δ

4. Limits of Set

The previous analysis has been carried out in the context of the fundamental set $E^{o} = \bigcup_{r \geqq 1} E^{r}$. It is of interest to see if the results may be obtained in terms of 'limits' of sequences of sets, rather than in terms of 'unions' of sequences of sets. This is a natural thing to do particularly where sets are nested, as in the sequence $\{S^r\}$. We will deal with the concepts of 'set theoretic' limits and limits defined in terms of distances between sets. The latter is particularly important when it comes to devising actual approximating computational schemes.

Although, as we shall see, everything works out quite nicely for the sequence $\{S^r\}$, things are not quite so nice for the sequence $\{E^r\}$. Let $S^o = \bigcap_{r \geqq 1} S^r$.

Let $A, B \subset R^n$, and consider the following Hausdorf distance for sets (see Kelly [8]). Note that we are not assuming any metric properties.

$$\tau(A,B) = \max[d(A,B), d(B,A)]. \tag{59}$$

where

$$d(A,B) = \sup_{x \in A} \inf_{y \in B} [\|a-b\|] \tag{60}$$

$\|a-b\|$ is the Euclidean norm.

We then have the following theorem.

Theorem 5

$$\lim_{r\to\infty} \tau(S^o, S^r) = 0. \tag{61}$$

Proof

$$S^r \subseteq S^o \to \sup_{x\in S^r} \inf_{y \in S^o} [\|x-y\|] = 0 \to (d(S^r,S^o) \to 0), \ \forall\ r \geqq 1. \tag{62}$$

Now suppose, given $\varepsilon > 0$, $\forall\ u \geq 1$, $d(S^o, S^r) \geqq \varepsilon$ for some $r \geqq u$. Then $\exists$ sequence $\{r_t\} \to \infty$, such that for each r_t $\exists$ $x_t \in S^o$ such that $d(x^{r_t}, S^{r_t}) > \varepsilon$, where A is the singleton, written x^{r_t}.

Since X is compact we can choose a subsequence $\{r_q\} \subseteq \{r_t\}$ such that $\{x^{r_q}\} \to x^o$, some $x^o \in X$. Then

$$d(x^o, S^{r_q}) \geqq d(x^{r_q}, S^{r_q}) - d(x^o, x^{r_q}), \ \forall r_q. \tag{63}$$

Then, $\exists\ r^* \geqq 1$ such that

$$d(x^o, x^{r_q}) \leqq \varepsilon/4, \quad \forall\ r_q \geqq r^* \tag{64}$$

and hence

$$d(x^o, S^{r_q}) \geqq 3\varepsilon/4, \quad \forall\ r_q \geqq r^*. \tag{65}$$

Now

$$S^o = \bigcup_{r \geqq r_q} S^{r_q}, \quad \text{for any } r_q \tag{66}$$

$$\bigcup_{r \geqq r^*} S^r. \tag{67}$$

Hence

$$\alpha(x^o, S^o) = \inf_{r_q \geqq r^*} [d(x^o, S^{r_q})] \geqq 3\varepsilon/4\ . \tag{68}$$

Then

$$d(x^o, x^{r_q}) + d(x^{r_q}, S^o) \geqq 3\varepsilon/4, \quad \forall r_q \tag{69}$$

and hence

$$d(x^{r_q}, S^o) \geqq \varepsilon/2, \quad \forall\, r_q \geqq r^*. \tag{70}$$

This contradicts the fact that $x^{r_q} \in S^o$, $\forall\, r_q$.

Hence the requisite result follows. Δ

S^o is therefore a limit of $\{S^r\}$, written $L(\{S^r\})$, in the Hausdorf sense. Such a limit is unique in the sense that if S^* were any other limit, then

$$\tau(S^o, S^*) = 0 \tag{71}$$

This is easily established.

It is possible to consider set theoretic limits (see Halmos [9]). For a sequence $\{A^r\}$, the following sets are defined.

$$A^o = \bigcap_{s=1}^{\infty} \bigcup_{r=s}^{\infty} A^r \tag{72}$$

$$A_o = \bigcup_{s=1}^{\infty} \bigcap_{r=s}^{\infty} A^r . \tag{73}$$

We have $A_o \subseteq A^o$, and, if $A_o = A^o$, either is said to be the limit of $\{A^r\}$. For nested sets, limits exist, and hence $\{S^r\}$ has a limit. It is trivial to show that this limit is S^o.

The important limit is however, for our purposes, the one arising from the Hausdorf distance, since computational approximations need some such distance.

We may use this result to reinterpret Theorem 4 in terms of S^o. First of all we prove a lemma.

Lemma 3

$$\text{(i)} \quad \text{Eff}(E^o) = \text{Eff}(S^o) \tag{74}$$

$$\text{(ii)} \quad I(\text{Eff}(\bar{E}^o)) = I(\text{Eff}(\bar{S}^o)). \tag{75}$$

Proof

(i) Let $x \in \text{Eff}(E^o/\text{Eff}(S^o)$. Then, since $E^o \subseteq S^o$, $\exists\, y \in S^o/E^o$ with yPx. Since $y \notin E^o$, $y \notin E^r$ for any r. Since $y \in S^o$, $y = x^{r+1}$ for some r (note $y \notin E^1$), and $\exists\, z \in E^r$ with zPy. Then zPx, with $z \in E^r \subseteq E^o$, contradicting

$x \in \mathrm{Eff}(E^o)$.

Let $x \in \mathrm{Eff}(S^o)/\mathrm{Eff}(E^o)$ then $x \in E^o$, $\exists\ y \in E^o \subseteq S^o$, with yPx, contradicting $x \in \mathrm{Eff}(S^o)$. If $x \notin E^o$, Then $y \notin E^r$ for any r. Since $y \in S^o$,, $y = x^{r+1}$ for some r (note $y \notin E^1$), and $\exists\ z \in E^r$ with zPy. Since $y \in S^o$, this implies that $x \notin \mathrm{Eff}(S^o)$, contrary to hypothesis.

(ii) Let $y \in I(\mathrm{Eff}(\bar{S}^o))/((\mathrm{Eff}(\bar{E}^o))$. Then $yIx \in \mathrm{Eff}(\bar{S}^o)$. If $x \in S^o$ then it is easy to show that $\exists\ y \in \bar{S}^o$ with yPx, contradicting $x \in \mathrm{Eff}(\bar{S}^o)$. If $x \notin S^o$, then x is a limit point of S^o. Hence either $\exists$ subsequence of points $\{x^{r_t}\} \subseteq S^o/E^o$ converging to x, or $\exists$ subsequence of points $\{x^{r_t}\} \subseteq E^o$ converging to x. In the latter case $x \in \bar{E}^o \subseteq \bar{S}^o$, and $\exists\ \bar{y} \in \bar{E}^o \subseteq \bar{S}^o$ with yPx, contradicting $x \in I(\mathrm{Eff}(\bar{S}^o))$. In the former case, $\exists$ subsequence of points $\{y^{r_t}\} \subseteq E^o$, with $y^{r_t} P x^{r_t}$, $\forall\ r$. Since X is compact, $\exists$ sub-subsequence $\{y^{r_s}\} \subseteq \{y^{r_t}\}$ converging to a limit point $\bar{y} \in \bar{E}^o \subseteq \bar{S}^o$ and $\bar{y}Rx$. Since $x \in \mathrm{Eff}(\bar{S}^o)$ we must have $\bar{y}Ix$, and $\bar{y} \in \mathrm{Eff}(\bar{E}^o)$, contradicting $x \notin I(\mathrm{Eff}(\bar{E}^o))$.

Let $x \in I(\mathrm{Eff}(\bar{E}^o))/I(\mathrm{Eff}(\bar{S}^o))$. Then $\bar{y} \in \mathrm{Eff}(\bar{E}^o)$ with $xI\bar{y}$, and $\exists\ z \in \bar{S}^o$ with $zP\bar{y}$. If $z \in S^o$, then $z = x^{r+1}$ for some $r \geq 1$, since if $r = 0$, then $x^1 \in E^1 \subseteq E^o$, and this contradicts $\bar{y} \in \mathrm{Eff}(\bar{E}^o)$. If $z \in E^o$ we get the same contradiction. If $z \notin E^o$, then $\exists\ u \in E^o$ with uPz, and then $uP\bar{y}$, and again we get a contradiction to $\bar{y} \in \mathrm{Eff}(\bar{E}^o)$. Now let $z \notin S^o$. Then $\exists$ subsequence $\{z^{r_t}\} \subseteq S^o$ converging to z. Then either $\exists$ subsequence $\{w^{r_s}\} \subseteq E^o$ converging to z, or $\exists$ subsequence $\{w^{r_s}\} \subseteq S^o/E^o$ converging to z. In the former case $z \in E^o$, and this again contradicts $\bar{y} \in \mathrm{Eff}(\bar{E}^o)$. In the latter case, $\exists$ subsequence $\{u^{r_p}\} \subseteq E^o$, converging to some $u \in \bar{E}^o$ with $u^{r_p} P z^{r_p}$, $\forall p$, and uRz, and hence uPy, again contradicting $\bar{y} \in \mathrm{Eff}(\bar{E}^o)$. Δ

Using the Hausdorf limit, Lemma 3 takes the form

$$\text{(i)}\quad \mathrm{Eff}(E^{o}) = \mathrm{Eff}(L(\{S^{r}\})) \tag{76}$$

$$\text{(ii)}\quad I(\mathrm{Eff}(\bar{E}^{o})) = I(\mathrm{Eff}(\overline{L(\{S^{r}\})})) \tag{77}$$

and, from (ii) and Theorem 4, we have

$$E = I(\mathrm{Eff}(\overline{L(\{S^{r}\})})). \tag{78}$$

It is to be noted that, in general, $\overline{L(\{A^{r}\})} \neq L(\{\overline{A^{r}}\})$.

If $E^{r} \subseteq E^{r+1}$, some $u \geqq 1$, $\forall\, r \geqq u$, a similar analysis will give

$$= I(\mathrm{Eff}(\bar{E}^{o})) = I(\mathrm{Eff}(\overline{L(E^{r})})). \tag{79}$$

Unfortunately it is not always the case that $\{E^{r}\}$ is nested, and (79) can fail even in some relatively nice situations, e.g. in convex problems. Thus consider the following example.

Let: $\{a_i\}$, $i = 0,1,2,\ldots$, $\{b_i\}$, $i = 0,1,2,\ldots$ be two sequences of non-negative rational numbers with

$$a_o = 0,\quad \{a_i\}\ \text{monotonically increasing to 1,}$$
$$b_o = 3,\quad \{b_i\}\ \text{monotonically decreasing to 2;}$$

$\{p_i\}$, $\{q_i\}$ be two sequences, of non-negative rational numbers with

$$p_o = 0,\quad \{p_i\}\ \text{monotonically increasing to e,}$$
$$q_o > e,\quad \{q_i\}\ \text{monotonically decreasing to e;}$$

$\{y_i\}$, $\{z_i\}$ be two sequences of numbers defined by

$$y_o = 1,\quad y_{i+1} = y_i - p_i(a_{i+1} - a_i),\quad \forall\, i \geqq 0$$
$$z_o = \lim_{i\to\infty}[y_i] - e - \sum_{i=0}^{\infty} q_i(b_i - b_{i+1})$$
$$z_{i+1} = z_i - q_i(b_i - b_{i+1}),\qquad z \geqq 0.$$

Then let: $X = \{x \in R^2\colon 0 \leqq x_1 \leqq 3$, and $x_1 \in [a_i, a_{i+1}] \to z_o \leqq x_2 \leqq ((x_1 - a_i)y_{i+1} + (a_{i+1} - x_1)y_i)/(a_{i+1} - a_i)$, $x_1 \in [b_{i+1}, b_i] \to z_o \leqq x_2 \leqq ((b_i - x_1)z_{i+1} + (x_1 - b_{i+1})z_i)/(b_i - b_{i+1})$, $1 \leqq x_1 \leqq 2 \to z_o \leqq x_2 \leqq ((2 - x_1)y_\infty + (x_1 - 1)z_\infty)\}$; $f(x) = x$, $\forall\, x \in X$; $\Lambda = \{\lambda^*\}$, $\lambda^* = (e/(1+e),\ 1/(1+e))$.

In effect X is a convex region bounded above by an infinite number of piecewise linear segments, with a middle part of slope e.

Beginning with $x^1 = (3,z_0)$, we move to the point $x^2 = (0,1)$. The slope of the line joining these is a rational number, h_1 say, giving λ^{21} and λ^{22} having rational components. At the next step we must pick up a point to the left of $(1,y_\infty)$ or the right of $(2,z_\infty)$. The process continues. We never pick up these points or any point on the line joining them, which constitutes E. We must also visit the left hand side and the right hand side indefinitely, as is easily demonstrated. The sets $\{E^r\}$ are not nested. They consist of singletons $\{z^r\}$. Clearly they do not converge in either of the two senses given.

It is possible to get some results of a similar kind to those for $\{S^r\}$ for $\{E^r\}$. Thus if we define $\eta^r = \bigcup_{s \geq r} E^s$, $\eta^o = \bigcap_{r \geq 1} \eta^r$, then if $\eta^o \neq \emptyset$, we have $\tau(\eta^o, \eta^r) \to 0$ as $r \to \infty$, and $E = I(\mathrm{Eff}(\bar{\eta}^o))$.

5. Efficiency with Respect to Λ^o and Λ^r

In Yu [5], the method involved finding efficient sets of X with respect to a sequence of cones $\{D^r\}$. Let us now similarly look at efficiency, in our paper, with respect to the sets $\{\Lambda^r\}$. Let, for any $Y \subseteq X$,

$$\mathrm{Eff}^r(Y) = \{x \in Y : \nexists\ y \in Y,\ yP^r x\} \tag{80}$$

where P^r is defined as in (2) or (3) with Λ^r replacing Λ, and

$$F^r = \mathrm{Eff}^r(X), \quad \forall\ r \geqq 0 \tag{81}$$

$$\Lambda^o = \cap_r \Lambda^r. \tag{82}$$

P^o is defined with respect to Λ^o.

Since each Λ^r is compact and non-empty, $r \geqq 1$, Λ^o is compact and non-empty.

In general $\Lambda^o \neq \Lambda$, as has already been demonstrated. Nor is $F^o = E$ in general for $P = P_1$ or P_2.

Consider the following example for $P = P_1$. $X = \{x \in R^2 : 0 \leqq x_1 \leqq 1, x_2 = 0\}$, $f(x) = x$, $\forall\, x \in X$, $\Lambda = \{\lambda^*\}$, $\lambda^* = (0,1)$. Then $E = X$. Let us begin with $x^1 = (1,0)$. Then $E^1 = \{x^1\}$, $\Lambda^1 = \{\lambda \in R^2 : \lambda \geqq 0,\ \lambda_1 + \lambda_2 = 1\}$, $\lambda^{11} = (1,0)$, $\lambda^{12} = (0,1)$. $\sigma_1 = 0$ and $\Lambda^o = \Lambda^1$, in which case $F^o = \{x^1\}$, and $F^o \subset E$.

Consider the following example for $P = P_2$. Let everything be as for the previous example, but $\Lambda = \{\lambda^*\}$, $\lambda^* = (1,0)$. Then $E = \{x^1\} = \{(1,0)\}$. If we begin with x^1, we have $\sigma_1 = 0$.

Then $\Lambda^o = \{\lambda \in R^2 : \lambda \geqq 0,\ \lambda_1 + \lambda_2 = 1\}$, $\lambda^{01} = (0,1)$, $\lambda^{02} = (1,0)$ $F^o = X$ and $E \subset F^o$.

The next lemma is important in what follows.

Lemma 4

For $P = P_1$ or P_2, $x \in F^o \rightarrow \exists\, z \in \bar{E}^o$ with

$$\lambda f(x) \leqq \lambda f(z), \quad \forall\, \lambda \in \Lambda^o. \tag{83}$$

Proof

$$\begin{aligned} \forall\, r \geqq 1,\ x \in F^o \rightarrow 0 &\leqq \min_{x \in X} \max_{\lambda \in \Lambda^o} [\lambda f(x) - \lambda f(z)] \\ &\leqq \min_{z \in \bar{E}^o} \max_{\lambda \in \Lambda^o} [\lambda f(x) - \lambda f(z)] \\ &\leqq \max_{y \in X} \min_{z \in E^r} \max_{\lambda \in \Lambda^r} [\lambda f(y) - \lambda f(z)] \\ &= \sigma_r. \end{aligned} \tag{84}$$

Since $\sigma_r \rightarrow 0$ as $r \rightarrow \infty$ (from Lemma 2), we have, for some $z \in \bar{E}^o$,

$$\max_{\lambda \in \Lambda^o} [\lambda f(x) - \lambda f(z)] = 0. \tag{85}$$

This gives the desired result. Δ

The next theorem shows that, for $P = P_1$, in special cases we have $F^o \subseteq E$. It seems to be very difficult to find a situation in which $E \subset F^o$. Such a situation would require E^o not to be closed.

Theorem 6

For $P = P_1$, $\# E^o < \infty$, we have

$$F^o \subseteq E. \tag{86}$$

Proof

Let $x \in F^o/E$. Then, from Lemma 4, $\exists\, z \in E^o$ with $\lambda f(x) = \lambda f(z)$, $\forall\, \lambda \in \Lambda^o$, and xIz. Since $x \notin E$, $\exists\, y \in E \cap E^o$ (from Theorem 4), with $yPxIz$. Since $y,\ z \in E^o$, by construction, for some $r \geqq 1$ we will have $\lambda^{rk} f(y) \geqq \lambda^{rk} f(z)$, $\forall\, k \in K^r$. Then $\lambda f(y) \geqq \lambda f(z) = \lambda f(x)$, $\forall\, \lambda \in \Lambda^o$. Since $x \in F^o$, we must have $\lambda f(y) = \lambda f(x)$, $\forall\, \lambda \in \Lambda^o$, and hence, in particular, $\lambda f(y) = \lambda f(x)$, $\forall\, \lambda \in \Lambda$. Hence yIx contrary to hypothesis. Δ

Corollary 6

For $P = P_1$, $\# X < \infty$

$$F^o \subseteq E. \tag{87}$$

Proof

Obvious. Δ

Note that even here we may not have $F^o = E$. Thus in the example given to show that we can have $F^o \subset E$, the same result would apply if X were replaced by its end points only.

Theorem 7

For $P = P_1$, if Λ is the interior of a polytope,

$$E \subseteq F^o. \tag{88}$$

Proof

Let $x \in E/F^o$. Then $\exists\, y \in X$ with $\lambda f(y) \geqq \lambda f(x)$, $\forall$

$\lambda \in \Lambda^o$, $\lambda f(y) > \lambda f(x)$, some $\lambda \in \Lambda^o$. Then $\exists\, \lambda \in \Lambda$ with $\lambda f(y) > \lambda f(x)$, and hence yPx, contradicting $x \in E$.

Corollary 7

For $P = P_1$, if Λ is the interior of a polytope and E^o is closed then

$$E = F^o. \tag{89}$$

Proof

Combine Theorems 7 and 8.

Note that, even in the simplest case when $\# X < \infty$, or when $\Lambda^r = \Lambda^o$ for some $r \geq 1$, we need not have $E = F^o$. The first example of this section gives $\Lambda^o = \Lambda^1$, but $F^o \subset E$. If, for this example, X is restricted to the end points in the above example, we again get $F^o \subset E$.

For $P = P_2$ we have a stronger result than that of Theorem 7 for $P = P_1$.

Theorem 8

For $P = P_2$

$$E \subseteq F^o. \tag{90}$$

Proof

Let $x \in E/F^o$. Then $\exists\, y \in X$ with $\lambda f(y) > \lambda f(x)$, $\forall\, \lambda \in \Lambda^o$. Hence $\lambda f(y) > \lambda f(x)$, $\forall\, \lambda \in \Lambda$, contradicting $x \in E$. Δ

For $P = P_2$, it is difficult to obtain conditions for which $F^o = E$, since even when $\# X < \infty$, perhaps the simplest case, we can have $E \subset F^o$. Thus let $X = \{(0,0), (1,0)\} \subseteq R^2$, $f(x) = x$, $\forall\, x \in X$, $\Lambda = \{\lambda^*\}$, $\lambda^* = (1,0)$. Then $E = \{(1,0)\}$, but no matter how we begin, $\Lambda^o = \{\lambda \in R^2 : \lambda \geqq 0,\ \lambda_1 + \lambda_2 = 1\}$, $\lambda^{01} = (1,0)$, $\lambda^{02} = (0,1)$, $F^o = X$.

If we know that every member of E will be picked up by some x^r at some stage r, we have the following theorem, valid for $P = P_1$ or P_2.

Theorem 9

For $P = P_1$ or P_2, if $E \subseteq E^o$,

$$E \subseteq F^o. \tag{91}$$

Proof

We consider the case $P = P_1$ initially.

Let $x \in E/F^o$. Then $\exists\ y \in X$ with $\lambda f(y) \geq \lambda f(x)$, $\forall\ \lambda \in \Lambda^o$, $\lambda f(y) > \lambda f(x)$, some $\lambda \in \Lambda^o$. Since $x \in E$, we have yIx, and $y \in E \subseteq E^o$, $x \in E \subseteq E^o$, $y \neq x$. Then, by construction, for some $r \geq 1$, $\lambda^{rk} f(x) = \lambda^{rk} f(y)$, $\forall\ k \in K^r$.

Hence $\lambda f(y) = \lambda f(x)$, $\forall\ \lambda \in \Lambda^o$, contrary to hypothesis.

The case $P = P_2$ comes from Theorem 8. Δ

Let us consider $\{\Lambda^r\}$ and the corresponding sets F^r. We will not consider counter examples to various propositions as we did for Λ^o and F^o, but concentrate on two main theorems which are modifications of Theorems 8 and 9.

Theorem 10

For $P = P_1$, if Λ is the interior of a polytope, then

$$E \subseteq F^r, \quad \forall\ r \geq 1. \tag{92}$$

Proof

Replace Λ^o by Λ^r in Theorem 7. Δ

Theorem 11

For $P = P_2$

$$E \subseteq F^o \subseteq F^{r+1} \subseteq F^r, \quad \forall\ r \geq 1. \tag{93}$$

Proof

From Theorem 9, $E \subseteq F^o$. Let $x \in F^{r+1}/F^r$. Then $\exists\ y \in X$, with $\lambda f(y) > \lambda f(x)$, $\forall\ \lambda \in \Lambda^r$. Then, from Lemma 1, $\lambda f(y) > \lambda f(x)$, $\forall\ \lambda \in \Lambda^{r+1}$, contradicting $x \in F^{r+1}$. Hence $F^{r+1} \subseteq F^r$. Now let $x \in F^o/F^{r+1}$. Then $\exists\ y \in X$, $\tau^{r+1} > 0$, such that $\lambda f(y) - \lambda f(x) \geq \tau^{r+1}$, $\forall\ \lambda \in \Lambda^{r+1}$. Then $\lambda f(y) - \lambda f(x) \geq \tau^{r+1} > 0$, $\forall\ \lambda \in \Lambda^o$, contradicting $x \in F^o$. Δ

The previous results are of some significance if it is intended to try to find E by finding Λ. In the vast majority of cases $\Lambda^o \neq \Lambda$. However one might seek for F^o, hoping that this might give E. The counter examples show that this is only valid in special circumstances.

The results may be useful computationally however, since, when $E \subseteq F^o$, or $E \subseteq F^r$, as is the case in some instances, then, since E is a kernel, from White [1], Theorem 11, we will have, respectively,

$$E = \text{Eff}(F^o) \quad \text{or} \quad \text{Eff}(F^r). \tag{94}$$

In the case when $F^o = F^r$ for some $r \geqq 1$, we have no problem. When this is not the case, some approximation to F^o is needed, and F^r is used when F^r has converged "sufficiently".

It is to be noted that, in the case of P_2, from Theorem 11 we have

$$E = \text{Eff}(F^o) = \text{Eff}(F^r), \quad \forall\, r \geqq 1. \tag{95}$$

Thus as soon as $\# F^r$ is small enough, the decision-maker may be left to make his choice directly.

6. Summary and Comments

This paper has been concerned with mathematical properties of a special multi-objective interactive algorithm. The assumption made about the decision-maker's preference structure is different from the majority of assumptions usually made, and allows for the decision-maker to be unsure about his preferences between any two members x, y of X, as does, for example, Yu [5]. In effect the assumption is equivalent to the decision-maker having a set of objective functions, linear in the objectives, and being prepared to state preferences between a pair x, y if and only if one is at least as good as the other for all such objective functions. There is, of course, the question of knowing, in advance, whether this structure is valid in the given circumstances. Some conditions for this are given in White [4]. However other structures may be more reasonable and this raises the question of whether similar approaches may be developed for other structures.

The central theory of the method is given in Section 3, with Theorem 2 giving the nicest results when $\# X < \infty$, showing termination in a finite number of steps. Theorem 4 is the main theorem characterising E in terms of $\bar{E}^o$, with theorem 3 being the special result for $\# X < \infty$.

One bad feature of the method is that it does not enable us to test whether a given solution is actually the optimal one. As is indicated by point (ii) following Theorem 2, we may, unknowingly, obtain E after a finite number of steps, and yet our indicator, σ_r, be positive and cause us to continue further. This feature is common to almost all methods known. The method of this paper will only conclude that we effectively have E at stage r if $\sigma_r = 0$.

The second bad feature of the method is the computational one in calculating σ_r given by (20). In actual fact for $\# X < \infty$ we only need to determine if $\sigma_r > 0$ or $\sigma_r = 0$, and the method can proceed with a non optimal x^{r+1}, i.e. one not giving σ_r but one for which for some $z \in E^r$, $k \in K^r$ we have

$$\lambda^{rk} f(x^{r+1}) - \lambda^{rk} f(z) > 0.$$

It is also to be noted that

$$\max_{k \in K^r} [\lambda^{rk} f(x) - \lambda^{rk} f(z)]$$

may be replaced by

$$\max_{\lambda \in \Lambda^r} [\lambda f(x) - \lambda f(z)].$$

For the case $\Lambda = \lambda^*$, σ_r may be replaced by

$$\max_{\lambda \in \Lambda^r} \max_{x \in X} [\lambda f(x) - \lambda f(z)].$$

Clearly some computational developments are needed.

It is to be noted that for the standard special case, when $\Lambda = \{\lambda \in R^m : \sum_{i=1}^{m} \lambda_i = 1, \lambda \geqq 0\}$, the method leads to the possibility of using the method for getting E even when Λ is known. This possibility is valid even for the more general Λ.

Section 4 studies the problem from the point of limit sets. The Hausdorf limit is particularly important since, when $\# X = \infty$, computational schemes will involve limit concepts. It is unfortunate that the limits have to be expressed in terms of $\{S^r\}$, and not in terms of $\{E^r\}$, unless the latter is nested. In general, even for well behaved problems this is not so.

Section 5 suggests an alternative method based on $\{F^r\}$, which is analogous to the method of Yu, and is essentially concerned with the relationships between E and F^o, seeing the latter as an alternative target for getting E.

Acknowledgements

I would like to thank my colleagues for their helpful comments on this paper, and Lyn Thomas in particular for his thorough refereeing of the paper.

References

1. D.J. White (1977), "Kernels of Preference Structures", *Econometrica*, 45, 91-100.

2. D.J. White (1980), "Multiple-Objective Interactive Programming", *Journal of the Operational Research Society*, 31, 517-523.

3. D.J. White (1982), *Optimality and Efficiency*, Wiley.

4. D.J. White (1972), Uncertain Value Functions, *Management Science, Theory*, 19, 31-41.

5. P.L. Yu (1973), "Introduction to Domination Structures in Multi-criterion Decision Problems", in *Multiple Criteria Decision Making* (eds.) J.L. Cochrane, M. Zeleny, University of South Carolina Press.

6. R.T. Rockafellar (1972), *Convex Analysis*, Princeton University Press.

7. F.D. Di Guglielmo (1977), "Non-convex Duality in Multiobjective Optimisation", *Mathematics of Operations Research*, 2, 285-291.

8. J.L. Kelly (1955) *General Topology*, Van Nostrand Reinhold.

9. P. Halmos (1950) *Measurement Theory*, Springer.

10. S. Karlin (1959), *Mathematical Methods and Theory in Games, Programming and Economics*, Addison Wesley.

11. O. Mangasarian (1969), *Non-linear Programming*, McGraw-Hill.

ANALYSIS OF STEM-LIKE SOLUTIONS TO MULTI-OBJECTIVE PROGRAMMING PROBLEMS

Y. Crama

(University of Liège, Belgium)

ABSTRACT

This paper generalizes the auxiliary problem as introduced by Benayoun et al. in the well-known method STEM, and studies some properties of the associated solution set. It then makes precise the structure of this set, and also deals with the issue of redundant objectives.

1. A THEORETICAL MODEL

We consider in this paper the problem of a unique decision-maker DM who wishes to maximise p real-valued objective functions on a set of feasible programs.

This general vector-maximization problem may be formulated as follows:

$$\max x$$

$$\text{s.t. } x \in A$$

where A is a subset of the objective space R^p.

Let us now assume the DM has also chosen two particular points in R^p: the goal-point G and the constraint-point c.

The jth component of G represents an ideal value, which the DM would like his jth objective to achieve. On the contrary, the constraint-point gives the minimum acceptable level of achievement for each objective.

We shall assume that G strictly dominates c, and that A contains at least one point which dominates c*.

---

* If $y,z \in R^p$, y is said to dominate $z(y \geq z)$, if $y_j \geq z_j$ $(j=1,\ldots,p)$ and $y \neq z$, y strongly dominates $z(y>z)$ if $y_j > z_j$ $(j=1,\ldots,p)$.

Now, if x is a point in A, we define the weighted loss $\varepsilon_j(x)$ incurred by the jth objective at point x as $\varepsilon_j(x) = \frac{G_j - x_j}{G_j - c_j}$, and the auxiliary problem (A;G,c) associated with the general vector-maximization problem may be written as follows:

$$\begin{aligned} &\min_j \max \varepsilon_j(x) \\ &\text{s.t. } x \in A \\ &\qquad x \geq c \end{aligned}$$

The solutions of the auxiliary problem are called quasi-balanced solutions of the general problem, and the set of all quasi-balanced solutions is denoted by S(A;G,c).

Finally, we shall use a last concept: if all the weighted losses at point x are equal, x is said to be a balanced point in A. The set B(A;G,c) of all balanced points in A is obviously the intersection of A with the straight line (c;G), and so it can be empty.

2. SOME PARTICULAR MODELS

The auxiliary problem just described may be seen as a generalization of the problem introduced in STEM method by Benayoun et al. (1). In this method, the goal is the maximum-point of A, M(A), where $M_j(A) = \max_{x \in A} x_j$, and the constraint level c_j is a fractional part of $M_j(A)$.

Another possible choice, suggested by Zeleny (5), is G = M(A) and c = m(A), where the minimum-point m(A) is defined by $m_j(A) = \min_{x \in A} x_j$.

The auxiliary problem has also been used in some related areas. For instance, Kalai-Smorodinsky's solution to the two-person bargaining problem is defined as the only efficient and balanced point in A (the goal is the maximum-point of A, and the constraint is the conflict point) (3), and Thomson makes use of the same solution in the problem of fair division of a fixed supply among a growing population (4).

But, as we already noticed, the set of balanced points may be empty, and even if it is not, there may exist no efficient balanced point †.

In these cases, quasi-balanced solutions provide a useful generalization of balanced solutions, as made precise below:

Property 1:

If x^* is a balanced and weakly efficient point in A, then x^* is a quasi-balanced solution of (A;G,c).

Proof ≠:

For any x in A, we can find k such that $x_k \leq x_k^*$.
So, $\max_j \varepsilon_j(x^*) = \varepsilon_k(x^*) \leq \max_j \varepsilon_j(x)$.

Moreover, if y belongs to A and y dominates c, there exists k such that $y_k \leq x_k^*$. Then, $c_k \leq x_k^*$, and we can easily conclude that x^* dominates c, since x^* is a balanced point in A. ■

Property 2:

If x^* is a balanced and efficient point in A, then x^* is the unique quasi-balanced solution of (A;G,c).

Proof:

Let x be any point in A such that $x \neq x^*$. We can write $x_k < x_k^*$ for some k, and complete the proof as above. ■

3. PROPERTIES OF THE SOLUTION SET

No restriction has been made so far about the set of feasible values A. But to ensure the existence of quasi-balanced solutions, we shall assume from now on that the set of all points in A which dominate c is compact.

---

† If $B \subset R^p$, y^* is efficient in B if $y^* \in B$ and if B contains no point which dominates y^*; y^* is weakly efficient in B if $y^* \in B$ and B contains no point which strongly dominates y^*. The efficient boundary of B is the set of all points efficient in B.

≠ Some proofs have been shortened or omitted in this paper. The reader will find these proofs as well as a few examples in reference (2).

So, denoting, respectively, by $E(A)$ and $E(S)$ the efficient sets of A and $S(A;G,c)$, we get the following two properties:

Property 3:

$S(A;G,c)$ is non-empty.

Property 4:

$E(S)$ is non-empty and $E(S) = E(A) \cap S$.

If x^* is any quasi-balanced solution, and if $d = \max_j \varepsilon_j(x^*)$, we can state:

Theorem 1: If $S(A;G,c)$ is convex, there exists $j(S)$ in $\{1,..,p\}$ such that, for any quasi-balanced solution x,

$$\varepsilon_{j(S)}(x) = d, \text{ and } \varepsilon_k(x) \leq \varepsilon_{j(S)}(x) \text{ if } k \neq j(S).$$

Proof:

It is clear that $S(A;G,c) = \{x \in A | x \geq c \text{ and } \max_j \varepsilon_j(x) = d\}$.

If the theorem is false, we can associate with each j a quasi-balanced solution $x^{(j)}$ such that $\varepsilon_j(x^{(j)}) < d$. Moreover, since $x^{(j)} \in S(A;G,c)$, $\varepsilon_i(x^{(j)}) \leq d$, $\forall i$.

Now, let us define the quasi-balanced solution y as a convex combination of $x^{(1)},\ldots,x^{(p)}$: $y = \frac{1}{p} \sum_{j=1}^{p} x^{(j)}$.

Then, for each i, $\varepsilon_i(y) < d$, which is contradictory with $y \in S(A;G,c)$. ∎

So this theorem expresses the fact that all quasi-balanced solutions are equivalent with respect to one objective at least. It suggests the following procedure to determine an efficient quasi-balanced solution.

Step 1: - solve the auxiliary problem

- let $S^1 = S(A;G,c)$ and $I^1 = \{1,\ldots,p\}\backslash\{j(S^1)\}$

Then, consecutively for $k = 1,\ldots,p-1$:

Step k+1: - solve the problem

$$\min_{j \in I^k} \max \varepsilon_j(x)$$

s.t. $x \in S^k$

- let $S^{k+1} = S(S^k;G,c)$ and $I^{k+1} = I^k \setminus \{j(S^{k+1})\}$.

Property 5:

The above procedure provides a unique efficient quasi-balanced solution when $S(A\ ;\ G,\ c)$ is convex.

Proof:

Trivial.■

4. REDUNDANT OBJECTIVES

In this section, we intend to study the effects of adding a redundant objective to the multiobjective function f.

In fact, it seems important for the solution of a multi-objective problem to remain invariant after such a transformation.

Restricting ourselves to linear combinations of the objectives, we will denote throughout by K the function K: $R^p \to R^{p+1}$; $x \mapsto (x, \sum_{j=1}^{p} k_j x_j)$, where k_j are non-negative real numbers, $\forall\ j \in \{1,\ldots,p\}$, and the redundant objective $u_{p+1} = \Sigma k_j\ u_j$ is supposed to be non-identically null.

A first result may be easily obtained: if the goal and the constraint are transformed like f, the solution set is invariant in the following sense.

Theorem 2: $K(S(A;G,c)) = S(K(A);K(G),K(c))$

Proof:

For any $x' = (x,x_{p+1})$ in $K(A)$,

$$\varepsilon_{p+1}(x') \leq \max_{j=1,..,p} \varepsilon_j(x') = \max_{j=1,..,p} \varepsilon_j(x),$$

and so, $\displaystyle\max_{j=1,..,p+1} \varepsilon_j(x') = \max_{j=1,..,p} \varepsilon_j(x)$.■

But this result still holds when the goal G_{p+1} - associated with the redundant objective x_{p+1} - only fulfils the milder condition

$$G_{p+1} \leq \Sigma k_j \; G_j$$

In particular, if we only consider problems of the form $(A;\; M(A),\; m(A))$, the hypothesis $M_{p+1} = \sum_{j=1}^{p} k_j \; M_j$ is generally false (because it implies $M(A) \in A$ when $k_j > 0,\; \forall j$), and so the scope of theorem 2 is considerably narrowed in this case.

Nevertheless, the inequality $M_{p+1} \leq \Sigma k_j \; M_j$, which is always true, suffices to prove the following theorem.

Theorem 3: If $m_{p+1} = \sum_{j=1}^{p} k_j \; m_j$, then

$$K(S(A;M(A),\; m(A))) = S(K(A);\; M',m'),$$

where $M' = M(K(A))$ and $m' = m(K(A))$.

Proof:

The proof is similar to the preceding one.■

Let us remark that the condition $m_{p+1} = \Sigma k_j \; m_j$ is certainly fulfilled when $m(A) \in A$, and that theorem 3 is generally incorrect without this hypothesis (see counter-example in (2) p. 29). It only remains true in the case of a two-objective problem.

Theorem 4: If A is convex and x^* is the unique quasi-balanced solution of the bi-objective problem $(A;\; M(A),\; m(A))$, then $K(x^*)$ is the unique quasi-balanced solution of $(K(A);\; M',\; m')$, where $M' = M(K(A))$ and $m' = m(K(A))$.

Proof:

It is sufficient to prove that

$$\varepsilon_3'(K(x^*)) \leq \max\; (\varepsilon_1(x^*),\; \varepsilon_2(x^*)) \qquad (1)$$

If k_1 (or k_2) is null, condition (1) is fulfilled as an equality.

So, we assume that $K: u \mapsto (u, u_1+u_2)$ and that $m_1 = m_2 = 0$ (quasi-balanced solutions are of course invariant with respect to affine transformations of the objectives).

Let v be a solution of $\max_{x \in X} (x_1+x_2)$. We have

$$v_1 + v_2 = M_3 \leq \max (M_1 + x_2^*, x_1^* + M_2),$$

otherwise $x_1^* < v_1$ and $x_2^* < v_2$, which is contradictory with the hypothesis that x* is a quasi-balanced solution.

So, assuming that $M_3 \leq M_1 + x_2^*$, we obtain:

$$\varepsilon'_3(K(x^*)) = \frac{M_3 - (x_1^* + x_2^*)}{M_3} \leq \frac{M_1 + x_2^* - x_1^* - x_2^*}{M_1 + x_2^*}$$

$$\leq \frac{M_1 - x_1^*}{M_1} = \varepsilon_1(x^*),$$

which entails condition (1) ■

REFERENCES

(1) Benayoun R., de Montgolfier J., Tergny J., Laritchev G., (1971) "Linear Programming with Multiple Objective Functions: Step Method (STEM)", *Math. Programming*, **1**, 366-375.

(2) Crama Y., (1981) "Etude Générale des Solutions Basées sur la Notion de Pertes Pondérées en Programmation à Objectifs Multiples", Working Papers "Cahiers du SMASH", Fac. Univ. St-Louis, Bruxelles.

(3) Kalai E., Smorodinsky M., (1975) "Other Solutions to Nash's Bargaining Problem", *Econometrica*, **43**, 513-518.

(4) Thomson W., (1981) "The Fair Division of a Fixed Supply Among a Growing Population", Working Paper, Univ. Minnesota.

(5) Zeleny M., (1974) "Linear Multiobjective Programming", Springer Verlag, New York.

COMPARING APPROACHES FOR MULTI-CRITERION OPTIMIZATION

E.E. Bischoff

(Department of Management Science, University College of Swansea)

1. INTRODUCTION

One of the central issues of the literature on multi-objective decision making is the question of how to determine an optimal course of action in a situation where the choices available are described by multiple heterogeneous attributes and the decision maker is unable to express his preference structure explicitly in the form of a single overall objective function. In other words, it is assumed that the decision maker seeks to find the maximum of a subjective utility function with respect to the values of the attributes involved, but cannot specify a function which adequately reflects his preferences. At a conceptual level this problem can be represented as

$$\begin{aligned} &\text{Max.} \quad U(f_1(x), f_2(x), \ldots, f_r(x)) \\ &\text{s.t} \quad x=(x_1, x_2, \ldots, x_n) \in A \quad , \end{aligned} \qquad \text{(UM)}$$

where x denotes the vector of decision variables, A stands for the set of feasible decisions, $f_1(x), f_2(x), \ldots, f_r(x)$ are the attributes that describe the outcome of a decision and U is the decision maker's - unknown - preference function.

Following Geoffrion, Dyer and Feinberg (8) and many others, a decision problem of this form will here be referred to as a "multi-criterion optimization problem". Numerous methods for tackling such problems have been suggested. These vary in procedural complexity from fairly simple approaches, such as asking the decision maker to assign weighting factors to the attributes considered and using their weighted sum as an approximation to his utility function, to relatively complicated interactive methods where information about the decision maker's preferences is required not only at the beginning of the analysis but also at several stages during the procedure. The development of approaches in this field has been traced by a number of surveys of which Roy (16), MacCrimmon (14), Starr and Zeleny (18) and Hwang and Masud (11) are only a few examples. White (22), in this volume, presents a selection of interactive procedures which, especially in recent years, have received some attention.

Whilst research into techniques for multi-criterion optimization has provided the potential user with a wide range of tools, this multitude of possible approaches also presents him with the difficult task of choosing a method, or a set of methods, to apply to the specific problem to be solved. As many approaches make fairly restrictive additional assumptions about the structure of problem (UM) - such as, for instance, monotony of U in each argument (e.g. Fandel (7), Haimes and Hall (10)) or linearity of U (e.g. White (21)) or the attribute functions f_i (e.g. Zionts and Wallenius (24), Steuer (19)) - he may often be able to narrow down significantly the alternatives that need to be considered. However, the number of methods that could theoretically be applied to a problem will typically be far in excess of the number that can actually be tried in the environment in which the decision has to be made. Not infrequently there will only be the opportunity to use one single approach.

The problem of making a suitable choice between different methods is the focal point of this paper. The existing literature provides little assistance in this respect. Applications of multi-criterion optimization methods to actual decision problems have been described by a number of authors, but very few papers deal with comparative evaluations. Of these, Wallenius (20) is probably the one most often quoted. He discusses the results of a series of laboratory experiments in which a group of business school students and managers were asked to use the two interactive procedures proposed by Geoffrion et al. (8) and Benayoun et al. (2) as well as an ill-structured trial-and-error approach to try to solve a hypothetical decision problem involving three conflicting criteria. The subjects were asked to make their own assessment of the methods used and the solutions they obtained. Whilst the study provides some interesting insights into the advantages and disadvantages of the methods examined - the unstructured approach was found to compare well, in many respects, with the two interactive procedures - it is, however, doubtful how far the results of such an investigation can be generalized. Its findings do not, for example, agree with those of an earlier study in a similar vein by Dyer (6), and, as Wallenius himself points out (20, p. 1394), the performance of a method may crucially depend, amongst other factors, on the experience of a decision maker with that method and with the type of problem to be solved.

The present paper has a different orientation. Instead of trying to evaluate different methods on the basis of the actual experiences of an individual or a group of people, it takes the approach of simulating applications of the methods under various assumptions in terms of the (fictitious) decision maker's utility function and his ability to provide information about his preferences. As in the case of an explicitly known utility function it is possible to calculate an optimal solution to problem (UM), such an approach enables the quality of the results obtained with different methods to be measured objectively. Moreover, it permits a systematic analysis of the robustness of the procedures with respect to inaccuracies in the preference information supplied by the user.

The test problems used in the simulation experiments are concerned with Research and Development (R&D) project selection, i.e., the compilation of a suitable portfolio of R&D projects form a given set of project opportunities. The data describing the opportunities available were generated randomly, but all the problems involve the same number of decision variables and have an identical basic structure. Details of the test problems used are discussed in section 3 of this paper.

Three approaches to multi-criterion optimization are examined in this framework. These are:

(1) Additive weighting of the attributes,

(2) Goal programming using the L_1-norm $\|d\|_1 = \sum_{i=1}^{r} |d_i|$ as a measure of the weighted deviations from the targets set (often referred to as MINSUM goal programming), and

(3) Goal programming using the L_∞-norm $\|d\|_\infty = \max_{i=1,\ldots,r} |d_i|$ as a measure of the weighted deviations from the goals (MINMAX goal programming).

The following section deals with particulars of the formulations used.

2. THE METHODS EXAMINED

The choice of the three methods analyzed here was motivated by two considerations. First, weighting and goal programming approaches to multi-criterion optimization have been widely adopted in practical applications. Secondly, whilst themselves relatively simple in nature, these methods form the conceptual basis of a large number of more sophisticated procedures.

Studying their performance may therefore also provide insights into the merits and weaknesses of several other techniques.

All three procedures require the active involvement of the decision maker only at the start, i.e., what is often referred to as an "a priori articulation of preference information" (cf. Hwang and Masud (11)). In the case of the weighted sum approach this is simply the set of weighting factors w_i, i=1,...,r. Given these, the problem is reduced to the ordinary mathematical programming problem:

$$\text{Max} \quad \sum_{i=1}^{r} w_i f_i(x) \qquad \text{s.t.} \quad x \in A \tag{WS}$$

Some authors make the additional stipulation that $\sum_{i=1}^{r} |w_i| = 1$. This is, however, clearly not an essential requirement.

Goal programming in its most general form uses both cardinal and ordinal preference information (cf. Ignizio (12), Lee (13)). The cardinal information required consists of target values for the attributes involved together with a set of weighting factors indicating the degree of importance the decision maker attaches to the attainment of these goals. The ordinal information takes the form of a ranking of the attributes by assigning them to several priority classes. The formulation considered here uses only cardinal preference information, i.e., assumes that all attributes are of a comparable degree of importance and can therefore be regarded as belonging to the same priority class. Using the symbols I_L and I_U to distinguish the cases where the target has the nature of a lower and an upper limit, respectively, on desirable values for an attribute and I_I to denote targets which represent an ideal level, the formulation chosen can be expressed as:

$$\text{Min } z = \Big[\sum_{i=1}^{r} (d_i)^p + \sum_{i \in I_I} (\hat{d}_i)^p\Big]^{1/p}$$

$$\begin{aligned}
\text{s.t.} \quad & \text{(i)} & f_i(x) + d_i/v_i &\geqslant g_i \ , \ i \in I_L \\
& \text{(ii)} & f_i(x) - d_i/v_i &\leqslant g_i \ , \ i \in I_U \\
& \text{(iii)} & f_i(x) + d_i/v_i - \hat{d}_i/\hat{v}_i &= g_i \ , \ i \in I_I \\
& \text{(iv)} & x &\in A \\
& \text{(v)} & d_i \geqslant 0 \ , \ i=1,\dots,r \ &; \ \hat{d}_i \geqslant 0 \ , \ i \in I_I .
\end{aligned} \tag{GP}$$

Here the values g_i are the goals set, the parameters v_i and $\hat{v}_i$ are the associated (positive) weighting factors, the variables d_i and $\hat{d}_i$ stand for the weighted deviations from the target values and the scalar p is the order of the L_p-norm used to aggregate these deviations in the single distance measure z.

For p=1 formulation (GP) becomes the MINSUM model:

$$\begin{aligned} \text{Min} \quad & \sum_{i=1}^{r} d_i + \sum_{i \in I_I} \hat{d}_i \\ \text{s.t.} \quad & \text{(i)-(v)} \quad , \end{aligned} \tag{MS}$$

and for $p \to \infty$ one obtains the MINMAX model:

$$\begin{aligned} \text{Min} \quad & \text{Max}\{d_i, \hat{d}_j \mid i=1,\ldots,r \ , \ j \in I_I\} \\ \text{s.t.} \quad & \text{(i)-(v)} \quad . \end{aligned} \tag{MM}$$

While there is no simple, general relationship between the three problems (WS), (MS) and (MM), it is easy to see that under certain conditions one of the formulations becomes equivalent to another. If, for example, all goals are attainable simultaneously then the problems (MS) and (MM) obviously have the same solutions. In the equally extreme case where $I_I = \emptyset$ and none of the goals is attainable in A, it can easily be shown that an optimal solution x^* to problem (MS) is also obtained by using model (WS) with weighting factors of $w_i = v_i$ for $i \in I_L$ and $w_i = -v_i$ for $i \in I_U$. In fact, the same is true under the weaker condition that $I_I = \emptyset$ and that x^* does not satisfy any of the goals set.

A number of authors have examined analytical relationships between goal programming and/or weighting models and the utility maximization problem (UM). Dyer (5), for instance, discusses the assumptions underlying the MINSUM model - more precisely the "one-sided" model where no constraints of type (iii) are present - and demonstrates that this approach is equivalent to the piecewise linear approximation of an additively separable utility function. Stadje (17) analyzes a generalized form of model (GP) which allows for distance measures other than L_p-metrics to be used in the objective function. Making the basic assumption that the decision maker's utility function is isotonic he derives conditions under which the solutions of a goal programming model can also be obtained by maximizing an appropriate utility function, and vice versa. Hwang and Masud (11, Ch. 2.1), to take another example, point out the close connection between the weighting factors w_i of model (WS) and the values of the partial derivatives $\partial U/\partial f_i$ of the utility function at an optimum x^*, i.e. that, under certain conditions regarding the functions involved, model (WS) with weighting factors $w_i = \partial U/\partial f_i \,|\, (f_1(x^*),\ldots,f_r(x^*))$, $i=1,\ldots,r$, leads to the solution x^*.

The knowledge of analytical relationships of this kind may obviously in certain special situations be of help in evaluating the suitability of different approaches. In general, however, such relationships are of only limited practical value. To know, for example, that under certain, strong conditions the models (MS) and (MM) have the same solutions is of little assistance if these conditions do not hold. Similarly, the knowledge that there exists a set of weighting factors for which model (WS) leads to an optimal solution of the utility maximization problem provides little help in the task of investigating how the method will perform with inappropriate weighting factors. As will be illustrated in the following sections, an empirical approach is a practicable way of tackling questions to which purely analytical approaches cannot provide an answer.

3. THE TEST PROBLEMS USED

As mentioned earlier, the simulation experiments were conducted in the framework of an assumed R&D project selection situation. Several reviews of prescriptive models for this type of problem have commented that the majority of models fail to take adequate account of the existence of multiple decision-relevant criteria (cf. Baker and Freeland (1), Ritchie (15)). One of the few papers dealing explicitly with the criteria involved in an assessment of project opportunities is a case study by Hart (9), in which he describes the development of a scoring chart based on twelve criteria. The construction of the test problems used in this study was loosely based on the criteria listed by Hart and some of the data he provides about the projects from amongst which a selection had to be made. One important difference between the problem he describes and the test problems constructed for the simulation experiments is that in the latter the attributes describing the outcome of a decision relate to the project portfolio as a whole rather than to individual projects as in Hart's formulation. Another significant modification concerns project costs, which Hart incorporates into his model as one of the twelve criteria, whereas the test problems involve rigid constraints on the resources available for an R&D program.

Ten problems of an identical structure were constructed, using the following attributes:

f_1 - Expected net sales revenue, year 2

f_2 - Expected net sales revenue, year 3

f_3 - Expected net sales revenue, years 4 and 5

f_4 - Expected net sales revenue, years 6-10

f_5 - Production know-how (cost-weighted)

f_6 - Subjective probability of success (cost-weighted)

f_7 - Expected additional fixed capital investment requirements

f_8 - External competition (cost-weighted)

f_9 - Internal competition (cost-weighted)

f_{10} - Marketing requirements (cost-weighted).

The comment "cost-weighted" means that the raw score of a project - which for f_5 and f_6 is a value between 0 and 1 and for f_8 to f_{10} is expressed on a scale between 0 and 10 - is multiplied by the cost of the project.

All f_i are assumed to be linear functions of the decision variables, i.e. if the variable x_j, $j=1,\ldots,n$, is used to denote the decision about whether to accept ($x_j=1$) or to reject ($x_j=0$) project proposal j, then the functions f_i can be written as $f_i(x_1,\ldots,x_n) = \sum_{j=1}^{n} a_{ij}x_j$. The coefficients $\{a_{ij}\}$ were generated randomly using a computer model, as were the resource requirements of the projects - three types of resources are distinguished - and a number of interdependencies between projects, which prevent some from being accepted unless, or if, others are adopted. The constraints arising from such interdependencies are of a linear form and, as the resource requirements of an R&D program are assumed to be the sums of the requirements of the projects included in it, the resource constraints are also linear. The only other constraints are the bounds on the individual decision variables which, in order to keep the amount of computer time required for the experiments within reasonable limits, were expressed in the continuous form $0 \leq x_j \leq 1$, rather than in the, from a theoretical viewpoint more appropriate, form $x_j=0$ or 1. All ten problems constructed involved 100 decision variables and between 29 and 42 constraints (excluding the two bounds for each variable), depending on how many interrelationships were generated in each case.

4. THE SIMULATION EXPERIMENTS

The simulation approach applied requires two sets of assumptions about the fictitious decision maker:

(a) A model of his preference structure, i.e. a utility function (Preference Model).

(b) A model of his responses to different questions about his preferences (Response Model).

Four different utility functions were used in the experiments. The simplest of these was an additively separable function of the form

$$U(f_1,\ldots,f_{10}) = \sum_{i=1}^{4} k_i f_i + \sum_{i=5}^{6} k_i \ln(f_i+c_i) + \sum_{i=7}^{10} k_i \ln(c_i-f_i) \quad \text{(I)}$$

where $k_1,\ldots,k_{10}$ and $c_5,\ldots,c_{10}$ are constants. The constants used ensure that the logarithms in the expression are defined throughout the range of values the attributes can take. This model implies that the decision maker's preferences with respect to one attribute are independent of the values of the other attributes and that he would always prefer higher values for attributes f_1-f_6 (sales revenue etc.) and lower ones for f_7-f_{10} (investment expenditures etc.). Using this explicit preference model the optimal solutions of the test problems can be calculated by means of a nonlinear programming technique. The technique used here was S.U.M.T. (cf. Bischoff (3) for a discussion of suitable choices for the parameters of the procedure in the case of problems involving a large number of variables.) The optimal utility values obtained for nine of the test problems are shown in the second column of Table Ia.

The reason why only nine - and not ten - values are shown is due to the fact that the solution of one of the problems is needed for the construction of the response model adopted here. More precisely, the preference information required by the three methods examined was derived from the optimal solution to the problem not listed in the Table. The conceptual basis of this model is the assumption that the decision maker, while not knowing an optimal solution to the problem he is facing, has some experience with similar problems and bases his weighting of the attributes and the target values he specifies on the solutions obtained in these other situations. The details of

Table I

Utility Function I, Accurate Weighting Factors

(a) Actual results

Test Problem	Optimal Value	WS Approach	MINSUM Appr.	MINMAX Appr.
1	25146	25140	24509	24396
2	24361	24361	24055	23892
3	22852	22852	22809	22077
4	24321	24313	24095	23846
5	24015	24011	23623	23649
6	24608	24608	24193	23777
7	24912	24912	24421	24200
8	23816	23815	23674	23512
9	23223	23223	23187	22591

(b) Normalised deviations

Test Problem	MINSUM Appr.	MINMAX Appr.
1	27.8%	32.7%
2	13.3%	20.4%
3	1.9%	33.8%
4	9.9%	20.7%
5	17.1%	15.9%
6	18.1%	36.2%
7	21.4%	31.0%
8	6.2%	13.3%
9	1.6%	27.6%
Average	13.0%	25.7%

the approach can best be explained by reference to Table Ia: Column 3 shows the results obtained by using model (WS) with the weighting factors w_i defined as the values of the partial derivatives $\partial U/\partial f_i$ at the optimum of the tenth - the "reference" problem. Columns 4 and 5 list the results of applications of models (MS) and (MM) with the same weighting factors, apart from a sign change where required (as follows from (I), the partial derivatives with respect to $f_1,\ldots,f_6$ are always positive, while those with respect to $f_7,\ldots,f_{10}$ are always negative, which implies that $I_L=(1,\ldots,6)$, $I_U=(7,\ldots,10)$, $I_I=\emptyset$), and the goals g_i defined as the values $f_i(x^*)$ at the optimum x^* of the reference problem. With this preference information all three methods, when applied to the reference problem itself, would produce an optimal solution. As can be seen from the Table, the weighted sum approach produces optimal or very nearly optimal solutions in all nine cases, whereas none of the solutions obtained through the MINSUM goal programming model is optimal and the results using the MINMAX model are in all but one case inferior to those of the MINSUM model. A number of similar experiments, using different reference problems, showed that the results listed in Table Ia are representative of the performance of the three methods in this situation.

If the same preference model is used in a series of experiments of this kind, then a comparison of different methods can be based simply on the actual utility values obtained. In analyzing the performance of certain methods with a number of different preference models, however, it is obvious that the results must be normalised in some way to allow a comparison. The approach taken here is to express the difference between the result obtained and the optimal value as a percentage of the difference between the highest and the lowest optimum value amongst the ten test problems. In other words, if $u(f)$ is the result obtained for a problem, u^* is the optimal value for this problem and u^*_{min} and u^*_{max} are the lowest and highest optimal values for all the test problems, then the normalised deviation y (of $u(f)$ from u^*) is defined as $y = \dfrac{u^* - u(f)}{u^*_{max} - u^*_{min}}$. As can easily be seen, the value of y is not changed if a constant term is added to the utility function or if the latter is multiplied by a constant. Table Ib shows the values obtained if this concept is applied to the results in section a of the same Table.

Table II contains the (normalised) results obtained with the same preference model, but a slightly different response model. The experiments used the same reference problem as that underlying Table I, but it was assumed that the decision maker can only distinguish between two categories of attributes - "important ones" (with a weighting factor of 2) and "less important ones" (with a weighting factor of 1). The distinction between the two categories was made on the basis of whether the value of the corresponding derivative $\partial U/\partial f_i$ at the optimum of the reference problem was higher or lower than the mean of these values (which were in the range of 1.9 to 13.0). It can be seen that the relative performance of the three methods is very similar to that exhibited in Table I. Again, repetitions of the experiments under slightly different assumptions confirmed this conclusion.

Table II

Utility Function I, Limited Accuracy of Weighting Factors.

Test Problem	WS Approach	MINSUM Appr.	MINMAX Appr.
1	4.5%	21.7%	31.2%
2	9.0%	6.6%	7.7%
3	5.6%	4.4%	42.4%
4	3.9%	13.9%	18.9%
5	10.2%	11.6%	16.4%
6	4.3%	21.2%	37.2%
7	1.4%	24.0%	29.2%
8	7.9%	15.1%	22.7%
9	2.6%	3.3%	32.2%
Average	5.5%	13.5%	26.4%

As mentioned above, four different utility functions were used in the experiments. The second one was not additively separable, but, like the first one, monotonic in every attribute. The third utility function used had a similar form, but was not monotonic in attribute f_5, and the fourth one was dependent on only five of the attributes (f_3, f_4, f_5, f_6, and f_{10}). A large number of experiments were conducted with these functions. All suggest the same conclusions:

(i) that the weighted sum approach, in most cases, produces much better results than the goal programming approaches, even when the weighting factors used are far from optimal; and
(ii) that the MINMAX approach, on average, leads to solutions that are significantly inferior to those obtained by the MINSUM model.

Tables III and IV show some of the results obtained with utility functions IV and II, respectively. In the case described by Table III the response model used was the same as the one underlying Table II, i.e., only weighting factors of 1 and 2 were permitted. In the case shown in Table IV the weighting factors used in model (WS) were all set equal (instead of values between 1.5 and 22.0). This is compared to the first phase of the (interactive) STEM approach (cf. Benayoun et al. (2)), in which no information is required from the decision maker, but which is based on calculations regarding the range of values taken on by the attributes over the feasible region. As can be seen from the Table, the results of the first phase of STEM are, on average, no better than those obtained with the rather crude weighting approach.

5. CONCLUSIONS

The results described in the previous section highlight the shortcomings of abstract comparisons based only on qualitative aspects of different approaches. They show that methods which require less information about the decision maker's preferences do not necessarily lead to inferior solutions. In fact, the implication is that the constraints introduced by the targets used in a goal programming formulation may prevent better solutions from being reached. Zeleny and Cochrane (23) make comments along similar lines.

Similarly, the results illustrate the weaknesses of comparisons between MINSUM and MINMAX goal programming approaches that have been made by a number of authors. These centre primarily on the fact that a small change in the weighting factors may cause the solution of a MINSUM model to change drastically,

Table III

Utility Function IV, Limited Accuracy of Weighting Factors.

Test Problem	WS Approach	MINSUM Appr.	MINMAX Appr.
1	1.1%	28.8%	28.4%
2	0.6%	13.0%	32.2%
3	0.0%	0.1%	8.0%
4	0.0%	0.0%	2.1%
5	0.0%	0.0%	25.3%
6	0.3%	11.3%	12.7%
7	3.7%	11.9%	17.2%
8	22.2%	25.0%	6.7%
9	0.1%	0.1%	20.0%
Average	3.1%	10.0%	17.0%

Table IV

Utility Function II, Model (WS) and STEM.

Test Problem	WS Approach	1st Phase of STEM
1	16.5%	10.5%
2	23.2%	11.6%
3	9.6%	6.9%
4	7.9%	21.0%
5	7.5%	23.6%
6	10.0%	19.1%
7	6.4%	11.8%
8	23.0%	19.7%
9	23.4%	19.9%
10	18.1%	22.0%
Average	14.6%	16.6%

whereas the MINMAX solution is more stable (cf. De Kluyver (4)). As is obvious from the results of this study, this does not imply that the MINMAX formulation is necessarily the better approach.

In concluding it should, however, also be pointed out that a study such as this cannot claim to demonstrate that one approach is generally better than another. The structure of the feasible set, the shape of the utility function, the number of decision variables and attributes and many other factors all have a certain, and possibly crucial, influence on the performance of a method. How the performance of an approach depends on such factors remains to be investigated.

REFERENCES

1. Baker, N. and Freeland, J. 1975 "Recent Advances in R&D Benefit Measurement and Project Selection Methods", *Management Science,* Vol. **21**, No. 10, June, pp. 1164-1175.

2. Benayoun, R., de Montgolfier, J., Tergny, J. and Larichev, O. 1971, "Linear Programming with Multiple Objective Functions: Step Method (STEM), *Mathematical Programming,* Vol. **1**, No. 3, Dec., pp. 366-375.

3. Bischoff, E. 1979 "The Application of S.U.M.T. to Relatively Large Systems", *Methods of Operations Research,* Vol. **35**, Athenaeum/Hain/Scriptor/Hanstein, Koenigstein, pp. 53-65.

4. De Kluyver, C.A. 1979 "An Exploration of Various Goal Programming Formulations - with Application to Advertising Media Scheduling", *Journal of the Operational Research Society,* Vol. **30**, No. 2, Feb., pp. 167-171.

5. Dyer, J.S. 1972 "Interactive Goal Programming", *Management Science,* Vol. **19**, No. 1, Sept., pp. 62-70.

6. Dyer, J.S. 1973 An Empirical Investigation of a Man-Machine Interactive Approach to the Solution of the Multiple Criteria Problem, In: "Multiple Criteria Decision Making", (J.L. Cochrane, and M. Zeleny, Eds.), University of South Carolina Press, Columbia, South Carolina, pp. 202-216.

7. Fandel, G. 1972 "Optimale Entscheidung bei mehrfacher Zielsetzung", Lecture Notes in Economics and Mathematical Systems, Vol. **76**, Springer, Berlin.

8. Geoffrion, A.M., Dyer, J.S. and Feinberg, A. 1972 "An Interactive Approach for Multicriterion Optimization with an

Application to the Operation of an Academic Department", *Management Science,* Vol. **19**, No. 4, Dec., pp. 357-368.

9. Hart, A. 1966 "A Chart for Evaluating Product Research and Development Projects", *Operational Research Quarterly,* Vol. **17**, No. 4, Dec., pp. 347-358.

10. Haimes, Y.Y. and Hall, W.A. 1974 "Multiobjectives in Water Resources Systems Analysis: The Surrogate Worth Trade-Off Method", *Water Resources Research,* Vol. **10**, No. 4, Aug., pp. 615-624.

11. Hwang, C.L. and Masud, A.S. 1979 "Multiple Objective Decision Making: Methods and Applications (A State-Of-The-Art Survey)", Lecture Notes in Economics and Mathematical Systems, Vol. **164**, Springer, Berlin.

12. Ignizio, J.P. 1976 "Goal Programming and Extensions", Lexington Books, Massachussetts.

13. Lee, S.M. 1972 "Goal Programming for Decision Analysis", Auerbach, Philadelphia, Pennsylvania.

14. MacCrimmon, K.R. 1973 An Overview of Multiple Objective Decision Making. In: "Multiple Criteria Decision Making", (J.L. Cochrane and M. Zeleny, Eds.), University of South Carolina Press, Columbia, South Carolina, pp. 18-44.

15. Ritchie, E. 1970 "Research on Research: Where Do we Stand", *R&D Management,* Vol. **1**, No. 1, Oct., pp. 3-9.

16. Roy, B. 1971 "Problems and Methods with Multiple Objective Functions", *Mathematical Programming,* Vol. **1**, No. 2, Nov., pp. 239-266.

17. Stadje, W. 1979 "On the Relationship of Goal Programming and Utility Functions", *Zeitschrift fuer Operations Research,* Vol. **23**, pp. 61-69.

18. Starr, M.K. and Zeleny, M. 1977 MCDM - State and Future of the Arts. In: "Multiple Criteria Decision Making", (M.K. Starr and M. Zeleny, Eds.), North Holland, New York, pp. 5-29.

19. Steuer, R.E. 1977 An Interactive Multiple Objective Linear Programming Procedure. In: "Multiple Criteria Decision Making", (M.K. Starr and M. Zeleny, Eds.), North Holland, New York, pp. 225-239.

20. Wallenius, J. 1975 "Comparative Evaluation of Some Interactive Approaches to Multicriterion Optimization", *Management Science,* Vol. 21, No. 12, Aug., pp. 1387-1396.

21. White, D.J. 1980 "Multi-Objective Interactive Programming", *Journal of the Operational Research Society,* Vol. 31, No. 6, June, pp. 517-523.

22. White, D.J. 1982 A Selection of Multi-Objective Interactive Programming Methods, Paper presented at the Conference on "Multi-Objective Decision Making", University of Manchester, April.

23. Zeleny, M. and Cochrane, J.L. 1973 A Priori and A Posteriori Goals in Macroeconomic Policy Making. In: "Multiple Criteria Decision Making", (J.L. Cochrane, and M. Zeleny, Eds.), University of South Carolina Press, Columbia, South Carolina, pp. 373-391.

24. Zionts, S. and Wallenius, J. 1976 "An Interactive Programming Method for Solving the Multiple Criteria Problem", *Management Science,* Vol. 22, No. 6, Feb., pp. 652-663.

A MULTI-OBJECTIVE DECISION PROBLEM: THE FURNITURE MANUFACTURER'S 2-DIMENSIONAL CUTTING OR TRIM PROBLEM

P. Harrison

(Joint Consultancy on Patterns and Systems Ltd., Bishops Stortford, Herts.)

BACKGROUND TO THE PROBLEM

Since 1978 we have been actively engaged in researching into the area of Operational Decision Making within the wood based industries in the U.K., Sweden, Finland and the USA. Part of this research has centred around the operational decision associated with cutting the large, predominately rectangular, boards into the smaller panel sizes required within the manufacture of furniture, i.e. the well known cutting or trim problem (2DCP).

The Furniture Manufacturer's 2DCP requires the conversion of large, composite, board materials into the smaller "sized" panels which are then subjected to additional manufacturing operations before they are assembled into (a) units of furniture, or (b) packed, to be despatched as DIY self-assemble kits of furniture. The sawing technology and the "box-like" design of modern day furniture constrains the sawing operation to guillotine cuts only. The cutting operation can be considered as a two or three staged process. The first stage is to cut the board into length strips. The second stage is to cut across these length strips thereby effecting an actual panel - smaller rectangle or square size. The third stage, known as off-line cutting or Z cutting, occurs when an additional cutting operation has to be performed, after stages 1 and 2, to obtain the correct panel size. In addition, the Planner (decision maker - DM) also has the option of Head-Cutting. If the H-Cutting option is taken, then the first cut will be across the width of the board. Thereafter the two "smaller" boards are machined separately.

APPROACHES TO THE CUTTING STOCK PROBLEM

The majority of the published work on the cutting stock problem has focused attention on the one and two dimensional trim problems of the paper, glass and steel industries, only minor references having been made to the furniture industries 2DCP. In this published work to date, the general emphasis has been clearly toward defining the problem as having a single objective function, i.e., that of waste minimisation. However, although there appears to be an abundance of mathematical solution methods available to solve the 2DCP, the number of companies actually using computerised approaches are few. The main reason we suggest for this is centred around the fact that the current solution methods only satisfy a small proportion of the Planner's actual cutting problems. Even where sophisticated multi-objective linear programming solutions, which incorporate novel back tracking sub-algorithms, are used the computerised results are rarely better than the manually generated cutting patterns of the Planner.

A MULTI-OBJECTIVE PROBLEM: WASTE AND OTHER CONSEQUENCES

During our research it has become evident that the Furniture Manufacturer's 2DCP cannot be formulated and solved as a normative trim-loss problem, where the predominant goal is one of waste minimisation. In practice the Furniture Manufacturer's 2DCP encompasses a complex, inter-related, set of problem issues which require wastage and other consequences to be considered. These "other consequences" include:

- costs associated with edge waste;
- cutting costs associated with level of complexity of cutting patterns;
- volume throughput (i.e. the amount of m^3 cut per hour):
- number of cutting patterns to number of panel inputs;
- the spread of panels (i.e. panel "A" appearing on too many cutting patterns).

The main objective of the Planner is to generate cutting patterns which satisfactorily take account of these consequences and other industrial characteristics, whilst maintaining a balance between them all, rather than optimising one objective at the expense of the remainder.

THE PLANNERS PREFERENCE SYSTEM

It is tempting to suggest that these other consequences can be treated on similar lines to multiple-attribute decision making. That presupposes, however, that the Planner can fully identify the attributes of the problem and that these attributes fully describe his goals. As we have discovered, Planners do not think in such terms. Determining the number and type of attributes that will describe an alternative is a difficult and complex task; even more so when the problem is complex and as inter-related as the 2DCP. If we assume that the attributes that the Planner focuses on are determined by his underlying goal structure, the problem still remains of how to identify and measure these values. Clearly one approach could be the use of numerical scales. However, although making the problem somewhat easier to deal with, not all the consequences of the 2DCP are easily formulated into scales of numerical values. In addition our research has shown that Planners are basically non-numerate, in the mathematical sense, and often have difficulty in verbalising their value system of preferences.

TRADE-OFF APPROACH

Where it is difficult to relate nominal and numerical attributes, suggestions in the literature advocate that the problem be structured using the concept of trade-offs. For example, in the 2DCP this could be achieved by considering the change in waste costs that would be required for a given change, in say, the reduction in the number of cutting patterns, i.e. the notion of trade-offs between differing sets of cutting patterns which produce the same set of panels. However, in practice it is not that simple. In our research we have found that Planners' preferences and the trade-offs upper and lower bounds, tend to change given certain circumstances. For example, the starting goal is just as likely to be the minimisation of the number of cutting patterns as the minimisation of waste. This preference for a low number of cutting patterns may be modified, even discarded after the generation of the first few cutting patterns, the explanation for this simply being that the possibility of cutting patterns with high order closures existing is greatest at the start point, not half way through the pattern generation routine. Given that the Planner has, in these initial few cutting patterns, sacrificed potential savings in material costs for high panel order closure per cutting pattern, then the over-riding objective would now become one of waste minimisation. This would then require that a new set of preferences, centred around the waste minimisation objective be adopted.

A PARAMETERISED APPROACH

Planners, then, do not use just one set of ordered preference values in sorting through their cutting problem, but many. More importantly, the ordering of these preferences and the level and activity of trade-offs between them tend to change, dependent upon the actual position that the Planner perceives himself to be in, i.e., if there is pressure from the Production Manager for increased volume, due to high product demand, then the waste objective might very well be modified for an increase in volume throughput. Thus, although the concept of simple preferences and trade-offs between two or three alternatives is theoretically easy to handle, in many practical cases, as the 2DCP indicates, this is likely to be unrepresentative of the actual decision situation faced by the decision maker.

In practice we find that decision makers require to be able to direct the problem solution, i.e., if volume is the primary goal then the solution approach has to rank the other consequences in relation to this goal and then determine the solution. Often only part of the solution is acceptable and hence the offending solutions are required to be re-calculated with the initial goal being ranked lower. The problem solution then is derived from successive iterations, each iteration imparting additional information which may or may not result in the decision maker restructuring the actual problem.

Given this situation, our approach to structuring the decision maker's preference system was to parameterise the main objectives and consequences and to allow the decision maker to select interactively his preferred solution direction. At this stage we add that our results are encouraging in as much as the parameters allow the decision maker to approach the cutting problem from a variety of different goals. Also the Decision maker is in control of the direction of the eventual solution - not the programme - and it is probably this aspect of our approach which has resulted in our successful implementation record. We now proceed to detail our heuristic approach to the Furniture Manufacturer's 2DCP.

AN INTERACTIVE HEURISTIC APPROACH TO THE 2DCP

Central to our approach to the Furniture Manufacturer's 2DCP is the belief that the real decision problem confronting the Planner is far more complex than the normative 2DCP cited in the literature. Furthermore, our experiences, gained from numerous installations, suggest that Planners require help and support to sort through the conflicting, inter-related set of objectives, not answers which claim to be optimal from a pure mathematical standpoint. What has to be understood is that the 2DCP affects a wide range of decision makers within the same system, and although there may be a general consensus about the necessity to minimise the wastage within the cutting operation - the rational economical objective - for each decision maker the 2DCP will raise quite different issues. High cutting pattern complexity, for example, means different things to different decision makers. For the Production Manager there is the prospect of less volume, due to high cutting pattern complexities; for the Planner, the complexity of the sequencing of panels which are spread across the complex cutting patterns; for the Mill Manager, a no win situation where no single objective has preference; all are equal! For the Sawyer, complex cutting patterns equate to more aggravation, not less, and the Purchasing Manager, who views the problem as one relating to material costs and order processing issues.

THREE STAGES

The approach that has been developed and which is now briefly outlined consists of three stages and follows very closely the heuristic methods and ideas that are used and which work in practice.

Stage 1 - User Defined Patterns

It became evident from our research that Planners stored, at a sub-conscious level, sets of good cutting patterns, good meaning acceptable wastage levels, high order closure per pattern with high or low open orders. When presented with a cutting list that required cutting patterns to be calculated, Planners automatically scanned the order listing in an attempt to identify and match orders to their library file of good cutting patterns. Often subtle changes would take place to the order list - in effect a relaxation of some of the restrictions - so that these good cutting patterns could be utilised. This pattern matching first stage then goes some of the way in explaining why manual approaches generally result in less cutting patterns, with slightly higher wastage levels, than the computer generated solutions. Quite simply, the objective function, at the initial stage is to select cutting patterns that close a high proportion of the order list and have acceptable levels of waste. Subsequent iterations will have less combinations that will satisfy these two goals and hence wastage levels will inevitably become the dominant goal. Having unearthed this User Defined Approach it seemed correct that the first stage of our algorithm should have a User Defined Routine so that the Planner could easily define his good cutting pattern set and store for later use, if required. Hence the first stage of our approach is an interactive User Defined pattern routine. In this routine the Planner is able to input his initial good set easily and to modify that set to reflect the current order requirements. Typically the current order requirement is matched to this set of good cutting patterns and then the order list is decremented.

Stage 2 - Strip Generation

The second stage of the algorithm is the generation of strip candidates to match the order requirements, i.e. it is necessary to determine the possible partitions of the panel lengths - and widths if there is no grain direction - into the given board lengths. To limit the generation to only feasible strip combinations a set of strip parameters is used. The concepts of additional panel inclusion and open orders are formally incorporated into the evaluation of the strip candidates by the use of a mathematical expression which allows the non-linear aspects of the 2DCP to be introduced explicitly into the evaluation procedure. These non-linear aspects are parameterised within the programme and are controllable by the Planner.

Stage 3 - Cutting Pattern Enumeration

The third stage is the enumeration of the cutting pattern. This uses the previously generated and evaluated strip candidates from Stage 2. Once again the concept of a cutting pattern value, similar to the one for strips, is used to generate and evaluate the best cutting pattern combination. The panel order list is then decremented and lexico-graphically re-ordered. The algorithm continues in this iterative manner, with alternative second and third stages, until the order list is satisfied, i.e. a problem reduction method. As many readers will no doubt realise, the problem reduction method can often result in the later cutting pattern tending to have higher waste and often low quantities of boards, i.e. unacceptable solutions. These patterns, which tend to exist in practice, force the Planner to adopt certain strategies to make these cutting patterns more acceptable, i.e.

- an additional panel type not previously included in the order list may be brought into consideration ... or
- accept higher amounts of extras ... or
- be prepared to use a different board size than initially stated ... or
- cancel the offending panel order - if possible

and there are other strategies.

Stage 1 then offers the Planner the facility to amend these poorer, later cutting patterns, and hence the major problem associated with the problem reduction method does not arise.

ACKNOWLEDGEMENTS

The author would like to thank Dr. R. Green, for his encouragement in the preparation of this paper. In addition thanks are also extended to the members of Homeworthy Furniture Limited and to Professor D.J. White for their helpful comments. The original systems programming design of the COPS Software was carried out by J. Wiltshire.

SOLVING A MULTI-OBJECTIVE PRODUCTION PLANNING PROBLEM BY AN INTERACTIVE PROCEDURE

W. Michalowski and A. Piotrowski

(Instytut Organizacji Zarzadzania i Doskonalenia Kadr, Poland)

1. DESCRIPTION OF THE UNION OF CONSTRUCTION MACHINERY INDUSTRIES

The Union of Construction Machinery Industries (UCMI) consists of several industrial enterprises. The basic line of production of UCMI is as follows [2]:

machinery for building and earth works;

self propelled machinery

cranes;

rollers;

power units, spare parts, etc., for the machinery.

High material consumption, close cooperation with other industries, and import dependency are the main characteristics of UCMI production. The major part of production is used by the building industry, and exported. Having in mind the improvement of short term planning, UCMI headquarters decided to use a mathematical programming model as one of the planning tools. It was an optimization model, constructed without feedbacks, concerned with the production plans of industrial enterprises constituting the UCMI. It was decided that the planning problem could be sufficiently described by linear programming (LP). Additionally, the existence of effective computer codes implied the utilization of an LP model.

2. DESCRIPTION OF THE INTERACTIVE PROCEDURE

We consider the following multiobjective (MOLP) model.

$$\max \quad C\bar{x}$$

$$\text{s.t.} \quad x \in X$$

where $X = \{x \in R^n | Ax = b, x \geqq 0\}$

$$C = (c^1, \ldots, c^\ell)^T$$

c^i is the vector of coefficients of the ith objective function.

C, A, x, b have dimensions $\ell \times n$, $m \times n$, $n \times 1$, $m \times 1$, respectively. X is a convex polyhedron.

While applying our interactive procedure we make the following assumptions [1]:

(i) the decision maker (DM) does not have a priori knowledge of the relative importance of the objective functions;

(ii) it is possible to define the accomplishment levels corresponding to the worst compromise.

Let us denote the efficient solutions by $\{x^i\}$, $i=1,\ldots,\ell$, where the objective functions reach their optimal values (we assume here that they are unique solutions). When it is impossible to define the worst compromise on the basis of the DM's preferences, we suggest a simple rule for its computation. We propose to define the worst compromise for the kth objective function, as the function's lowest value reached on the set $\{x^i\}$ $i=1,\ldots,\ell$ i.e.

$$m_k^1 = \min_{1 \leq i \leq \ell} \{c^k x^i\} \text{ (when objective function is maximized);}$$

$$m_k^1 = \max_{1 \leq i \leq \ell} \{c^k x^i\} \text{ (when objective function is minimized).}$$

So here we assume that the DM is not interested in the efficient solutions where the values of any objective function are worse than the given $\{m_k^1\}$ values although this may exclude some efficient solutions. We assume also that the DM can, at every iteration, evaluate the outcomes of different objective functions.

The interactive procedure is initiated with the calculation of an initial basic efficient solution of the MOLP problem. Let us denote it by $\bar{x}$. In the first iteration $\bar{x}$ is an initial basic efficient solution, while further on it is a basic solution computed in step 3.

Step 1

It is the step of interaction between the decision and computing phases. In this step we obtain the information concerning the DM's local preferences. On the basis of this information we distinguish the following subsets in the set of objective function indices, viz:

W the subset of objective function indices whose values should be improved in reference to the values reached at $\bar{x}$;

P the subset of objective function indices whose values may be made worse in reference to the values reached at $\bar{x}$;

Z the subset of objective function indices whose values should not be made worse in reference to the values reached at $\bar{x}$.

In order to help the DM to make up his mind, the following decision table is presented to him. The row A O F is for him to assign the objective functions to one of the sets W, P or Z.

TABLE 1

Decision Table

Objective Function Level \ Objective Function Number	1	2	. . .	ℓ
Optimal level	c^1x^1	c^2x^2		c^1x^ℓ
Worst compromise	m_1^1	m_2^1		m_ℓ^1
Actual attained level	$c^1\bar{x}$	$c^2\bar{x}$		$c^3\bar{x}$
A O F				

Letter

W denotes objective functions whose values are to be improved;
P denotes objective functions whose values may be made worse;
Z denotes objective functions whose values are to be maintained;

In order to fill in the last row of the decision table, the DM answers the following question.

"Are the objective function values presented in this table satisfactory to you? If YES, it is the final solution. Otherwise please indicate (writing letter P) the values which may be worsened, the values to be improved (writing letter W), and the values to be maintained (writing letter Z)."

Step 2

A certain modification of the feasible solutions set is performed in this step. It is accomplished by the introduction of three groups of constraints.

First group of constraints

$$c^i x - h_i w \geqq c^i \bar{x}, \ \forall i \in W$$

where h_i is a normalisation factor computed according to the following formulae.

$$h_i = 1/|c^i x^i - m_i^1|, \ \forall i \in W.$$

Second group of constraints

$$c^i \bar{x} \geqq c^i x \geqq m_i^1, \ \forall i \in P.$$

The first inequality may be relaxed although the DM should be aware that some worsening of the objective functions may arise in this group.

Third group of constraints

$$c^i x \geqq c^i \bar{x} \qquad \forall i \in Z.$$

For the general iteration we will denote by m^r the worst compromise vector m where r is the iteration number. It results from the changes of components of vector m^{r-1} while moving from one iteration to another. So, at the rth iteration, the worst compromise is defined as follows.

$$m_k^r = f_k \text{ with } f_k \in [m_k^{r-1}, c^k \bar{x}^{r-1}]$$

where

f_k is the kth objective function value which can be specified by the DM;

$\bar{x}^{r-1}$ is the basic efficient solution obtained at the r-1th iteration.

Step 3

A new, basic efficient solution which is presented later on to the DM, is derived from the solution of the following problem

$$\max w$$

s.t.

$$x \in X$$

$$c^i x - h_i w \geqslant f_i \qquad i \in W$$

$$\left.\begin{array}{l} c^i x \geqq f_i \\ c^i x \leqq c^i \bar{x} \end{array}\right\} \quad i \in P$$

$$c^i x \geqq c^i \bar{x} \qquad i \in Z.$$

This solution is basic efficient with respect to the new problem. It is efficient in the original problem if we relax the left hand side inequalities in group P.

The procedure is terminated when the DM finds the solution presented to him satisfactory, or when the same optimal solution of the above problem is obtained in two consecutive iterations.

3. THE MOLP PROBLEM DESCRIPTION

In a MOLP problem constructed for UCMI there are 120 decision variables and four objective functions, given below.

(i) Volume of sales (denoted by SALES);

(ii) net profit from sales (denoted by PROFIT);

(iii) import of raw materials (denoted by IMPORT);

(iv) utilization of production capacities (denoted by PRODUCT).

The functions SALES, PROFIT, PRODUCT are maximised, while the function IMPORT is minimized. The MOLP problem is constructed under the assumption that the given article is produced by one manufacturer.

3.1 The Notation

We use the following notation.

j an index of article (decision variable), $j=1,\ldots,120$;

c_j^1 selling price of jth article;

c_j^2 net profit per unit of jth article;

c_j^3 value of import per unit of jth article;

c_j^4 total volume of manufacturing time required to produce a unit of jth article;

x_j a volume of jth article to be produced (decision variable);

I set of indices of imported raw materials;

a_{ij}^1 $(i \in I)$ a quota of ith imported raw material per unit of jth article;

R_i $(i \in I)$ total value of ith imported raw material;

M set of indices of domestic raw materials in short supply;

a_{ij}^2 $(i \in M)$ a quota of ith domestic raw material in short supply per unit of jth article (in value terms);

D_i $(i \in M)$ total amount of ith domestic raw material in short supply;

K the set of indices of spare parts and machinery bought under cooperation agreements;

a_{ij}^3 $(i \in K)$ a quota of ith cooperation elements per unit of jth article;

W_i $(i \in K)$ total amount of ith cooperation element;

p a manufacturer index;

S_p the set of indices of articles produced by pth manufacturer;

T_i $(i \in S_p)$ total amount of time available for ith production stands in pth manufacturer;

a^4_{ij} $(i \in S_p)$ amount of time of ith production stands in pth manufacturer required to produce a unit of jth article;

d_j, g_j lower and upper limits on production of jth article.

3.2 MOLP Problem

3.2.1 Objective Functions

(i) Maximization of volume of sales (SALES).

$$\sum_{j=1}^{120} c^1_j x_j \longrightarrow \max.$$

(ii) Maximization of net profit from sales (PROFIT).

$$\sum_{j=1}^{120} c^2_j x_j \longrightarrow \max.$$

(iii) Minimization of import of raw materials (IMPORT).

$$\sum_{j=1}^{120} c^3_j x_j \longrightarrow \min.$$

(iv) Maximization of utilization of production capacities (PRODUCT).

$$\sum_{j=1}^{120} c^4_j x_j \longrightarrow \max.$$

3.2.2 Constraints

(i) The balance of imported raw materials

$$\sum_{j=1}^{120} a^1_{ij} x_j \leq R_i, \ i \in I.$$

(ii) The balance of domestic raw materials in short supply.

$$\sum_{j=1}^{120} a^2_{ij} x_j \leq D_i, \ i \in M.$$

(iii) Constraints resulting from the cooperation requirements.

$$\sum_{j=1}^{120} a_{ij}^{3} x_j \leqq W_i, \quad i \in K.$$

(iv) Constraints resulting from the production capacities.

$$\sum_{j=1}^{120} a_{ij}^{4} x_j \leqq T_i, \quad i \in S_p.$$

(v) Lower limites (d_j) imposed on production resulting from the agreements, and upper limits (g_j) resulting from the cooperation conditions.

$$d_j \leqq x_j \leqq g_j, \quad j=1,\ldots,120.$$

(vi) Nonnegativity constraints.

$$x_j \geqq 0, \qquad j=1,\ldots,120.$$

(vii) Additionally one should impose integer constraints on the decision variables, but, having in mind the order of magnitude of these variables, we took the integer part of x_j as the actual decision instead.

4. THE SOLUTION

The MOLP problem discussed in Section 3 was solved by our interactive programming procedure. We cooperated with the DM from the Planning Department of UCMI. He was briefed on the interactive procedure rules and general principles of the decision making situation. We used the MPSX computer code in the optimization phase, and all computations were performed on an IBM 370/142 computer. All necessary data were stored on a magnetic disc, and corrected with a proper utility program.

According to the initial step requirements we made the following calculations.

(i) We solved four LP problems;

(ii) we computed values of all objective functions for the optimal solutions of these problems.

Table 2 is the result of these calculations.

TABLE 2

Objective Function \ Optimal Solution Number	1	2	3	4
$SALES_{max}$	22256581	18027076	17615308	18885456
$PROFIT_{max}$	5261700	8197967	4509282	5316584
$IMPORT_{min}$	7482000	8015600	3735200	9198800
$PRODUCT_{max}$	10652711	9745870	8402829	11285651

The vector m^1 representing the worst compromise is following:

$$m^1 = (17615308;\ 4509282;\ \ 9198800;\ 8402829)^T$$

The normalisation factors are computed according to the formulae

$$h_i = (1/|c^i x^i - m_i^1|).10^6$$

and are as follows.

i	1	2	3	4
h_i	.215	.271	.183	.347

The MOLP problem defined in Section 3 is modified by the introduction of the following constraints

$$\sum_{j=1}^{120} c_j^1 x_j - 0.215w \geqslant 17615308$$

$$\sum_{j=1}^{120} c_j^2 x_j - 0.271w \geqslant 4509282$$

$$\sum_{j=1}^{120} c_j^3 x_j + 0.183w \leqslant 9198800$$

$$\sum_{j=1}^{120} c_j^4 x_j - 0.347w \geqslant 8402829$$

and taking the following objective function.

$$w \longrightarrow \max.$$

The first decision table presented to the DM after solving a modified MOLP problem is as follows in Table 3.

TABLE 3

First Decision Table

	SALES	PROFIT	IMPORT	PRODUCT
Optimal level	22256581	8197967	3735200	11285651
Worst compromise	17615308	4509282	9198800	8402829
Actual attained level	19372499	6724164	7703142	9383524
A O F	Z	P	W	Z

The new worst compromise vector is as follows.

$$(19372499;\ 4509282;\ 7703142;\ 9383524)^T$$

The set of feasible solutions is modified by the introduction of the following constraints.

For functions SALES and PRODUCT

$$\sum_{j=1}^{120} c_j^1 x_j \geqslant 19372499$$

$$\sum_{j=1}^{120} c_j^4 x_j \geqslant 9383524.$$

For function PROFIT

$$6724164 \sum_{j=4}^{120} c_j^2 x_j \geqslant 4509282.$$

For function IMPORT

$$\sum_{j=1}^{120} c_j^3 x_j + 0.252w \leqslant 7703142.$$

A new decision table related to the solution of a new, modified, problem is presented in Table 4

TABLE 4

Second Decision Table

	SALES	PROFIT	IMPORT	PRODUCT
Optimal level	22256581	8197967	3735200	11285651
Worst compromise	19372499	4509282	7703142	9383524
Actual attained level	19372499	5371051	6777185	11238858
A O F	W	Z	Z	P

The worst compromise vector is as follows.

$$(19372499;\ 5371051;\ 6777185;\ 11000000)^T$$

The value 11000000 was proposed by the DM.

The constraints of this iteration are as follows.

$$\sum_{j=1}^{120} c_j^1 x_j - 0.347w \geqslant 19372499$$

$$\sum_{j=1}^{120} c_j^2 x_j \geqslant 5371051$$

$$\sum_{j=1}^{120} c_j^3 x_j \leq 6777185$$

$$11238858 \geq \sum_{j=1}^{120} c_j^4 x_j \geq 11000000.$$

New values of four objective functions, together with all accompanying information, are collected in the decision table presented in Table 5.

TABLE 5

Third Decision Table

	SALES	PROFIT	IMPORT	PRODUCT
Optimal level	22256581	8197967	3735200	11285651
Worst compromise	19372499	5371051	6777185	11000000
Actual attained level	21650080	5371051	6777185	11000000
A O F	Z	Z	Z	Z

The DM decided that the solution presented to him during the third iteration was satisfactory. So, this solution was taken as the final one of the MOLP problem. In Table 6 we present a comprehensive list of objective function values reached at every iteration, and the optimal solution of the LP problem with the SALES objective function.

5. CONCLUSIONS

In our final solution of the MOLP problem, the value of the SALES function is only 2.7% inferior to its optimal value (to some extent, SALES is the leading criterion to the DM). Moreover, the values of all remaining objective functions computed with our interactive procedure are better than those in the SALES optimal solution. In general the DM's opinion on our procedure was favourable. He accepted the scheme of the decision table, and the rules of objective function value judgements. The DM criticized the lack of calculations for different values of MOLP problem parameters, resulting from computer system and software limitations. Due to the positive

TABLE 6

A Comprehensive List

Solution \ Objective Function	SALES	PROFIT	IMPORT	PRODUCT
1	19372499	6724164	7703142	9383524
2	19372499	5371051	6777185	11238858
3	21650080	5371051	6777185	11000000
$SALES_{max}$	22256581	5261700	7482000	10652711

practical evaluation of our interactive procedure it was decided to incorporate it into the planning system being prepared for UCMI.

ACKNOWLEDGEMENTS

The authors wish to thank Doug White for his refereeing of this article and the useful points made.

REFERENCES

1. Michalowski, W. 1980 "Poszukiwanie rozwiazan optymalnych w wielokryteriowych modelach liniowych", SGPiS, Warsaw.

2. Piotrowski, A. and Rotkiel, T. 1979 "Automatyzacja funkcji planowania: Zalozenia projektowe - model matematyczny", PIMAB, Warsaw.

LUBRICANT BLENDING AS A MULTI-OBJECTIVE PROBLEM

M.K-S. Tso

(University of Manchester Institute of Science and Technology)

and

M.L.R. Price

(Operational Research Group, Wales Gas)

ABSTRACT

The problem of determining a minimum cost blend subject to quality constraints which have been empirically determined by regression analysis is reformulated as a multi-objective optimization. We show that Pareto-optimal solutions may be obtained by solving a set of quadratic programming sub-problems.

INTRODUCTION

A lubricant may be regarded as a blend of base oil and a number of additive components, chemicals included to improve the oil's technical performance. If a linear cost function is assumed and performance can also be considered as depending linearly on composition, then the determination of a minimum cost blend to satisfy multiple performance criteria is the archetypal example of linear programming (LP).

It must be assumed, conventionally, that the coefficients relating performance to composition are known. In this paper we take account of the uncertainty present in this relationship arising from the estimation of the coefficients by regression analysis. Emphasis is placed on a reformulation as a multi-objective decision problem.

BASIC NOTATION

A blend is represented by a real p-vector $\underline{x} \in S$ where S is the simplex

$$S = \{\underline{x} \mid \underline{1}^T\underline{x} = 1,\ \underline{x} \geq 0\} \tag{1}$$

and $\underline{1}$ is a p-vector of ones. That is, $\underline{x}$ is a vector of proportions that we wish to determine. For example x_1 may be the proportion of base oil in the blend and $\{x_k | k = 2,\ldots,p\}$ the proportions of each of p-1 additives that may be included in the blend.

The technical performance of a lubricant is assessed by a set of m tests and it is assumed that the outcome $y_j(\underline{x})$ of the jth test on a blend $\underline{x}$ gives a satisfactory result if $y_j(\underline{x}) \geq b_j$, where b_j is given constant.

UNCERTAINTY IN PERFORMANCE

If we assume that performance is related to composition by the linear regression relationship

$$y_j = \underline{x}^T \underline{\beta}_j + \varepsilon_j \qquad j = 1,\ldots,m \tag{2}$$

where $\underline{\beta}_j$ is a vector of contant regression coefficients and ε_j is an additive normally distributed error, (ε_j distributed independently for $j = 1,\ldots,m$), then the uncertainty in predicting the outcome of a future test on $\underline{x}$ arises from two sources. First, there is the uncertainty in estimating $\underline{\beta}_j$. Secondly, it is impossible to predict the outcome of a future test to a greater precision than the inherent standard deviation σ_j of ε_j. Specifically, let X(nxp) be a matrix containing a sample of n blends and let $\{\underline{y}_j | j = 1,\ldots,m\}$ be the vectors of test performance observed on these blends (assumed complete). The mean μ and variance V of a future test result $y_j(\underline{x})$ on a blend $\underline{x}$ are estimated by

$$\begin{aligned} \mu &= \underline{x}^T \underline{a}_j \\ V &= s_j^2\, [\underline{x}^T S \underline{x} + 1] \end{aligned} \tag{3}$$

where $S = (X^T X)^{-1}$. Here $\underline{a}_j$ and s_j^2 are the usual unbiased estimates of $\underline{\beta}_j$ and σ_j^2 based on the sample $\{X, \underline{y}_j\}$. An empirical Bayesian argument can be employed to derive a subjective probability distribution for a future observation y_j:

$$\frac{y_j - \underline{a}_j^T \underline{x}}{s_j(\underline{x}^T S \underline{x} + 1)^{\frac{1}{2}}} \sim t_{n-p} \tag{4}$$

where t_ν denotes Student's t-distribution on ν degrees of freedom. Hence the probability that a future blend $\underline{x}$ satisfies the jth test based on the sample $\{X, y_j\}$ is

$$p_j(\underline{x}) \triangleq P\left[y_j(\underline{x}) \geq b_j\right] = T_{n-p}\left[\frac{\underline{a}_j^T \underline{x} - b_j}{s_j(\underline{x}^T S \underline{x} + 1)^{\frac{1}{2}}}\right] \tag{5}$$

where T_ν is the cumulative distribution function of Student's t-distribution on ν degrees of freedom. Equation (5) may also be derived using the notion of a classical confidence limit (see [2]).

MINIMUM-COST FORMULATION

Replacing the deterministic linear constraints of the standard LP formulation by their probabilistic counterpart, we obtain

$$\begin{aligned} &\text{minimise } \underline{c}^T \underline{x} \\ &\text{subject to } p_j(\underline{x}) \geq \alpha_j \qquad j = 1,\ldots,m \\ &\qquad\qquad \underline{x} \in S \end{aligned} \tag{6}$$

where $p_j(\underline{x})$ is given by (5) and $\{\alpha_j\}$ are given constants representing the minimum acceptable probability of passing each test satisfactorily. The jth constraint of (6) may be written

$$\underline{a}_j^T \underline{x} - b_j \geq t_{n-p}(\alpha_j)\ s_j(\underline{x}^T S \underline{x} + 1)^{\frac{1}{2}} \tag{7}$$

where $t_{n-p}(\alpha)$ is the 100α % point of t_{n-p}. It is easily seen that the r.h.s. of (7) is a convex function of $\underline{x}$ provided that $t_{n-p}(\alpha_j) \geq 0$, i.e. provided that $\alpha_j \geq 0.5$. If this holds for each j, then the feasible region for (6) will be convex and numerical optimization should result in a global minimum. Note that $\alpha_j \geq 0.5$ would not seem to be a severe limitation in practice, as $\alpha_j < 0.5$ corresponds to a blend more likely to fail than to pass the jth test. We also note that the case $\alpha_j = 0.5$ reduces to the standard LP formulation, so that ignoring the stochastic nature of the constraints results in blends having perhaps only a 50% chance of passing each test. In classical terms, one is adopting a 50% confidence limit as a constraint boundary for the LP.

MAXIMUM PROBABILITY FORMULATION

The minimum cost formulation results in a non-linear optimization which has the features that (i) the non-linearity is in the constraints and (ii) a set of minimum probability levels $\{\alpha_j\}$ must be specified. An alternative approach is to maximise in some sense the probabilities of passing each test subject to an upper limit constraint on the cost of an acceptable blend. We now have the multi-objective optimization problem

$$\left.\begin{aligned} P:\ &\text{maximise } p_j(\underline{x}) = T_{n-p}[z_j(\underline{x})] \\ &\text{where } z_j(\underline{x}) = \frac{\underline{a}_j^T\underline{x} - b_j}{s_j(\underline{x}^T S \underline{x} + 1)^{\frac{1}{2}}} \qquad j = 1,\ldots,m \\ &\text{subject to } \underline{c}^T\underline{x} \le K \\ &\underline{x} \in S \end{aligned}\right\} \tag{8}$$

and we see that the non-linearity has been transferred to the objective functions. The specification of $\{\alpha_j\}$ in the previous formulation which amounted to an implicit subjective assessment of the relative importance of passing each test is now avoided. Instead we are faced with an explicitly multi-objective problem. Comparing the alternative formulations (6) and (8), perhaps (8) is more in keeping with the cost-directed approach of industrial research and development. Making use of the monotonic increasing nature of $T_{n-p}(\cdot)$, a standard theorem ([3], Theorem 3.6) informs us that a <u>strictly</u> optimal solution to the scalarised sub-problem

$$\begin{aligned} P_\lambda:\ &\text{maximize } \Sigma\lambda_j z_j(\underline{x}) \\ &\text{subject to } \underline{c}^T\underline{x} \le K \\ &\underline{x} \in S \end{aligned} \tag{9}$$

where $\{\lambda_j > 0,\ j = 1,\ldots,m\}$ is an arbitrary set of positive weights, will be an efficient (Pareto-optimal) solution to (8).

A USEFUL TRANSFORMATION

Given a choice of positive weights $\{\lambda_j\}$ summing to unity, both the numerator and the denominator of the objective function in (9) can be expressed as functions homogeneous of degree 1 on the blend simplex S. A transformation given by Bradley and Frey [1] may be used to solve (9) by quadratic programming. Writing the objective function as

$$\frac{\underline{a}^T\underline{x} - b}{(\underline{x}^T S\underline{x} + 1)^{\frac{1}{2}}} \quad \text{where } \underline{a} = \sum_j \frac{\lambda_j \underline{a}_j}{s_j} \text{ and } b = \sum_j \frac{\lambda_j b_j}{s_j} \tag{10}$$

the transformation $\underline{y} = \underline{x}/(\underline{a}^T\underline{x} - b)$ restricted to $\{\underline{x} | \underline{a}^T\underline{x} - b > 0\}$ leads to the convex quadratic programming problem

$$\left.\begin{aligned} &\text{minimise } \underline{y}^T(S + \underline{1}\,\underline{1}^T)\underline{y} \\ &\text{subject to } (\underline{c}^T - K\,\underline{1}^T)\underline{y} \le 0 \\ &\qquad (\underline{a}^T - b\,\underline{1}^T)\underline{y} = 1 \\ &\qquad \underline{y} \ge 0 \end{aligned}\right\} \tag{11}$$

The optimal blend $\underline{x}$ is given by the back-transformation

$$\underline{x} = \underline{y}/(\underline{1}^T\underline{y}) \tag{12}$$

The restriction of the forward transformation to the half-space $\{\underline{x} | \underline{a}^T\underline{x} - b > 0\}$ is unimportant provided (11) is feasible (see [2] for a fuller discussion of this point).

DISCUSSION

We have considered the stochastic version of the standard LP blending problem in which the constraint hyperplanes are replaced by confidence surfaces derived from regression analysis. Two formulations have been proposed, both requiring an implicit or explicit weighting of the probabilities of meeting each constraint. One approach is to find a blend to maximise these probabilities subject to an upper bound on blend cost. This is a vector maximisation problem for which efficient solutions may be found by solving scalarised sub-problems $\{P_\lambda\}$ parametrised by a positive vector of weights $\underline{\lambda}$. Different efficient solutions may be generated by varying $\underline{\lambda}$. We have seen that P_λ may be solved by an algorithm for quadratic programming. There appear to be two important practical aspects requiring further investigation:

1. Is there a strategy for choosing the weights $\{\lambda_j\}$ in order to select the best blend (in some subjective sense) from the efficient set? White's algorithm [4] for multi-objective interactive programming might be applicable here.

2. Under what circumstances, if any, do the solutions to $\{P_\lambda\}$ form precisely the efficient set for (8). It is well known ([3], Theorem 3.7) that concavity of the feasible cost set

$$\Gamma \triangleq \{\underline{z}(\underline{x}) \mid \underline{c}^T\underline{x} \leq K,\ \underline{x} \in S\} \tag{14}$$

is sufficient, where $\underline{z}(\underline{x})$ is the vector with jth component $z_j(\underline{x})$ given in (8). However, it seems unlikely that Γ is concave in the majority of cases and then it would be useful to know how much of the efficient set is achievable by solving $\{P_\lambda\}$.

ACKNOWLEDGEMENT

The work described in this paper was carried out while the first author was at Thornton Research Centre, Chester (Shell Research Ltd.). Some of this work was also submitted by M.L.R. Price in fulfilment of the degree of Ph.D. at the University College of Wales, Aberystwyth [2].

REFERENCES

1. Bradley, S.P. and Frey, S.C. 1974 "Fractional programming with homogeneous functions", *Operations Research*, **22**, p. 350.

2. Price, M.L.R. 1982 "Optimisation under statistically derived constraints", Ph.D. Thesis submitted to the University College of Wales, Aberystwyth.

3. Vincent, T.L. and Grantham, W.J. 1981 "Optimality in parametric systems", Wiley, New York.

4. White, D.J. 1980 "Multi-objective interactive programming", *J.O.R.S.*, **31**, p. 517-523.

A PLEA FOR INTERACTIVE VISUALISATION TECHNIQUES AS MULTI-CRITERIA AIDS

A. Jaeger

(Bochum)

In order to cope with multi-objective decision problems, a great variety of interactive methods has been proposed, for example those reported in this volume. From a purely mathematical standpoint, they are certainly interesting, elegant, exciting, even impressive; but much less can be said about their practical applicability.

At least in the Federal Republic of Germany, decisions are generally made not by professional mathematicians and in most cases not by people with a strong mathematical background, but by managers who might possibly have some reservations about the wisdom of applying sophisticated mathematics directly as a decision aid. Many German managerial decision makers are lawyers by training if not attitude. Because of the codetermination law, blue collar workers, mostly trade unionists, who might not have college training participate in company group decision-making, and in parliamentary bodies many representatives are professional politicians.

What all these people have in common is that they are very busy and hence uninterested, or unwilling to spend considerable time in becoming familiar with involved and opaque questioning techniques of a multi-criteria decision analyst. While they are much more ready to engage in eloquent pleas for their own cause, they may perhaps at best be willing to answer three or four easy quantitative questions, unless they suspect that their replies could be counterproductive.

One very promising way to assist the busy decision maker for the preparation of his answer consists in presenting him with relevant data in the form of geometrical (not numerical) figures on a monitor generated by computer programs (see Booth 1979, Newman et al 1979 and Robinson 1981). For example in the case of a linear vector optimisation problem: the efficient faces in the neighbourhood of an efficient solution may be visualised by means of three dimensional projections on interesting criteria spaces (Winkels 1981, Winkels 1982); for every pair of aspiration levels in two criteria the corresponding efficient values of the other criteria can be represented (Winkels 1982); the line segment between an initial efficient solution and a new target point can be projected on the efficient border to simplify the improvement of a compromise (Winkels 1981 and 1982); stability regions of interesting efficient solutions can be visualised to provide information on the corresponding sensitivity with respect to changes of data (Winkels1982).

The theoretical foundations for these visualisation methods listed above have been developed at the Ruhr University of Bochum by H.-M. Winkels in such a way that computer implementation could be executed immediately. In collaboration with M. Meika and R. Colman, the corresponding computer programs have been written in FORTRAN 77 for a CYBER 175 and in BASIC for a microcomputer of the type TRS 80 (Level II). Further current research activities at Bochum in the area of visualisation include the development of interactive techniques for the construction of outranking relations and utility functions.

These examples may serve as promising paradigms for multi-objective decision mathematicians to intensify or even concentrate their future work on such interactive methods which are compatible with monitor visualisation techniques, although the use of computer graphics in operational research is just beginning (Johnson et al 1980, Lucas 1981, Schilling 1980 and Schilling et al 1982) and much theoretical research and practical implementation has still to be carried out. However it cannot be over-emphasised that relationships between numerical variables can be grasped by non-mathematicians much more easily and much more intuitively if they are presented by means of curves or more complex geometric figures and not by formulae or by verbal explanations. After all the acceptance of the multi-objective decision procedure by a real and very busy decision maker is at stake.

REFERENCES

BOOTH, K.S. 1979 Tutorial in Computer Graphics, The Institute of Electrical and Electronic Engineers, Inc., New York.

JOHNSON, L.E. and LOUCKS, D.P. 1980 "Interactive Multi-objective Planning Using Computer Graphics", *Computers and Operations Research*, 7(1-2), pp. 89-97.

LUCAS, H.C. 1981 "An Experimental Investigation of the Use of Computer-Based Graphics in Decision Making", *Management Science*, 27(7), pp. 757-768.

NEWMAN, W.M., SPROULL, R.F. 1979 Principles of Interactive Computer Graphics (2nd Ed.), McGraw-Hill, London.

ROBINSON, P. 1981 "Trends in Computer Graphics", *Journal of the Operational Research Society,* **32**, pp. 303-316.

SCHILLING, D.D. 1980 An Approach to the Display and Analysis of Multi-objective Problems, Working Paper Series WPS 80-61, College of Administrative Science, Ohio State University, Columbus OH.

SCHILLING, D.D.; McGARITY, A. and REVELLE, C. 1982 "Hidden Attributes and the Display of Information in Multi-objective Analysis", *Management Science,* **28**(3), pp. 236-242.

WINKELS, H.-M. 1981 Efficiency Projections, Working Paper on Economathematics No. 8103, Departments of Economics and Mathematics, Ruhr University Bochum (submitted for publication in OR-Spektrum).

WINKELS, H.-M. 1981 Visualisation and Discretisation for Convex Polyhedral Sets, Working Paper on Economathematics No. 8104, Departments of Economics and Mathematics, Ruhr University Bochum (submitted for publication in Zeitschrift fur Operations Research).

WINKELS, H.-M. 1982 A Flexible Decision Aid Method for Linear Multi-criteria Systems, IIASA-Proceedings of the Conference on Multi-objective and Stochastic Optimisation.

WINKELS, H.-M. 1982 Visualising the Neighbourhood of an Efficient Solution, Working Paper on Economathematics No. 8205, Departments of Economics and Mathematics, Ruhr University Bochum.

A SURVEY AND INTERPRETATION OF MULTI-ATTRIBUTE UTILITY THEORY

Simon French
(Department of Decision Theory, University of Manchester)

INTRODUCTION

During the last decade there have appeared a number of excellent surveys of multi-attribute utility theory: Farquhar [1,2], Fishburn [3,4], Keeney and Raiffa [5], Krantz et al [6], and Roberts [7]. So why another? Part of the answer is that I was the outvoted member of the organising committee; but, more seriously, with the notable exception of Keeney and Raiffa, earlier surveys have concentrated on the mathematical aspects of multi-attribute utility functions with little mention of how the theory fits into a normative decision analysis. I believe that it is this concentration on the mathematics with an emphasis of axioms and assumptions that has led many to reject the theory as too precise and quite impractical for applications. For instance, Zeleny in his foreword to a special issue of Computers and Operations Research [8] on multiple objectives in mathematical programming chastises utility theory because:

> "Considering a single objective function (profit, cost, utility, etc.), as in the classical mathematical optimisation, presupposes that the decision maker's preferences and values are both complete and definite *at the beginning* of the decision process. Once the objective function is specified there is no further demand on the decision maker's involvement The decision was *implicitly* made; it only remains to be explicated through mathematical search or algorithms. The decision maker can then only say yes or no to the final outcome. The solution to mathematical optimisation is usually unique and no further decision making effort is required."
> (His emphasis)

Zeleny goes on to sing the praises of interactive multi-objective programming because this methodology involves the decision maker throughout the process in a way that multi-attribute utility analysis apparently does not. Zeleny is not alone in making this criticism; many others agree with him, although they may champion alternative methodologies, e.g. fuzzy sets.

I do not share Zeleny's views. I believe that decision analysis or multi-attribute utility analysis - call it what you will - is a far more delicate, interactive, exploratory tool than Zeleny will allow, one that involves the decision maker at all stages and moreover one that does not prescribe a single best choice. The primary function of a decision analysis is to help the decision maker understand his situation, his preferences and his beliefs better so that through this understanding he may make a more informed decision. It is my purpose in this paper to argue that this is so and, in particular, to emphasise and explore the role played by multi-attribute utility theory and its underlying independence conditions.

WHAT IS A NORMATIVE THEORY?

It is often said that utility theory is a normative theory in contrast to a descriptive one; and perhaps the best place to begin this paper is by discussing this distinction. In simple terms, normative analyses tell us how we should behave in particular circumstances, whereas descriptive theories conjecture how things are or how they are behaving. Although essentially correct this simple distinction is, I believe, too naive; it seems to grant normative analyses almost dictatorial powers over our behaviour. Yet surely the role of such analyses is that of providing guidance and advice. To see how they achieve this let us explore the difference between descriptive and normative theories more closely.

Essentially a descriptive theory is simply a conjectured picture of reality. It is a proposition which mirrors possible relations between possible objects or classes of object in the external world. It may be tentative, a scientific hypothesis, i.e. the merest suggestion of how the world may be, unsupported as yet by comparison with empirical knowledge; or it may be something in which more trust may be placed, i.e. a scientific model that has been tested against data and that in some sense has passed sufficiently well to be deemed satisfactory for making predictions.

Normative theories do not describe how things are; instead they provide guidance in a choice or judgement which has yet to be made. Here I confine attention to normative decision theories. The normative aspects of logic as a guide to mathematical argument are discussed from a similar viewpoint by Feferman [9], and I discuss normative models to aid an examiner's judgement elsewhere [10,11]. I shall assume that the decision is faced by a single person, that I am that person, and that I face the decision alone. Later I shall briefly extend the argument to a group of decision makers who take advice from an analyst. There is an advantage in assuming that I am the decision maker. I shall shortly introduce a model decision maker to whom I shall refer in the third person, thus creating a natural contrast with the actual decision maker - me.

At the simplest level I believe that a normative analysis guides my choice by example. It constructs a model decision problem (m.d.p.), which describes the alternatives facing me and predicts their consequences. Thus the m.d.p. is a descriptive model of my actual decision problem. In the context of the m.d.p. the analysis erects a model decision maker (m.d.m.), who in one sense is idealised and in another reflects me. He is idealised in that his logical structure is always consistent with certain axioms, which embody principles which I believe to be canons of rational behaviour. Thus he is idealised in a way which I admire; the consistency embodied in his behaviour is one that I would like to emulate. Subject to this constraint of consistency he reflects me in that his preferences and beliefs model my own. If I prefer more money to less then so does he; if I believe that it is more likely to rain tomorrow than snow then so does he. At least he does providing that my preferences and beliefs are 'reasonably' consistent in terms of the canons of rationality. If they are not I must either modify them as discussed below or reject the entire analysis since I clearly do not wish to emulate the behaviour embodied in the m.d.m. Using the logical structure I can determine the m.d.m.'s choice in the m.d.p. Thus I may see how an idealised decision maker with preferences and beliefs similar to mine will choose in a situation which parallels that in which I find myself. Because I admire the idealisation present in him, his choice will be a pointer - but only a pointer - to my choice in my real problem. If you like, a normative analysis provides a modern day parable carefully tailored to my current situation and thus helps me to choose a course of action.

To give these ideas more substance, consider a Bayesian decision analysis. Here the m.d.p. takes the form of a decision table, which predicts the outcome for each possible action under each possible set of external factors. The m.d.m. is composed of two functions: a subjective probability distribution and a utility function. His choice is determined by maximising his expected utility. The canons of rationality embodied by his behaviour are well known; for instance, they are formulated by Savage's postulates [12]. Other schools of normative analysis may be discussed within this m.d.p./m.d.m. framework [13,14].

It is not only by example that a normative analysis advises. There is another, arguably more important process involved. The construction of the m.d.m. as a reflection of me enables me to explore and clarify my preferences and beliefs. Indeed, in many cases it guides their evolution in that it encourages me to think about aspects of the problem which hitherto I had not considered and, therefore, about which I have no pre-existing beliefs and preferences. Before I undertake a decision analysis my thoughts are likely to be muddled, conflicting, and in need of 'straightening-out'. As I articulate my beliefs and preferences during the construction of the m.d.m., my attention is drawn to any inconsistency between these and the canons of rationality. The procedure brings into focus those areas in which I need to think my position through more carefully. Note that the procedure leaves me to reconcile any inconsistencies. It does not tell me what to think; it just tells me where I am not thinking clearly.

In summary, a normative analysis advises me in two ways. First, in constructing the m.d.m. I am guided through a process of evolving and clarifying my preferences and beliefs. Second, it shows me what a totally rational decision maker would do when faced by a choice which parallels mine. In both these ways it leads me to an understanding of where the balance of my beliefs and preferences lies. It is through this understanding that I make the decision. A normative analysis improves my perception of the problem and of my feelings about it, but I make the decision.

For the remainder of the paper attention is confined to just one aspect of the process, namely the construction of a utility function to represent the m.d.m.'s preferences and, hence, to represent my preferences within the constraints of consistency.

THE STRUCTURING OF OUTCOMES AS A VECTOR OF ATTRIBUTES

In the very simplest of decision analyses the m.d.p. is structured as a decision table with each possible outcome stated holistically. Consequences are not represented by a single number, or even a vector of numbers, but rather described verbally. In more complex cases such holistic representation of the consequences is not possible. However desirable it might be to give a long, complete, verbal description of each outcome, one is limited to a few summary statistics, or attribute levels as they are known in decision analysis. I shall not consider the methodology of choosing the set of attribute dimensions along which to measure each of the possible consequences. Others have already given exemplary discussions [5,7,15-22]. However, for the development within this paper there are a number of points which should be noted.

First, the structure of the process by which the attribute dimensions are defined is typically hierarchical. A global and loosely stated objective is gradually analysed into more and more detailed subobjectives. The attributes are the dimensions along which success in these subobjectives is measured. Many illustrations of hierarchies of objectives may be found in Keeney and Raiffa [5].

Second, using a set of attributes to summarise the consequences in a decision table has implications for the preference structures that may be considered rational, because there is an implicit, albeit not binding, assumption that preferences between all pairs of outcomes should always be determined by comparisons along the same set of dimensions. In terms of the m.d.p./m.d.m. format, I am saying that I find the m.d.m.'s behaviour more ideal if in complex situations he uses a multi-attribute rather than holistic representation of the consequences. And, indeed, I do find this the more rational. However, many would disagree saying that no multi-attribute formulation can ever capture the subtlety and delicacy of the human mind's ability to compare holistic alternatives. Hence the m.d.m.'s behaviour cannot be considered ideal. Persuasive though this argument may be in the abstract - it is always pleasant to be told that ones intuitive processes cannot be bettered - there is an unfortunate lack of empirical evidence to support it. Unguided human judgement is susceptible to many failings [23]. In particular, a number of studies have shown that holistic assessments give weight to fewer value attributes than a guided multi-attribute approach [24,25]. In short, I am reluctant to trust my human holistic judgement and would prefer to emulate the analytic approach of the m.d.m.

Thus, without further discussion here, outcomes will be represented by a vector of attribute levels, e.g.

$$\underset{\sim}{x} = (x_1, x_2, \ldots, x_n) \in X_1 \times X_2 \times \ldots \times X_n = X,$$

where X_i is the set of possible levels for the ith attribute and x_i is the level attained for the particular outcome. On the subject of notation, it is convenient here to introduce *decompositions* of X. Let $I \subset \{1,2,..,n\}$, $I \neq \phi$, and define

$$Y = \times_{i\in I} X_i, \qquad Z = \times_{i\notin I} X_i.$$

Thus with reordering $X = Y\times Z$ and $\underset{\sim}{x} = (\underset{\sim}{y},\underset{\sim}{z})$. We shall use the term 'decomposition' to mean this particular form of restructuring of X. It will correspond to focusing attention on just some of the attributes.

MULTI-ATTRIBUTE VALUE THEORY: THE CASE OF CERTAINTY

Suppose that I am happy that the n attributes describe the outcomes in terms of all the factors that are important for their discrimination. Moreover, suppose that there is no (or negligible) uncertainty in the external factors. Thus each course of action has only one possible outcome. What qualitative properties would I consider ideal in the m.d.m.'s preference structure over X? The answer to this question will determine the form of the multi-attribute value function for this particular problem. (N.B. I adopt the now standard convention of using the term 'value function' in the case of certainty and utility function for a von Neumann-Morgenstern utility function.) By 'qualitative property' I mean a property of the form: all other things being equal, a higher level of X_1 is always preferred to a lower level. Such properties are known by the generic term 'independence (or dependence) conditions'. Consider the simplest of these for a decomposition (Y,Z) of X:

> Y is *preferentially independent* of Z if the preference between $(\underset{\sim}{y}_1,\bar{\underset{\sim}{z}})$ and $(\underset{\sim}{y}_2,\bar{\underset{\sim}{z}})$ does not depend on the level $\bar{\underset{\sim}{z}}$.

If I believe that Y should be preferentially independent of Z for all decompositions (Y,Z) of X, then under fairly nonrestrictive conditions it may be shown [3,5,6,7] that the m.d.m.'s preferences should be represented by the additive form:

$$v(\underset{\sim}{x}) = \sum_{i=1}^{n} v_i(x_i),$$

where $v_i(.)$ are single attribute value functions.

It is worth pausing and explaining better what I mean by "Y should be preferentially independent of Z". I have suggested that, when I look to a normative analysis for guidance, I begin with an awareness that my initial, raw, unthinking preferences may be muddled, conflicting, and in need of 'straightening-out'. In particular, I may be aware of, and undoubtedly am susceptible to, all the failings of holistic judgement. To 'straighten-out' my preferences I need first to consider and define what I mean by 'straight' for the particular problem. In judging which preferential independence conditions should hold I am essentially doing just this, and in adopting an appropriate form of multi-attribute value function I am ensuring that the m.d.m.'s are 'straight', thus being in a form that I wish to emulate. Note also that in thinking about which preferential independence conditions should be obeyed I am exploring and clarifying my own preferences.

Of course, there are few problems in which it is reasonable to assert that all decompositions should be mutually preferentially independent. A more plausible condition in many cases is that of sign dependence [6], namely:

> Y is *sign dependent* on Z if there exists a partition of Z, $Z = Z_1 \cup Z_2 \cup Z_3$, and if the preference between $(\underset{\sim}{y}_1, \bar{\underset{\sim}{z}})$ and $(\underset{\sim}{y}_2, \bar{\underset{\sim}{z}})$ depends on which of the subsets Z_1, Z_2, and Z_3 contains $\bar{\underset{\sim}{z}}$. Specifically, if $\bar{z} \in Z_3$ the preference is the reverse of that when $\bar{\underset{\sim}{z}} \in Z_1$, and if $\bar{\underset{\sim}{z}} \in Z_2$ $(\underset{\sim}{y}_1, \bar{\underset{\sim}{z}})$ and $(\underset{\sim}{y}_2, \bar{\underset{\sim}{z}})$ are indifferent.

Given various combinations of sign dependence and preferential independence, it may be shown [6] that the appropriate forms of the multi-attribute value function are simple polynomials of single attribute value functions, e.g.

$$v(x_1, x_2, x_3) = (v_1(x_1) + v_2(x_2)).v_3(x_3).$$

Further generalisations of sign dependence in which $Z = Z_1 \cup Z_2 \cup \ldots \cup Z_m$ for $m>3$ have recently been studied by Farquhar and Fishburn [26,27].

It should be emphasised that multi-attribute value functions only represent preferences ordinally unless further assumptions are made. They do not represent value differences between outcomes. Recent work by Dyer, Sarin and Kirkwood has provided the extra conditions that must hold before a value difference representation is obtained [28,29]. A value difference interpretation may be particularly useful in providing a metric in which to undertake a sensitivity analysis. However, it should be noted that the cognitive appreciation of comparable value differences is by no means established. I, the decision maker, may not be able to make the judgements asked of me.

What happens if there are no sets of preference independence/dependence conditions which I feel should be adopted? Morris and Oren have developed one approach [30]. However, I would suggest that the question is ill-posed. To say that there are no conditions that should be adopted is essentially to demand a return to holistic judgement of the outcomes, and I am reluctant to follow such a path. It removes much of the guidance that a normative analysis may bring and provides no mechanism for exploring and clarifying my preferences.

MULTI-ATTRIBUTE UTILITY THEORY: THE CASE OF UNCERTAINTY

In most problems it is unreasonable to assume that the external factors are known with certainty. Thus it is usually necessary to construct the m.d.m.'s preferences so that they are appropriate for making choices in the case of uncertainty. Since I am personally convinced that Ramsay [31], Savage [12], and others have identified canons of rationality appropriate to this context, I will wish to emulate an m.d.m. whose preferences are representable by a von Neumann-Morgenstern utility function. Over and above this, there will be further independence/dependence conditions, which I will consider appropriate for the particular problem and which will limit the form of the utility function in much the same way as they limited the form of the value functions discussed above. Typical of the independence conditions in this case are the following.

> In the decomposition (Y,Z) of X, Y is *utility independent* of Z if preferences for lotteries over $(Y,\bar{\underset{\sim}{z}})$ for a fixed level $\bar{\underset{\sim}{z}} \in Z$ dependent only on the marginal probability distributions over Y and do not depend on the fixed level $\bar{z}$.
>
> In the decomposition (Y,Z) of X, Y and Z are *additively (or absolutely) independent* of each other if preferences between lotteries on both Y and Z depend only on the marginal probability distributions over Y and Z.

If I feel that Y and Z should be utility independent for all decompositions of X, then it may be shown that the m.d.m.'s preferences should be represented by either the multi-linear form [1-5,7]:

$$1 + ku(\underset{\sim}{x}) = \prod_{i=1}^{n} (1+kk_i u_i(x_i)),$$

or, if in addition additive independence should hold for all decompositions, the additive form:

$$u(\underset{\sim}{x}) = \sum_{i=1}^{n} k_i u_i(x_i),$$

where the $u_i(.)$ are single attribute utility functions and the k's are scaling constants.

Again it is not always reasonable to assume that independence conditions should apply whatever the partition, and there are several generalisations of these independence conditions that are less restrictive. Generalised utility independence corresponds to the sign dependence condition above [32,33]. Still more general conditions have been developed by Farquhar and Fishburn [26,27,34,36]. If there are subsets of attributes for which no such conditions are appropriate, then the approximation method of Bell [35] may be used to estimate a marginal utility function over these dimensions.

Keeney [21] has recently developed a problem-oriented methodology in which the structuring of the hierarchy of objectives is undertaken with an eye to dependency conditions that will be appropriate among the resulting attributes. In some cases this approach may generate rather artificial attributes that have little cognitive meaning, but in other cases it will most certainly be valuable. In particular, as may be seen from his paper, Keeney's method does much to help me explore and clarify my preferences.

GROUP DECISION MAKING

So far the discussion has been addressed to single person decision making. What happens when, as is more usual, a group of individuals share responsibility for the decision? Several writers [5,37,38,39] have noted the similarity between the aggregation of the individuals' preferences into a group utility function and the assessment of a multi-attribute utility function for one individual. Suppose that there are N individuals in the group and that each individual j has a utility function $u_j(\underset{\sim}{x})$ over the consequences (which may be multi-attributed). Then the group utility function $u_g(\underset{\sim}{x})$ should surely be a composition of these:

$$u_g(\underset{\sim}{x}) = u_g(u_1(\underset{\sim}{x}), u_2(\underset{\sim}{x}), \ldots, u_N(\underset{\sim}{x})).$$

However, I do not find these approaches persuasive. One is invariably left with the problem of determining mutliplicative constants by which to put the $u_j(.)$ on the same scale, i.e. one is forced to conduct an interpersonal comparison of preferences, and quite simply I do not know how to operationalise the concepts necessary to achieve this. Moreover, Arrow's impossibility theorem and its later extensions [40,41] convince me of the futility of trying to do so. To me these results suggest that it is fallacious to believe that a group can act as a single entity and decide upon a course of action. A group does not possess a mind of its own and so cannot choose; in which case there is no rationale for forming a group utility function.

A group should not be seen as a single decision maker, but as a social process which translates a voting pattern into a course of action. There is no single decision present; there are many, one for each member of the group: how should he vote. So it is not necessary to extend single person theory to groups; it is only necessary to consider its use in the context of a group. As a consequence, decision analysts should see their role as to advise the individual members of the group and to help communication and understanding between the members. In this latter respect multi-attribute utility analysis has an important part to play, because the identification of the independence/dependence conditions which a particular individual feels should be obeyed enables him or her to express general properties of his or her preferences in a way that simply stating particular preferences could not.

DISCUSSION

Given that this is supposed to be a survey paper, there are some remarkable omissions in its coverage. Had I not adopted such an idiosyncratic, interpretive style, there are a number of topics that I could not have failed to discuss. First, I have made little mention of the mathematics that underlies multi-attribute utility and value theory; but, as I have remarked, this aspect is well surveyed elsewhere [1-7,26-29, 32,36].

Second, there are a number of fields of application in which the context suggests the introduction of special independence conditions. Meyer [5,42] and a number of other writers [6,43] have considered a number of conditions that may be appropriate to the expression of preferences over timestreams of monetary returns. Richard [43] has developed concepts of risk attitude appropriate to multi-attribute circumstances. Recently, Keeney [44-46] has discussed the preference conditions that may be required in governmental decision making in cases where members of the public may be required to bear some risk to life and limb. As reported at this conference, Marilena Vassiloglou and I have recently considered the application of multi-attribute value theory to aid examiners in their judgement of multicomponent examinations.

Third, no mention has been made of the interactive, introspective procedures by which first the appropriate dependence/independence conditions for the decision problem are identified and then the necessary single attribute utility functions and scaling constants are determined. Such procedures are presented in detail by Keeney and Raiffa [5]. Returning to my role as the decision maker, it should be noted that these procedures are specifically designed to help me reflect upon my preferences, discover any inconsistencies between them and the ideals of behaviour that I wish to emulate, and thus identify those areas where I need to think my position through more carefully.

Lastly, I have made little mention of case histories. Much of the subtlety and delicacy of decision analysis can best be appreciated by studying its application to specific problems. It is noteworthy that the result of most decision analyses is not the identification of a single best course of action. Instead the available actions are ranked with two or three front-runners and, more importantly, the decision maker(s) understand their problem much more clearly than they did prior to the analysis [5,17-19,22].

To close this paper let me recap on the distinction, as I see it, between descriptive and normative analyses, and let me particularly emphasise their differing approaches to the modelling of preferences. In a descriptive analysis my preferences are taken as immutable data; I am given no chance to reconcile any inconsistency between them and certain canons of rationality. Indeed, in a descriptive study there are no such canons; the purpose is simply to report how I do make my decisions. On the other hand, in a normative analysis it is very much part of the purpose that my preferences should evolve. The procedures are designed to help me explore and develop my preferences.

Zeleny [8] might do well to consider this distinction and look to the methods of multi-objective interactive programming that he champions. In these there is no attempt to help me explore and develop my preferences. I am simply asked to state my preferences between pairs of alternatives. Furthermore, these pairs of alternatives may often differ slightly in many attributes, but not be much different overall (because of being adjacent vertices of a simplex in attribute space). It is precisely because I find it so difficult to make such choices that I turn to a normative analysis for guidance. Thus I should be very reluctant to use multi-objective programming until I had spent much time in introspection, asking myself questions about preferential independence, monotonicity of preference, etc. But in doing this I would have all but carried out a multi-attribute value analysis. So why not complete that rather than switch to interactive multi-objective programming?

REFERENCES

[1] Farquhar, P.H. "A Survey of multi-attribute utility theory and applications." *TIMS Studies in the Management Sciences*, Vol.6, 59-89, 1977.

[2] Farquhar, P.H. "Advances in multi-attribute utility theory" *Theory and Decision*, Vol.12, 381-394, 1980.

[3] Fishburn, P.C. *Utility Theory for Decision Making*. Wiley, New York, 1970.

[4] Fishburn, P.C. "Multi-attribute utilities in expected utility theory." Bell, D.E., Keeney, R.L., and Raiffa, H. (eds.) *Conflicting Objectives in Decisions*. Wiley, New York, 1977.

[5] Keeney, R.L. and Raiffa, H. *Decisions with Multiple Objectives*. Wiley, New York, 1976.

[6] Krantz, D.H., Luce, R.D., Suppes, P., and Tversky, A. *Foundations of Measurement. Vol.1*. Academic Press, New York, 1971.

[7] Roberts, F.S. *Measurement Theory*.Addison Wesley, Reading, Mass, 1979.

[8] Zeleny, M. "Foreword" *Computers and Operations Research* Vol.7, 1-4, 1980.

[9] Feferman, S. "What does logic have to tell us about mathematical proofs?" *The Mathematical Intelligencer*, Vol.2, 20-24, 1979.

[10] French, S. "Measurement theory and examinations" *British Journal of Mathematical and Statistical Psychology*, Vol.34, 38-49, 1981.

[11] French, S. "The weighting of examination components" Presented to the Royal Statistical Society Conference, York, March 22nd-26th, 1982.

[12] Savage, L.J. *The Foundations of Statistics*. 2nd Edition, Dover, New York, 1972.

[13] French, S. "Fuzzy decision analysis: some criticisms" *TIMS Studies in the Management Sciences*, Volume on Fuzzy Decision Analysis (in press).

[14] French, S. "On various non-Bayesian decision aids" Notes in Decision Theory No.89, Department of Decision Theory, University of Manchester, 1980.

[15] Baecher, G.B., Gross, J.C. and McCusker, K. "Methodologies for facility siting decisions" in Bunn, D.W. and Thomas, H. (eds.) *Formal Methods in Policy Analysis*. Birkhäuser, Basel, 1978.

[16] Byer, P. and De Neufville, R. "Choosing the dimensions and uncertainties of an evaluation" in Bunn, D.W. and Thomas, H. (eds) *Formal Methods in Policy Analysis*. Birkhäuser, Basel, 1978.

[17] De Neufville, R. and Keeney, R.L. "Systems evaluation through decision analysis: Mexico City Airport" *Journal of Systems Engineering*, Vol.3, 34-50, 1972.

[18] Ellis, H.M. and Keeney, R.L. "A rational approach for government decisions concerning air pollution" in Drake, A.W., Keeney, R.L., and Morse, P.M. (eds.) *Analysis of Public Systems*. MIT Press, 1972.

[19] Keefer, D.L. and Kirkwood, C.W. "A multi-objective decision analysis: budget planning for production engineering" *Journal of the Operational Research Society*, Vol. 29, 435-442, 1978.

[20] Keeney, R.L. "Measurement scales for quantifying attributes" *Behavioural Science*, Vol.26, 29-36, 1981.

[21] Keeney, R.L. "Analysis of preference dependencies among objectives" *Operational Research*, Vol.29, 1105-1120, 1981.

[22] Keeney, R.L. and Nair, K. "Selecting nuclear power plant sites in the Pacific Northwest using decision analysis" in Bell, D.E., Keeney, R.L. and Raiffa, H. (eds) *Conflicting Objectives in Decisions*. Wiley, New York, 1977.

[23] Hogarth, R.M. *Judgement and Choice*. Wiley, New York, 1980.

[24] Slovic, P., and Lichtenstein, S. "Comparison of Bayesian and regression approaches to the study of information processing in judgement" *Organizational Behaviour and Human Performance*, Vol.6, 649-744, 1971.

[25] Fischer, G.W. "Utility models for multiple objective decisions: do they accurately represent human preferences?" *Decision Sciences*, Vol.10, 451-479, 1979.

[26] Farquhar, P.H. "Multivalent preference structures" *Mathematical Social Sciences*, Vol.1, 1981.

[27] Farquhar, P.H. and Fishburn, P.C. "Equivalences and continuity in multivalent preference structures" *Operations Research*, Vol.29, 282-293, 1981.

[28] Dyer, J.S. and Sarin, K. "Measurable multi-attribute value functions" *Operations Research*, Vol.27 810-822, 1979.

[29] Kirkwood, C.W. and Sarin, R.K. "Preference Conditions for multi-attribute value functions" *Operations Research*, Vol.29, 225-232, 1980.

[30] Morris, P.A. and Oren, S.S. "Multi-attribute decision making by sequential resource allocation" *Operations Research*, Vol.29, 233-252, 1980.

[31] Ramsay, F.P. "Truth and probability" in *The Logical Foundation of Mathematics and other Essays*. Keegan Paul, London, 1931.

[32] Fishburn, P.C. and Keeney, R.L. "Seven independence concepts and continuous multi-attribute utility functions" *Journal of Mathematical Psychology*, Vol.11, 294-327, 1974.

[33] Fishburn, P.C. and Keeney, R.L. "Generalised utility independence and some implications" *Operations Research*, Vol.23, 928-940, 1975.

[34] Farquhar, P.H. "A fractional hypercube decomposition theorem for multi-attribute utility functions" *Operations Research*, Vol.23, 941-967, 1975.

[35] Bell, D.E. "Multi-attribute utility functions: decompositions using interpolation" *Management Science*, Vol.25, 744-753, 1979.

[36] Farquhar, P.H. "Pyramid and semicube decompositions for multi-attribute utility functions" *Operations Research*, Vol.24, 256-271, 1976.

[37] Keeney, R.L. and Kirkwood, C.W. "Group decision making using cardinal social welfare functions" *Management Science*, Vol.22, 430-437, 1975.

[38] Dyer, J.S. and Sarin, R.K. "Group preference aggregation rules based on strength of preference" *Management Science*, Vol.25, 822-832, 1979.

[39] Eliasberg, J. and Winkler, R.L. "Risk sharing and group decision making" *Management Science*, Vol.27, 1221-1235, 1981.

[40] Arrow, K.J. *Social Choice and Individual Values*. 2nd Edition. Wiley, New York, 1963.

[41] Kelly, F.S. *Arrow Impossibility Theorems*. Academic Press, New York, 1978.

[42] Meyer, R.F. "State-dependent time preference" in Bell, D.E., Keeney, R.L., and Raiffa, H. (eds.) *Conflicting Objectives in Decisions*. Wiley, New York, 1977.

[43] Richard, S.F. "Multivariate risk aversion, utility independence, and separable utility functions" *Management Science*, Vol.22, 12-21, 1975.

[44] Keeney, R.L. "Evaluating alternatives involving potential fatalities" *Operations Research*, Vol.28, 188-205, 1980.

[45] Keeney, R.L. "Utility functions for equity and public risk" *Management Science*, Vol.26, 345-353, 1980.

[46] Keeney, R.L. "Equity and public risk" *Operations Research*, Vol.28, 527, 1980.

FUNDAMENTAL DEFICIENCY OF EXPECTED UTILITY DECISION ANALYSIS

M. McCord and R. de Neufville

(Massachusetts Institute of Technology, Cambridge, MA, USA)

INTRODUCTION

Decision analysis, as most commonly practised today, rests upon the axiomatic theory presented by von Neumann and Morgenstern in 1947. Various writers have since presented alternative sets of axioms in efforts to render them more intuitively appealing (see, for example, the review by MacCrimmon and Larsson, 1979), but these variants all lead to the same two results. The axioms imply: (1) the existence of a cardinal (or vNM) utility function, independent of the probability distributions, which orders the set of outcomes; and (2) that actions leading to outcomes with specified probabilities can be ranked by taking, for each action, the expectation of the vNM utilities of its outcomes. For this reason the theory is also known as expected utility theory. One can also speak of expected utility decision analysis, distinguishing it from other forms of decision analysis, for example that advocated by Roy (1982).

Expected utility decision analysis has become very popular over the last twenty years and is now widely used for analyzing and ordering complex choices. This success is partly due to the attractiveness of the axioms. But this is certainly not a sufficient explanation: first of all, a large fraction of the users and practitioners of decision analysis only dimly remember its axiomatic foundations; secondly, the axioms are quite controversial on several grounds. The more likely reason for the dominance of the practice of decision analysis is that this methodology now embodies simple, routine and apparently reliable procedures that make it easy to apply. The short of the matter is that the prevalence of expected utility decision analysis is more due to its pragmatic appeal than to its theoretical strength -- which is contested.

Popularity is not ultimately a sufficient justification for a method. If decision analysis is to be a standard element of systems analysis, it must be validated in each of its essential elements. It is in this spirit that we have attempted to identify critical aspects of expected utility decision analysis and to test them empirically.

We believe that we have identified a critical experiment for decision analysis and have carried out this test with extreme care. The results of our tests, which we believe to be easily replicable, indicate that expected utility decision analysis, as practised currently, embodies fundamental inconsistencies which must severely limit its appropriateness. To what extent these difficulties stem from deficiencies in the operational methods for carrying out the analysis or from insufficient theory is debatable. Either way the conclusion appears to be the same: solutions to the problems of expected utility decision analysis are beyond the state-of-the-art.

The organization of the paper is as follows. First, the literature to date is summarized, as a prelude to identifying a critical element of expected utility decision analysis. Next, the over-all research strategy, the procedures to be applied, and the protocol of the experiments are described. The empirical results are then reported and analyzed. Finally, the implications of this work are discussed.

THE DEBATE TO DATE

Traditional criticisms of expected utility decision analysis have been both theoretical and practical. On theoretical grounds, many thoughtful persons argue that the axioms underlying expected utility theory, which supposedly describe "rational" behaviour, do not actually do so; that while they are superficially appealing, deeper reflection indicates that they miss several subtleties (see Machina, 1982, for a recent review of these arguments, and also Allais, 1953; Roy, 1982; Slovic and Tversky, 1974; and Tversky, 1972). The classic illustration of this argument is the Allais paradox, which shows how informed, intelligent (in short, "rational" by all usual standards) persons choose actions in violation of the axioms of expected utility theory. The "paradox" consists of the fact that people rank similar pairs of simple lotteries having different probability distributions on the outcomes, in a manner which is incompatible with the axioms (Allais, 1953; Allais, 1979 a and b; and MacCrimmon and Larsson, 1979). Naturally, the "paradox" only exists if one accepts the axioms of expected utility theory; the "paradox" disappears for alternative axiomatic formulations, specifically for those that allow the utility functions to depend on the probability distributions of the outcomes.

On the pragmatic side, an array of experiments demonstrates that people left to their own devices systematically choose in ways other than those indicated by expected utility decision analysis. (Lichtenstein and Slovic, 1971, 1973; Slovic, 1975; and Slovic and Lichtenstein, 1968).

Both critics and defenders of expected utility decision analysis agree on the empirical observations. But, whereas the critics see them as convincing evidence that the method is fundamentally flawed, the defenders do not -- quite the contrary!

In fact, the defenders of expected utility decision analysis see the empirical evidence as yet another justification of the method! The reasoning can be paraphrased as follows: "It is obvious that people choose inconsistently and otherwise make mistakes. And it is quite true that our analysis indicates that they should do otherwise. This discrepancy is precisely why our decision analysis is so useful. If people normally chose well, or if we could not alter their choices, the analysis would provide no contribution. The strength of decision analysis is that it is normative, telling people how they should act, rather than being descriptive of their idiosyncracies." By such arguments many proponents of expected utility decision analysis manage to reject the whole gamut of critical arguments. They essentially cloak themselves with what may be called a "normative immunity" to empirical evidence.

CRITICAL VULNERABILITY

Careful thought indicates that although expected utility decision analysis is presented as a normative method, not to be confused with a description, it must in fact contain a crucial descriptive element for all practical applications. This element is so fundamental to the use of the method, moreover, that if it is not accurate the entire procedure as now conceived may collapse.

The situation is as presented in Fig. 1. Every normative prescription produced by expected utility decision analysis rests upon a vNM utility function for the decision-maker. This function can only be obtained through interactions with this person; the vNM utility function is a description of attitudes of that person.

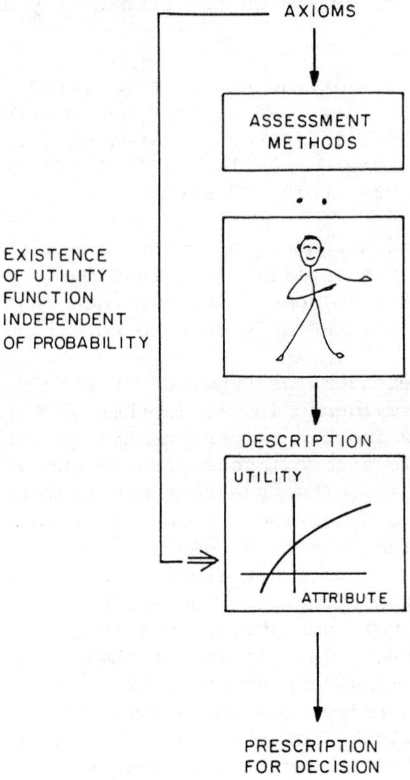

Fig. 1 Organization of Expected Utility Decision Analysis in Practice.

It is now important to recognize that the axioms imply definite limits on the nature of the utility functions: they should be independent of the probabilistic situation in which they are developed. This feature, which is implicitly presumed to hold, is crucial to the application of expected utility decision analysis. It is what makes the method a practical proposition. First, it allows the analyst to obtain a utility function in one probabilistic setting and then use it in all others, rather than having to attempt the hopeless task of obtaining a new utility function for the decision-maker for each circumstance. Second, it permits the substitution of certain equivalents for probabilistic outcomes and thus greatly simplifies the calculations involved in the process.

Contrary to what the axioms would have, there is evidence that the utility functions do depend on the probability distribution. Karmarkar's (1974, 1978) results can be interpreted this way. Also, Allais (1979b) found that two theoretical equivalent methods did not encode the same vNM utility function.

The possibility that the utility functions that are assessed are dependent on the probabilistic situation must be seen as a critical issue. Indeed, suppose they are. The analyst is then placed in a dilemma, where both choices are extremely unattractive.

He then either: Rejects the axioms and thus the whole expected utility decision analysis;

or: Retains his belief in the axioms by dismissing the evidence as invalid (either as yet another instance of people being muddled or because the assessment procedures are inadequate). But if he does so the decision analysis is impossible as he has no utility function to work with (alternatively, he might consider that he has too many, each implying different choices, and not know how to choose between them).

Either way, an empirical relationship between the utility functions and their probabilistic setting invalidates the practical application of expected utility decision analysis.

We may conclude that the decision analyst should care deeply whether the axioms are descriptively correct with regard to the utility functions, even though he may propose that his is really a prescriptive method. The practical application of decision analysis as we generally know it today is critically vulnerable to this issue.

RESEARCH DESIGN

The central objective of the experiments was to test if vNM utility functions depend significantly on the probabilistic situation in which they are assessed. This involved three basic elements:

(1) Assessment of the utility functions by methods using different probability distributions which ought, theoretically, to give the same results;

(2) Analysis of the evidence to determine if the differences observed were significant; and

(3) Extreme care in executing the study to ensure replicability and to avoid the attribution of any differences to extraneous factors.

The vNM utility functions were assessed using standard lotteries in the usual way. As described in detail in the next section, we investigated different probabilistic situations by using the fractile method with different pairs of complementary probabilities, and the varying probability method in which the outcomes of the lottery remain fixed but the probability of obtaining them changes. Also, as a special case, we assessed the deterministic value function in which outcomes occur with certainty.

The analysis required imagination because there are no standard statistical methods to investigate differences in curves such as utility functions. Our approach consisted of two parts. First, we developed a standard means to measure the differences between the curves obtained. We could then determine the relative accuracy of the procedures. Second, we looked at the distribution of the differences between the functions to see if they were Gaussian, in which case they could be attributed to random errors of measurement, or if they were systematically skewed, which would demonstrate a more interesting relationship between the utility functions and the probability distributions. The analysis is described in detail subsequently.

Extreme care was exercised at three levels. First, the analysts were skilled and experienced. We were, in fact, associated with one of the major demonstrations of the applicability of decision analysis, the case of the Airport for Mexico City (de Neufville and Kenney, 1973), and have taught and practised the techniques for many years. Second, we worked with technically competent decision-makers who could not be accused of not understanding probability. Third, we paid special care to the details of the measurements, using the best available psychometric procedures, as indicated in the protocol for the experiments.

ASSESSMENT METHODS

Two distinct modes of assessment were used in the experiments, one to estimate the vNM utility functions and the other to estimate the deterministic value functions.

vNM utility function

The vNM function, U(X), is a mapping, unique to a positive linear transformation and specific to an individual at a given moment, of the level of the attribute, X, into a real number. It is a description of how a person feels about probabilistic situations. It is a construct which permits, within the context of the axioms, an ordering of the uncertain prospects.

The assessment of U(X) is obtained through personal interviews between the analyst and the decision-maker. This process proceeds from two ideas:

(1) Since vNM utility is constant up to a positive linear transformation, two points on the function can be assumed arbitrarily; and

(2) The utility of a probabilistic situation is, according to the axioms, equal to the expectation of the utility of the possible outcomes.

The analyst thus works with the client to determine for what amount the client is indifferent between having this amount for sure (thus, the name certainty equivalent) and possession of a gamble or lottery which has two possible outcomes whose probabilities must be complementary. Specifically, if the client states indifference between X_1 and the lottery involving the upper and lower bounds of the range of the attribute, X^* and X_*, whose probabilities of occurrence are p and (1-p), respectively, we have:

$$U(X_1) = U(\text{lottery}) = pU(X^*) + (1-p)U(X_*) \qquad (1)$$

Assuming the utility for the two points X^* and X_*, Eq. (1) gives the utility of the third point, X_1. (If X is a desirable attribute, it is normal to set $U(X^*) = 1.0$ and $U(X_*) = 0$, so that $U(X_1) = p$.) In such a way, as many points as desired of the utility function can be obtained.

The most common form of interview technique uses the "fractile method", so named because the probabilities used in the two lotteries are fixed, and thus the differences in the utilities of the outcomes of the lotteries are split into constant fractions. The procedure starts with Eq. (1) and then sets up a second lottery identical to the first except that X_1 replaces X^*. A second certainty equivalent, X_2, is obtained, such that $U(X_2) = p^2$, and so on. Points in the upper portion of the curve are similarly determined by replacing the less desirable outcome by the certainty equivalent of the preceding lottery.

In the fractile method, the most frequently used probability is 0.5, resulting in "50-50" lotteries. There is no theoretical reason why p should equal 0.5. Indeed, it follows from the axioms that the utility functions obtained by the fractile method using different values of p, say p' and p", should be equal. Theoretically,

$$U_{p'}(X) = U_{p''}(X) \qquad (2)$$

This is a proposition we tested empirically.

The "varying probability" method of assessment differs from the fractile method in that the probability used in the sequence of lotteries varies, while the outcomes remain fixed at X^* and X_*. Typically the analyst expresses probabilities in fractions that are easy to understand (one half, one third, one quarter, ...) and obtains the utilities of corresponding values.

Again, the axioms indicate that the utility function encoded using the variable probability method, U_{pv}, should equal the utility functions obtained by the fractile method:

$$U_{pv}(X) = U_{p'}(X) = U_{p''}(X) \qquad (3)$$

This is the other theoretical result we tested.

Deterministic Value functions

A special case of the dependence of the vNM utility on the probability distribution is that in which one outcome occurs with certainty: some believe that the vNM utility of a certain outcome is equivalent to the subjective value of this outcome determined by methods in which no uncertainty is present (Halter and Dean, 1971; Allais, 1979 a and b). This equivalence is controversial, however.

The value function determined by deterministic methods is similar in many respects to the vNM utility function. It is a positive linear transformation, specific to an individual at a particular time, of the level of an attribute into a real number indicating the degree of satisfaction with that level. The clear difference is that the value function is determined without reference to any probabilities. The value function, therefore, cannot incorporate any "risk attitude" whatever that nebulous concept actually is. In any event, there seem to be empirical differences between the two functions, as Allais (1979b) indicates. Sarin et al. (1980) attempt to demonstrate empirical relationships between the two functions which they show to be different. Similarly, Krzysztofowicz (1982) compares the two functions and addresses the differences with a behavioural interpretation.

Single attribute value functions have been determined in several ways. These appear to differ from one another more with respect to assumptions made and the method of assessment, than to the interpretation of the resultant value function. The methods fall into two main classes, those which determine the single attribute value functions from multi-attribute functions (Fishburn, 1967; Keeney and Raiffa, 1976; Sarin et al., 1980) and those which determine the single attribute function directly. This second category can be further divided into methods requiring direct allocation of value to an attribute (Fishburn, 1967; Huber et al., 1971; Keeney and Raiffa, 1976), and those requiring the evaluation of value differences (Allais, 1979b; Sarin et al., 1980; Krzysztofowicz, 1982; and also mentioned in Weldon, 1950; Keeney and Raiffa, 1976; and Bell, 1981).

We used the concept of equal value differences since it seemed both most effective and most prevalent. The basic idea is that, if the degree of satisfaction obtained from a change in the level of an attribute from X_i to X_j is considered equivalent to that associated with a change from X_r to X_s, then the differences in the respective subjective values are equal. Notationally:

$$X_i \rightarrow X_j \sim X_r \rightarrow X_s$$

$$\Rightarrow V(X_j)-V(X_i) = V(X_s)-V(X_r) \qquad (4)$$

where $X_i \rightarrow X_j$ indicates the change from X_i to X_j, and $V(X)$ is the deterministic value of the level of X.

In our experiments we developed $V(X)$ by a procedure similar to the fractile method using 50-50 lotteries. Starting with the extremes of the attribute range, X_* and X^*, we determined X_1 as the point which divided that range into two ranges of equal value difference. Scaling the end points of the value function as $V(X_*) = 0.0$ and $V(X^*) = 1.0$, as we did for the vNM utility, we obtain $V(X_1) = 0.5$. By further subdivision of the ranges X_* to X_1 and X_1 to X^* we obtained quarter and eighth points.

PROTOCOL OF THE EXPERIMENT

Utility functions using the varying probability method and two or more fractile methods were assessed for twenty-three subjects, and deterministic value functions were obtained for twenty-two. Most subjects were technically trained, being MIT professors, graduate students and undergraduates in engineering or science. There were two non-science college graduates.

The interviews were designed, supervised and carried out by persons with extensive theoretical and field experience in such matters.

The interviews were limited to one hour, to limit boredom, fatigue and inattention. The first half of the session was devoted to explaining the experiment, gathering general information, and to assessing a deterministic value function. The rest of the session was spent on assessing the vNM utility functions. When time remained, we presented the subject with some of his responses which contradicted the axioms of expected utility theory, to determine if he were still comfortable with his response. Alteration of responses at this point was virtually non-existent.

To facilitate responses, the situations presented to the subjects were as realistic, and as representative of situations they understood, as possible. The utility and value functions were assessed for money so that a wider range of people could be tested with a minimal effort required to familiarize them with the nuances of the attribute. The range of money considered was 0 to $10,000 gained. Losses were not discussed since we felt that time would be better spent, in this experiment, assessing the vNM utility functions over a wider range of probabilities. The upper bound of $10,000 was selected to present a significant gain which was still sufficiently realistic to allow subjective evaluation.

Responses were obtained from the subjects by the bracketing method; that is, in the search for the point which made the subject indifferent between two choices, he was first asked to consider points which were likely to be much too large or too small and which were, consequently, easy to respond to. Gradually, the interviewer reduced the range between the possible responses, proceeding from one extreme to the other, until the point of indifference for the subject was found. Psychometrically, this procedure has been found to be essential in eliminating biases caused by any subject's tendency to anchor his responses toward the direction of approach, and the bracketing procedure is now standard in all measurement of responses to stimuli.

The interviewer prepared charts in advance to display the responses, both to expedite the interviews and to focus the attention of each subject.

The entire experimental procedure was pretested on a number of other subjects to establish the consistency, clarity and replicability of the experimental protocol.

vNM utility functions

We attempted to encode at least three and sometimes four utility functions for each subject. For most subjects, we first obtained the varying probability utility function $U_{pv}(X)$, then the fractile utility functions $U_p(X)$ with the following probabilities: $p = 0.500$; one of either $p = 0.250$ or $p = 0.0625$; and a few points for either $p = 0.125$ or $p = 0.750$. The order in which the fractile methods were presented was equally distributed among subjects to curtail any bias due to the order of presentation.

Scenarios were described at the beginning of the assessment to define a realistic context. For a student, the scenario consisted of being considered for a fellowship. If this were granted, he would receive the higher of the two cash prizes in the lottery, tax-free, without any obligation as to how it should be spent. If he were not awarded the fellowship, he would receive the lower prize of the lottery, either a lesser fellowship or nothing, depending on whether the lower prize was greater than or equal to zero. The scenarios were essentially the same for non-students. For professors, the prize was suggested to be a grant from a research sponsor; for others, a one-time cash bonus. It was emphasized in all cases that there was no difference in prestige in winning the lottery, losing it, or accepting a certain equivalent; but that the only difference was the amount of money received.

The subjects were to consider their chances no better or worse than any of the other hypothetical candidates for the grants. The number of candidates, then, defined the probability of receiving the grant. In an attempt to avoid casual consideration of the probabilities, each subject was shown a number of playing-cards equal to the number of candidates. The number of winning cards defined the probability that the subject would be chosen. The cards were shuffled and placed face down in front of the subject. Occasionally, he was allowed to draw a card to give him a feeling for the probabilities involved, but it was quickly emphasized that the drawings were independent events and that winning or losing in one case should not affect the perception of chances to win or lose in another case.

Finally, in determining the certainty equivalent of the lottery, the subject was asked not to try "to get the best deal" from the interviewer in the sense that, by refusing to take a specific amount, he could force the interviewer to raise the offer. Rather, subjects were to consider leaving the answers to questions with an agent, who would do the bargaining with the prospective grantor. The indifference points were to indicate to the agent that, when the negotiations were finished, a final offer should be accepted if superior to the indifference point, otherwise not. It was emphasized throughout that there was no right or wrong answer to any questions, and that each should be considered carefully according to individual preferences.

Consistency checks on the certainty equivalents were obtained by comparing the first lottery of each fractile method with the identical lottery presented in the varying probability method. Small differences (for example, $500 for high probabilities, a few hundred dollars for low probabilities) were mentioned but not emphasized. Large differences were reconciled. In general, the subjects gave consistent results, which was especially encouraging since most did not remember which value they had given previously but rather thought through their preference again. This would validate the existence of at least a fairly narrow range for certainty equivalents.

Deterministic Value functions

The procedure here is rather straightforward. The essential methodological issue centres on the fact that direct comparison of the psychological value of changes in asset positions may be difficult. To circumvent this problem we introduced a surrogate measure of this psychological value. The approach was inspired by the procedures described by Keeney and Raiffa (1976) and Sarin et al. (1980).

The surrogate measure of the value of changing from one asset position to another was the maximum amount of time, outside current working hours, that the subject would engage in a job of no personal value other than the monetary remuneration represented by the change in asset position. At the same time, it was mentioned that the job was not morally objectionable.

For this procedure to be valid, working hours and dollars must be value additive. This assumption seems reasonable over the small range of working hours, and it is also unimportant compared to the others used in the assessment.

RESULTS

The experimental data lead to two immediate conclusions:

(1) large descriptive differences exist between the functions resulting from the various methods of assessment; and

(2) individuals preferred to deviate in a fairly consistent fashion from the behaviour presumed by the axioms.

The deviations are qualitatively apparent when free-hand curves are traced through the data. No sophisticated curve-fitting techniques were needed; the differences are too striking. Some examples are displayed in the subsequent figures.

The effect of probability differences in the methods of assessment is, somewhat caricaturally, to make risk averters more risk averse and risk seekers more risk seeking. This notion is refined subsequently. For the moment, the essential point to retain is that the differences between two functions tend to be directionally opposite, depending on whether a person is a risk seeker or is risk averse. Therefore, these two distinct populations should not generally be pooled in analyzing the data.

Measure of Differences between functions

To summarize the deviations, portray their order of magnitude, and facilitate discussion, we had to develop special indices.

Statistical tests were considered but rejected as impractical, if not useless, for this study. Although some work has been done in this area (Eliashberg and Hauser, 1980), the assumptions appear too restrictive and the procedures too involved to be of value here.

We sought illustrative measures with a clear operational meaning, which would also be sufficiently general to allow repeatable analyses, and which would permit comparison both between functions and pairs of functions. Variations of the Gini index, as well as other such measures, were rejected because they did not fulfil these criteria.

The index we developed for this analysis is based on the notion of relating the difference between two purportedly equivalent levels of value to a normalizing standard. The measure is thus one of "relative difference" between two functions $f(X)$ and $g(X)$, associated with a specific ordinate A. The differences themselves are taken along the abscissa and are normalized with reference to a standard function h(X) also associated with A. Notationally:

$$W(A)_{f,g} = (f^{-1}(A) - g^{-1}(A)) \;/\; h^{-1}(A) \qquad (5)$$

In practice h(X) may be chosen as any reference function, including either f(X) or g(X), and it may be useful to do exactly that. Fig. 2 illustrates the definition of the measure. As a rule, we express W(A) as a percentage.

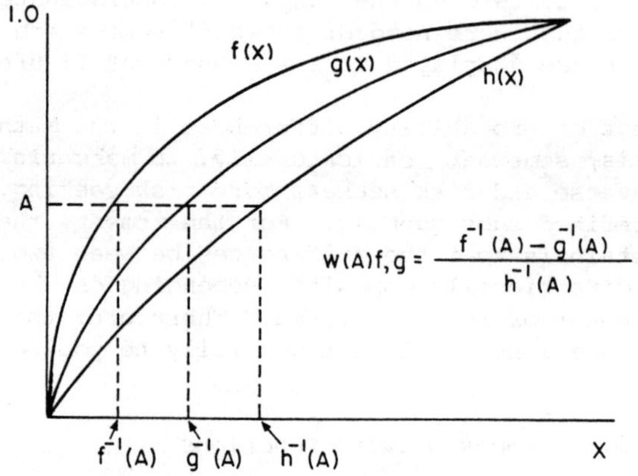

Fig. 2 Illustration of Definition of Measure of Relative Difference between Functions.

The interpretation of the measure in our situation is straightforward. It represents the relative difference in the value of the attribute indicated by different functions at a common level of utility or value. More largely, it indicates the percentage error to be made with respect to a choice in the attribute, when inappropriately using one function instead of another.

To portray the size of the discrepancies between two functions for a set of N individuals, we resorted to the concept of average absolute differences:

$$\overline{|W(A)_{f,g}|} = \frac{1}{N} \sum_i |W_i(A)_{f,g}| \qquad (6)$$

Likewise, we can speak of average differences taking signs into account. We can also apply either formula to specific subsets of the sample, such as the risk averters and the risk seekers.

General considerations

To pursue the idea that the differences between functions depended systematically on whether a person was risk averse or risk seeking, we had to classify all subjects into these groups. We did so on the basis of the certainty equivalent each furnished for the 50-50 lottery over the extreme range of outcomes, 0 and \$10,000. As such there were seventeen risk averters and five risk seekers. There was only one person who was risk neutral. Naturally, since risk attitudes can -- and did -- change for each person over the range of the attribute, the classification scheme we adopted is not absolute. An alternative approach might slightly alter the partition among the subjects. As indicated by the evidence, however, we do not believe that our results would be significantly affected by any marginally different classification.

Comparisons between the functions were made at levels of utility or value of A = 0.25, 0.50, and 0.75 where these functions were scaled between 0.0 and 1.0. More comparisons could be made, of course.

Comparison of vNM utility functions

Two sets of comparisons of the utility functions were made: first, between the functions elicited with the varying probability method and the 50:50 fractile method; and second, between functions elicited with fractile methods of different probabilities. In both cases the normalizing standard, h(X), was taken as the utility obtained with the 50:50 fractile method, for the simple reason that it is the most commonly used vNM utility function.

The function f(X) was either $U_{pv}(X)$, V(X), or the utility obtained by the fractile method with the higher probability of gaining the greater prize.

The absolute discrepancies between these utility functions, which should be equivalent axiomatically, are very large. They are extraordinary, in fact. The <u>average</u> differences in certainty equivalents easily exceed 50% and were often close to 100%. Table I gives the details.

The effect is visually striking. The results for one subject, in Fig. 3, give the idea. It is to be noted that, as shown here, the utility function obtained using the higher probability of getting the higher outcome of the lottery lies above the utility function obtained using a lower probability.

Table I

Average percent relative differences, $\overline{|W(X)|}$, between vNM utility functions

FUNCTIONS COMPARED		DIFFERENCES IN CERTAINTY EQUIVALENTS (%) AT UTILITY LEVEL		
Theoretically Equivalent?	Type	0.25	0.50	0.75
Yes	$U_{p'}(X)$, $U_{p''}(X)$ p', p" vary	99	86	49
	$U_{pv}(X)$ and $U_p(X)$, p=0.50	54	--	31
No	$V(X)$ and $U_p(X)$, p=0.50	56	34	21

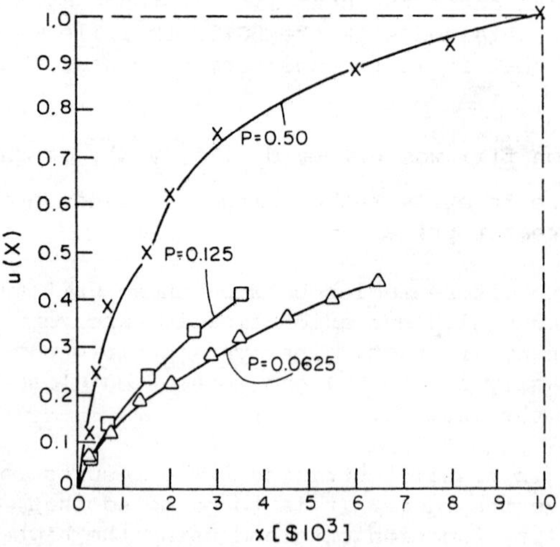

Fig. 3 Different vNM Utility Functions obtained by various Fractile Sequences (Subject 34).

The results also tend to support the observations by Kahnemann and Tversky (1979), and the hypothesis by Munera (1978), indicating that there might be a discontinuity in the functions. Indeed, for smaller values of probability used in the fractile method, the curves definitely show such a trend. This is a further point to be explored.

The discrepancies between the functions are, furthermore, systematic rather than random. This effect is evident from the distributions of these differences, which are clearly skewed rather than Gaussian, both for the risk averters and the risk seekers (Figs. 4 and 5). To quantify this effect, we calculated $\bar{W}$, the average relative difference -- taking sign into account -- for each set of observations. If the discrepancies were random, the values of $\bar{W}$ would be close to zero. They are not. The average discrepancies have a consistent bias, as indicated in the figures.

Comparison of Value and Utility Functions

In comparing the graphs, it was readily apparent that the deterministic value function did not replicate, even approximately, any of the vNM utility functions. To limit the discussion, analytic comparisons were only made between the preference function and the most commonly used utility function, that obtained by the fractile method with probability of one half. The relative differences were large, but not as large as the differences between the utility functions obtained using different fractile methods, as Table I shows. Put another way, the results indicate that functions assessed with methods which theoretically must produce the same curves perform as badly as methods which are not axiomatically equivalent.

A striking aspect of the differences is the great frequency with which most of the utility functions differ systematically from the value function. As a general rule, they are far above for risk averters and far below for risk seekers. This effect is illustrated by Fig. 6. For those who propose that the vNM utility function correctly combines both risk attitude and strength of preference and that the preference function only incorporates strength of preference, they can find an indication of this difference in our measure of relative difference. We normalized this difference with respect to the value function instead of the utility function since the value function would then have a simpler interpretation. Thus, the corresponding values in Table I are a measure of the risk aversion associated with the 50:50 lotteries. Since utility functions for different assessment methods are quite different, different levels of risk aversion could be associated with different probability distributions used in the assessment lotteries. The systematic

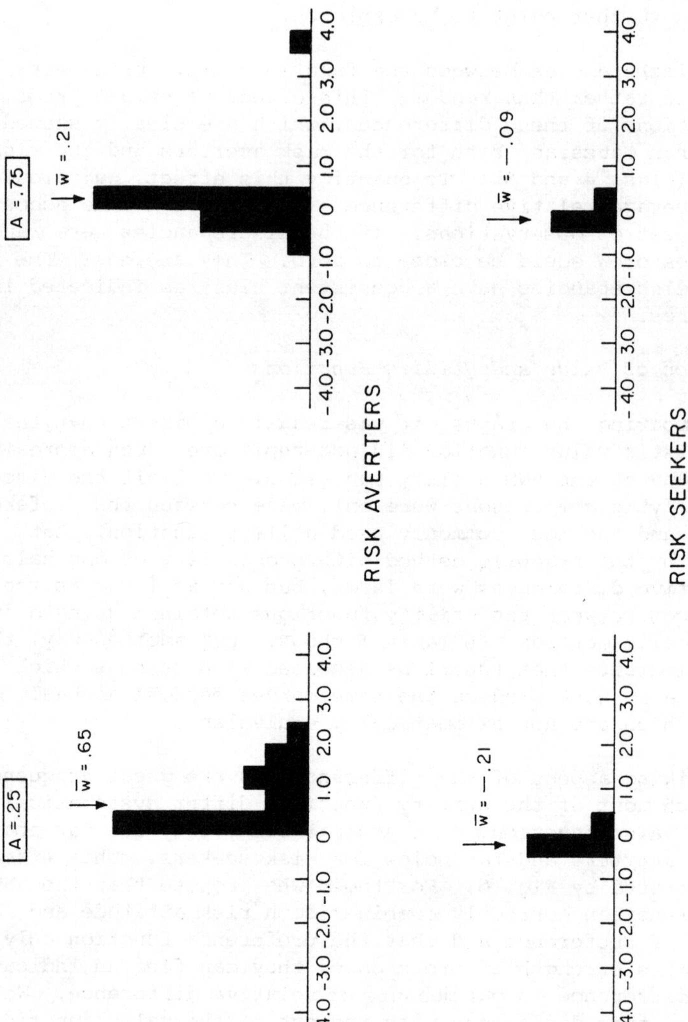

Fig. 4 Frequency Diagram of Relative Differences between Utility Functions obtained by the Varying Probability and 50:50 Fractile Methods.

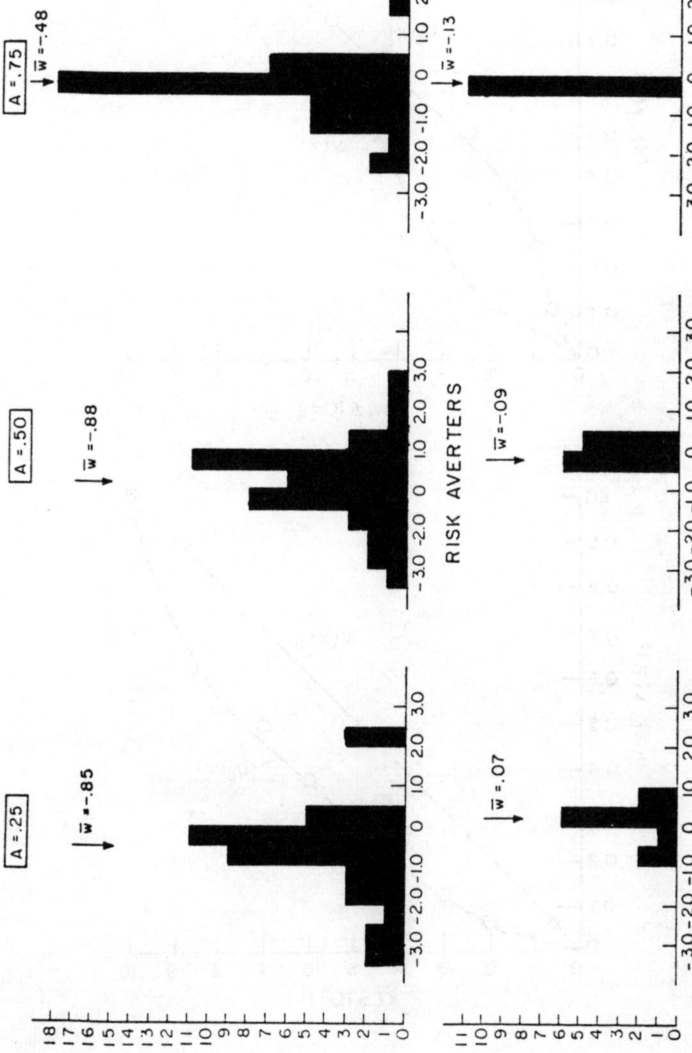

Fig. 5 Frequency Diagram of Relative Differences between Utility Functions obtained using Fractile Methods with Different Probabilities.

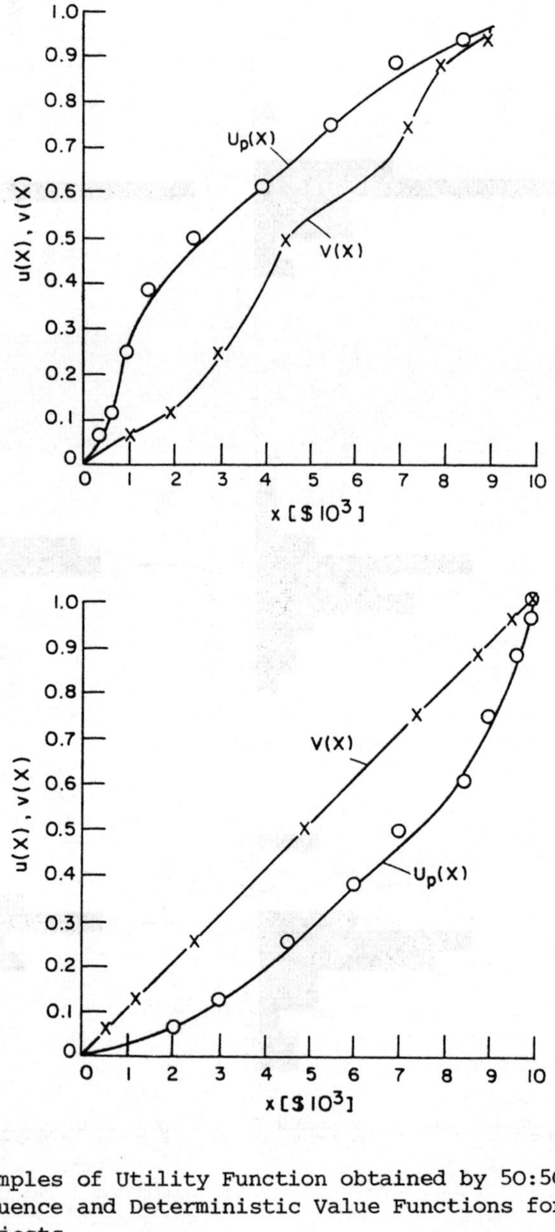

Fig. 6 Examples of Utility Function obtained by 50:50 Fractile Sequence and Deterministic Value Functions for Two Subjects.

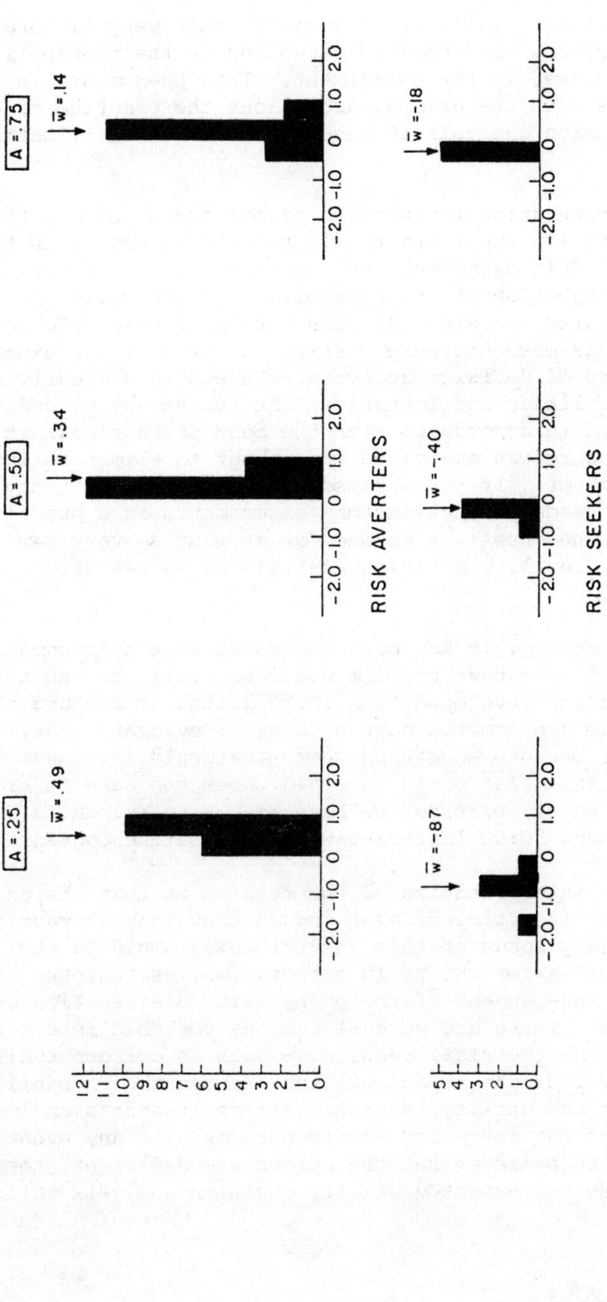

Fig. 7 Frequency Diagram of Relative Differences between Value and Utility Functions, obtained by the 50:50 Fractile Method.

nature of the differences between the value and utility functions is shown in Fig. 7.

DISCUSSION

The empirical result is, in summary, that very different utility functions are obtained depending on the probability distribution used in the assessment. This phenomenon is quite incompatible with the axioms, and places the practice of expected utility decision analysis in a quandary. This is illustrated by Fig. 8.

One interpretation is that the axioms are sound and that different utility functions result from deficiencies in the assessment. This might well be the case but, in effect, implies a complete rejection of the possibility of any valid use of expected utility decision analysis for the foreseeable future. Indeed, our assessments were carried out by skilled, experienced practitioners of decision analysis; the subjects clearly understood probabilities and lotteries; the assessment procedures were executed in accordance with the best professional standards; and extreme care was exercised throughout to eliminate extraneous sources of error. If our assessments are not sufficient, who can hope to execute satisfactory assessments in a practical situation? The answer is no one, or at most so very few as to make expected utility decision analysis an unrealistic proposition.

Parenthetically, it has been suggested that a "pragmatic" resolution of the above problem would be simply to use the utility function developed from 50:50 lotteries because these probabilities are somehow more natural or evident. But, of course, just because something seems "natural" (as sun worship or a belief in a flat earth once did) does not make it right. More to the point, perhaps, we have as yet no axiomatic justification to endow 50:50 lotteries with a normative content.

The other interpretation of the results is that the axioms are, somehow, insufficient even though they look attractive. The most likely locus of this insufficiency would be the "substitution" axiom which, in effect, implies that the utility function is independent of the probability distribution over the outcomes. There are several reasons for this interpretation: one is that the empirical results -- such as our own typified in Fig. 3 -- indicate an association between the probability distribution and utility; another is that it offers an immediate resolution of the so-called Allais paradox. In any event, if one chooses to believe that the axioms are deficient, then the justification for expected utility decision analysis falls.

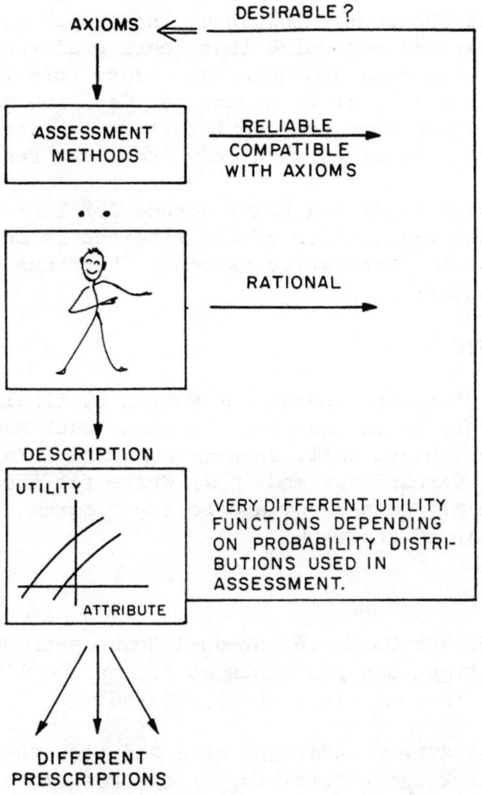

Fig. 8 Critique of Practice of Expected Utility Decision Analysis in light of Experimental Results.

It seems that we have here a classic case of being damned if you do, and damned if you do not.

CONCLUSION

The conclusion is that the justification of the practical use of expected utility decision analysis as it is known today is weak. Specifically, the whole computational side of the method, which seeks to define a best choice by means of calculus based on a description of a person's utility, does not appear valid: either we do not know how to encode this vNM utility or it does not exist.

This conclusion does not mean that the concept of decision analysis -- in some form -- should be discarded. Professional experience confirms that there is much value in helping people structure their choices; think about the probabilistic nature of the outcomes; and recognize that their preferences are a non-linear response to risk and quantity. Just this limited exercise is often valuable in that it encourages decision makers to identify strategies that provide insurance against calamities or opportunities to obtain particularly excellent results.

This work also implies a heavy agenda for further work. Confirmation and replication of our findings is one major task. The development of alternative axiomatic hypotheses for use in practice is another.

ACKNOWLEDGEMENTS

Roman Krzycztofowicz and Hector Munera particularly helped us formulate this investigation. We also thank Maurice Allais, Gregory Baecher, David Bell, Jean-Yves Jaffray, Ralph Keeney, Howard Raiffa, Bernard Roy and D.J. White for their advice and comments. The MIT Technology and Policy Program and the French Government financed the work.

REFERENCES

Allais, M. 1953 "Le Comportement de l'Homme Rationel devant le Risque: Critique des postulats et Axiomes de l'Ecole Américaine", *Econometrica,* **21** (4), 503-46.

Allais, M. 1952 "The Foundations of a Positive Theory of Choice Involving Risk and a Criticism of the Postulates and Axioms of the American School", pp. 27-148 in Allais and Hagen (1979).

Allais, M. 1979 "The So-Called Allais Paradox and Rational Decisions Under Certainty", pp. 437-682 in Allais and Hagen.

Allais, M. and Hagen, O. 1979 Eds. "Expected Utility Hypotheses and The Allais Paradox, D. Reidel Publishing Company, Dordrecht, Holland.

Bell, D.E. Regret in Decision Making Under Uncertainty, draft 4-11-81.

de Neufville, R. and Keeney, R. 1973 "Multiattribute Preference Analysis for Transportation Systems Evaluation", *Transportation Research,* **7**, No. 2, 1-16.

Eliashberg, J. and Hauser, J.R. "A Measurement Error Theory for von Neumann-Morgenstern Utility Assessment, Working Draft, 2, September, 1980.

Ellsberg, D. 1954 "Classic and Current Notions of 'Measurable Utility'", *Economic Journal,* **64**, 528-56.

Ellsberg, D. 1961 "Risk, Ambiguity, and the Savage Axioms", *Quarterly Journal of Economics,* **75** (4), 643-69.

Fishburn, P.C. 1967 "Methods of Estimating Additive Utilities", *Management Science,* **13** (7), 435-53.

Halter, A.N. and Dean, G.W. 1971 Decision Under Uncertainty, South-Western Publishing Co., Cincinnati, OH.

Howard, R.A., 1977 Risk Preference, pp. 429-66 in "Readings in Decision Analysis", Decision Analysis Group, Stanford Research Institute, Menlo Park, CA.

Huber, G.P., Daneshyar, R. and Ford, D.L. 1971 "An Empirical Comparison of Five Utility Models for Predicting Job Performances", *Organizational Behavior and Human Performance,* **6**, 267-82.

Kahneman, D. and Tversky, A. 1979 "Prospect Theory: An Analysis of Decision Under Risk", *Econometrica,* 47(2), 263-91.

Karmarkar, U.S. 1974 "The Effect of Probabilities on the Subjective Evaluation of Lotteries", MIT Working Paper No. 698-74, Sloan School of Management, MIT, Cambridge, MA, February.

Karmarkar, U.S. 1978 "Subjectively Weighted Utility: A Descriptive Extension of the Expected Utility Model", *Organizational Behavior and Human Performance,* **21**, 61-72.

Keeney, R.L. and Raiffa, H. 1976 Decisions with Multiple Objectives: Preferences and Value Tradeoffs, John Wiley & Sons, New York.

Krzysztofowicz, R. 1982 "Strength of Preference and Risk Attitude in Utility Measurement", *Organizational Behavior and Human Performance,* **28**.

Krzysztofowicz, R. and Duckstein, L. 1980 "Assessment Errors in Multi-attribute Utility Functions", *Organizational Behavior and Human Performance*, **26**, 326-48.

Lichtenstein, S. and Slovic, P. 1973 "Response-Induced Reversals of Preference in Gambling: An Extended Replication in Las Vegas", *Journal of Experimental Psychology,* **101**(1), 16-20.

Lichtenstein, S. and Slovic, P. 1971 "Reversals of Preference between Bids and Choices in Gambling Decisions", *Journal of Experimental Psychology,* **89** (1), 46-55.

MacCrimmon, K.R. and Larsson, S. 1979 Utility Theory: Axioms versus "Paradoxes", pp. 333-410 in Allais and Hagen.

Machina, M.J. 1982 "Rational" Decision Making versus "Rational" Decision Modelling?, *Journal of Mathematical Psychology*.

Munera, H.A. 1978 Modeling of Individual Risk Attitudes in Decision Making Under Uncertainty: An Application to Nuclear Power, Ph.D. Thesis, University of California, Berkeley, CA.

Raiffa, H. 1970 Decision Analysis: Introductory Lectures on Choices Under Uncertainty, Addison-Wesley Publishing Company, Reading, MA.

Roy, B. and Hugonnard, J.C. 1982 "Ranking of Suburban Line Extension Projects on the Paris Metro System by a Multicriteria Method", *Transportation Research,* **16A** (4), 301-12.

Sarin, R.K., Dyer, J.S. and Nair, K. 1980 A Comparative Evaluation of Three Approaches for Preference Function Assessment, Presented at the Joint National Meeting TIMS/ORSA, Washington DC, May 4-7.

Savage, L.J. 1972 The Foundations of Statistics, Dover Publications, New York.

Slovic, P. 1975 "Choice Between Equally Valued Alternatives", *Journal of Experimental Psychology: Human Perception and Performance,* **1** (3), 280-87.

Slovic, P. and Lichtenstein, S. 1968 "Relative Importance of Probabilities and Payoffs in Risk Taking", *Journal of Experimental Psychology Monograph,* **78** (3), Part 2, 1-18.

Slovic, P. and Tversky, A. 1974 "Who Accepts Savage's Axioms?", *Behavioral Science,* **19**, 368-73.

Swalm, R.O. 1966 "Utility Theory - Insights into Risk Taking", *Harvard Business Review,* **44** (Nov.-Dec.), 123-36.

Tversky, A. 1972 "Elimination by Aspects: A Theory of Choice", *Psychological Review,* **79** (4), 281-99.

Tversky, A. 1969 "Intransitivity of Preferences", *Psychology Review,* **76** (1), 31-48.

von Neumann, J. and Morgenstern, O. 1947 Theory of Games and Economic Behavior, 2nd ed., Princeton University Press, Princeton, NJ.

Weldon, J.C. 1950 "A Note on Measures of Utility", *The Canadian Journal of Economic and Political Science,* **16**, 227-33.

EXAMINATIONS AND MULTI-ATTRIBUTE UTILITY THEORY

S. French and M. Vassiloglou

(Department of Decision Theory, University of Manchester)

INTRODUCTION

Examinations are used as means of assessing the achievements and abilities of candidates in a certain group. This assessment is not obtained from a unique test in which the candidates "compete", but from a series of tests, the components of the examination. An examination can be separated into components at many levels; for example, it might consist of a set of papers, each of which consists of a number of essays or questions, each of which is again divided into parts. At all these levels the examiners mark the components separately and then combine the component marks to get overall marks.

The ideas behind this combining process have seldom been discussed explicitly. It has, however, been realized that the simple summation of component marks is inadequate, since it does not reflect the relative importance of components. Even so, no other method that has been suggested has been found universally acceptable (French, 1982).

In this paper it is suggested that the problem facing examiners who have to judge candidates on the basis of a number of examination components can be seen as a close parallel to the problem dealt with in multi-attribute utility theory (see also French, 1981, 1982). The components can be seen as attributes along which an aspect of the candidates' performance is measured and then the examiners' task is similar to assessing a multi-attribute value function.

There is, however, one important difference between the two problems. In multi-criteria decision making it is assumed that all the alternatives are measured along all the relevant attributes - an assumption that does not hold in examinations.

In examinations usually candidates are given a choice of questions within papers and, perhaps, of the papers themselves. In this way not all the candidates are assessed by all the components. This kind of examination is called differentiated papers and there the task of the examiners is similar to assessing an n-dimensional value function, where each alternative is only measured along $m < n$ attributes.

Some ways of assessing candidates' performances on the basis of differentiated papers are discussed by Backhouse (1976) and Wood and Wilson (1980). Backhouse considers the case of two groups; one sat Papers One and Two and the other sat Papers Two and Three. The problem then is to determine the grades for two groups sharing a common paper. Backhouse compares the rankings reached by examiners on intuitive, qualitative grounds to those obtained by three formal quantitative methods: ranking, scaling and regression. The ranking method ranks the candidates within each group according to the sum of their marks on the pair of papers they have taken and uses the common paper to compare candidates from different groups. The scaling method equalises the means and standard deviations of the papers, based on the idea that the weight of a paper depends on the spread of the candidates' marks in it. It then ranks the candidates according to the sum of their modified marks. The regression method uses the marks in the common paper to predict the hypothetical scores of the candidates in the paper they have not taken and then takes the "complete" data and ranks the candidates according to the sum of their three marks. The first comment to be made on all these methods is that, whatever their individual characteristics, they all assume that a simple linear combination of the marks is adequate for the overall assessment of the candidates.

Wood and Wilson (1980) on the other hand, propose a method of assessment involving paired comparisons. They suggest that, in the case where all pairs of candidates have been compared an equal number of times, an adequate measure of performance is the sum of the number of times each candidate has performed better than other candidates. In the general case, where the number of paired comparisons is not constant, they propose the maximum likelihood estimator of the probability of a candidate being assessed higher than others. There are many important comments to be made about this method, but the only point we would like to make here is that they consider marking to be on an ordinal scale and hence they only use rankings in their assessment.

EXAMINATION ASSESSMENT AND SOCIAL CHOICE THEORY

Before turning to multi-attribute value theory let us first look at the idea of assessing candidates just by the component rank orders. As we have seen such "ranking" methods have been proposed by Backhouse (1976) and Wood and Wilson (1980).

It has been shown that it is not possible to construct an assessment method, based purely on rank orders, that will be fair and consistent. Many social choice theory ideas are very close to this problem; Vassiloglou and French (1982) have studied the similarities of the two problems. If the component rank orders are seen as individuals' orderings of alternatives, then the problem of assessing the overall rank order of the candidates from the component rank orders is similar to that of obtaining the society's ordering of alternatives from the individuals' orderings. A very important result in social choice theory is Arrow's impossibility theorem. Arrow defined a social welfare function to be the process through which the society's ordering is derived from the individual's orderings. He then developed five axioms that most people would consider necessary for a social welfare function to satify and proved they were incompatible. The axioms, stated informally for our present context, are:

(1) (i) <u>Non triviality</u>: The problem involves at least three candidates and two components.

(ii) <u>Weak ordering</u>: Both the component rank orders and the overall rank order are comparable and transitive.

(2) <u>Universal domain</u>: There is no combination of component rank orders for which the overall rank order cannot be determined.

(3) <u>Independence of irrelevant candidates</u>: The relative ranking of any two candidates does not depend on who the other candidates are.

(4) <u>Pareto optimality</u>: If candidate A is ranked higher than B in all components, then A is ranked higher than B overall.

(5) <u>Non-dictatorship</u>: There is no component whose rank order always determines the overall rank order.

After some thought it can be seen that all these axioms describe properties that most examiners would consider necessary for the assessment procedure. This implies therefore that no method of assessment that only considers rank orders is consistent and hence that marks must always be taken into consideration in some way.

The above analysis at no point mentions differentiated papers. However, it is obvious that it applies there too, since a set of marks in differentiated papers can be broken down to groups that do not involve any differentiation. Arrow's theorem now applies to the first stage of ranking the candidates within these groups. For example, both Backhouse's ranking method and Wood and Wilson's simple version of their method have been shown to break the Independence of Irrelevant Candidates axiom. We should also mention that Backhouse's scaling and regression methods, even though they do not only use rank orders, can be criticized on a similar basis, since they both break the Axiom of Independence of Irrelevant Candidates by basing the procedure upon statistical properties of the marks obtained by the population of candidates.

A FRAMEWORK FOR THE DIFFERENTIATED PAPERS ASSESSMENT SCALING PROBLEM

Having suggested the inadequacy of pure ranking methods we can now turn to multi-attribute value theory. We look at the relevance to this context of the ideas developed by Ducamp and Falmagne (1969). For simplicity we will assume that there are only two streams of candidates, A and B, but the theory can be extended. The context will be that described by Backhouse (1976); i.e. group A have taken Papers One and Two and group B Papers Two and Three. Let us ignore the problem of ranking the candidates within a group (where they are all assessed by the same two papers) and simply state that we have weak orders R_A, R_B of the candidates in groups A and B respectively. The problem now is to combine these two rank orders in an overall rank order.

Define Q_{AB} and Q_{BA} to be orders of performance on $A \times B$ and $B \times A$ respectively. In other words, if a is a member of A and b is a member of B, $aQ_{AB}b$ means that the examiners have judged the performance of a on Papers One and Two to be at least as good as the performance of b on Papers Two and Three. The properties we will demand of Q_{AB} and Q_{BA} will be very similar to those of a weak order. We want to construct S, a weak order of performance of the combined group

$A \cup B$. Let us first state three axioms representing obvious fairness and consistency properties.

<u>A1</u>: R_A and R_B are comparable and transitive.

<u>A2</u>: $\nexists$ $(a \in A, b \in B)$ such that $a\overline{Q_{AB}}b$, $b\overline{Q_{BA}}a$.

<u>A3</u>: R_A, Q_{AB}, R_B, Q_{BA} are consistent:

(α) $\forall\, a,a' \in A$, $\forall\, b \in B$: $aR_A a'$, $a'Q_{AB}b \Rightarrow aQ_{AB}b$

(β) $\forall\, a,a' \in A$, $\forall\, b \in B$: $bQ_{BA}a$, $aR_A a' \Rightarrow bQ_{BA}a'$

(γ) $\forall\, a \in A$, $\forall\, b,b' \in B$: $bR_B b'$, $b'Q_{BA}a \Rightarrow bQ_{BA}a$

(δ) $\forall\, a \in A$, $\forall\, b,b' \in B$: $aQ_{AB}b$, $bR_B b' \Rightarrow aQ_{AB}b'$

(ε) $\forall\, a,a' \in A$, $\forall\, b \in B$: $aQ_{AB}b$, $bQ_{BA}a' \Rightarrow aR_A a'$

(ζ) $\forall\, a \in A$, $\forall\, b,b' \in B$: $bQ_{BA}a$, $aQ_{AB}b' \Rightarrow bR_B b'$.

We can now construct S to be:

	A	B
A	R_A	Q_{AB}
B	Q_{BA}	R_B

<u>Table 1</u>

i.e. $aSa' \Leftrightarrow aR_A a'$, S restricted to $A\times A$ is R_A;
$aSb \Leftrightarrow aQ_{AB}b$, S restricted to $A\times B$ is Q_{AB}; etc.

Obviously S is a weak order (comparable and transitive). This construction of S is intuitively logical: the final ranking of all candidates preserves the group rankings and simply joins them together through Q_{AB} and Q_{BA}. The axioms too, even though they are many, do not demand unreasonable properties from the rank orders. However, this set of assumptions simply catalogues properties of S without giving a useful understanding of the structure. We will therefore construct S from Q_{AB} and Q_{BA} to attempt to gain an insight as to why this simple, intuitive construction works. Clearly the axioms will have to be modified too. We will keep A1, A2 and A3 α-δ, but we will delete A3 ε and ζ and add two new ones.

These two are analogous to BQ_1 from Ducamp and Falmagne (1969). There they consider the representation of a relation $S \subset A\times B$ such that aSb if and only if $f(a)>g(b)$ for all a in A and b in B. They show that the representation problem has no solution in the case where there exist elements $a,a' \in A$ and $b,b' \in B$ with the property aSb, $a'Sb'$, but $a\bar{S}b'$ and $a'\bar{S}b$. If such elements did exist the functions f and g would have to obey the contradictory conditions:

$$\left.\begin{array}{l} f(a) > g(b) \\ f(a') > g(b') \\ f(a) \leq g(b') \\ f(a') \leq g(b) \end{array}\right\} \Rightarrow f(a) > f(a).$$

Hence they prove that the representation problem has a solution if and only if for all $a,a' \in A$ and $b,b' \in B$:

$$aSb,\ a'\bar{S}b,\ a'Sb' \Rightarrow aSb' \qquad (BQ_1)$$

The modified set of axioms is:

C1: R_A and R_B are comparable and transitive

C2: $\nexists\ (a\in A,\ b\in B)$ such that $\overline{aQ_{AB}b},\ \overline{bQ_{BA}a}$

C3: Consistency

(α) $\forall\ a,a'\in A,\ \forall\ b\in B$: $aR_Aa',\ a'Q_{AB}b \Rightarrow aQ_{AB}b$

(β) $\forall\ a,a'\in A,\ \forall\ b\in B$: $bQ_{BA}a,\ aR_Aa' \Rightarrow bQ_{BA}a'$

(γ) $\forall\ a\in A,\ \forall\ b,b'\in B$: $aQ_{AB}b,\ bR_Bb' \Rightarrow aQ_{AB}b'$

(δ) $\forall\ a\in A,\ \forall\ b,b'\in B$: $bR_Bb',\ b'Q_{BA}a \Rightarrow bQ_{BA}a$

C4: $aQ_{AB}b,\ bQ_{BA}a',\ a'Q_{AB}b' \Rightarrow aQ_{AB}b'$

C5: $bQ_{BA}a,\ aQ_{AB}b',\ b'Q_{BA}a' \Rightarrow bQ_{BA}a'$.

As we already said C4 and C5 are analogous to BQ_1 modified by C2, so that they are in terms of weak relations.

We now want to restructure S so that its restrictions to $A\times A$ and $B\times B$ are in terms of Q_{AB} and Q_{BA}. We will show the logic behind the relation in the restriction to $A\times A$ and by symmetry the case $B\times B$ will follow. aSa' means that candidate a is ranked at least as high as candidate a' in the overall rank order $(a,a'\in A)$. aSa' should hold whenever for all b one of the following is true: either a's performance is judged to be strictly better than b's, or b's performance is judged to be strictly better than a''s or a's performance is at least as good as b's and b's performance is at least as good as a''s. This is so because, if none of the above is true, then either a''s performance is judged to be at least at good as b's and b's strictly better than a's or a''s performance is judge to be strictly better than b's and b's at least as good as a's – in both cases a' should be ranked higher than a overall.

Therefore let S be

Table 3

	A	B
A	$\forall b$ either $b\overline{Q_{BA}}a$ or $a'\overline{Q_{AB}}b$ or $(aQ_{AB}b, bQ_{BA}a')$	$aQ_{AB}b'$
B	$bQ_{BA}a'$	$\forall a$ either $a\overline{Q_{AB}}b$ or $b'\overline{Q_{BA}}a$ or $(bQ_{BA}a, aQ_{BA}b')$

We must first show that S is a weak order:

(1) <u>Comparability</u>:

Suppose $\exists\ a, a' \in A$ such that $a\bar{S}a'$, $a'\bar{S}a$.

$a\bar{S}a' \Rightarrow \exists\, b$ such that $bQ_{BA}a$ (i)

and $a'Q_{AB}b$ (ii)

and $(a\overline{Q_{AB}}b$ or $b\overline{Q_{BA}}a')$ (iii)

$a'\bar{S}a \Rightarrow \exists\, b'$ such that $b'Q_{BA}a'$ (iv)

and $aQ_{AB}b'$ (v)

and $(a'\overline{Q_{AB}}b'$ or $b'\overline{Q_{BA}}a)$ (vi)

If we apply C4 to (v), (iv), (ii) we get $aQ_{AB}b$. C5 on (i), (v), (iv) implies $bQ_{BA}a'$. But these two together contradict (iii). So we cannot possibly have $a\bar{S}a'$, $a'\bar{S}a$.

A similar proof can be used for $b\bar{S}b'$.

The comparability proof for the other two cases is given directly by C2.

Hence S is comparable.

(2) Transitivity:

To prove transitivity we need to look at four typical cases; symmetry will imply the other four

(a) aSa', a'Sa"

$aSa' \Rightarrow \forall b$ either $b\overline{Q_{BA}}a$ (i)

or $a'\overline{Q_{AB}}b$ (ii)

or $(aQ_{AB}b, bQ_{BA}a')$ (iii)

$a'Sa'' \Rightarrow \forall b$ either $b\overline{Q_{BA}}a'$ (iv)

or $a''\overline{Q_{AB}}b$ (v)

or $(a'Q_{AB}b, bQ_{BA}a'')$ (vi)

Suppose then that $a\bar{S}a'' \Rightarrow \exists b'$ such that $b'Q_{BA}a$ (vii)

and $a''Q_{BA}b'$ (viii)

and $(a\overline{Q_{AB}}b'$ or $b'\overline{Q_{BA}}a'')$ (ix)

For b', (vii) implies (i) does not hold,
(viii) implies (v) does not hold
(xi) implies (iii) and (vi) do not hold.

Therefore $a'\overline{Q_{AB}}b$, $b\overline{Q_{BA}}a'$ must hold. But this contradicts C2.
Hence $aSa', a'Sa'' \Rightarrow aSa''$.

(b) aSa', a'Sb

$aSa' \Rightarrow \forall b'$ either $b'\overline{Q_{BA}}a$ (i)

or $a'\overline{Q_{AB}}b'$ (ii)

or $(aQ_{AB}b', b'Q_{BA}a')$. (iii)

$a'Sb \Rightarrow a'Q_{AB}b$ (iv)

(iv) implies (ii) cannot hold for b.

(i) implies by C2 that $aQ_{AB}b'$.

So in both possible cases for b, $aQ_{AB}b \Rightarrow aSb$.

(c) aSb, bSb'

$aSb \Rightarrow aQ_{AB}b$ (i)

$bSb' \Rightarrow \forall a'$ either $a'\overline{Q_{AB}}b$ (ii)

or $b'\overline{Q_{BA}}a'$ (iii)

or $(bQ_{BA}a', a'Q_{AB}b')$ (iv)

(i) implies (ii) cannot hold for a.
(iii) implies by C2 that $a'Q_{AB}b'$.

So in both possible cases for a, $aQ_{AB}b' \Rightarrow aSb'$.

(d) aSb, bSa'.

We want to show that $aSa' \Rightarrow \forall b'$ either $b'\overline{Q_{BA}}a$

or $a'\overline{Q_{AB}}b'$

or $(aQ_{AB}b', b'Q_{BA}a')$.

$aSb \Rightarrow aQ_{AB}b$

$bSa' \Rightarrow bQ_{BA}a'$.

Suppose that $\exists b'$ such that $b'Q_{BA}a$ and $a'Q_{AB}b'$. Using C4 and C5 we then get: $(aQ_{AB}b', b'Q_{BA}a')$. Therefore aSa'.

Hence S is transitive.

We have now proved that S constructed simply by Q_{AB} and Q_{BA} is a weak order. All that remains is to find the relationship between S on A and R_A (and S on B and R_B). What we will prove is that S on A is the same as R_A, except for the cases where, even though two members of A are not ranked equally by R_A, S cannot discriminate between them, because there is no B candidate lying between them. This means that: $a'\bar{S}a \Rightarrow a'\bar{R}_Aa$.

Suppose the above was not true. Then we could have $a'\bar{S}a$, $a'R_Aa$.

$$a'\bar{S}a \Rightarrow \exists b' \text{ such that } b'Q_{BA}a' \quad \text{(i)}$$
$$\text{and } aQ_{AB}b' \quad \text{(ii)}$$
$$\text{and } (a'\overline{Q_{AB}}b' \text{ or } b'\overline{Q_{BA}}a) \quad \text{(iii)}$$

$a'R_Aa$ and (ii) imply by C3α that $a'Q_{AB}b'$.
(i) and $a'R_Aa$ imply by C3β that $b'Q_{BA}a$.
These two together contradict (ii). Therefore there cannot occur $a'\bar{S}a$, $a'R_Aa$.

Hence S on A is related to R_A by the relationship described above. So, if we construct A by Q_{AB} and Q_{BA} and in the cases where S ranks two candidates equally distinguish between them if R_A or R_B do so, the final rank order of the candidates will be the same as that obtained by S as constructed in the first place. Therefore we can go back to the simpler definition of S.

By the Birkhoff-Milgram Theorem (see Roberts, 1979, Chapter 3) we can define a function g such that xSy if and only if $g(x) \geq g(y)$. Therefore:

$$aSa' \Leftrightarrow aR_Aa' \Leftrightarrow g(a) \geq g(a')$$
$$aSb \Leftrightarrow aQ_{AB}b \Leftrightarrow g(a) \geq g(b)$$
$$bSa \Leftrightarrow bQ_{BA}a \Leftrightarrow g(b) \geq g(a)$$
$$bSb' \Leftrightarrow bR_Bb' \Leftrightarrow g(b) \geq g(b')$$

Suppose also that there are functions ϕ_A and ϕ_B corresponding to the rank orders R_A and R_B in the following manner:

$$aR_Aa' \Leftrightarrow \phi_A(a) \geq \phi_A(a')$$
$$bR_Bb' \Leftrightarrow \phi_B(b) \geq \phi_B(b').$$

$\phi_A(x)$ and $\phi_B(x)$ can be seen as the marks of candidate x on the corresponding pair of papers for each group.

From the definitions of ϕ_A, ϕ_B and g we get:

$$g(a) \geq g(a') \Leftrightarrow \phi_A(a) \geq \phi_A(a')$$
$$g(b) \geq g(b') \Leftrightarrow \phi_B(b) \geq \phi_B(b').$$

Therefore in general:

$$g(c) = \begin{cases} f[\phi_A(c)] & \text{if } c \in A \\ h[\phi_B(c)] & \text{if } c \in B \end{cases}$$

where f and h are strictly increasing functions. That f and h are strictly increasing is to be expected from the physical context because surely strictly more marks imply a strictly better performance.

So f^{-1} exists and it is also strictly monotonic increasing. Therefore S can also be represented by $f^{-1}[g(c)]$. Hence:

$$f^{-1}[g(c)] = \begin{cases} \phi_A(c) & \text{if } c \in A \\ \ell[\phi_B(c)] & \text{if } c \in B \end{cases}$$

where $\ell[\phi_B(c)] = f^{-1}[h[\phi_B(c)]]$.

So, without loss of generality, we can simplify our notation to:

$$g(c) = \begin{cases} \phi_A(c) & \text{if } c \in A \\ h[\phi_B(c)] & \text{if } c \in A \end{cases}$$

where h is monotonic increasing.

So we have come to the conclusion that the overall rank order of two groups sharing a common paper can be given by a monotonic increasing function g which leaves the marks of the one group constant and scales those of the other group to reflect the differences in difficulty of the papers.

Look for example at the case where group A has taken a pair of more difficult papers than group B. A method that is often considered reasonable is that of allowing members of A to obtain any mark, but restricting members of B from obtaining the top marks. However if we used the process described above, we could leave the marks of group A as they are and scale those of group B. Then we would have h being a concave function, so that it would be very difficult, but not impossible, for members of B to obtain the top grades (see figure 1).

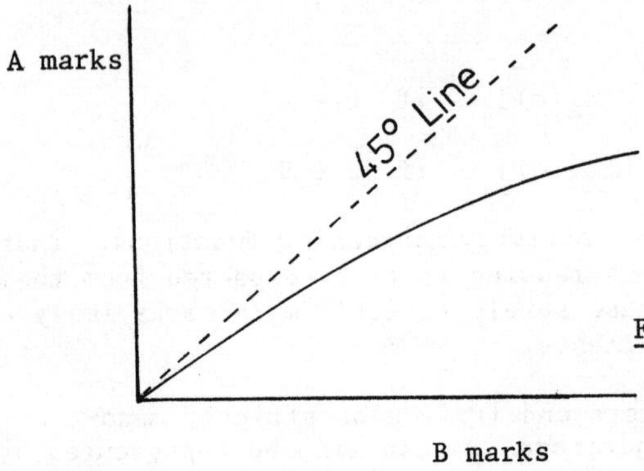

Figure 1

It is easy to see from figure 1 that one mark in B has less value than one mark in A and also that the marks in B have diminishing marginal "returns". This method seems to be not as ad hoc and discontinuous as limiting the top grades to group A.

In more general terms, the derivation of g at no point implied that h (the scaling function) should be linear or, more correctly for our purposes, affine. If, as in Backhouse (1976), h is taken to be affine, there must be some more assumptions to be made that will induce this linearity.

Consider the following six candidates:

	Marks in Group A	Marks in Group B
C_1	-	96
C_2	77	-
C_3	-	80
C_4	65	-
C_5	-	24
C_6	23	-

Table 4

Given that group A take the more difficult papers, it is not unreasonable to think that the examiners might judge that C_1 and C_2 perform equally well (i.e. C_1SC_2, C_2SC_1), and that C_3 and C_4 perform equally well (i.e. C_3SC_4, C_4SC_3). If the function h is strictly increasing and affine, i.e. $h(x) = \alpha x+\beta$ with $\alpha > 0$, then this implies

$$\left.\begin{array}{l}\alpha 96+\beta = 77\\ \alpha 80+\beta = 65\end{array}\right\} \Rightarrow \quad \alpha = \tfrac{3}{4}, \quad \beta = 5.$$

If this is so it immediately follows that the examiners must judge C_5 and C_6 to have performed equally because $\frac{3}{4}\times 24 + 5 = 23$. Moreover, it also follows that a mark of 0 on the easy papers is equivalent to a mark of 5 on the harder papers.

It seems to us that this example makes two points. Firstly, if h is to be affine, then perhaps β should be constrained to be non-positive. Secondly, the assumption that h is affine is a very strong assumption for it insists that examiners judgements about high scoring group B candidates are literally in line with their judgements of low scoring candidates.

It will be apparent that the above applies whether groups A and B take a common paper or whether they are assessed on entirely distinct components. Let us now structure the problem so that the analysis explicitly includes the common paper.

Let x_i be the candidate's mark on paper i. So for each candidate in group A we have x_1 and x_2 and for each candidate in group B we have x_2 and x_3. On the basis of these marks we want to rank the candidates of the combined group $A \cup B$. An initial reaction might be to rank them according to the scheme

$$g(x_1,x_2) = x_1 + x_2$$
$$g(x_2,x_3) = x_2 + h(x_3)$$

where the higher the value of $g(x_i,x_j)$ for a candidate, the higher this candidate will be placed in the overall rank order.

What we have done by taking function h of the marks on Paper Three is to put Paper One and Paper Three on the same scale (the assumptions underlying this are precisely those discussed earlier in the paper). This way the problem is reduced to two papers and the differentiation has disappeared. We can therefore use linear utility theory to compare the performances of the candidates, by constructing the overall mark of a candidate from group A to be x_1+x_2 and that of a candidate from group B to be $x_2+h(x_3)$.

We should however investigate the assumptions that lie behind this method. An obvious one is that it assumes that the judgement of performance on Papers One and Three is independent of performance on Paper Two. See, for example, the following case.

	1	2	3
C_1	40	80	
C_2		80	80
C_3	40	30	
C_4		30	80

Table 5

Suppose the examiners judge C_1 and C_2 to have performed equally well (when Paper One is considered to be more difficult than Paper Three). C_1SC_2, C_2SC_1 implies that $h(80) = 40$. If this is the case, then the examiners would have to rank C_3 and C_4 equally too. However, some people might object to this, because of the great difference in marks on Paper Two, which might put the marks on the other papers into a different light.

DISCUSSION

In this paper we have studied the problem in the context of choice of papers rather than questions. As we noted in the introduction, similar arguments apply to the case of questions too. However, the problem there is somewhat more complex: questions are carefully set and discussed at examiners' meetings, until the examiners are satisfied that the questions are of equal difficulty (approximately). Furthermore, the marking scheme is designed with this in mind and adjusted during the assessment. So it would not be unreasonable to assume that h, the scaling function between questions is the identity function. On the other hand differentiated papers are usually designed to be of unequal difficulty and there our initial research becomes more relevant.

Throughout the paper we have ignored the question of the actual measurement of h; ideas that could prove useful in that area can be found in Chapter 3 of Keeney and Raiffa (1976),

MacCrimmon's trade-off analysis (MacCrimmon, 1969) and Kruskal's monotonic regression (Kruskal, 1965).

A comment that may help in the interpretation of this work is the following: additive and polynomial conjoint representations of relations on $A \times A$ are based on the primitive assumption that the relations are weak orders (French, 1981; Roberts, 1979). Here we have been investigating the corresponding assumption for relations on $A \times B$.

Our work in the area of examination assessment and multi-attribute utility theory is just beginning. There is a lot still to be investigated. However, we feel that we have begun the introduction of a formal structure into an area that until now has lacked such a framework.

BIBLIOGRAPHY

Backhouse, J.K. (1976): Determination of grades for two groups sharing a common paper. *Educational Research*, 18, 126-137.

Ducamp, A. and Falmagne, J.C. (1969): Composite measurement. *Journal of Mathematical Psychology*, 6 , 359-390.

French, S. (1981): Measurement theory and examinations. *British Journal of Mathematical and Statistical Psychology*, 34, 38-49.

French, S.(1982): The weighting of examination components, Notes in Decision Theory No. 117, Department of Decision Theory, Manchester University.

Keeney, R.L. and Raiffa, H. (1976): *Decisions with Multiple Objectives*. Wiley, New York.

Kruskal, J.B. (1965): Analysis of factorial experiments by estimating monotone transformation of the data. *Journal of the Royal Statistical Society (B)*, 27, 251-263.

MacCrimmon, K.R. (1969): Improving the system design and evaluation process by the use of trade-off information: an application to north-east corridor transportation planning. RM-5877-DOT, The Rand Corporation, Santa Monica, Cal.

Roberts, F.S. (1979): *Measurement Theory*. Addison-Wesley, Reading, Mass.

Vassiloglou, M. and French, S. (1982): Arrow's theorem and examination assessment. Notes in Decision Theory, No. 110, Department of Decision Theory, University of Manchester. Accepted by *British Journal of Mathematical and Statistical Psychology*.

Wood, R. and Wilson, D.T. (1980): Determining a rank order when not all individuals are assessed on the same basis. In L.J. Th. van der Kamp, W.F. Langerak and D.M. de Gruijter (eds.), *Psychometrics for Educational Debates*. Wiley, New York.

AGENCY RELATIONSHIPS AND INCENTIVE STRUCTURE

H.L. Dhingra

(University of Saskatchewan and University of Warwick)

Portfolio Theory (Markowitz 1952, Sharpe 1963) of investment suggests that the optimal portfolio for any risk averting investor is likely to be diversified across securities of many firms. The implication of this is that the efficient allocation of risk bearing gives rise to separation of ownership function from the control function with effective decision making residing with the management (Williamson 1963, Fama 1980). When decision making authority is delegated to one party (agent) to act on behalf of other party (principal), there are agent-principal relationships commonly known as an agency model (Ross 1973). This model captures many important aspects of a contracting arrangement in which parties to the contract are motivated by both self interest and joint interest - as their destinies depend to some extent on the survival of the team (e.g. the firm) in competition with other teams.

In a normative decision theoretic context of the agency relationships the service performed by agent who perhaps is relatively more knowledgeable about the decision environment than the principal, consists of choosing an act from a set of feasible actions. Subsequent to the choice, a state of nature is realized yielding both pecuniary and non-pecuniary consequences which are shared between the two parties - with the agent receiving a compensation or fee schedule, and the principal receiving the uncertain and possibly negative payoff. Assuming that both the agent and principal possess separate utility functions, they act so as to maximize their expected utility. In other words, the agent acts to maximize the expected utility of the compensation he receives and the principal seeks to maximize over both his choice of agents and compensation schedules. A market imposed minimum expected utility of compensation by the agent would be one desirable constraint to this optimization problem.

Due to asymmetry of information (e.g. the management of a firm possesses inside information) (Haugen et al 1979), and high monitoring and bonding agency costs (Jensen et al 1976), individual security holders of a firm may not have strong interest in directly overseeing the management of a particular firm. Further, many managers, even if they own a fraction of the total assets of their firm, do not bear the full cost of any non-pecuniary benefits they consume. Because of these reasons, the managerial models of the firm suggest that the management of a large firm enjoys discretionary behaviour and powers, that is, managers have incentives to shirk work and consume more on the job than is agreed in the contract. Since in such situations, agents (management) may not always act to the best interest of principals (security holders), the problem of moral hazard (Arrow 1970, Holmstrom 1979) is evident. This gives rise to an incentive problem, that is structuring an incentive contractual relationship, including compensation incentives (Ross 1978, Shavell 1979, Harris et al 1979, Haugen et al 1979), between the principal and agent to induce the latter to behave as if he were maximizing the former's welfare given that uncertainty and monitoring costs exist. In other words, the managers of a firm are induced to display appropriate financial signals (Ross 1977, 1978) of their firm so that with the help of these signals, the investors can easily assess their performance or read the firm's type.

When we observe that millions of investors are willing to turn over a significant part of their wealth to corporations which are controlled by managers and who have little interest in their well-being, the development of an incentive structure which, in order to resolve the problem of moral hazard, simultaneously motivates managers to make optimal activity choice and to signal correctly the firm's type, is an important topic for future research in the area of "multi-objective decision making".

REFERENCES

ARROW, K.J. 1970 Essays in the Theory of Risk Bearing, North Holland Publishing Company, Amsterdam.

FAMA, E.F. 1980 "Agency Problems and the Theory of the Firm", *Journal of Political Economy*, pp. 288-307.

HARRIS, M. and RAVIV, A 1979 "Optimal Incentive Contracts with Imperfect Information", *Journal of Economic Theory,* pp. 231-259.

HAUGEN, R.A. and SENBENT, L.W. 1979 "New Perspectives on Informational Asymmetry and Agency Relationship", *Journal of Financial and Quantitative Analysis*, pp. 671-694.

HOLMSTROM, B. 1979 "Moral Hazard and Observability", *Bell Journal of Economics*, pp. 74-91.

JENSEN, M.C. and MECKLING, W.M. 1976 "Theory of the Firm: Managerial Behaviour, Agency Costs and Ownership Structure", *Journal of Financial Economics*, pp. 305-360.

MARKOWITZ, H.M. 1952 "Portfolio Selection", *Journal of Finance*, pp. 77-91.

ROSS, S.A. 1973 "The Economic Theory of Agency: The Principal's Problem", *American Economic Review*, pp. 134-139.

ROSS, S.A. 1977 "Determinants of Financial Structure: The Incentive-Signalling Approach", *Bell Journal of Economics*, pp. 23-40.

ROSS, S.A. 1978 "Some Notes on Financial Incentive-Signalling Models, Activity Choice and Risk Preferences", *Journal of Finance*, pp. 777-792.

SHARPE, W.F. 1963 "A Simplified Model for Portfolio Analysis", *Management Science*, pp. 277-293.

SHAVELL, S. 1979 "Risk Sharing and Incentive in the Principal Agent Relationships", *Bell Journal of Economics*, pp. 55-73.

WILLIAMSON, O.E. 1964 The Economics of Discretionary Behaviour: Managerial Objectives in the Theory of the Firm, Prentice Hall, New Jersey, USA.